*Iron Men,
Wooden Women*

Gender Relations in the
American Experience

Joan E. Cashin and Ronald G. Walters,
Series Editors

Iron Men, Wooden Women
Gender and Seafaring in the Atlantic World, 1700–1920

Edited by
Margaret S. Creighton
and Lisa Norling

The Johns Hopkins University Press
Baltimore and London

© 1996 The Johns Hopkins University Press
All rights reserved. Published 1996
Printed in the United States of America on acid-free paper
05 04 03 02 01 00 99 98 97 96   5 4 3 2 1

The Johns Hopkins University Press
2715 North Charles Street
Baltimore, Maryland 21218-4319
The Johns Hopkins Press Ltd., London

ISBN 0-8018-5159-9
ISBN 0-8018-5160-2 (pbk.)

Library of Congress Cataloging-in-Publication Data
will be found at the end of this book.

A catalog record for this book is available
from the British Library.

Contents

Introduction   vii
Contributors   xv

1 MARCUS REDIKER
Liberty beneath the Jolly Roger
The Lives of Anne Bonny and Mary Read, Pirates   1

2 DIANNE DUGAW
Female Sailors Bold
Transvestite Heroines and the Markers of Gender and Class   34

3 RUTH WALLIS HERNDON
The Domestic Cost of Seafaring
Town Leaders and Seamen's Families in Eighteenth-Century Rhode Island   55

4 LISA NORLING
Ahab's Wife
Women and the American Whaling Industry, 1820–1870   70

5 HASKELL SPRINGER
The Captain's Wife at Sea   92

6 MARGARET S. CREIGHTON
Davy Jones' Locker Room
Gender and the American Whaleman, 1830–1870   118

7 W. JEFFREY BOLSTER
"Every Inch a Man"
Gender in the Lives of African American
Seamen, 1800–1860   *138*

8 LAURA TABILI
"A Maritime Race"
Masculinity and the Racial Division of Labor
in British Merchant Ships, 1900–1939   *169*

9 LILLIAN NAYDER
Sailing Ships and Steamers, Angels and Whores
History and Gender in Conrad's Maritime Fiction   *189*

10 MELODY GRAULICH
Opening Windows toward the Sea
Harmony and Reconciliation in American
Women's Sea Literature   *204*

Notes   *227*
Index   *287*

Introduction

IN 1924 FREDERICK WILLIAM WALLACE published *Wooden Ships and Iron Men*, neatly summing up in the title what he considered to be the salient features of maritime history and what he saw as the link between seafaring and rugged masculinity.[1] Wallace's assumptions were hardly formed in isolation: the notions that maritime history and literature amounted to tales of men, ships, and the sea, and that sailors were universally tough, have long enjoyed wide currency. The complementary premise that women and shoreside institutions were tangential to maritime experience has been equally tenacious. Women have found their way into some scholarship, but they appear mostly on the periphery, as stiff and objectified as the wooden figureheads that faced the sea at the bows of sailing ships.

This collection challenges the reduction of maritime culture to the stereotypical "iron" men and "wooden" women. The contributors argue that sailors' masculinity has varied in form and meaning, that women have played active and important roles in maritime enterprise, and that the shore has been vital in shaping seafaring experience. Taken together, the work included here demonstrates decisively that gender is a fundamental component of seafaring, as it is of all human society.

Iron Men, Wooden Women examines the formulation of gender within seafaring communities, among sailors, and by authors of sea fiction; and it considers how these formulations have influenced or reflected gender norms created elsewhere. Such close attention to gender gives both maritime history and sea criticism deeper nuance and substance, and helps connect maritime scholarship to current historical and literary investigation more generally. The various essays scrutinize such seemingly natural and universal categories as gender, race, class, and age; and they examine how these constructs have been used to explain inequality and to assert domination in a range of political, economic, and social relationships.

At the same time, this collection suggests how many of these central concerns might be considered afresh or further illuminated through attention to maritime cultures and contexts. Over the two centuries and more covered here, English and American vessels carried vast numbers of people and tons of goods. Their captains, crews, and passengers took with them commercial schemes and colonial ambitions, competing concepts of individualism and community, sovereignty and revolution. And they transported, too, changing ideas about manhood and womanhood.[2] The scholars represented in this volume are attentive to the crucial role which seafarers and seafaring played in disseminating these ideas around the Atlantic world.

While the range of sources, topics, and approaches is broad, all of the essays address the "iron men / wooden women" convention in the English-speaking North Atlantic from 1700 to about 1920. These two centuries encompassed the apex of both the age of sail and Anglo-American domination of international shipping.[3] By the end of the seventeenth century, ships and seamen from England and its American colonies had successfully seized control of the lucrative Atlantic trade routes from every foreign competitor. After the American Revolution, the British and American merchant marines vied for global maritime supremacy: by 1850, fully 47 percent of the world's merchant shipping sailed under British registry and another 40 percent under the American flag.[4] Though temporarily achieving a leading position during the Napoleonic Wars, American shipping declined after the Civil War and virtually ceded the competition. British maritime dominance itself collapsed under the impact of World War I.

British success and American failure on the seas in the decades before the Great War derived in large part from Britain's more rapid adoption of a revolutionary new technology, the steam engine. Over the course of the nineteenth century, the technology of sail was eclipsed by steam propulsion, which dramatically altered the design of vessels and the skills needed to operate them. By the turn of the twentieth century, further technological developments, economies of scale, and an international labor market combined with the demands of domestic and international politics to produce a complicated phenomenon: British- and American-owned shipping operating with largely foreign crews and often under foreign registry. By the early 1900s, sail and an unambiguously national merchant marine had drastically declined on both sides of the English-speaking Atlantic. The nature of seafaring as an occupation had utterly and irrevocably changed.

Like every specialized occupation, labor under sail evolved with its own distinctive language, rhythms, rituals, and lore. Most readers today learn of that seafaring subculture through the accounts provided by writers like

Richard Henry Dana, Herman Melville, and Joseph Conrad. Although these portrayals are rich and detailed, they must be understood as framed by the authors' literary and reform ambitions. Other sources suggest that seafaring experience was shaped by the close confines, intermittent isolation, and strict hierarchy of authority of the ship; the mobility inherent in a transportation industry; and the natural dangers that were inescapably part of the deep-sea workplace. But just how distinctive sailors and shipboard societies really were, in what ways, and why, remain points of disagreement even among the authors represented in this collection.

Virtually all maritime scholars agree, however, that for centuries seafaring has been one of the most exclusively male-dominated occupations. Women have certainly traveled on ships, but the vast majority of them put to sea as passengers or, more horrifically, as human cargo rather than as a part of the blue water workforce. The actual numbers of women who were employed on shipboard, either disguised as men or in such specific positions as stewardess or cook, have as yet been difficult to establish.[5]

Although we still do not clearly understand why or how ocean labor was originally designated as men's work, the association of masculinity and seafaring clearly strengthened in the last two hundred years. Influencing the linkage were new notions of sexual difference which emerged out of the seismic shifts in European social, political, economic, and intellectual life in the late seventeenth and eighteenth centuries. These new concepts of gender centered around claims that male and female behaviors and roles derived from basic biological distinctions. Enlightenment science, which stressed binary oppositions, promoted ideas of male activity and female passivity, male strength and female frailty, male rationality and female emotionality, qualities that were defined as universal and permanently rooted in nature.[6]

By the early nineteenth century in England and the United States, these ideas took on geographical form through distinctive middle-class definitions of gender. This set of cultural meanings, values, and norms, sometimes referred to by historians as the ideology of the "separate spheres," prescribed domesticity for women and public activity for men.[7] As several of the contributors to this volume suggest, the "iron men / wooden women" convention seems to have derived from this new spatial configuration of gender difference. The view of the ocean as a single-sex masculine space, in contrast to a feminized and domesticated society on land, reflected the nineteenth-century projection of bourgeois social mores onto a time-honored division of seafaring labor.[8]

Middle-class theorists also promoted the idea that maritime work bred

Introduction

toughened "iron" men. A particularly hardy and physical style of manhood seems to have been an enduring ideal in many working-class subcultures, including that of sailors.[9] In the late 1800s, this model of male muscularity and aggressiveness was appropriated by some elements in the middle class. Some scholars suggest that this was in part an antidote to the perceived weakening of men in an industrializing society or, as others argue, a reaction to the equally feared intrusion of women into male institutions and professions. Whatever the reason, social commentators and critics increasingly described the sea, along with the battlefield, the frontier, and the sports arena, as a male proving ground.[10] Historians ever since have unquestioningly linked the ocean with boldness and virility, regardless of the eras they investigated or the subjects they studied. They have thus perpetuated "iron" manhood as both natural and inevitable. Much of the scholarship on sea literature has likewise contrasted male adventure at sea with female domesticity on land. Critics have highlighted the misogyny of the most widely studied maritime authors without fully contextualizing it.[11]

The handful of scholarly studies and published narratives of those few women who went to sea have, ironically, contributed to the "iron men / wooden women" convention.[12] Accounts of female sailors in disguise and captains' wives who followed their husbands to sea have stressed how unusual these women were, in effect rendering them as curiosities. With a few recent exceptions, these accounts document women's experiences onboard ship without questioning the gender assumptions that framed them. Shoreside women have suffered much the same fate. References to nameless prostitutes—the nautical equivalents of military camp followers, found between decks on naval ships in port—or to stylized sweethearts left weeping on the docks reduce such women to caricatures and actually tell us more about the imagination of the men who left them behind. Until now, most maritime historians and critics have followed suit, relegating women to passing comments, sometimes comic, sometimes poignant, sometimes remarkable, but always marginal to the maritime enterprise and culture they entered almost as if by mistake. The impression left by this literature ends up reinforcing rather than questioning or complicating the rigid polarization of ocean and land, underscoring the idea of the ship as a self-contained "total institution" and dismissing sailors as rootless and alienated from shore society.[13]

The estrangement of seafarers and maritime experience from the mainstream of American historiography may be rooted in the late nineteenth

Introduction

century, when Frederick Jackson Turner, speaking at the 1893 World's Fair in Chicago, noted the importance of the *terrestrial* frontier to the course of American history and the American character. Turner's assertion of his "Frontier Thesis" coincided, not by accident, with the dramatic decline of the American maritime industries as both intellectual and financial capital shifted away from the sea. Even though the particulars of his theories were widely criticized, Turner's fundamental orientation to the land pervaded the scholarship. For generation after generation, students of American history emphasized westward expansion and internal economic and demographic growth as the most critical forces in American development.[14] They in large part dismissed the degree to which an oceanic frontier linked America to other landward polities, societies, and economic systems around the world.

To a far greater extent, British scholarship has acknowledged the importance of maritime components in their country's national and international development. In studying the heritage of an island nation, its long-lived overseas colonial empire, and its continued dominance of international shipping, many British historians and critics have remained sensitive to the nexus between sea and shore. Yet they, too, have generally accepted rather than critiqued the gender assumptions embodied in the "iron men / wooden women" construction.[15]

Beginning in the late 1960s, historians launched an effort to integrate the history of sailors with that of society ashore. In his 1968 article, "Jack Tar in the Streets," American historian Jesse Lemisch called for a revised look at the relationship between seafaring and shoreside history as he demonstrated that seamen played a central role in the radical protests of the American Revolution.[16] Over the past two decades, scholars on both sides of the Atlantic have followed Lemisch's lead in challenging the characterization of sailors as outsiders and in arguing for the integration of maritime topics into analyses of society and culture ashore.[17] In the 1989 inaugural issue of the *International Journal of Maritime History*, the editors called for maritime studies to become more international, to focus more on social and economic subjects, and to be revitalized by the important debates in the academy as a whole.[18]

With this collection, we hope to extend these efforts still further by applying the critical tools developed in gender studies. The contributors to this volume define gender as those cultural meanings and values that societies attribute to anatomical sex differences, that define women's and men's social and cultural roles, and that express underlying relations of power. The ideals and the experiences of masculinity and femininity, then, are socially constructed and historically variable.

Iron Men, Wooden Women makes clear that any thorough analyses of maritime culture and enterprise must include study of how gender norms and behaviors affected and were modified by sea and shore experience. But while the contributions share an attention to gender, they do not necessarily fit themselves to a uniform theory or method. To the contrary, they draw upon differing epistemological traditions and in some cases represent sharply contrasting points of view. Historians and literary critics bring the multiple visions of their disciplines to the subject at hand and they employ an impressive variety of sources, from popular ballads, fiction, and poetry to logbooks, account books, diaries, and a range of public records. Some of the contributors recover and examine the experiences of male and female historical subjects at sea and on shore, while others explore the ways that fictive sailors and fictive ships reflected and influenced gender and class tensions within a society.

The collection as a whole reflects the compelling utility of an interdisciplinary approach. By illuminating the context in which fictional and nonfictional texts were produced and received, we can better appreciate their authors both as literary artists and as historical informants. And by juxtaposing social history, cultural history, and literary analysis, we can gain a fuller understanding of the interplay between material conditions, politics, and cultural influences within a specific historical period. The essays appear chronologically to highlight from different perspectives issues commmon to a particular period, and to indicate development over time. Each one is self-contained and can be read individually. As the headnotes suggest, however, many of them cluster around certain themes or topics and can be read in pairs or groups to explore comparative, complementary, or sometimes contrasting analyses.

The works included in this volume challenge the parallel "iron men / wooden women" and "sea / land" divisions. Taken together, they broaden our understanding of maritime experience by including the societies onshore that set ships in motion, that affected shipboard culture, and that in turn were shaped by the distinctive experiences of seafaring life. Some of the authors challenge the characterization of maritime enterprise as strictly male by examining the importance of women's work in shoreside economies and communities. Just as importantly, others argue for the diverse social character of men at sea, demonstrating conclusively that the lack of flesh-and-blood females aboard ship did not mean that shipboard society lacked gender. All of these contributions find in the sea an arena in which dominant constructions of gender and sexuality might be mirrored, contested, rearranged, or established anew.

Iron Men, Wooden Women reflects substantive work in new areas and demonstrates the opportunities and rewards in applying the lens of gender to maritime topics. But by bringing to life some of the "wooden" women and "iron" men of the past, the volume also highlights the numbers who yet remain immobilized through lack of scrutiny. One of the most glaring gaps is in the area of sexuality. A few pioneering scholars have begun to uncover and examine certain kinds of sexual relations between men at sea, but we still know frustratingly little about sailors' sexual relations with women—or indeed about gender and sexuality in portside settings more generally.[19] Future study must also fully acknowledge seafaring as the site of multiracial and multicultural interactions. Analysis of material culture and folklore will help us as we chart the gendered spaces of ship and shore. Behind these disparate approaches lie several fundamental questions. How did men and women coming together from different racial, class, and cultural backgrounds define gender and sexuality, and how did they express them in maritime settings? When gender is added, how must the maritime experience be rewritten? How, then, will the history of the rest of society be modified? The exploration of seafaring and gender must continue to be dynamic, investigating the shore and the sea in ways that intersect and overlap.

Contributors

W. JEFFREY BOLSTER is assistant professor of history at the University of New Hampshire. A licensed master mariner with ten years of seafaring experience, he has published articles on a variety of maritime subjects and is currently writing a book on African American seamen in the Atlantic world, 1740–1865.

MARGARET S. CREIGHTON is associate professor of history and chair of American cultural studies at Bates College. She is the author of *Rites and Passages: The Experience of American Whaling, 1830–1870*, and her present research projects include a study of sailors and maritime women in American popular culture.

DIANNE DUGAW is associate professor of English at the University of Oregon. Her published articles focus on the areas of eighteenth-century literature and music, women's studies, and Anglo-American folklore and popular culture. She is the author of *Warrior Women and Popular Balladry, 1650–1850*, and the editor of *The Anglo-American Ballad: A Folklore Casebook*. She is completing a book on eighteenth-century popular culture and the social satire of John Gay.

MELODY GRAULICH is professor of English and women's studies at the University of New Hampshire. Her research centers on western American women writers, including Mary Hallock Foote, Leslie Marmon Silko, and especially Mary Austin. She has introduced and edited three Austin works, *Western Trails*, *Cactus Thorn*, and *Earth Horizon*, and is editing a collection of critical essays on Austin.

RUTH WALLIS HERNDON is a research fellow at the Philadelphia Center for Early American Studies. She has published a number of articles on early New England social history; her forthcoming book is titled *Childhood in Colonial America*.

Contributors

LILLIAN NAYDER is assistant professor of English at Bates College. She has published numerous articles on Charles Dickens and Wilkie Collins and is currently writing the volume on Collins for the Twayne English Authors series.

LISA NORLING is assistant professor of history at the University of Minnesota. She has published a number of articles on gender in maritime communities and is currently revising her dissertation, "Captain Ahab Had a Wife: Ideology and Experience in the Lives of New England Maritime Women, 1790–1870," for publication.

MARCUS REDIKER teaches history at the University of Pittsburgh. He is the author of *Between the Devil and the Deep Blue Sea: Merchant Seamen, Pirates, and the Anglo-American Maritime World, 1700–1750*, and is a contributing author of volume 1 of *Who Built America: Working People and the Nation's Economy, Politics, Culture, and Society*. He is currently working with Peter Linebaugh on a book manuscript, "The Many-Headed Hydra: Explorations in the History of the Atlantic Working Class."

HASKELL SPRINGER is professor of English at the University of Kansas. He has published books and articles on Henry David Thoreau, Washington Irving, Herman Melville, and other American authors. In recent years he has been area chair for sea literature for both the American Culture and Popular Culture associations.

LAURA TABILI is associate professor of modern European history at the University of Arizona. She is the author of *"We Ask for British Justice": Workers and Racial Difference in Late Imperial Britain*.

*Iron Men,
Wooden Women*

MARCUS REDIKER

I

Liberty beneath the Jolly Roger
The Lives of Anne Bonny and Mary Read, Pirates

The book opens with two contributions that take as their subject an early modern phenomenon somewhat surprising to modern readers: women who disguised themselves as men and went to sea as sailors. Their actual numbers are extremely difficult to establish but appear relatively few; however, a range of evidence documents both their existence and their significance to their contemporaries and modern scholars alike. In the first essay, Marcus Rediker recovers the lives and considers the legacy of two specific seagoing women, the famed eighteenth-century female pirates Anne Bonny and Mary Read. Most of what we know about Bonny and Read is drawn from a Captain Charles Johnson's accounts of them published in 1724; these narratives are reprinted in full at the end of Rediker's essay.

In the first section of his study, Rediker explores what the experiences of the two female freebooters tell us about the sexual division of labor on shipboard and about the class specificity—at sea and on land—of gender markers like physical strength, personal initiative, and courage in combat. Rediker has argued elsewhere that the male pirates of the Atlantic world defined their lives in opposition to the emergent capitalist social relations of work represented in the British merchant marine and the Royal Navy; here he suggests that the pirate subculture may have also offered to a few daring women the possibility for rebellion against the concomitant evolution of gender norms.

The popularity among their contemporaries of Anne Bonny, Mary Read, and other women like them prompts Rediker to consider their legacy in the second part of his essay. He traces their continued reappearance in cultural forms ranging from ballad and broadside to historical narrative, novel, drama, and visual images in engraving and painting. Though the celebration of female sailors waned with the growing dominance of bourgeois feminine ideals—as Dianne Dugaw describes in the following essay—Rediker contends that specific images of Bonny and Read may have inspired and served as symbol in highly influential representations of liberty and resistance in the revolutions of the late eighteenth and early nineteenth centuries.

Marcus Rediker

JAMAICA'S MEN OF POWER gathered at a Court of Admiralty in St. Jago de la Vega in late 1720 and early 1721 for a series of show trials. Governor Nicholas Lawes, members of his Executive Council, the chief justice of the Grand Court, and a throng of minor officials and ship captains confirmed the gravity of the occasion by their concentrated presence. Such officials and traders had recently complained of their "Coasts being infested by those Hell-hounds the Pirates." In this Jamaica's coasts were not alone: pirates had plagued nearly every colonial ruling class as they made their marauding attacks on mercantile property across the British empire and beyond. The great men came to see a gang of pirates "swing to the four winds" upon the gallows. They would not be disappointed.[1]

Eighteen members of Calico Jack Rackam's crew had already been convicted and sentenced to hang—three of them, including Rackam himself, afterward to dangle and decay in chains at Plumb Point, Bush Key, and Gun Key, as moral instruction to the seamen who passed their way. Once shipmates, now gallowsmates, they were meant to be "a Publick Example, and to terrify others from such-like evil Practices."[2]

Two other pirates were also convicted, brought before the judge, and

"Ann Bonny and Mary Read *convicted of Piracy Novr 28th 1720 at a Court of Vice Admiralty held at St. Jago de la Vega in ye Island of Jamaica.*" The women pirates as imagined by an unknown English artist, 1724.

Captain Charles Johnson, *A General History of the Robberies and Murders of the Most Notorious Pyrates* (London, 1724)

Liberty beneath the Jolly Roger

"asked if either of them had any Thing to say why Sentence of Death should not pass upon them, in like manner as had been done to all the rest." These two pirates, in response, "pleaded their Bellies, being Quick with Child, and pray'd that Execution might be staid." The Court then "passed Sentence, as in Cases of Pyracy, but ordered them back, till a proper Jury should be appointed to enquire into the Matter."[3] The jury inquired into the matter, discovered that they were indeed women, pregnant ones at that, and gave respite to these two particular "Hell-hounds," whose names were Anne Bonny and Mary Read.

This essay explores some of the meanings of the lives of the two women pirates, during their own times and long after. It surveys the contexts in which Bonny and Read lived and discusses how these women made a place for themselves in the rugged, overwhelmingly male world of seafaring. It concludes by considering their many-sided and long-lasting legacy. Any historical account of the lives of Anne Bonny and Mary Read must in the end be as picaresque as its subjects, ranging far and wide across the interrelated and international histories of women, seafaring, piracy, labor, literature, drama, and art. Theirs was ultimately a story about liberty, whose history they helped to make.

Much of what is known about the lives of these extraordinary women appeared originally in *A General History of the Pyrates*, written by a Captain Charles Johnson and published in two volumes in 1724 and 1728. Captain Johnson (who may or may not have been Daniel Defoe)[4] recognized a good story when he saw one. He gave Bonny and Read leading parts in his study, boasting on the title page that the first volume contained "the remarkable Actions and Adventures of the two female Pyrates, Mary Read and Anne Bonny." (Johnson's accounts are reprinted in their entirety at the end of this essay.) *A General History* proved a huge success: it was immediately translated into Dutch, French, and German and published and republished in London, Dublin, Amsterdam, Paris, Utrecht, and elsewhere, by which means the tales of the women pirates circulated to readers around the world.[5] Their stories had doubtless already been told and retold in the holds and on the decks of ships, on the docks, and in the bars and brothels of the sailortowns of the Atlantic by the maritime men and women of whose world Bonny and Read had been a part.

As the narrative in Johnson's *General History* relates, Mary Read was born an illegitimate child outside London; her mother's husband was not

A well-armed Mary Read as depicted by an unknown Dutch artist, 1725
Capiteyn Charles Johnson, *Historie der Engelsche Zee-Roovers* (Amsterdam, 1725)

her father. In order to get support from the husband's family, Mary's mother dressed her to resemble the recently deceased son she had by her husband, who had died at sea. Mary apparently liked her male identity and decided eventually to become a sailor, enlisting aboard a man-of-war, then a soldier, fighting with distinction in both infantry and cavalry units in Flanders. She fell in love with a fellow soldier, allowed him to discover her secret, and soon married him. But he proved less hardy than she, and before long he died. Mary once again picked up the soldier's gun, this time serving in the Netherlands. At war's end she sailed in a Dutch ship for the West Indies, but her fate was to be captured by pirates, whom she joined, thereafter plundering ships, fighting duels, and beginning a new romance. Her new lover one day fell afoul a pirate much more rugged than himself and was challenged to go ashore and fight a duel in the pirates' customary way, "at sword and pistol." Mary saved the situation by picking a fight with the same rugged pirate, scheduling her own duel two hours before the one to involve her lover, and promptly killing the fearsome pirate "upon the spot." Her martial skills were impressive, but still they alone were no match for the naval vessel that captured and imprisoned her and her comrades in 1720.

Anne Bonny was also born an illegitimate child (in Ireland), and she too was raised in disguise, her father pretending that she was the child of a relative entrusted to his care. Her father eventually took the lively lass with him to Charleston, South Carolina, where he became a merchant and planter. Anne grew into a woman of "fierce and courageous temper." Once, "when a young Fellow would have lain with her against her Will, she beat him so, that he lay ill of it a considerable time." Ever the rebel, Anne soon forsook her father and his wealth to marry "a young Fellow, who belong'd to the Sea, and was not worth a Groat." She ran away with him to the Caribbean, where she dressed "in Men's Cloaths" and joined a band of pirates that included Mary Read and, more importantly, Calico Jack Rackam, who was soon the object of Anne's affections. Their romance too came to a sudden end, when one day in 1720 she and her mates fell into battle with a vessel sent to capture them. When they came to close quarters, "none [of the pirates] kept the Deck except Mary Read and Anne Bonny, and one more"; the rest of the pirates scuttled down into the hold in cowardice. Exasperated and disgusted, Mary Read fired a pistol at them, "killing one, and wounding others." Later, as Calico Jack was to be hanged, Anne said that *"she was sorry to see him there, but if he had fought like a Man, he need not have been hang'd like a Dog."* Anne, who had "fought

Anne Bonny firing a pistol, as drawn by an unknown Dutch artist, 1725
Capiteyn Charles Johnson, *Historie der Engelsche Zee-Roovers* (Amsterdam, 1725)

like a Man," was forced to plead her belly to prolong her days among the living.

Of the existence of two women pirates by the names of Anne Bonny and Mary Read there can be no doubt, for they were mentioned in a variety of historical sources, all independent of *A General History of the Pyrates*. The names first appeared in a proclamation by Woodes Rogers, governor of the Bahama Islands, who on 5 September 1720 declared Jack Rackam and his crew to be pirates and warned all authorities to treat them as "Enemies to the Crown of *Great Britain*." He named the pirates involved and noted "Two women, by name, Ann Fulford alias Bonny, & Mary Read." The second mention came in a rare pamphlet, *The Tryals of Captain John Rackam and Other Pirates*, published in Jamaica in 1721. At about the same time, Governor Lawes wrote from Jamaica to the Council of Trade and Plantations that *"the women, spinsters of Providence Island, were proved to have taken an active part in piracies, wearing men's clothes and armed etc."* Finally, newspaper reports in the *American Weekly Mercury*, the *Boston Gazette*, and the *Boston News-Letter* mentioned but did not name the two women pirates who were members of Rackam's crew.[6]

The Tryals of Captain John Rackam contains testimony from the trial and verifies crucial parts of the narratives in Johnson's *General History*, independently establishing Anne Bonny and Mary Read as fierce, swashbuckling women, genuine pirates in every sense.[7] One of the witnesses against Bonny and Read was a woman, Dorothy Thomas, who had been captured and made prisoner by Rackam's crew. She claimed that the women "wore Mens Jackets, and long Trouzers, and Handkerchiefs tied about their Heads, and that each of them had a Machet[e] and Pistol in their Hands." Moreover, they at one point "cursed and swore at the Men," their fellow pirates, "to murther the Deponent." "They should kill her," they growled, "to prevent her coming against them" in court, as was indeed now happening before their very eyes. Bonny and Read were at the time dressed as men, but they did not fool Thomas: "the Reason of her knowing and believing them to be Women was, by the largeness of their Breasts."[8]

John Besnick and Peter Cornelius, likewise captives of Rackam and crew, testified that Bonny and Read "were very active on Board, and willing to do any Thing." Anne Bonny apparently worked as a powder monkey in times of engagement: she "handed gun-powder to the Men."[9] When Rackam and crew "saw any vessel, gave Chase or Attack'd," Bonny and Read "wore Men's Cloaths," but "at other Times," presumably times free of military confrontation, "they wore Women's Cloaths." According to these witnesses, the women "did not seem to be kept, or detain'd by Force," but rather took part in piracy "of their own Free-Will and Consent." Thomas Dillon, a captured master of a merchant vessel, added that they "were both very profligate, cursing, and swearing much, and very ready and willing to do any Thing on board."[10]

Despite the general authenticity of the tales of Anne Bonny and Mary Read,[11] many modern readers must surely have doubted them, thinking them descriptions of the impossible. After all, women never went to sea; seafaring was a man's world and a man's world only. But recent research throws doubt upon such uncritical assumptions. Linda Grant De Pauw has shown that women went to sea in many capacities: as passengers, servants, wives, prostitutes, laundresses, cooks, and occasionally—though certainly much less often—even as sailors, serving aboard naval, merchant, whaling, privateering, and pirate vessels.[12] Dianne Dugaw has written: "Perhaps the most surprising fact about eighteenth-century female soldiers and sailors is their frequency, not only in fiction but in history as well."[13] An anonymous British writer, possibly the dramatist and poet Oliver Goldsmith, wrote in 1762 that there were so many women in the British army that they deserved their own separate battalion, perhaps not unlike the contemporaneous women warriors who fought for the African kingdom of Dahomey.[14]

So Anne Bonny and Mary Read rigged themselves out in men's clothes and carried their bold imposture into the always rough, sometimes brutal world of maritime labor. Their cross-dressing adventures were not as unusual among early modern women as previously believed, but they nonetheless directly challenged customary maritime practice, which forbade women to work as seamen aboard deep-sea vessels of any kind. The reasons for the exclusion are not yet clear, but the evidence of it is incontrovertible: the ship was a sharply gendered workplace, reserved almost exclusively for male labor. Seafaring was a line of work long thought to "make a man" of anyone who entered.[15]

One reason why women found no berth would have been the sheer physical strength and stamina required for early modern maritime labor. Employing at this time a low level of machine power, the ship depended on brute strength for many of its most crucial operations—assisting in the loading and unloading of cargo (using pulleys and tackle), setting heavy canvas sails, and operating the ship's pump to eliminate the water that oozed through the seams of always-leaky vessels. A few women, obviously, did the work and did it well, earning the abiding respect of their fellow workers. But not everyone—certainly not all men—was equal to its demands. It was simply too strenuous, leaving in its wake lameness, hernias, a grotesque array of mutilations, and often premature death.[16]

A second and perhaps more important reason for the segregation of the sexes was the apparently widespread belief that women and sexuality more generally were inimical to work and social order aboard the ship. Arthur N. Gilbert has convincingly shown that homosexual practice in the eighteenth-century British Royal Navy was punished ruthlessly because it was considered subversive of discipline and good order.[17] Minister John Flavel made the same point when he wrote of seamen to merchant John Lovering, "The *Death* of their Lusts, is the most *Probable* Means to give *Life* to your Trade." Flavel, like many sea masters, saw the saving of souls and the accumulation of capital as complementary parts of a single disciplinary process.[18] But some version of his view apparently commanded acceptance at all levels of the ship's hierarchy. Many sailors saw women as objects of fantasy and adoration but also as sources of bad luck or, worse, as dangerous sources of conflict, as potential breaches in the male order of seagoing solidarity. Early modern seafarers seem to have agreed among themselves that some kind of sexual repression was necessary to do the work of the ship.[19]

The assumption was strong enough to command at least some assent from pirates, who were well known for organizing their ships in ways dramatically different from the merchant shipping industry and the Royal Navy. The freebooters who sailed the Mediterranean in the early seventeenth century refused to allow women aboard the ships because their presence was "too distracting."[20] The refusal was continued into the eighteenth century. The articles drawn up by Bartholomew Roberts and his crew specified: "No Boy or Woman to be allowed amongst them." Moreover, should a woman passenger be taken as a captive, "they put a Centinel immediately over her to prevent ill Consequences from so dangerous an Instrument of Division and Quarrel." The crew of John Phillips reasoned likewise: "If at any Time we meet with a prudent Woman, that Man that offers to meddle with her, without her Consent, shall suffer present Death." William Snelgrave, a slave trader held captive by pirates off the west coast of Africa in 1719, explained: "It is a rule amongst the Pirates, not to allow Women to be on board their Ships, when in the Harbour. And if they should Take a Prize at Sea, that has any Women on board, no one dares, on pain of death, to force them against their Inclinations. This being a good political Rule to prevent disturbances amongst them, it is strictly observed."[21]

Black Bart Roberts was more straitlaced than most pirate captains (he banned gambling among his crew, this too to reduce conflict), so it may be unwise to hold up his example as typical.[22] Another, perhaps more important doubt arises from evidence that Anne Bonny and Mary Read did not cross-dress all of the time aboard the pirate ship. As John Besnick and Peter Cornelius testified in court, "when [the pirates] saw any vessel, gave Chase or Attack'd, [Bonny and Read] wore Men's Cloaths, and, at other Times, they wore Women's Cloaths." In other words, they dressed as men only during times of chase or engagement, when a show of "manpower" and strength might help to intimidate their prey and force a quick surrender. Other times, presumably during the daily running of the ship, they dressed as women.[23]

The strongest test of the attitudes of male pirates toward the female would be the actual number of women who appeared on the sea rovers' ships in the early eighteenth century; the surviving evidence suggests that there were few. Two other women pirates appeared in this era, both in Virginia, where authorities tried Mary Harley (or Harvey) and three men for piracy in 1726; they sentenced the three men to hang but released the woman.[24] Three years later they tried a gang of six pirates, including Mary Crickett (or Crichett), all of whom were ordered to the gallows. Crickett and Edmund Williams, the leader of the pirates, had been transported as felons to Virginia aboard the same ship in late 1728.[25] It is not known whether Harley and Crickett cross-dressed to become pirates, nor if they were moved to do so by tales of Anne Bonny and Mary Read. The very presence of all four women among the pirates came to light only because their vessels were captured. Thus the pirate ship may have offered more room to women than either the merchant or naval vessels of the day, but still it was little enough. And in any case it existed only because radical female action created it in the first place.[26]

Bonny and Read were able to undertake such action in part because their class experiences and personal characteristics had prepared them to do so. They both drew upon and perpetuated a deeply rooted underground tradition of female cross-dressing, pan-European in its dimensions but especially strong in early modern England, the Netherlands, and Germany. Such disguise was usually, though not exclusively, undertaken by women of the working class.[27] Like other female cross-dressers, Bonny and Read were young, single, and humble of origin; their illegitimate births were not uncommon. Moreover, Bonny and Read perfectly illustrated what historians Rudolf M. Dekker and Lotte C. van de Pol have identified as the two main reasons why some women cross-dressed in the early modern era: Read did it largely out of poverty and economic necessity, while Bonny, turning her back on her father's fortune, followed her instincts for love and adventure.[28]

Anne Bonny may have been drawn to the sea and to piracy in particular by the popular lore in her native Ireland about Grace O'Malley, a pirate queen who in the late sixteenth century marauded up and down the Emerald Isle's western coast. O'Malley was fierce of action and visage: the face of this literally commanding figure had been badly scarred in her youth by the talons of an eagle. Sir Henry Sydney wrote in 1577 that O'Malley was "a notorious woman in all the coasts of Ireland." Such coasts would have included the port of Cork, where O'Malley had often attacked the merchant ships that sailed to the Iberian Peninsula and where Bonny was born to a family with seafaring experience.[29]

In any event, Bonny and Read became part of a larger tradition that included such famous women as Mrs. Christian Davies, who, dressed as a man, chased her dragooned husband from Dublin to the European continent; survived numerous battles, wounds, and capture by the French; and returned to England and military honors bestowed by Queen Anne.[30] Ann Mills went to sea "about the year 1740," serving as "a common sailor onboard the Maidstone frigate" during the War of Austrian Succession. She distinguished herself in hand-to-hand combat against "a French enemy" and "cut off the head of her opponent, as a trophy of victory."[31] Perhaps the best known cross-dressing sailor of the eighteenth century was Hannah Snell, who ran away to sea in 1745 in search of a seafaring husband who had abandoned her pregnant self. Accounts of her life appeared in the *Gentlemen's Magazine,* the *Scots Magazine,* and in books long and short, in English and in Dutch.[32]

Women such as Mrs. Christian Davies, Ann Mills, and Hannah Snell were also, significantly, celebrated in popular ballads around the Atlantic world. A "semi-literate lower class" of "apprentices, servants, charwomen, farmworkers, laborers, soldiers, and sailors" sang the glories of "warrior women" at the fairs, on the wharves, around the street corners, and amid the mass gatherings at hangings.[33] Anne Bonny and Mary Read came of age in an era when female warrior ballads soared to the peak of their popularity.[34]

Dianne Dugaw has pointed out that ballads about warrior women gave "a surprisingly accurate, if conventionalized, reading of lower-class [female] experience," which as a matter of course bred physical strength, toughness, independence, fearlessness, and a capability of surviving by

Ann Mills with one of the spoils of war, c. 1740; artist unknown
James Caulfield, *Portraits, Memoirs, and Characters of Remarkable Persons from the Revolution in 1688 to the End of the Reign of George II* (London, 1820)

one's wits. The prevailing material reality of working women's lives made it possible for some women to disguise themselves and enter worlds dominated by men; the same reality then assured that such women would be familiar enough within early working-class culture to be celebrated. Bonny and Read represented not the typical, but the strongest side of popular womanhood.[35]

Their strength was a matter of body and mind, for they were well suited to maritime labor and piracy in ways both physical and temperamental. By the time she was a teenager Read was already "growing bold and strong." Bonny was described as "robust" and of "fierce and couragious temper." In "times of Action, no Person amongst [the pirates] was more resolute, or ready to board or undertake any Thing that was hazardous" than Bonny and Read, not least because they had, by the time they sailed beneath the Jolly Roger, already endured all manner of hazard. Read's mother had been married to "a Man who used the Sea" but who was himself apparently used up by it; Anne Bonny's mother was a "Maid-Servant." As illegitimate children, both faced shifting, precarious circumstances early in life. The art of survival in a rough proletarian world included a capacity for self-defense, which both Bonny and Read had mastered.[36] Read's experience in the British infantry and cavalry helped make her a fearsome duelist among the pirates. Bonny's training was less formal but no less effective, as the would-be rapist suddenly and painfully discovered.[37]

Bonny and Read were thus well prepared to adopt the sailor's and even the pirate's cultural style, which they did with enthusiasm. They cursed and swore like any good sailor. They were, moreover, armed to the teeth, carrying their pistols and machetes like those well trained in the ways of war. They also affirmed one of the principal values and standards of conduct among both seamen and pirates, that is, an unwritten code of courage. Calico Jack Rackam got his big boost in the pirate world when his captain, Charles Vane, refused to engage a French man-of-war, which led immediately to charges of cowardice, a democratic vote of no confidence, and Rackam's promotion from quartermaster to captain. Among sailors and especially pirates, courage was a principal means of survival; cowardice was an invitation to disaster and ultimately death.[38]

Courage was traditionally seen as a masculine virtue, but Mary Read and Anne Bonny proved that women might possess it in abundance. They demonstrated it in the mutinies that launched each of them into piracy and again in the skirmish after which they were captured, when Mary Read fired a pistol into the hold at her quivering comrades. Read dreaded to hear her lover called a coward; Bonny called her own lover as much as the noose neared his neck in Port Royal. The strongest evidence of the importance of courage came in Mary Read's class-conscious answer to a captive's question about facing an "ignominious Death" upon the gallows, when she gamely insisted that "Men of Courage"—like herself—would not fear it. She indicted the cowardly rogues ashore who used the law as an instrument of oppression; in so doing she commented indirectly on the broad, violent redefinition of property relations that was taking place in her native England at the very moment she uttered her condemnation.[39]

Read considered courage a resource, something akin to a skill that offered the poor some protection in a vicious labor market. The same idea was expressed more fully by pirate captain Charles Bellamy, who lectured a captured captain thusly: "damn ye, you are a sneaking Puppy, and so are all those who will submit to be governed by Laws which rich Men have made for their own Security, for the cowardly Whelps have not the Courage otherwise to defend what they get by their Knavery; but damn ye altogether: Damn them for a Pack of crafty Rascals, and you, who serve them, for a Parcel of hen-hearted Numskuls. They villify us, the Scoundrels do, when there is only this Difference, they rob the Poor under the Cover of Law, forsooth, and we plunder the Rich under the Protection of our own Courage."[40] Courage was thus the antithesis of law; the working class had to have it in order to make their way in a world of sneaking puppies, hen-hearted numbskulls, crafty rascals, and scoundrels. This was the secularized eighteenth-century voice of the radical antinomian who had taken the law into his or her own hands during the English Revolution.

An antinomian disdain for state authority was evident in another part of the class experience of Anne Bonny and Mary Read, that is, their marital and family situations. Both women engaged in what John Gillis has called the "proletarian practice of self-marriage and self-divorce." Mary Read happily wedded herself to her husband. Anne Bonny, once she had prospects for a life of some wealth and class privilege, promptly turned her back on them, married a poor sailor, and headed off to a place known to be "a Receptacle and Shelter for Pirates & loose Fellows." The property-preserving marriage practices of the middle and upper classes were not for her. Nor, apparently, was the marriage to James Bonny, for she soon tried, with the help of her new lover, Calico Jack Rackam, to arrange a popular form of divorce known as a "wife sale" in order to end an old relationship and begin a new one. Calico Jack was to give her husband "a Sum of Money, in Consideration he should resign her to the said *Rackam* by a Writing in Form, and she even spoke to some Persons to witness the said Writing." When Governor Woodes Rogers refused to validate the popular custom, threatening instead to whip and imprison Anne for such "loose Behaviour," she and Calico Jack, "finding they could not by fair Means enjoy each other's Company with Freedom, resolved to run away together, and enjoy it in Spight of all the World." Bonny and Read thus exercised marital liberty, the collective choice of which helped to generate the passage of England's Hardwicke Act of 1753, designed to restrict legal marriage to public ceremonies conducted in the church.[41]

Anne Bonny and Mary Read threw down their greatest challenge to state authority by choosing the life of the pirate, which was yet another class experience and no less, in its way, about liberty. Captain Charles Johnson recognized piracy as a "Life of Liberty" and made the matter a major theme of his book. Bonny and Read took part in a utopian experiment beyond the reach of the traditional powers of family, state, and capital, one that was carried out by working men and at least a few women. They added another dimension altogether to the subversive appeal of piracy by seizing what was regarded as male liberty. In so doing they were not merely tolerated by their male compatriots, for they clearly exercised considerable leadership aboard their vessel. Although not formally elected by their fellow pirates to posts of command, they nonetheless led by example—in fighting duels, in keeping the deck in time of engagement, and in being part of the group designated to board prizes, a right always reserved to the most daring and respected members of the crew. They proved that a woman could find liberty beneath the Jolly Roger.[42]

Did Anne Bonny and Mary Read, in the end, make their mark upon the world? Did their daring make a difference? Did they leave a legacy? Dianne Dugaw argues in this volume that the popular genre of ballads about warrior women like Bonny and Read was largely suffocated in the early nineteenth century by a new bourgeois idea of womanhood. Warrior women, when they appeared, were comical, grotesque, and absurd, since they lacked the now-essential female traits of delicacy, constraint, and frailty. The warrior woman, in culture if not in actual fact, had been tamed.[43]

But the stubborn truth remained: even though Bonny and Read did not transform the terms in which the broader societal discussion of gender took place, and even though they apparently did not see their own exploits as a call for rights and equality for all women, their very lives and subsequent popularity nonetheless represented a subversive commentary on the gender relations of their own times as well as "a powerful symbol of unconventional womanhood" for the future. The frequent reprinting of their tales in the romantic literature of the eighteenth, nineteenth, and twentieth centuries surely captured the imaginations of many girls and young women who felt imprisoned by ideologies of femininity and domesticity.[44] Julia Wheelwright has shown that nineteenth-century feminists used the examples of female soldiers and sailors "to challenge prevailing notions about women's innate physical and mental weakness." Bonny and Read, like many others, offered ample disproof of then-dominant theories of women's incapacity.[45]

Anne Bonny, Mary Read, and women like them had captured many an imagination in their own day, including those at work in the realm of literature. Bonny and Read were real-life versions of Defoe's famous heroine, Moll Flanders, with whom they had no small amount in common. All were illegitimate children, poor at birth and for years thereafter. All were what Defoe called "the offspring of debauchery and vice." Moll and Anne were born of mothers who carried them in the womb while in prison. All three found themselves on the wrong side of the law, charged with capital crimes against property, facing "the steps and the string," popular slang for the gallows. All experienced homelessness and roving transiency, including trips across the great Atlantic. All recognized the importance of disguise, the need to be able to appear in "several shapes." Moll Flanders too had cross-dressed: her governess and partner in crime "laid a new contrivance for my going abroad, and this was to dress me up in men's clothes, and so put me into a new kind of practice."[46] Moll even had a brush with pirates during her passage to Virginia, though she encountered no women on board. Had she decided to join up with those who sailed beneath the Jolly Roger, the lives of Anne Bonny and Mary Read might be read as one possible outcome to the novel, which was published the year after our heroines' adventures in any case.

Christopher Hill has written, "The early novel takes its life from motion." Writing of the seventeenth and early eighteenth centuries, he concludes that "the novel doesn't grow only out of the respectable bourgeois household. It also encompasses the picaro, the vagabond, the itinerant, the pirate—outcasts from the stable world of good householders—those who cannot or will not adapt." Peter Linebaugh has agreed, emphasizing the proletarian origins of the picaresque novel in the early modern age, especially in England where the literary form "reached an apogee in the publication of *Moll Flanders* in 1722." Thus the experiences of the teeming, often dispossessed masses in motion—people like Anne Bonny and Mary Read—were the raw materials of the imagination. Hannah Snell's contemporary biographer made the connection when he insisted that his subject was "the real *Pamella*," referring to Richardson's famous novel. The often-desperate activity of working-class women and men in the age of nascent capitalism thus helped to generate one of the world's most important and durable literary forms, the novel, which indeed is inconceivable apart from them.[47]

Anne Bonny and Mary Read also affected another major area of literary endeavor, that is, drama. It is widely known that John Gay's *The Beggar's Opera* was one of eighteenth-century England's most popular and successful plays. It is less widely known that in 1728–29 Gay wrote *Polly: an Opera, being the Second Part of the Beggar's Opera*. The sequel's obscurity was a matter of political repression, for it was censored by none other than Prime Minister Robert Walpole, who was less than happy that he had appeared in *The Beggar's Opera* as "Bob Booty." Disliking Gay's effort to establish moral equivalence between highway robbers and the prime minister's own circle in government and considering the new play to be a still-seditious continuation of the old, Walpole had *Polly* banned. But in so doing, he may have made *Polly* even more popular. Demand for the new play was clamorous: thousands of subscriptions brought Gay a handsome sum of money, though not nearly as much as would have been his if twenty-odd pirate printers and booksellers had not produced and sold their own editions. *Polly* achieved a popular presence and visibility well before its first performance in 1777.[48]

The namesake of the play was the daughter of a Jonathan Wild–type character called Peachum. Polly came to the New World, the West Indies in particular, in search of her love, Macheath, the highwayman of *The Beggar's Opera*, who had been transported for his crimes. Macheath, Polly discovered, had turned pirate, disguised as Morano, a "Negro villain" and captain of a crew of freebooters.[49] En route to America, Polly's money was stolen, which forced her to indenture herself as a servant. She was bought by a Mrs. Trapes, who ran a house of prostitution, then sold by the madame to a wealthy sugar planter, Mr. Ducat. Polly escaped the situation by cross-dressing "in a man's habit," going to sea as a pirate in search of Macheath. She did it, she explained, "To protect me from the violences and insults to which my sex might have exposed me."[50]

The very act of writing a play that featured women pirates only a few years after Anne Bonny and Mary Read had stood trial suggests that Gay knew of and drew upon the adventures of the real women pirates. The likelihood is made even stronger by specific similarities between the play and the freebooting reality of the Caribbean earlier in the decade. Jenny Diver, a prostitute in *The Beggar's Opera* and Macheath's (Morano's) "doxy" aboard the pirate ship, may have, in the new play, been modeled on Anne Bonny. Like Anne, Jenny is the lover of the pirate captain; she also falls for another pirate who turns out to be a disguised woman, in this case the cross-dressed Polly rather than Mary Read. For her part, Polly resembles Mary Read in her modest, even "virtuous" sexual bearing.[51]

Anne Bonny and Mary Read may have influenced posterity in yet another, more indirect way, through an illustration by an unknown artist that appeared as the frontispiece of the Dutch translation of Captain Charles Johnson's *A General History of the Pyrates*, now called *Historie der Engelsche Zee-Roovers*. It featured a bare-breasted woman militant, armed with a sword and a torch, surging forward beneath the Jolly Roger, the international flag of piracy. In the background at the left hangs a gibbet with ten executed pirates adangling; at the right is a ship in flames. Trampled underfoot are an unidentifiable document, perhaps a map or a legal decree; a capsizing ship with a broken mainmast; a woman still clutching the scales of justice; and a man, possibly a soldier, who appears to have his hands bound behind his back. Hovering at the right is a mythic figure, perhaps Aeolus, Greek god of the winds, who adds his part to the tempestuous scene.[52] Bringing up the rear of the chaos is a small sea monster, a figure commonly drawn by early modern mapmakers to adorn the aquatic parts of the globe. The illustration is an allegory of piracy, the central image of which is female, armed, violent, riotous, criminal, and destructive of property—in short, the very picture of anarchy.[53]

The characteristics of the allegory of piracy were equally those of the lives of Anne Bonny and Mary Read, who were, not surprisingly, featured prominently in the *Historie der Engelsche Zee-Roovers*, not only in its pages but in separate illustrations and even on the cover page, directly opposite the frontispiece, where the book proudly advertised its account of their lives. It seems almost certain that these two real-life pirates, who lived, as their narrative claimed, by "Fire or Sword," inspired the illustrator to depict insurgent piracy in the allegorical form of a militant, marauding woman holding fire in one hand, a sword in the other.

It is instructive to compare the work to a famous painting, Eugène Delacroix's *Le 28 juillet: la Liberté guidant le peuple*, for the similarities are striking.[54] Compositionally the works are remarkably similar: a central female figure, armed, bare-breasted, and dressed in a Roman tunic, looks back as she propels herself forward—upward, over, and above a mass of bodies strewn below. The working-class identity of each woman is indicated by the bulk, muscle, and obvious strength of her physique; Parisian critics in 1831 were scandalized by the "dirty" Liberty, whom they denounced as a whore, a fishwife, a part of the "rabble."[55] Moreover, flags and conflagrations help to frame each work: the Jolly Roger and a burning ship at the right give way to the French tricolor and a burning building in almost identical locations. An armed youth, a street urchin, stands in for the windmaker.[56] Where the rotting corpses of pirates once hung now mass "the people." Two soldiers, both apparently dead, lie in the forefront.

There are differences: Liberty now has a musket with bayonet rather than a sword and torch. Still she leads but now takes her inspiration from the living rather than the dead. "The people" in arms have replaced "the people"—as a ship's crew was commonly called in the eighteenth century—who are hanging by the neck in the Dutch illustration.[57]

More importantly, Delacroix has softened and idealized both the female body and the face, replacing anger and anguish with a tranquil, if determined, solemnity. His critics notwithstanding, Delacroix has also turned a partially naked woman into a partially nude woman, exerting over the female body an aesthetic control that parallels the taming of the warrior woman in popular balladry. Liberty thus contains her contradictions: she is both a "dirty" revolutionary born of action and an otherworldly, idealized female subject combining a classical artistic inheritance and a new nineteenth-century definition of femininity.[58]

It cannot be proven definitively that Delacroix saw the earlier graphic and used it as a model. The artist discontinued his journal—where he might have noted such an influence—in 1824 and did not return to it until 1847. And in any case, both the Dutch and the French artist probably drew upon classical depictions of goddesses such as Athena, Artemis, and Nike as they imagined their subjects.[59] Regardless, there is a great deal of circumstantial evidence to suggest that the allegory of piracy may have influenced Delacroix's greatest work.

First, it is well known that Delacroix drew upon the experiences of real people in his rendition of *Liberty Leading the People*, including Marie Deschamps, who during the hottest of the July days seized the musket of a recently killed citizen and fired it against the Swiss guards, and "a poor laundry-girl" known only as Anne-Charlotte D., who was said to have killed nine Swiss soldiers in avenging her brother's death.[60] These real women, like Anne Bonny and Mary Read, were bound to appeal to the romantic imagination.[61]

An allegory of piracy, probably inspired by the tales of Mary Read and Anne Bonny; artist unknown, 1725

Capiteyn Charles Johnson, *Historie der Engelsche Zee-Roovers* (Amsterdam, 1725)

Liberty beneath the Jolly Roger

Second, Delacroix himself noted in his journal that he often studied engravings, woodcuts, and popular prints as he conceptualized his paintings and sought to solve compositional problems. By the time Delacroix composed his famous painting, late in 1830, at least twenty editions of *A General History of the Pyrates* had appeared, six (or more) of these in French and many containing the Dutch illustration. The majority of these editions, which, including the French, advertised the stories of Bonny and Read on their title pages, would have been available to the artist in Paris.[62]

Third, and most importantly, it can be established that piracy was on

"Le 28 juillet: la Liberté guidant le peuple," by Engène Delacroix. Delacroix may have drawn upon knowledge of the lives of Mary Read and Anne Bonny in creating one of the world's most famous images of liberty.

The Louvre, Paris

Delacroix's mind at the very moment he was painting *Liberty*. The English romantic poet Lord Byron was, according to art historian George Heard Hamilton, "an inexhaustible source of inspiration" for the painter. Delacroix engaged the work of Byron intensely during the 1820s, exhibiting three major paintings on subjects from Byron's poetry in 1827 and executing several others on the Greek civil war, in which Byron ultimately lost his life. More crucially still, Delacroix was reading Byron's poem *The Corsair*—about piracy—as he was painting *Liberty*. At the very same salon in which he exhibited his greatest painting, in 1831, Delacroix also entered a watercolor based on Byron's poem.[63]

The image of piracy (1725) preceded the image of liberty (1830) by more than a century. And yet it seems that the liberty seized by Anne Bonny and Mary Read—the liberty they found so briefly, so tantalizingly, beneath the Jolly Roger—took a strange, crooked, still poorly understood path from the rough, rolling deck of a ship in the Caribbean to the polished, steady floor of an art salon in Paris. It was a case of liberty seized in action; of low culture affecting high; of New World struggles supplying and driving what once would have been seen as the genius and originality of European art and culture. It would be a fitting tribute to Anne Bonny and Mary Read if the example of these two women who seized liberty beneath the Jolly Roger in turn helped to inspire one of the most famous depictions of liberty the modern world has ever known.

Liberty beneath the Jolly Roger

The Narratives of Mary Read and Anne Bonny,
as they appeared in Captain Charles Johnson,
A General History of the Pyrates (London, 1724).

The LIFE of Mary Read

Now we are to begin a History full of surprizing Turns and Adventures; I mean, that of *Mary Read* and *Anne Bonny*, alias *Bonn*, which were the true Names of these two Pyrates; the odd Incidents of their rambling Lives are such that some may be tempted to think the whole Story no better than a Novel or Romance; but since it is supported by many thousand Witnesses, I mean the People of *Jamaica*, who were present at their Tryals, and heard the Story of their Lives, upon the first Discovery of their Sex; the Truth of it can be no more contested, than that there were such Men in the World, as *Roberts* and *Black-beard*, who were Pyrates.[64]

Mary Read was born in *England*, her Mother was married young, to a Man who used the Sea, who going a Voyage soon after their Marriage, left her with Child, which Child proved to be a Boy. As to the Husband, whether he was cast away, or died in the Voyage, *Mary Read* Could not tell; but however, he never returned more; nevertheless, the Mother, who was young and airy, met with an Accident, which has often happened to Women who are young, and do not take a great deal of Care; which was, she soon proved with Child again, without a Husband to Father it, but how, or by whom, none but her self could tell, for she carry'd a pretty good Reputation among her Neighbours. Finding her Burthen grew, in order to conceal her Shame, she takes a formal Leave of her Husband's Relations, giving out, that she went to live with some Friends of her own, in the Country: Accordingly she went away, and carry'd with her young Son, at this Time, not a Year old: Soon after her Departure her Son died, but Providence in Return, was pleased to give her a Girl in his Room, of which she was safely delivered, in her Retreat, and this was our *Mary Read*.

Here the Mother liv'd three or four Years, till what Money she had was almost gone; then she thought of returning to *London*, and considering that her Husband's Mother was in some Circumstances, she did not doubt but to prevail upon her, to provide for the Child, if she could but pass it upon her for the same, but the changing a Girl into a Boy, seem'd a difficult Piece of Work, and how to deceive an experienced old Woman, in such a Point, was altogether as impossible; however, she ventured to dress it up as a Boy, brought it to Town, and presented it to her Mother-in-Law, as her Husband's Son; the old Woman would have taken it, to have bred it up, but the Mother pretended it would break her Heart, to part with it; so it was agreed betwixt them, that the Child should live with the mother, and the supposed Grandmother should allow a Crown a Week for its maintenance.

Thus the Mother gained her Point, she bred up her Daughter as a Boy, and when she grew up to some Sense, she thought proper to let her into the Secret of her Birth, to induce her to conceal her Sex. It happen'd that the Grandmother died, by which Means the Subsistance that came from that Quarter, ceas'd, and they were more and more reduced in their Circumstances; wherefore she was obliged to put her Daughter out, to wait on a *French* Lady, as a, Foot-boy being now thirteen Years of Age: Here she did not live long, for growing bold and strong, and having also a roving Mind, she enter'd herself on board a Man of War, where she served some Time, then quitted it, went over into *Flanders,* and carry'd Arms in a Regiment of Foot, as a *Cadet;* and tho' upon all Actions, she behaved herself with a great deal of Bravery, yet she could not get a Commission, they being generally bought and sold; therefore she quitted the Service, and took on in a Regiment of Horse; she behaved so well in several Engagements, that she got the Esteem of all her Officers; but her Comrade, who was a *Fleming,* happening to be a handsome young Fellow, she falls in Love with him, and from that Time, grew a little more negligent in her Duty, so that, it seems, *Mars* and *Venus* could not be served at the same Time; her Arms and Accoutrements which were always kept in the best Order, were quite neglected: 'Tis true, when her Comrade was order'd out upon a Party, she used to go without being commanded and frequently run herself into Danger, where she had no Business, only to be near him; the rest of the Troopers little suspecting the secret Cause which moved her to this Behaviour, fancy'd her to be mad, and her Comrade himself could not account for this strange Alteration in her, but Love is ingenious, and as they lay together in the same Tent, and were constantly together, she found a Way of letting him discover her Sex, without appearing that it was done with Design.

He was much surprized at what he found out, and not a little pleased, taking it for granted, that he should have a Mistress solely to himself, which is an unusual Thing in a Camp, since there is scarce one of those Campaign Ladies, that is ever true to a Troop or Company; so that he thought of nothing but gratifying his Passions with very little Ceremony; but he found himself strangely mistaken, for she proved very reserved and modest, and resisted all his Temptations, and at the same Time was so obliging and insinuating in her Carriage, that she quite changed his Purpose, so far from thinking of making her his Mistress, he now courted her for a Wife.

This was the utmost Wish of her Heart, in short, they exchanged Promises, and when the Campaign was over, and the Regiment marched into Winter Quarters, they bought Woman's Apparel for her, with such Money as they could make up betwixt them, and were publickly married.

The Story of two Troopers marrying each other, made a great Noise, so that several Officers were drawn by Curiosity to assist at the Ceremony, and they agreed among themselves that every one of them should make a small Present to the Bride, towards House-keeping, in Consideration of her having been their Fellow-Soldier. Thus being set up, they seemed to have a Desire of quitting the Service, and settling in the World; the Adventure of their Love and Marriage had gained them so much Favour, that they easily obtained their Discharge, and they immediately set up an Eating-House or Ordinary, which was the Sign of the *Three Horse-Shoes*, near the Castle of *Breda*, where they soon run into a good Trade, a great many Officers eating with them constantly.

But this Happiness lasted not long, for the Husband soon died, and the Peace of *Ryswick* being concluded, there was no Resort of Officers to *Breda*, as usual, so that the Widow having little or no Trade, was forced to give up House-keeping, and her Substance being by Degrees quite spent, she again assumes her Man's Apparel, and going into *Holland*, there takes on in a Regiment of Foot, quartered in one of the Frontier Towns: Here she did not remain long, there was no Likelihood of Preferment in Time of Peace, therefore she took a Resolution of seeking her Fortune another Way; and withdrawing from the Regiment, ships herself on board of a Vessel bound for the *West-Indies*.[65]

It happened this Ship was taken by *English* Pyrates, and *Mary Read* was the only *English* Person on board, they kept her amongst them, and having plundered the Ship, let it go again; after following this Trade for some Time, the King's Proclamation came out, and was published in all Parts of the *West-Indies*, for pardoning such Pyrates, who should voluntarily surrender themselves by a certain Day therein mentioned.[66] The Crew of *Mary Read* took the Benefit of this Proclamation, and having surrender'd liv'd quietly on the Shore; but Money beginning to grow short, and hearing that Captain *Woodes Rogers*, Governor of the Island of *Providence*, was fitting out some Privateers to cruise against the *Spaniards*, she, with several others, embark'd for that Island, in order to go upon the privateering Account, being resolved to make her Fortune one way or other.[67]

These Privateers were no sooner sail'd out, but the Crews of some of them, who had been pardoned, rose against their Commanders, and turned themselves to their old Trade: In this Number was *Mary Read*.[68] It is true, she often declared, that the Life of a Pyrate was what she always abhor'd, and went into it only upon Compulsion, both this Time, and before, intending to quit it, whenever a fair Opportunity should offer it self; yet some of the Evidence against her, upon her Tryal, who were forced Men, and had sail'd with her, deposed upon Oath, that in Times of Action, no Person amongst them was more resolute, or ready to board or undertake any Thing that was hazardous, than she and *Anne Bonny*; and particularly at the time they were attack'd and taken, when they came to close Quarters, none kept the Deck except *Mary Read* and *Anne Bonny*, and one more; upon which, she, *Mary Read*, called to those under Deck, to come up and fight like Men, and finding they did not stir, fired her Arms down the Hold amongst them, killing one, and wounding others.

This was part of the Evidence against her, which she denied; which, whether true or no, thus much is certain, that she did not want Bravery, nor indeed was she less remarkable for her Modesty, according to the Notions of Virtue: Her Sex was not so much as suspected by any Person on board till *Anne Bonny*, who was not altogether so reserved in Point of Chastity, took a particular Liking to her; in short, *Anne Bonny* took her for a handsome young Fellow, and for some Reasons best known to herself, first discovered her Sex to *Mary Read*; *Mary Read* knowing what she would be at, and being very sensible of her own Incapacity that Way, was forced to come to a right Understanding with her, and so to the great Disappointment of *Anne Bonny*, she let her know she was a Woman also; but this Intimacy so disturb'd Captain *Rackam*, who was the Lover and Gallant of *Anne Bonny*, he would cut her new Lover's Throat, therefore, to quiet him, she let him into the Secret also.

Captain *Rackam* (as he was enjoined) kept the Thing a Secret from all the Ship's Company, yet, notwithstanding all her Cunning and Reserve, Love found her out in this Disguise, and hinder'd her from forgetting her Sex. In their Cruise they took a great Number of Ships belonging to *Jamaica*, and other Parts of the *West-Indies*, bound to and from *England*; and whenever they met any good Artist, or other Person that might be of any great Use to their Company, if he was not willing to enter, it was their Custom to keep him by Force.[69] Among these was a young Fellow of most engaging Behaviour, or, at least, he was so in the Eyes of *Mary Read*, who became so smitten with his Person and Address, that she could neither rest Night or Day; but there is nothing more ingenious than Love, it was no hard Matter for her, who had before been practiced in these Wiles, to find a Way to let him discover her Sex: She first insinuated herself into his Liking, by talking against the Life of a Pyrate, which he was altogether averse to, so they became Mess-Mates and strict Companions: When she found he had a Friendship for her, as a Man, she suffered the Discovery to be made, by carelessly shewing her Breasts, which were very white.

The young Fellow, who was made of Flesh and Blood, had his Curiosity and Desire so rais'd by this Sight, that he never ceas'd importuning her, till she confessed what she was. Now begins the Scene of Love; as he had a Liking and Esteem for her, under her supposed Character, it was now turn'd into Fondness and Desire; her Passion was no less violent than his, and perhaps she express'd it, by one of the most generous Actions that ever Love inspired. It happened this young Fellow had a Quarrel with one of the Pyrates, and their Ship then lying at an Anchor, near one of the Islands, they had appointed to go ashore and fight, according to the Custom of Pyrates: *Mary Read* was to the last Degree uneasy and anxious, for the Fate of her Lover, she would not have had him refuse the Challenge, because, she could not bear the Thoughts of his being branded with Cowardice; on the other Side, she dreaded the Event, and apprehended the Fellow might be too hard for him: When Love once enters into the Breast of one who has any Sparks of Generosity, it stirs the Heart up to the most noble Actions; in this Dilemma, she shew'd, that she fear'd more for his Life than she did for her own; for she took a Resolution of quarrelling with this Fellow her self, and having challenged him ashore, she appointed the Time two Hours sooner than that when he was to meet her Lover, where she fought him at Sword and Pistol, and killed him upon the Spot.[70]

It is true, she had fought before, when she had been insulted by some of those Fellows, but now it was altogether in her Lover's Cause, she stood as it were betwixt him and Death, as if she could not live without him. If he had no regard for her before, this Action would have bound him to her for ever; but there was no Occasion for Ties or Obligation, his Inclination towards her was sufficient; in fine, they plighted their Troth to each other, which *Mary Read* said, she look'd upon to be as good a Marriage, in Conscience, as if it had been done by a Minister in Church; and to this was owing her great Belly, which she pleaded to save her Life.

She declared she had never committed Adultery or Fornication with any Man, she commended the Justice of the Court, before which she was try'd, for distinguishing the Nature of their Crimes; her Husband, as she call'd him, with several others, being acquitted; and being ask'd, who he was? she would not tell, but, said he was an honest Man, and had no Inclination to such Practices, and that they had both resolved to leave the Pyrates, the first Opportunity, and apply themselves to some honest Livelihood.

It is no doubt, but many had Compassion for her, yet the Court could not avoid finding her Guilty; for among other Things, one of the Evidences against her, deposed, that being taken by *Rackam*, and detain'd some Time on board, he fell accidentally into Discourse with *Mary Read*, whom he was taking for a young Man, ask'd her, what Pleasure she could have in being concerned in such Enterprizes, where her Life was continually in Danger, by Fire or Sword; and not only so, but she must be sure of dying an ignominious Death, if she should be taken alive?—She answer'd, that as to hanging, she thought it no great Hardship, for, were it not for that, every cowardly Fellow would turn Pyrate, and so infest the Seas, that Men of Courage must starve:—That if it was put to the Choice of the Pyrates, they would not have the Punishment less than Death, the Fear of which kept some dastardly Rogues honest; that many of those who are now cheating the Widows and Orphans, and oppressing their poor Neighbours, who have no Money to obtain Justice, would then rob at Sea, and the Ocean would be crowded with Rogues, like the Land, and no Merchant would venture out; so that the Trade, in a little Time, would not be worth following.

Being found quick with Child, as has been observed, her Execution was respited, and it is possible she would have found Favour, but she was seiz'd with a violent Fever, soon after her Tryal, of which she died in Prison.

The LIFE of Anne Bonny

As we have been more particular in the Lives of these two Women, than those of other Pyrates, it is incumbent on us, as a faithful Historian, to begin with their Birth. *Anne Bonny* was born at a Town near *Cork*, in the Kingdom of *Ireland*, her Father an Attorney at Law, but *Anne* was not one of his legitimate Issue, which seems to cross an old Proverb, which says, *that Bastards have the best Luck*. Her Father was a married Man, and his Wife having been brought to Bed, contracted an Illness in her lying in, and in order to recover her Health, she was advised to remove for Change of Air; the Place she chose, was a few Miles distance from her Dwelling, where her Husband's Mother liv'd. Here she sojourn'd some Time, her Husband staying at Home, to follow his Affairs. The Servant-Maid, whom

Liberty beneath the Jolly Roger

she left to look after the House, and attend the Family, being a handsome young Woman, was courted by a young Man of the same Town, who was a *Tanner*; this *Tanner* used to take his Opportunities, when the Family was out of the Way, of coming to pursue his Courtship; and being with the Maid one Day as she was employed in the Household Business, not having the Fear of God before his Eyes, he takes his Opportunity, when her Back was turned, of whipping three Silver Spoons into his Pocket. The Maid soon miss'd the Spoons and knowing that no Body had been in the Room but herself and the young Man, since she saw them last, she charged him with taking them; he very stifly denied it, upon which she grew outragious, and threatned to go to a Constable, in order to carry him before a Justice of Peace: These Menaces frighten'd him out of his Wits, well knowing he could not stand Search; wherefore he endeavoured to pacify her, by desiring her to examine the Drawers and other Places, and perhaps she might find them; in this Time he slips into another Room, where the Maid usually lay, and puts the Spoons betwixt the Sheet, and then Makes his Escape by a back Door, concluding she must find them, when she went to Bed, and so next Day he might pretend he did it only to frighten her, and the Thing might be laugh'd off for a Jest.

As soon as she miss'd him, she gave over her Search, concluding he had carry'd them off, and went directly to the Constable, in order to have him apprehended: The young Man was informed, that a Constable was in Search of him, but he regarded it but little, not doubting but all would be well next Day. Three or four Days passed, and still he was told, the Constable was upon the Hunt for him, this made him lye concealed, he could not comprehend the Meaning of it, he imagined no less, than that the Maid had a Mind to convert the Spoons to her own Use, and put the Robbery upon him.

It happen'd, at this Time, that the Mistress being perfectly recovered of her late Indisposition, was returned Home, in Company with her Mother-in-Law; the first News she heard, was of the Loss of the Spoons, with the Manner how; the Maid telling her, at the same Time, that the young Man was run away. The young Fellow had Intelligence of the Mistress's Arrival, and considering with himself, that he could never appear again in his Business, unless this Matter was got over, and she being a good-natured Woman, he took a Resolution of going directly to her, and of telling her the whole Story, only with this Difference, that he did it for a Jest.

The Mistress could scarce believe it, however, she went directly to the Maid's Room, and turning down the Bed Cloaths, there, to her great

Surprize, found the three Spoons; upon this she desired the young Man to go Home and mind his Business, for he should have no Trouble about it.

The Mistress could not imagine the Meaning of this, she never had found the Maid guilty of any pilfering, and therefore it could not enter her Head, that she designed to steal the Spoons her self; upon the whole, she concluded the Maid had not been in her Bed, from the Time the Spoons were miss'd, she grew immediately jealous upon it, and suspected, that the Maid supply'd her Place with her Husband, during her Absence, and this was the Reasons why the Spoons were no sooner found.

She call'd to Mind several Actions of Kindness, her Husband had shewed the maid, Things that pass'd unheeded by, when they happen'd, but now she had got the Tormentor, Jealousy, in her Head, amounted to Proofs of their Intimacy; another Circumstance which strengthen'd the whole, was, that tho' her Husband knew she was to come Home that Day, and had no Communication with her in four Months, which was before her last lying in, yet he took an Opportunity of going out of Town that Morning, upon some slight Pretence:—All these Things put together, confirm'd her in her Jealousy.

As Women seldom forgive Injuries of this Kind, she thought of discharging her Revenge upon the Maid: In Order to [do] this, she leaves the Spoons where she found them, and orders the Maid to put clean Sheets upon the Bed, telling her, she intended to lye there herself that Night, because her Mother-in-Law was to lye in her Bed, and that she (The Maid) must lye in another Part of the House; the Maid in making the Bed, was surprized with the Sight of the Spoons, but there were very good Reasons, why it was not proper for her to tell where she found them, therefore she takes them up, puts them in her Trunk, intending to leave them in some Place, where they might be found by Chance.

The Mistress, that every Thing might look to be done without Design, lyes that Night in the Maid's Bed, little dreaming of what an Adventure it would produce: After she had been a Bed some Time, thinking on what had pass'd, for Jealousy kept her awake, she heard some Body enter the Room; at first she apprehended it to be Thieves, and was so fright'ned, she had not Courage enough to call out; but when she heard these Words, Mary, *are you awake?* she knew it to be her Husband's Voice; then her Fright was over, yet she made no Answer, least he should find her out, if she spoke, therefore she resolved to counterfeit Sleep, and take what followed.

The Husband came to Bed, and that Night play'd the vigorous Lover;

but one Thing spoiled the Diversion on the Wife's Side, which was, the Reflection that it was not design'd for her; however she was very passive, and bore it like a Christian. Early before Day, she stole out of Bed, leaving him asleep, and went to her Mother-in-Law, telling her what had passed; not forgetting how he had used her, taking her for the Maid; the Husband also stole out, not thinking it convenient to be catched in that Room; in the mean Time, the Revenge of the Mistress was strongly against the Maid, and without considering that to her she owed the Diversion of the Night before, and that one good *Turn* should deserve another; she sent for a Constable, and charged her with stealing the Spoons: The Maid's Trunk was broke open, and the Spoons found, upon which she was carry'd before a Justice of Peace, and by him committed to Gaol.

The Husband loiter'd about till twelve a-Clock at Noon, then comes Home, pretending he was just come to Town; as soon as he heard what had pass'd in Relation to the Maid, he fell into a great Passion with his Wife; this set the Thing into a greater Flame, the Mother takes the Wife's Part against her own Son, insomuch that the Quarrel encreasing, the Mother and Wife took Horse immediately, and went back to the Mother's House, and the Husband and Wife never bedded together after.

The Maid lay a long Time in the Prison, it being near half a Year to the Assizes; but before it happened, it was discovered she was with Child; when she was arraign'd at the Bar, she was discharged for want of Evidence; the Wife's Conscience touch'd her, and as she did not believe the Maid Guilty of any Theft, except that of Love, she did not appear against her; soon after her Acquittal, she was delivered of a Girl.

But what alarm'd the Husband most, was, that it was discovered the Wife was with Child also, he taking it for granted, he had no Intimacy with her, since her last lying in, grew jealous of her, in his Turn, and made this a Handle to justify himself, for his Usage of her, pretending now he had suspected her long, but that here was Proof; she was delivered of Twins, a Boy and a Girl.

The Mother falling ill, sent to her Son to reconcile him to his Wife, but he would not hearken to it; therefore she made a Will, leaving all she had in the Hands of certain Trustees, for the Use of the Wife and two Children lately born, and died a few Days after.

This was an ugly Turn upon him, his greatest Dependance being upon his Mother; however his Wife was kinder to him than he deserved, for she made him a yearly Allowance out of what was left, tho' they continued to live separate: It lasted near five Years; at this Time having a great Affection for the Girl he had by his Maid, he had a Mind to take it Home, to live with him; but as all the Town knew it to be a Girl, the better to disguise the Matter from them, as well as from his Wife, he had it put into Breeches, as a Boy, pretending it was a Relation's Child he was to breed up to be his Clerk.

The Wife heard he had a little Boy at Home he was very fond of, but as she did not know any Relation of his that had such a Child, she employ'd a Friend to enquire further into it; this Person by talking with the Child, found it to be a Girl, discovered that the Servant-Maid was its Mother, and that the Husband still kept up his Correspondence with her.

Upon this Intelligence, the Wife being unwilling that her Children's Money should go towards the Maintainance of Bastards, stopped the Allowance: The Husband enraged, in a kind of Revenge, takes the Maid home, and lives with her publickly, to the great Scandal of his Neighbours; but he soon found the bad Effect of it, for by Degrees he lost his Practice, so that he saw plainly he could not live there, therefore he thought of removing, and turning what Effects he had into ready Money; he goes to *Cork,* and there with his Maid and Daughter embarques for *Carolina.*[71]

At first he followed the Practice of the Law in that Province, but afterwards fell into Merchandize, which proved more successful to him, for he gained by it sufficient to purchase a considerable Plantation: His Maid, who passed for his Wife, happened to die, after which his Daughter, our *Anne Bonny,* now grown up, kept his House.

She was of a fierce and couragious Temper, wherefore, when she lay under Condemnation, several Stories were reported of her, much of her Disadvantage, as that she had kill'd an *English* Servant-Maid once in her Passion with a Case-Knife, while she look'd after her Father's House; but upon further Enquiry, I found this Story to be groundless: It was certain she was so robust, that once, when a young Fellow would have lain with her, against her Will, she beat him so, that he lay ill of it a considerable Time.

While she lived with her Father, she was look'd upon as one that would be a good Fortune, wherefore it was thought her Father expected a good Match for her; but she spoil'd all, for without his Consent, she marries a young Fellow, who belong'd to the Sea, and was not worth a Groat; which provoked her Father to such a Degree, that he turn'd her out of Doors, upon which the young Fellow, who married her, finding himself disappointed in his Expectation, shipped himself and Wife, for the Island of *Providence,* expecting Employment there.[72]

Here she became acquainted with *Rackam* the Pyrate, who making Courtship to her, soon found Means of withdrawing her Affections from her Husband, so that she consented to elope from him, and go to Sea with *Rackam* in Men's Cloaths; She was as good as her Word, and after she had been at Sea some Time, she proved with Child, and beginning to grow big, *Rackam* landed her on the Island of *Cuba;* and recommending her there to some Friends of his, they took Care of her, till she was brought to Bed: When she was up and well again, he sent for her to bear him Company.

The King's Proclamation being out, for pardoning of Pyrates, he took the Benefit of it, and surrender'd; afterwards being sent upon the privateering Account, he return'd to his old Trade, as has been already hinted in the Story of *Mary Read*. In all these Expeditions, *Anne Bonny* bore him Company, and when any Business was to be done in their Way, no Body was more forward or couragious than she, and particularly when they were taken; she and *Mary Read*, with one more, were all the Persons that durst keep the Deck, as has been before hinted.

Her Father was known to a great many Gentleman Planters of *Jamaica*, who had dealt with him, and among whom he had a good Reputation; and some of them, who had been in *Carolina*, remember'd to have seen her in his House; wherefore they were enclined to shew her Favour, but the Action of leaving her Husband was an ugly Circumstance against her. The Day that *Rackam* was executed, by special Favour, he was admitted to see her; but all the Comfort she gave him, was, *that she was sorry to see him there, but if he had fought like a Man, he need not have been hang'd like a Dog.*

She continued in Prison, to the Time of her lying in, and afterwards reprieved from Time to Time; but what is become of her since, we cannot tell; only this we know, that she was not executed.

DIANNE DUGAW

Female Sailors Bold
Transvestite Heroines and the Markers of Gender and Class

Dianne Dugaw extends our understanding of the significance of early modern female sailors with her study of the place of these transvestite heroines in two centuries of Anglo-American popular imagination. For Dugaw, the rise and fall in popularity of "bold" women who sailed in disguise serves as an important indicator of dramatically changing gender ideals and class dynamics. Surveying street ballads and other published accounts, she finds that the seafaring subculture was portrayed as a legitimate context for working-class heroines in the 1700s, but by the nineteenth century it had become a place where "proper" women did not belong.

At the core of Dugaw's argument is a close analysis of the textual encounters between three eighteenth-century female sailors and two nineteenth-century women writers. Her examination of these interactions in print addresses a key transformation: the shift in the dominant way femaleness was understood and experienced, from an external code of manipulable markers of dress and behavior to an internalized set of supposedly natural physical and psychological characteristics. Dugaw links this sea change in Anglo-American society to the consolidation of the dominance of the middle class, a group for whom gender identity becomes interwoven with property ownership, patterns of consumption, and other attributes of class status. Her essay demonstrates how probing an interaction between maritime experience and land-based cultural production—here, the "imaginative preoccupation" with the "female sailor bold"—vividly reveals both the historically constructed nature and the interrelatedness of gender and class.

> Come all ye good people, and listen to my song
> While I relate a circumstance that does to love belong,
> Concerning a pretty maid who ventured we are told,
> Across the briny ocean as a female sailor bold . . .
> —Sung by Ben Henneberry of Devil's Island, Nova Scotia (c. 1930)

Female Sailors Bold

THE "female sailor bold" disguises herself as a man and goes to sea, a popular heroine of the early modern era. Sailing fictional and actual oceans, celebrated women of song, story, and real life ventured into that seafaring realm which imagination had traditionally reserved for men, for the *sons* of Odysseus and Aeneas.[1] Popular for more than two centuries, especially among the lower classes, the cross-dressing heroine is for us an engaging if enigmatic figure—a gender-confounding ideal of womanly behavior who defies simpleminded explanations of human sexuality and gender identity. Surprising and subversive, she brings us to confront some of our deepest assumptions.

This transvestite heroine visits us, as it were, from another world, one whose understandings of gender and sexuality we only partially share.[2] In this essay I explore this world and its legacy to our own. After sketching as a backdrop the popularity of the cross-dressing heroine in Anglo-American literature, I examine connections between this imaginative preoccupation and accounts of actual women sailors of the eighteenth century who lived out this story of disguise. Because these heroines reached the privileged realms of print from the lower levels of pre-Victorian society, their stories resonate with questions, not only about gender, but about social and economic power as well. My discussion probes the interdependence of gender and class in these accounts of female sailors, the ways that these two categories of the modern world mutually depend upon and construct each other.[3] Reading accounts of transvestite heroines leads us to acknowledge how gender—that is, femaleness and maleness and attributes associated with these categories—is historically constructed.[4]

Key changes in circumstance and attitude stand between our world and that of the "female sailor bold."[5] One factor is crucial, not only because it influenced the waning of the transvestite heroine in the popular imagination,[6] but also because it contributes significantly to our own ideology of gender: an ethos of female delicacy. This value system requires of women such attributes as passivity, slightness, softness, and weakness of constitution; sensitivity of perception and feeling; and refinement, modesty, shame, and restraint in actions. For Euro-American culture since the eighteenth century, the organization of gender difference has rested upon the widespread acceptance of this ethos with its presupposition of physical and emotional frailty as the "natural" mark of a "woman," and the converse, physical and emotional invulnerability, the "natural" mark of a "man." This value system is an ideology tied to historical and social circumstance.

THE FEMALE SAILOR.

The following song is founded on fact, however romantick it may appear. In the month of Febuary 1835 this interesting girl arrived at Fresh Wharf London Bridge, on board the Sarah; her sex having been discovered a few days previous. Of course so singular a circumstance as that of a young Female Sailor could not long be kept a secret; and, as is always the case, the most exagerated reports were immediately propagated; at length this extraordinary history reached the ears of the Lord Mayor, who with the greatest humanity, ordered one of the police to ascertain the particulars of the case and see whether she was ill used. The officer brought her to the Lord Mayor to whom she related the following interesting particulars—She said her name was Ann Jane Thornton, that she was in the 17th year of her age: her father being a widower took her and the rest of the family from Gloucestershire, where she was born to Donegal, when six years old, where her father now resides; she regretted leaving home, as it must have caused him many a sorrowful hour, he being always affectionate to her. When she was only 13 years old she met Capt. Alexander Burk, an Englishman but whose father resided in New York, and before she was 15 they became strongly attached to each other; soon afterwards Alexander Burk was obliged to go to New York, and she resolved to follow him: she quitted her father's house, accompanied by a maid servant and boy; and having procured a cabin boy's dress, she obtained a passage direct to America by degrees she became reconciled to her new situation; and when she arrived at New York, she hastened to the father of her sweetheart, whom she learnt was dead, disconsolate as she was, she hastened from East Point in North America, to St. Andrew's a distance of 70 miles through the woods alone walking all the way on foot. She then obtained the situation of cook and steward on board the Adelaide, and next in the Rover, in which latter vessel she sailed to St Andrew's where she fell in with the Sarah, Cap. M'Intire, who engaged her as cook and steward, and in which ship she arrived in the port of London.—For 31 months she had been engaged in these remarkable adventures and participated in the most severe toils of the crews of which she performed a part, with the greatest propriety and decorum.

Good people give attention and listen to my song,
I will unfold a circumstance that does to love belong;
Concerning of a pretty maid who ventur'd we are told,
Across the briny ocean as a female sailor bold.

Her name was Ann Jane Thornton, as you presently shall hear,
And also that she was born in fam'd Gloucestershire;
Her father now lives in Ireland, respected we are told,
And grieving for his daughter—this female sailor bold.

She was courted by a captain when not fifteen years of age,
And to be joined in holy wedlock this couple did engage,
But the captain was bound to America, as I will now unfold
And she followed him o'er the ocean did this female sailor bold.

She dress'd herself in sailors clothes and was overcome with
When with a captain she did engage to serve as cabin boy,
And when New York in America this fair maid did behold
She determined to seek her true love did this female sailor bold.

Then to her true loves fathers she hastened with speed,
When the news that she did hear most dreadful indeed,
That her love had been dead some time they to her did unfold
Which very near broke the heart of this female sailor bold

Some thousand miles she was from home from friends far away
Alone she traveled seventy miles thro' woods in North America
Bereft of all her kindred nor no parent to behold,
In anguish she cried my true love did this female sailor bold.

Then she went on board the Adelaide, to cross the troubled wave
And in storms of hail and gales of wind, she did all dangers brave
She served as cook and steward in the Adelaide we are told
Then sailed on board the Rover did the female sailor bold.

From St. Andrew's in America, this fair maid did set sail,
In a vessel called the Sarah and brav'd many a stormy gale
She did her duty like a man did reef and steer we're told,
By the captain she was respected well—the female sailor bold.

With pitch and tar her hands were hard, tho' once like velvet soft
She weighed the anchor, heav'd the lead and boldly went aloft
Just one and thirty months she braved the tempest we are told,
And always did her duty did the female sailor bold.

'Twas in the month of Febuary eighteen hundred thirty five,
She in the port of London in the Sarah did arrive;
Her sex was then discovered which the secret did unfold,
And the captain gaz'd in wonder on the female sailor bold.

At the Mansion-House she appear'd before the Lord Mayor,
And in the public papers then the reasons did appear,
Why she did leave her father and her native land she told,
To brave the stormy ocean, did this female sailor bold.

It was to seek her lover that sailed across the main,
Thro' love she did encounter storms tempest wind and rain
It was love caused all her troubles and hardships we are told,
May she rest at home contented now the female sailor bold.

Printed and sold at No. 42, North Main street (opposite the Museum,) Providence. Where are kept for sale 100 other kinds.

American broadside (c. 1835) with the ballad "The Female Sailor," a woodcut illustration, and a journalistic prose account of the incident to which the ballad refers

Photo courtesy of the Brown University Library

Of course, a notion of female limitation did not spring up new with the modern era. However, the eighteenth century saw an increased emphasis upon women's physical and emotional frailty, with the fixing of this gendering as a universal in "Nature." In Britain, particularly after the spectacle of the French Revolution, this ideology went hand in hand with the development of a wage-based class-stratified society. Reformers and educators at the turn of the nineteenth century strove to inculcate and manage this delicacy at every social level, for the first time directing their efforts toward women of the lower ranks.[7] (Ironically, these "natural" traits required extensive training and enforcement.)[8] An increasingly commanding precept of female delicacy pulled against and ultimately put an end to the conventions and convictions that made possible such celebrated lower-class heroines as the "female sailor bold."

Cross-dressing heroines held sway in British commercial balladry from the seventeenth century to the Victorian age. Moreover, such heroines were an imaginative preoccupation in other genres as well: romance, epic, biography, picaresque, comedy, tragedy, opera, and ballad opera. But the ballad gives us the Female Warrior in her most explicit form, and the only form in which she survives today in folksongs like *Jack Monroe, The Cruel War Is Raging,* and *The Female Sailor Bold*. A ballad commonplace, disguising women sailors and soldiers appear in thousands of versions of over 120 separate songs sold to a genuinely popular market.[9] Carried about by peddlers and street vendors, cheap ballad sheets were sold on street corners and docks, at crossroads, markets, and fairs, to people from the lower orders—apprentices and laborers, milkmaids and servants, soldiers and sailors, small shopkeepers, artisans, adolescents, children, and so on.[10]

The "female sailor bold" conforms to an ideal type—a conventionalized heroine who, pulled from her beloved by "war's alarms" or a cruel father, goes off disguised as a man to sea or to war. The ballads are success stories. Their transvestite heroine, a model of beauty and pluck, is deserving in romance, able in war, and rewarded in both. The ballads are laudatory. Here, at the edge of the twenty-first century, we find transvestites—male or female—oddities at best. By contrast, this heroine is exemplary, a model of womanhood. She is a "fair and vertuous Maid," "a virtuous damsel," "a fearless maiden fair," and so on. The ballads do not depict a disturbing freak or a world tipped upside down. Rather, the world of the ballads and their heroine is in place. Hers is a romantic and heroic success story; she is a romantic and heroic ideal. But that ideal changed as the early modern world gave way to the modern and an ethos of feminine frailty was applied to women at all levels.[11]

These street ballads spoke to and for an audience of common people. This cross-dressing heroine of the ballads represents a social level of people whose life stories rarely surface in the annals of history as we know it. Furthermore, she poses contradictions between what must have been the experience of such actual fighting and sailing women and the retrospectively imagined world that polite scholarship usually constructs. Accounts of women sailors and soldiers present a subject mesmerizing in its mutability and unresolve. They often expose to our view telling disjunctions of value and thought as the shadowy figures of these women from the lower ranks filter through the ill-fitting lenses of the reports.

The biography of Hannah Snell is a case in point. In 1750 Robert Walker, a London newspaper printer, published *The Female Soldier*, an anonymous account of Snell's "life and adventures."[12] Although the outlines of her story are balladlike, Hannah Snell was a real person, the daughter of a Worcester hosier. Under the name "James Gray," she saw action as a British sailor and soldier from 1745 to 1750, serving as cook, assistant steward, and common seaman aboard ship and fighting intermittently on land. Through it all she maintained her masquerade, "as good a Man as any Seaman on board." When her ship's crew was paid off at Gravesend in 1750, Snell made known her "adventures," and Walker quickly printed them up as *The Female Soldier*.[13]

Snell herself was unlettered, for her "adventures" open with an affidavit of the truth of her story, sworn before the Lord Mayor and signed with an X, "Her Mark." Walker's booklet about her is an illuminating fabric of social and aesthetic discontinuities. With a mixture of admiration and squeamishness, the text introduces Snell to a middlebrow audience of novel readers.[14] Uneasy and ambivalent, it negotiates the social and cultural gap between these readers and the unschooled Hannah Snell.

Two incongruous designs shape *The Female Soldier*. On the one hand, it poses a heroine whose story suggests the outlines of the popular, lower-class ballads. On the other, it struggles to make sense of an unpalatable and curious tale, as the laudatory and straightforward ballads never do. A tough, risk-taking Hannah Snell can be inferred from what is known of the facts of her tumultuous life. But Walker's *Female Soldier* covers over this

Portrait of Hannah Snell from *The Female Soldier* (London: R. Walker, 1750)

Photo courtesy of the William Andrews Clark Memorial Library, University of California, Los Angeles

gritty truth, imagining Snell in the sentimental terms of upper-class literary tradition: "one of the tender Sex, who are afraid of Shaddows, and shudders at the Pressage of a Dream."[15] However, the timorous "tenderness" (in his words), the socially marked "femininity," of these literary types stands completely at odds with the facts of Snell's rambunctious story.

Seeking precedents to make the story understandable, Walker's narrator first places Snell in the realm of epic and romantic antiquity, imagining her in the company of the Amazons and of Cleopatra and Semiramis, on the one hand, and of the pastoral band of *"Arcadian* Shepherdesses," on the other.[16] Yet this summoning of heroic prototypes—lofty *"Rara Aves in Terris"*[17]—is actually short-lived. Rather, it is the bourgeois ethos of the newly emergent Richardsonian novel that ultimately informs *The Female Soldier*.

Printer and publisher Samuel Richardson (1689–1761) wrote several influential novels in the 1740s and 1750s. *Pamela* (1740), the first, depicts a young womanservant's struggle to fend off the sexual advances of her master, in which struggle she ultimately triumphs, winning his admiration for her virtue and his hand in marriage.[18] Articulating a new concern with working- and middle-class women, Richardson's novels imagine for them aspirations to a genteel virtue closely connected to the task of holding sexuality in check. They prescribe and map a world of female delicacy and bodily constraint generalized to include servants, at least upwardly mobile ones like Pamela.

Walker's *Female Soldier* aligns itself with this new novelistic realm. Ringingly it refers to Richardson as it brings its story to a close, saluting Snell as "the real *Pamella*" whose "Adventures and Virtues" surpass those of Richardson's "romantick" and "counterfeit" heroine. Unlike the fictional Pamela Andrews, Hannah Snell is "real Flesh and Blood." Moreover, while Pamela kept at bay only a single squire, Snell displays an even more heroic femininity, preserving "her Chastity by the most virtuous Stratagems," even "in the midst of thousands of the Martial Gentry" on land and "hardy resolute Tars" at sea, "who soon would have batter'd down the Fort of her Virtue, had they discovered that *James Gray* was Mrs. *Hannah Snell*."[19]

But Pamela Andrews's story is not really Hannah Snell's, the narrator's Richardsonian projections notwithstanding. Unlike Pamela, Hannah plays not the waiting "Fort" but the active warrior. Her masquerading sojourn into the conventional realm of male heroism discloses the extent to which behaving heroically and being an active protagonist in stories of any kind require "manliness" as a starting point. Moreover, unlike Pamela, Hannah remains in a lower-class context whose economic precariousness and gritty desperation seep up through the language of pastoral elevation, sexual titillation, and ill-fitted moralizing that encases her narrative.

Walker's *Female Soldier* starkly, if unwittingly, bespeaks social and cultural divisions of class in its representation of the sailing and soldiering of Hannah Snell. An obscure later glimpse of Snell adds an overtly economic dimension to this demarcation of class otherness. In 1778 the diarist James Woodforde met Snell, then a peddler, in the neighborhood of his Norfolk parsonage. His remarks capture both his admiring curiosity and the chasm between his clergyman's world and that of the unlettered woman before him. With a fixation on money, merchandise, and trade, he writes:

> I walked up to the White Hart with Mr. Lewis and Bill to see a famous Woman in Men's Cloaths, by name Hannah Snell, who was 21 years as a common soldier in the Army, and not discovered by any as a woman. Cousin Lewis has mounted guard with her abroad. She went in the Army by the name of John Gray. She has a Pension from the Crown now of 18.5.0 per annum and the liberty of wearing Men's Cloaths and also a Cockade in her Hat, which she still wears. She has laid in a room with 70 Soldiers and not discovered by any of them. The forefinger of her right hand was cut off by a Sword at the taking of Pondicherry. She is now about 60 yrs of age and talks very sensible and well, and travels the country with a Basket at her back, selling Buttons, Garters, laces etc. I took 4 Pr of 4d Buttons and gave her 0.2.6.[20]

Like Walker's, Woodforde's text is frustratingly opaque in its representation of this intriguing woman. Peering at the words, we squint for a further glimpse of Snell. What is she wearing? What does she look like? What does she say? Where has she been? Where is she going? And we cannot mistake the property ethos mediating the gap between her and Woodforde's idea of her. Like the buttons she sells, Snell is mute, an object in a world of objects floating in and out of the parson's ownership. The concept of property, as we know, underpins all modern relationships of power—not least of them, certainly, social class and gender identity. Personal dominion and the overseeing posture it implies shape the gendering of the modern self. Accounts of cross-dressing women sailors disclose the workings of this interdependence of gender and property relations.

The disguised heroine continued to flourish as a staple of popular culture, and the generation after Snell saw more cross-dressing women, among them one Mary Anne Talbot. Her story was first published as "The Intrepid Female" by R. S. Kirby in 1804 and then again in 1809 and 1820, part of *Kirby's Wonderful and Eccentric Museum; or, Magazine of Remarkable Characters, &c.*[21] Talbot's account reveals the connections between gender and class, showing in particular how female delicacy signifies womanly identity and value. Like Walker's presentation of Snell in *The Female Soldier,* "The Intrepid Female" encompasses but never reconciles the heroine's claims of female delicacy and suffering, on the one hand, and her successful and apparently satisfying masquerade, on the other. Unlike the lower-class ballads, these two accounts of Snell and of Talbot betray a gap between the phenomena of events and behaviors themselves, and the interpretive frames explaining them. As with Snell's story, social class plays an ongoing and crucial part in Talbot's. Moreover, Talbot's account has a complicated mix of purposes and ideological cross-currents.

Mary Anne Talbot did not hail from the lower levels of eighteenth-century society. Rather, she claimed to be the illegitimate daughter of an aristocrat. Thus, a complex and socially ambiguous upbringing shaped and filtered her attitudes. Unlike Snell, Talbot was fully literate and, to all appearances, contributed actively to the construction of her own story.[22] Class identity and social position further impinge on Talbot's autobiography because it aims simultaneously to appeal to a general popular readership and to elicit for its author some kind of aristocratic patronage, especially from particular members of the nobility implicated in the story: the duchess of Devonshire, Sir William Pulteney, the duke of Norfolk, and the duke and duchess of York. From the outset, Talbot's text speaks from a complex intersection of class worlds: her own ambivalently privileged upbringing, the lower-class realm of soldiering and seafaring life about which she writes, the middling level of novel readers who made up the audience for the various editions of *Kirby's Wonderful and Eccentric Museum,* and the aristocratic patrons whose attention and favor she hoped to gain.[23]

The story itself is fairly simple. Born in 1778, the illegitimate daughter of Lord Talbot, baron of Hensol, Mary Anne was orphaned at birth and raised in a provincial boarding school, with "nine years careful attention to [her] education and morals" (162). At the age of 14, with the death of her older sister, the young Talbot came under the guardianship of one "Captain Bowen" who, forcing a sexual relationship, made her "every thing he could desire" and carried her off in 1792 to the West Indies disguised as "his footboy" (166). Companion to Bowen, she learned sailing aboard ship and later in the year went with him to Flanders as a drummer with his regiment (167–70).[24] When Bowen was killed at the Siege of Valenciennes, Talbot deserted the army and in 1793 began her own career at sea, first on a French privateer, then on British warships, and finally on an American merchant vessel (171–84). After several voyages, she was accosted in London by a pressgang in 1796, whereupon she revealed her identity rather than be swept into the British war fleet as a common sailor (185–86). In the remainder of "The Intrepid Female," which relates events through 1803, Talbot describes her ongoing attempts to cope with chronic war wounds and to make a living in London, primarily by soliciting pay and patronage for her military service (188–221).[25] Throughout, Talbot's adventures in men's and women's clothing disclose in her experience a fascinating liminality with regard to both class and gender.

"The Intrepid Female" actually works against its own framing prescriptions of female limitation and suffering. (In this, it is like *The Female Soldier*, which incongruously imagines the hearty Snell in terms of pastoral shepherdesses and Richardsonian victims.)[26] An introduction by the publisher R. S. Kirby presents "The Intrepid Female" as "the extraordinary sufferings and adventures" of a "truly unfortunate female" in whom, he assures his readers, "we find no disposition to any masculine propensity" (161). This awkward disclaimer, like Walker's uneasily invoked allusion to shepherdesses, stands at odds with the active, bold, and manifestly successful "manliness" evident in most of Talbot's actions and discourse throughout the story.

Talbot herself occasionally invokes this image of suffering womanhood as an interpretive and framing device, but only obliquely. She concludes her account, for example, with an apology for "any deviation from the paths of propriety" (224), which we infer must mean some aspect of "femininity." But throughout the piece, her allusions to womanliness do not suggest, as we might expect, conceptions of physical delicacy or psychological limitation. Rather, in referring to her hardships, Talbot focuses on her vulnerability and youth and on the sufferings brought upon her by her villainous captor. Indeed, a story that might have been a novelistic sexual kidnapping along the lines of *Clarissa*, Samuel Richardson's other famous icon of female suffering, moves quickly in a rather opposite direction as Talbot tells the tale of a Female Warrior.[27]

"The Intrepid Female" discloses little about Talbot's experience of being a woman or of covering her gender, that is, disguising her "femininity." Rather, Talbot focuses on her adventures as "John Taylor": her learning to be a sailor; her battlefield experiences; her return to sea, and the scramble to advance from common sailor to apprentice officer; her struggle to survive once her masquerade is over. Like the Female Warrior ballads and other premodern stories of female transvestites, Talbot's account does not ask questions about physical limitations or difficulties in carrying out her disguise, or about psychological inhibition, shame, or doubt. Dressed as a man, Talbot is taken for a man. Matter-of-factly she describes her growing seaworthiness: "It was in [a tremendous gale] I first learnt the duty of a sailor; being obliged on some necessary occasion, first to go aloft, which frequent use rendered at last familiar, and by no means irksome" (167). With a hint of amazement, she tells of fighting in combat, "spectator as well as actor . . . though strange to add . . . not in the least intimidated" (177). Its framing prescriptions of female suffering notwithstanding, "The Intrepid Female" poses a heroine who engaged the world successfully and apparently with satisfaction as "John Taylor."[28]

Nonetheless, Talbot's disclosure of her womanhood to avoid the London pressgang reveals the contradictions of her masquerade. Describing herself corralled in a crowd of hapless seamen on the deck of the pressmen's tender, she says:

> I accosted the inspecting officers, and told them I was unfit to serve his Majesty in the way of my fellow-sufferers, being female. They both appeared greatly surprised . . . and sent me to the surgeon, whom I soon convinced of the truth of my assertion. The officers upbraided each other with ignorance at not discovering before my being a woman, and readily gave me a discharge. (186)

But of course, her previous years of service in the army and the navy—in both of which she proved herself perfectly "fit"—contradict this protestation of "unfitness." It is not a fact, but an agreed-upon idea. Imposed from without as a principle, it frees Talbot from this scene of trapped and belligerent sailors and bumbling press officers.

In Talbot's story, delineations of maleness and femaleness are prescribed from without; they are perceptual and relational rather than natural or self-generated. Matters of costume and manner, they are neither based in nor do they express personal identity. In the course of her masquerade, she gains an enlarging sense of competence and entitlement as "John Taylor." Looking back, she describes her continued enactment of "John Taylor" as an earned choice: "having been used to a male dress in the defence of my country, I thought I was sufficiently entitled to wear the same whenever I thought proper" (216). Talbot—and presumably her reader—takes for granted the largely conditioned nature of gender identity. She says:

> I was placed in a lodging at the house of Mrs. Jones, Falcon Court, Shoe Lane, with a strict injunction, if possible, to break me of the masculine habit I was so much used to.... I resumed the dress of my own sex, though at times I could not so far forget my seafaring habits, but frequently dressed myself, and took excursions as a sailor. (188)

The "habit" and "habits" of a sailor are interchangeable here—to wear the habit is to enact the habits. So habited, the woman Talbot remains unvexed by her disguise, however much it troubles her landlady. It needs no explaining. She herself seems oblivious to such paradoxes of the story as the contradiction in her declaring to the press officers her "unfitness" despite the "fitness" of years of sailing in masquerade. The histrionic Talbot negotiates a system of external rather than internal constraints, which leaves her with no need to mediate the contradictions within herself as we now must. Unencumbered by a conviction of her own physical delicacy, she stands equally clear of the guilt, shame, and personal constraint and contradiction that in the modern world constitute so much of gender politics, especially for women.

For us, gender is a highly internalized system, which we are taught and expected to generate from within and among ourselves as individuals. By contrast, Talbot's account suggests the external and social character of gender differences in her world.[29] Dressed as a man and behaving as a man, Talbot is taken for a man and to a large extent understands herself as "manly."[30] Or, more to the point of her story, as "John Taylor" she moves to advantage in her seafaring world. When disguise kept her gender from holding her in check, her background joined with her native wit to help her succeed at seafaring, rising in class from worker to manager, from common seaman to officer. Describing her promotion from powder monkey to cabin boy, she says:

> I was stationed on board the Brunswick.... The service allotted me, was to ... hand cartridge to the men; or, to speak in the seaman's phrase, to act in

> the capacity of *powder monkey*. I had not however been long on board before Captain Hervey, observing my cleanliness and manner different from many lads on board, called me to him, and questioned me. . . . finding by my answers I had been better brought up and educated than most in my present situation, he observed, if I would consider him as a confidential friend . . . I should find a protector in him. (175)

Here and elsewhere Talbot suggests the ingredients of her advancement in the market of her world, a virtual catalogue of bourgeois values: intelligence; quickness; social, physical, and psychological agility; diligence; hard work; initiative; the advantages of education; and cleanliness and other marks of social background. Talbot's social and educational advantages, that is, those marks of class which she displays, give her means for advancing to greater freedom, prestige, and power in her seafaring world—provided she is not known to be a woman.[31]

"The Intrepid Female" shows class to be manipulable as an external code system that, like gender, might be subject to disguise.[32] Talbot's final capture by the British pressgang results, ironically, from just such a class deception. As apprentice officer on an American merchant ship, she and a colleague plan a sojourn ashore while the ship anchors in London. The two set out, according to Talbot, in a masquerade of their rank, a ruse that ultimately ruins them because their lower-class garb leaves them prey to the press. Talbot's description conveys how firm were the boundaries of class—at least with regard to appearances—and the extent to which costume and manner coded these relations of power and opposition: "We put on a plain seaman's dress knowing the prejudices of most of the lower people about Wapping, against officers of any description, whom in general they consider as little better than spies on their actions. But while about to land at St. Catharine's, we were attacked by a press-gang" (185). Her account is poignant. Presenting herself as of "the lower people," she is subject to just such intrusive "spying" within moments of leaving her ship. Rather than be taken again into the British navy, she reveals that she is a woman, "unfit" for service.

Throughout "The Intrepid Female," Talbot remains undiscovered because she manipulates these codes of identity, relying upon the considerable overlap among women and men in appearance and capacities. She and the people around her read and construct identity from the outside, by means of external signs, extrinsic codes of costume and manner. Furthermore, Talbot traverses flexibly because she seems relatively without qualms about the morality and naturalness of her character. She becomes

"John Taylor" (or "Mary Anne Talbot," for that matter) in a world stratified more by extrinsic and habituated signification than by such marks of an innate "Nature" as individual physiology and the psychology of the self. These latter for women fall under the rubric of female delicacy. For her, gender and class markers are movable, externally imposed, learned, manipulable, and to some extent open to choices. These choices have since been legislated and educated out of our field of vision.[33]

In 1893, the accounts of both Hannah Snell and Mary Anne Talbot reappeared in an edition that illustrates not only the late-century sway of an ethos of natural delicacy for women but also the bias of socioeconomic class implicit in that ethos. In a collection entitled *Women Adventurers,* Menie Muriel Dowie presented—with considerable qualms and skepticism—the lives of four women soldiers and sailors: Snell; Talbot; Christian Davies, who fought in British wars of the early eighteenth century; and Loreta Janeta Velazquez, who served the Confederacy as an officer in the American Civil War.[34] In her introduction, Dowie voices an uneasiness with cross-dressing which infuses her trimming and taming of the accounts. Committed to the "Independence of Woman," Dowie nonetheless argues for the tutored poses of feminine identity, assuming their rootedness in "the conditions of being."

> Allowed now to understand the world in which they live, and the conditions of its and their own being, there is no longer any need for [women] to put on the garb of men in order to live, to work, to achieve, to breathe the outer air. . . . They do well to keep their own clothes. An air of masculinity, however slight, goes against the woman who would be successful in the eye of the public and on platforms. Her frills and her laces are, in the meantime, a weapon, or if not a weapon to fight with, at least an implement to work with. To have a character for enjoying tea and toast and the softnesses of life, to have it known that one is frightened at mice and spiders, assists greatly at the cordial reception of the most advanced intellectual display.[35]

In this passage Dowie remains oblivious to the manifest artifice of the womanly codes she cites, their watchful cultivation in a limited and circumscribed milieu, the middle and upper classes of Victorian England. Indeed, one can hardly be convinced of Dowie's claims for universal "conditions of being" in such phenomena as "frills and laces," "enjoying tea and toast," and "hav[ing] it known that one is frightened at mice and spiders."

Dowie discloses elements of her class bias as she contends with the otherness of the cross-dressing women sailors and soldiers who are her subjects. Much of their world is beyond her reach. At this distance, we can see in her dismissive perplexity the condescensions of class.

> It is difficult to take them quite seriously, these ladies of the sabre; they are to me something of a classic jest: their day is done, their histories forgotten, their devotion dead, and they have left us no genuine descendants. The socialist woman, the lecturing woman, the political woman, the journalising woman—none of these must call them ancestress. All these are too serious, too severe. Their high, stern code leaves no room for the qualities of "the female soldier." Plain living and high thinking were never the notion of Christian Davies, for instance. . . . Strip her of her beery halo, drag her from the tavern taproom, and she is but a dull and common wench enough, with few high qualities, little nobility of mind and character, and no great thoughts.[36]

Thus, Dowie separates these "classics" "finely from ourselves." Throughout, her discussion hints at the interbraiding of class values and her ideas of womanly "nobility of mind and character." Explaining her omission of the well-known chapbook story of Ann Bonny and Mary Read, found in *A General History of the Pyrates* (1724), Dowie says, "The account of their lives is freaked with so little genuine adventure or romance and smeared with so much coarseness and triviality that I have not thought it worthy to be included with those of the other adventurers."[37]

In this projection of otherness, the constructs of gender and class overlap as Dowie ponders the transvestite heroine. We see, on the one hand, Dowie's notion of our (genuinely womanly) selves with "high qualities," "nobility," "the softnesses of life," "genuine adventure or romance," and a "high, stern code," and, on the other, these puzzling visitants from another era—"dull and common wench[es]," "smeared with so much coarseness and triviality." Quite opposite a noble womanhood, the "Woman Adventurer," Dowie declares, was "of a coarse grimy sensuality."[38] Nor is Dowie finally unaware of the overlap of class values and this construction of gender and sexuality, which hinges on female delicacy, for she says, "Rarely . . . was she of the better class, and here is the singular and striking difference."[39]

Another report of an eighteenth-century female sailor further lays bare this braiding of gender identity and the values and behaviors encoding economic class. Writing in the nineteenth century, the novelist Amelia Opie describes a youthful encounter in the 1780s with a female sailor, one Anna Maria Real. With incongruities reminiscent of those in the accounts of Snell and Talbot, Opie's memoir records her troubled perplexity when the lower-class transvestite woman she meets does not match her expectations of a delicate, novelistic heroine. Indeed, Opie first frames her tale from the same bourgeois literary context invoked in Walker's *Female Soldier:* the world of romances and novels. Quickly, however, she recognizes the awkward fit. As her account continues, Opie shifts from romance to didacticism, settling in a moralistic warning the incongruities of class and gender identity which leap to her awareness. Projecting onto the cross-dressing Real an increasingly threatening otherness articulated in terms of indelicacy, Opie turns her tale into a lesson on her own foolish and youthful romanticizing. By the end of the account, Opie denies to Real any human subjectivity at all, objectifying her beyond the realm of identity altogether.

Opie's memoir begins with her first hearing of the sailor through a network of friends:

> A highly respected friend of mine, a member of the Society of Friends, informed me that she had a curious story. . . . her husband had received a letter from a friend at Lynn, recommending to his kindness a young man, named William Henry Renny, who was a sailor, just come on shore from a distant part. . . . [The husband] received the young man kindly, and ordered him refreshments in the servants' hall; and, as I believe, prepared for him a bed in his own house. But before the evening came, my friend had observed something in the young man's manner which he did not like; he was too familiar towards the servants, and certainly did not seem a proper inmate for the family of a Friend.[40]

From the outset, Opie's account falls into interconnected distinctions of propriety and class: "familiar" with the servants, "the young man" did not seem "a proper inmate" for the family.

The Quaker host expresses "his vexation" at these improprieties. When the young "man" responds to "the deserved rebuke" with "agitation," the vexed Friend wonders if "better meals than the sailor had been used to" might be "a sort of excuse for his behaviour."[41] Totally unprepared is he for the nervous guest's disclosure.

> Falling on his knees, the young man, with clasped hands, conjured his hearer to forgive him the imposition he had practised. "Oh, sir!" cried he, "I am an impostor, my name is not William Henry L. but Anna Maria Real, I am not a man, but a woman!" . . . She said, that her lover, when very young, had left her to go to sea, and that she resolved to follow him to Russia, whither he

was bound; that she did follow him, disguised as a sailor, and had worked out her passage undetected. She found her lover dead, but she liked a sailor's life so well, that she had continued in the service up to that time, when . . . she left the ship, and came ashore at Lynn, not meaning to return to it, but to resume the garb of her sex.⁴²

Real tells the familiar Female Warrior tale, echo of Snell's story and Talbot's, echo of dozens of popular ballads. However, Opie's is no laudatory lower-class song. Quickly the Quakers set about to reform their surprising visitor: "my friend and his wife were willing to assist her, and endeavour to effect a reformation in her. The first step was to procure her a lodging that evening, and to prevent her being seen, as much as they could, before she had put on woman's clothes." The Quakers' interdictions and reforms put into action the squeamishness evident in Walker's account of Snell, Kirby's disclaimers about Talbot, and Dowie's presentation of all of her "ladies of the sabre." Indeed, as already noted, this "charity" of Opie's "excellent friends" implies a larger program: the concerted social and religious policies in late eighteenth-century Britain which targeted the lower classes, encouraging such values as thrift, temperance, responsibility, regular and steady work, and in women the attributes of feminine delicacy.⁴³

But in Opie's face-to-face encounter with Real we see up close the intricate workings of this interlacing of class and gender values. Fired by romance, the young Opie is enthusiastic at first, imagining the trouser-clad Real a "romantic" object:

> But what an interesting tale was this for me, a Miss just entered into her teens! Of a female soldier's adventures I had some years previously heard, and once had seen Hannah Snelling [sic], a native of Norfolk, who had followed her lover to the wars. Here was a female sailor added to my experience. . . . What a romantic incident! The romance of real life too! How I wanted to see the heroine . . . as my parents gave leave, I . . . called at the adventurer's lodgings, who was at home!

Voicing the expectations of Walker's readers, Opie imagines "the adventurer" an elevated object from a pastoral romance: "a female sailor" to add to her "experience." (Notice how the projected image quickly turns into a personal possession.)

Soon Opie records her own disorientation and discomfort with the trouser-clad woman before her, as an ethos of property intrudes more

Female Sailors Bold

explicitly in the account. Her sentimentalized image of a romance heroine dissolves into a projection of threat. Breaking codes of female restraint—to which Opie herself subscribes—Real looks nothing like the novelistic heroine of Opie's imagination. Bold, indelicate, "unfeminine," she signals danger.

> Yes,—she was at home, and to our great consternation we found her in men's clothes still, and working at a trade which she had acquired on board ship, the trade of a tailor! Nor did she leave off though we were her guests, but went on stitching and pulling with most ugly diligence, though ever and anon casting her large, dark, and really beautiful, though fierce eyes, over our disturbed and wondering countenances, silently awaiting to hear why we came. We found it difficult to give a reason, as her appearance and employment so totally extinguished anything like sentiment in our young hearts.

Shuddering at Real's "men's clothes," Opie finds her employment outrageous. It is not sewing itself—that most traditionally female of activities—which offends, but that Real plies it "manfully" *as a trade*. Nor did she "leave off" her "stitching and pulling" as a leisured, domesticated, wifely woman should, to tend to her "guests." Real defies the constraints of female delicacy and detachment from trade that define Opie's bourgeois ideal, constraints by which she herself is of course bound.

Objects and objectification pepper the memoir, the same commodifying gaze evident in Woodforde's view of Snell. However, Opie, young and female, has none of the parson's cool complacence. At its climax the memoir fixes dramatically and anxiously on property. Her adulation darkened, Opie's sympathy disappears altogether amidst what she perceives as a threat to a possession. When her watch gets Real's attention, Opie imagines it (and herself) accosted.

> I wore a gold watch in my girdle, with a smart chain and seals, and the coveting eye with which she gazed, and at length clapped her hand upon them, begging to see them near, gave me a feeling of distaste; and, as I watched her almost terrible eyes, I fancied that they indicated a deranged mind; therefore, hastening to give her the money which I had brought for her, I took my leave . . . resolving not to visit her again.

Attention rivets on the watch, shiny emblem of personal dominion. As the sexually charged language attests, Opie identifies *with* the watch, *against* the woman before her. Recoiling from rapport, she defines herself as "watch-owner," convinced that her sovereignty is under siege. Too threatened is she to wonder why the watch interests Real. Hastily she tosses her money, an arresting further maneuver of defense in a world of objects thrown up as class barriers and controls.

That Opie saw Real herself as an object hardly needs remark. By the story's close the female sailor is wholly objectified, a point of detached observation: "she went to the Friends' meeting with them, and they were pleased to see her there in her woman's attire; but, when she walked away, with the long strides and bold seeming of a man, it was anything rather than satisfactory *to observe her* [emphasis mine]."

Codes of gender—"long strides and bold seeming of a man"—undergird the dismissal. Opie's choice of words—"bold *seeming*"—conveys with striking self-implication the perceptual and social construction that she herself undertakes as she identifies the "boldness" of Real as the "seeming" of a "man." In the course of the account, Opie defines Real's property-threatening otherness as an "unnatural" and increasingly objectified indelicacy. The next sentence pushes this reification further as Real becomes a "loathed object": "though this romance of real life occupied the minds of my young friend and myself . . . still the actress in it was becoming, justly, an object with whom we should have loathed any intercourse." The construction of otherness in Opie's account turns on objectification and ownership, even of romance heroines. Personal identity and personal property become necessary correlatives. Nowhere, not even in the eager opening, does Opie imagine Real as a young woman like herself—*what she in fact was*. A failed object of adulation, Real becomes a threat that Opie's imagination distances further from herself by rendering her another kind of object, and one pointedly removed from the realm of gendered delicacy: she is an untamed animal.[44]

Opie's reading of Real's body projects onto her a markedly indelicate, ungendered, and depersonalized animal nature. Hints of bestial imagery drift already into the first scene in which the "great agitation" of the supposed "young man" is imagined as a class-determined response of the body: indigestion from "better meals than he had been used to." Elsewhere Real is rendered in pointedly physical terms as fragmented body parts, her hands "stitching and pulling," her eyes "casting ever and anon." Indeed, no other features ever appear save these pawlike hands and her "large, dark, and really beautiful, though fierce eyes." This "fierceness" Opie presses further as a sexually tinged threat when she pictures her watch and herself accosted by the woman's "coveting eye" and "clapping" hand. Real's words are never represented, her thoughts never imagined.

Rather, she rises from the page a threatening and subhuman assemblage of "fierce," "bold," "casting," "coveting," "clapping" body parts. Without language, mind, manners, gender, and property, she is an untamed animal.

The story's ending clinches this objectification of the "untamed" Real and her lower-class world. Opie concludes: "I do not recollect how long she remained under the care of my excellent friends. . . . All that I know with certainty is, that a collection of wild beasts came to town, the shewman of which turned out to be Maria Real's husband, and with him she left Norwich!"

So departs the mysterious Real, with "a collection of wild beasts" and a husband mentioned only in passing, a flickering and seemingly contradictory hint of gender and human relationship. How little we know about her. But how much Opie divulges about her own sensibility and its gendered and propertied "reality" behind which the disguising Real and her story disappear.

As I have shown, the "female sailor bold" is a figure who defies modern femininity and its intersection with the bourgeois subject.[45] Accounts of Hannah Snell, Mary Anne Talbot, and Maria Real show how objectifying constructions of property and female delicacy serve each other to render the transvestite heroine a disturbing and puzzling affront.[46] Opie in particular objectifies Real in a circling and recircling effort to push her beyond the rim of the human altogether. Finally she sends her lower-class female sailor off with a "circus" of untamed animal curiosities. But of course, Opie's uneasiness itself suggests the precariousness of her own "feminine" self in this gendered and commodifying design of identity. With urgency and fright, her memoir constructs its own female subjectivity amidst an anxiously mounting distinction between "wild beasts" and "excellent friends." As it does so, it discloses with fascinating if unwitting candor the braiding of modern gender and class values.

In this essay, I have discussed the transvestite heroine of the early modern era with particular attention to what she reveals to us about the markers of gender and class. Through the pages of their stories, Hannah Snell and Mary Anne Talbot visit us from a world different from ours, a world in the process of reimagining its gender politics. An increasingly commanding concept of female delicacy pulled against and ultimately put an end to the conventions and convictions that made possible the celebrated sailing and soldiering of these cross-dressing women. As the nineteenth-century onlookers Dowie and Opie show, this delicacy is identified with class. But Opie's account is a remarkably compelling demonstration of how this braiding comes to be an internal and a generative construction—a lesson in personal identity fraught with urgency and conscience. In 1941, Mrs. Carrie Grover of Gorham, Maine, sang old songs of female sailors for the collector Alan Lomax. Asked if she ever had "daydreams" of being such a woman sailor, Mrs. Grover replied:

> I sure did. I had daydreams about a good many of these songs. . . . I imagine things like this happened in the days gone by . . . but now they've got laws, so they couldn't get by with it.[47]

We can hardly overestimate the importance of understanding what we today can and cannot "get by with" and why. It is the deeper subject of my discussion of female sailors of "days gone by."

RUTH WALLIS HERNDON

3

The Domestic Cost of Seafaring
Town Leaders and Seamen's Families
in Eighteenth-Century Rhode Island

The work by Ruth Herndon in this essay and Lisa Norling in the next stresses the importance of expanding the purview of maritime history to include land-based experience. Herndon takes as her subject the impact of seafaring on community life in eighteenth-century Rhode Island. Her rich research base centers on sources rarely touched by maritime historians: the day-to-day minutiae of town clerks' records, here covering fifty years in fourteen Rhode Island towns. Herndon uncovers a quantity of material, buried in the unpublished, handwritten accounts of local governance, testifying to the intimate connections between ship and shore.

Herndon finds that Rhode Island town fathers, to counter the extended absences, transience, and poverty so often associated with seafaring, relied on familiar methods for dealing with the town's needy. Implicit in these remedies, she argues, were "gendered notions of dependence and responsibility," patriarchal notions built into the very structure of colonial New England society. Herndon describes in detail how town fathers intervened to control and manage the lives of sailors and their families on shore—interventions that, she suggests, underscore the ironies and contradictions posed by maritime work. Her contribution offers the intriguing possibility that certain meanings accorded manhood in shipboard culture—autonomy and fraternity— were rendered irrelevant on land, where dominant norms linking manliness to heading households and supporting families prevailed. Herndon's work thus points toward a central theme pursued further in this volume by other contributors, especially Margaret Creighton and W. Jeffrey Bolster: the historicity, variability, and situational nature of masculinity.

ON A January day in 1775, the Jamestown, Rhode Island, Town Council met at William Wilbur's house in order to question an Indian sailor named Primus Thompson. A few weeks earlier, Thompson had fallen and broken his leg on Wilbur's icy wharf; he was unable to earn a living and would soon need public support unless the council made other arrangements. Anxious to determine which town had legal responsibility for Thompson's care, the councilmen engaged in the following conversation with him, which the town clerk recorded:

Q: Where was you born?
A: I was born at Capt. Joshua Thompson's in the town of Westerly in this colony.
Q: Where did you serve your time?[1]
A: At the said Capt. Joshua Thompson's.
Q: Did you ever, since your time was out, move out of that town of Westerly, into any other town or place, & there live for the space of one year or longer, whereby you might gain a settlement out of that town?
A: No, except over sea.
Q: How long is it since you came from Westerly?
A: About three months since.
Q: Has there been any surgeon to set your thigh?
A: Yes, I had Doctor Job Sweet to set my thigh, which he did on the 27th day of December last.
Q: Do you think your thigh is now so strong that you might be moved with safety, either on horseback or otherwise?
A: I cannot ride on horseback, but I do think my thigh is well enough for me to be moved with safety in a chaise or some carriage.
Q: Had you at the time you fell & broke your thigh, or at any time since, any money to pay the doctor for setting your thigh & defray the other expense which has arisen by that means?
A: I had no money by me then nor since, but a small matter that was charitably given me.

The Jamestown councilmen decided that Primus Thompson was a legal inhabitant of the town of Westerly; they ordered the town sergeant to rent a horse and chaise "or other suitable carriage" in Newport and transport Thompson back to his hometown.[2] In Westerly, William Greene, overseer of the poor, received Thompson and put him in the care of William Sweet Peckham, who received payment from the Westerly Town Council for "keeping" the injured sailor.[3] The responsibility for the unfortunate seaman's care had passed from the Jamestown Town Council to the Westerly Town Council. Thompson's injury illustrates one aspect of the domestic cost of seafaring for Rhode Island communities: a lame and penniless sailor was the responsibility not of his former employer but of his town of legal residence. The Jamestown council's response to Thompson was typical of the way town leaders countered seafaring problems:

they applied already existing remedies of removal and public support. Implicit in these remedies were gendered notions of dependence and responsibility.

This essay examines seafaring from the point of view of the towns where seafarers originated; it draws on town meeting and town council minutes from fourteen (about half) of Rhode Island's eighteenth-century communities. These records show that seafaring work presented particular problems for eighteenth-century towns and that town leaders responded with particular solutions that emphasized the dependence of seafaring families. Seamen, with their frequent and prolonged absences, necessitated the intervention of town leaders to see to both their public and their familial responsibilities. And because of what were often meager wages, seamen who came close to the edge of economic ruin found themselves and their families the object of discipline, control, and public charity monitored by town leaders. Seafaring thus presented a dilemma in gender roles for eighteenth-century New England communities and implicitly challenged the normative (white) pattern of male adulthood. While they shouldered the work of adult males, many seafarers—white men or men of color—never successfully shouldered the family and community responsibilities that New Englanders expected of adult males. When town leaders stepped in to govern and support an absent sailor's family or to provide poor relief to an ex-sailor, they implicitly announced to the community that a seafaring man was unable to fulfill that most basic requirement of manhood: heading his own household.[4]

The frequent intervention of town leaders thus revealed the ironies of seafaring as men's work: a man might earn wages at sea while his family fell into poverty on land; a man enjoyed a lively community aboard ship while his family was sent packing from their community on land. While at sea, sailors lived in a community that allowed them to forget—for a time— the fact that they existed on the margins of society because of their poverty and (for many) their race. But their families, and the towns where they lived, never enjoyed a similar illusion. For the wives and children who lived with the uncertain economic benefits of the job, and for the towns who supported seafaring families when all other resources failed, the costs of seafaring were high.

Town leaders' roles as providers and caretakers of seafaring families flowed out of the larger concept of patriarchy which dominated early American culture. Linda Kerber has defined this colonial patriarchy as "the assumption that it was natural for communities to be organized along the lines of families consisting of adult men and the people over whom they had power and for whom they had responsibility." The robe of patriarchy covered more than wives and children—it covered all inhabitants of a household, including slaves and servants. Kerber has also noted an important public aspect of patriarchy: "the head of the family represented the family in its relationship to the state."[5] Because of this public aspect, Stephanie Coontz has called patriarchy "the glue that bound individuals to households and households to community."[6]

New England town leaders acted within this communitarian understanding of patriarchy. Town councilmen, overseers of the poor, deputies, and other officials functioned as the heads of a public family, and all inhabitants within their town came under their power and had claim to their care. From the moment of their annual election, the fathers of the towns assumed it was their right to manage the lives of others within the town—to claim their labor for road maintenance or to claim their wealth for town taxes. Male heads of households were just as subject to the authority of the town fathers as their children, servants, and household members were to them. One instructive example occurred in Hopkinton in 1796, when the town councilmen put Rufus Button and David Button under guardianship (and so prevented them from spending their own money) because their *sons* had caused public complaint by being "idle, disobedient to parents, & mischievous."[7] Since the sons (one supposes) had not been responsive to parental discipline, the town council would discipline the fathers.[8]

Some members of this patriarchal "town family" appeared to need attention more than others, and town leaders spent the majority of their energies dealing with troublesome and suffering inhabitants—people whose race, poverty, and / or defiance of conventions resulted in their lives being managed and directed by others. Rhode Island towns were well organized around principles of patriarchy and dependence, and town leaders had at their disposal various institutions of control that brought order to the lives of those in dependent positions: indentured servitude, guardianship, removal of needy transients, the granting of departure certificates or poor relief.[9] It was with good reason that town leaders were called "fathers of the town"; they made it their business to act as surrogate fathers, husbands, and masters to all whose households did not function in accordance with European patriarchal tradition. Seamen fell into this needy category quite often. By their lack of wealth, they were already near

The Domestic Cost of Seafaring

a servant class. By their frequent and irregular absences, they left their families dependent on other sources of support. When married seafaring men left town, their wives and children no longer had a male head of household—hence the frequent need for councilmen and overseers of the poor to take on the responsibilities of financial provision and management. The poverty long associated with both seafaring and fatherless families caused the town fathers to keep these incomplete households under careful scrutiny. Leaders did not hesitate to apply the solutions of removal, indenture, or poor relief whenever they decided that such intervention was necessary.

An incident that took place in Jamestown in 1752 illustrates particularly well this patriarchal attitude toward seafaring men. One of the overseers of the poor reported to the town council that Indian seaman Aaron Stephenson had become ill and was "in a perishing condition" after his voyage with Capt. William Read. The councilmen ordered that care and support be provided for Stephenson; they also appointed a townsman to settle the sailor's accounts with the ship's captain, to "receive the balance" of his pay, and to "employ the money so received for [Stephenson's] relief & support."[10] In taking over the profits from Stephenson's labor, the councilmen revealed the paternal nature of their relationship to the ailing sailor and to all indigent and helpless inhabitants of their town. What had been Stephenson's now belonged to the town, and the fathers of the town would use it for Stephenson's (and their) best interests.

Town leaders stood ready to maintain a seafaring family when other sources had failed. Families and friends usually formed the first line of defense for seamen and their families. Primus Thompson had maintained himself during the first weeks following his accident because a friend had given him money "charitably." Where seafaring families constituted the majority of a town's population, widespread mutual support was the norm. Lisa Norling has shown how Nantucket women of the late eighteenth and early nineteenth centuries sustained an active and interdependent community during the frequent absences of their husbands. In fact, an economy separate from (but complementary to) the whalefishery developed within this mutually supportive female community.[11] Even in Providence, which ranked behind Newport in the significance of its maritime economy for most of the eighteenth century, the wives of seafarers found and supported each other. In 1757, the Providence Town Council called in and questioned three women who had come from other towns to live together in Providence. Mrs. Tower, Mrs. Meachins, and Mrs. Manning (the town clerk recorded no first names) faced the town leaders together and explained that they, with their eleven children, had been waiting over a year for their husbands to return from their voyages.[12] Their comradeship suggests the existence of an even larger community of women brought together by their common relationship to seafaring men.

If such communities could not save a family from disaster, there were other potential sources of support. The captain of the ship might be appealed to for a seaman's share of the profits. And later, in the nineteenth century, there would be another alternative in ships' agents to whom families might turn for credit or cash during long separations.[13] But when these other lines of defense gave way, families on the edge turned to public support. When all else failed, the town leaders would provide the bare necessities of life.

By race and economic status, Primus Thompson represented a significant portion of seafaring men.[14] Daniel Vickers has shown that in the early 1700s, Nantucket-based whaling captains drew heavily upon the local population of Indians for crewmen, having first entrapped them in a system of debt peonage to secure their labor.[15] Jeffrey Bolster has shown that by the early 1800s, seafaring's relatively integrated society and relatively steady wages attracted free black Americans, particularly in Rhode Island.[16] In the Revolutionary period bridging these two eras, it is likely that both Indians and blacks, for reasons of obligation or opportunity, followed the sea in disproportionate numbers, just as they were overrepresented as servants.[17]

Primus Thompson's indigence also marked him as typical of seafaring crews. What appeared as desirable wages to nineteenth-century men of color were meager and insecure wages to many eighteenth-century white men. Vickers has shown that when whites began to replace Indians as ships' crew members, it was largely because tough economic times drove poor Yankees to take on menial labor in the absence of any better alternatives on land.[18] Marcus Rediker has argued that the seasonal and casual nature of maritime labor in the eighteenth century rendered it unattractive to all but laborers willing to settle for an insecure wage.[19] Seamen could count on neither year-round employment nor wages high enough to avoid financial ruin. One historian discovered that between 1756 and 1828, seamen as an occupational group were fourth in frequency of bankruptcy in Rhode Island.[20]

When white seafaring men could not adequately govern or provide for their own households, they joined a dependent class already inhabited by men who had been relegated there by race. In eighteenth-century Rhode Island, most men of color in close contact with whites lived not as heads of households but in a dependent status as slaves, servants, or poor laborers constantly on the verge of needing town support.[21] For African American and Native American families, seafaring rarely offered a permanent escape from dependence; and for white families, it often brought a marginalized status long associated with servitude.

Servants and seafarers had much in common. Vickers notes that the "most serviceable" seamen were those who could "resign their spirits to continuous subordination"; for those first Indian crew members, whaling was nothing but institutionalized servitude.[22] Rediker has called seafaring work "virtual incarceration" and has summed up the relationship between crew and captain by crediting the ship's master with "near-absolute authority," which included meting out "necessary and bloody" discipline.[23]

The actions town leaders took in dealing with unfortunate seamen and their families were often the same as those taken on behalf of servants. In the eyes of the town fathers, both groups needed direction, care, and control. Rhode Island law specifically empowered town councils to send poor and problematic young men to sea instead of binding them out as indentured servants within the town's borders.[24] Councilmen did not hesitate to make use of this law. The Providence Town Council bound over Benjamin Champney to service aboard Capt. Monroe's ship during the Revolutionary War in order to check the man's "irregular, evil, and idle course of life," marked by frequent intoxication.[25] The South Kingstown Town Council voted to "ship Ichabod Sheffield a voyage to sea" to pay back the costs the town had incurred as a result of Sheffield's bringing smallpox into the community from Newport.[26] And Stephen Mott Jr. proved "such an indolent, idle person" that the East Greenwich Town Council decided to "ship him for the sea."[27] The sea could thus serve as a dumping ground for troublesome men and perhaps provide an incentive for more industrious behavior in the future.

Primus Thompson was not an Everyman for the seafaring community. Among the men who "followed the sea" were established residents and prosperous members of the communities from which they sailed. Such men were far more likely to be ships' captains or senior members of the crew; common seamen like Primus tended to be young.[28] Some of the older, settled sea veterans shared in town leadership. Wealthy John Eldred of Jamestown, who identified himself as a "mariner" in his will, had served intermittently in the important town offices of warden, town councilman, and deputy to the state legislature.[29] Eldred's election to town office was occasional rather than continuous, no doubt because of the seasonal nature of his maritime business. For such men, participation in local government sometimes clashed with seafaring. In 1761, John Gardner told the Jamestown town meeting that he planned to go "on a voyage to sea" and asked them to elect another tax assessor in his place.[30] In 1765, the Warwick freemen elected John Wickes to be a constable in the place of Thomas Warner, "who is lately gone a voyage to sea"; in 1785, the freemen elected Jonathan Gorton as an overseer of the poor in the middle of the election year because Gideon Arnold had gone to sea.[31] Even in landlocked and agrarian Glocester, seafaring interrupted town business. In 1794, Amasa Smith, Glocester's tax collector, went to sea, leaving "a considerable part of said taxes uncollected"; the freemen voted to have Ziba Smith replace his brother and finish collecting the tax.[32] In many similar incidents, the consequences of seafaring were borne by voters who had to find replacements for leaders whose business had taken them to sea.

When town leaders went to sea, political adjustments filled the gaps. When taxpayers and property owners went to sea, economic adjustments similarly followed. The economic structure of Rhode Island town governments depended on income produced through town taxes. Often the voters authorized a new tax while seafaring men were absent, and tax collectors faced a challenge if seamen had made no prior arrangements for paying their assessments. Ordinarily tax collectors could "seize" property and sell it at auction to pay taxes of absent men, but occasionally collectors found themselves stymied. East Greenwich tax collector George Pierce reported to the town meeting that he could not collect the rates of some men who had gone to sea because "they left no visible estate that could be found" to pay the tax bill.[33] The town decided to write off these taxes as "bad rates," a common solution for uncollectible taxes and one that did not raise the prestige of tax delinquents among their fellow townsmen.

A different economic problem arose over the business of administering and protecting estates of men who were absent at sea for long periods of time. Providence mariner Robert Scott lodged a document with the town clerk when he went to sea, giving "my trusty friend Miss Amey Mitchell" power of attorney over his estate in his absence and in case of his death.[34] Many seafaring men did not return from their voyages, and town councils decided who should administer these men's estates—and when. After William Tourtellot of Glocester had been at sea and "absent & unheard of for some years," the town council granted his uncle's request to administer Tourtellot's estate.[35] The wording in the Glocester records echoes a phrase from Rhode Island law, which provided that councils could treat estates as though the owner had died if he was "absent and unheard of for three years."[36]

Much could happen in those three years, as Sarah Tripp of Tiverton discovered. When her husband had been gone to sea "upwards of two years & never been heard of," she sought help from the town council to avert disaster. The council, certain that the ship was lost, petitioned the General Assembly on Tripp's behalf and secured permission for her to sell some of her husband's land to support herself and her four small children, all of whom were "in a poor, low, & deplorable state & condition."[37]

Occasionally the town fathers stepped in without invitation to protect a seaman's property in his absence. During the Seven Years' War, "sundry persons of good credit" reported to the Warren Town Council that Naomi Freeman was wasting her husband Joshua's estate while he was gone to sea. Fearful that Joshua Freeman had been "taken by the enemy and not likely to come home very soon, if ever," the council appointed a guardian over Naomi Freeman so that she could no longer sell any of her husband's goods without permission.[38]

To each of these political and economic problems presented by seafarers, town leaders applied already familiar solutions. Midterm election of officials occurred in cases of death or illness as well as when men went to sea. Tax delinquency occurred with depressing regularity among struggling farmers and shopkeepers as well as seamen throughout the latter half of the eighteenth century and had no special link to seafaring. Administration of estates and protection of property for men of all occupations constituted a significant chunk of council business in every town. Seafaring problems may have been distinctive, but the solutions applied by the town leaders were not.

Solutions like guardianship and administration of an estate reinforced patriarchal authority in that white male leaders assumed the role of husbands and fathers in seafaring families; but these solutions also suggested that a man's participation in patriarchal leadership (of a household or of a community) depended on his continuous presence in the community. A man who gave up his leadership position as overseer of the poor or town councilman in order to pursue his livelihood at sea might find the political dynamics changed and his old position no longer available when he returned. A man of lesser means might find that his household had been scattered during his absence. When Robert Leonard returned to Providence after a long voyage at sea, he discovered that the town council had solved his family's temporary poverty by binding out his son Robert Jr. as an indentured servant to a blacksmith. Robert Sr. petitioned successfully for the indenture to be canceled and his son returned to him, but the eighteen months that Robert Jr. spent in another household must have shaken the family's confidence in the father's authority over his own family.[39] In such ways, seafaring men were reminded of the fragile nature of their participation in the patriarchal structure of the community.

Primus Thompson was not a town leader; he was neither the owner of an estate nor a taxpayer. Thompson was a poor and transient Indian, and thus far more representative of common seamen. He was also injured. The potential cost of his wharf accident was a lifetime of public support due to perpetual lameness. Unlike a seafaring constable or an absent taxpayer, a seriously injured town dependent required more than a single vote of the freemen or a single dictate of the town council.

The Jamestown councilmen were eager first to question Thompson and then to remove him from their community, because they wanted to pass along to the proper town the responsibility of caring for the lame and indigent sailor. Because he was working in a town other than his home community, Thompson did not warrant support from Jamestown taxpayers. Since he belonged legally in Westerly, to Westerly he would go for care.

Throughout eighteenth-century Rhode Island, councilmen routinely questioned men and women in similar situations. The goal was always the same: to determine legal residence and thus legal responsibility to provide support. Once they were satisfied that a person belonged to their town, councilmen routinely authorized payments for food, clothing, housing, fuel, and medical care.[40] This commitment to support needy inhabitants did not stop at Rhode Island's borders—it permeated town life throughout New England.[41]

Of first importance, then, was establishing where a person properly belonged. Most councils began interrogations by asking, "Where was you born?" and "Where did you serve your time?" These questions reflected Rhode Island law, which set down the ways to become a legal, settled inhabitant of a particular town. The first was by birth: unless a person moved away, she or he would always be an inhabitant of that town. The second was by living in the town for an entire year without being removed by the town council; the third, by purchasing a freehold—real estate worth £40 or more in the late 1700s. The fourth was by having served an apprenticeship with a master who was an inhabitant of the town. At the end of apprenticeship, the ex-servant could choose between birth town or apprenticeship town for legal residence; but to secure that settlement, the ex-apprentice had to live continuously in the chosen town and not be absent for more than a year.[42]

Written explicitly into Rhode Island law and implicitly into the institutions of the towns were the particular circumstances of seafaring. Ex-apprentices who went to sea were an exception to the law of settlement: they did not lose residence in the town of apprenticeship when they were gone to sea for more than a year.[43] A seaman's legal residence remained the place where he was born or had served out his indenture, even if he sailed out of another town for years on end. For this reason, seafaring men often were "transients" while in port; a town elsewhere in the state claimed them as legal inhabitants.

The settlement laws often trapped seafaring families because those laws originated in the permanent, settled nature of agrarian communities. Even towns like Providence, Newport, and Bristol, which depended heavily on a maritime economy, applied settlement laws to men whose essential labor aboard the ships prevented them from living a settled life. The special dispensation granted to seafaring ex-apprentices acknowledged both the youth and the poverty of the majority of sailors, but did nothing to solve the long-term problems such men faced when trying to establish residence in the towns from which their ships sailed. Rarely could these men participate in the political, economic, and social relationships that maintained the communities which by law claimed them as inhabitants. Their dilemma revealed another of the ironies of seafaring: when young men asserted their manhood by cutting their ties with land and putting out to sea, they undercut their ability to achieve manhood by the traditional standards of their home communities—that is, by shouldering communal duties with fellow townspeople. Seafaring gave many young men the illusion of independence and adulthood, but in fact the personal cost was high. Cut off from the towns that claimed them, seafarers could not enter the adult male world of their home communities. When they returned to land, many sailors followed a pattern of transience that emphasized their separation from the place they once called home.

Seafaring families were not the only transients. Numerous people who were not legally settled inhabitants dwelled within the borders of every Rhode Island town. Some of these people eventually purchased land and became permanent members of the community. Some were itinerant tradespeople and artisans whose vocations would eventually take them on to other towns. But some were poor people with no way of acquiring settlement—they lived by their labor in a precarious existence, perpetually on the edge of distress.[44] Townspeople kept a close eye on such people and were quick to inform the council about anyone who looked "likely to become chargeable to the town." This common phrase indicated obvious poverty, illness, or lameness in people of all ages, or advanced pregnancy in a woman unaccompanied by a husband. Councilmen were equally quick to question these people and order them out of town if there was any hint of need in the near future.[45]

Seafaring often led to this kind of transience. Some seamen had already left their hometowns in order to follow the sea. When they married, they endowed their legal settlement on their wives and children, who thus shared their transient status. When the economic rigors of seafaring left these people in desperate circumstances, town leaders were likely to order them out of the very community where they had tried to establish a home. Thus it was that wives and children of absent sailors sometimes straggled from community to community. Mary Prew Wiley told the South Kingstown Town Council in 1772 that her husband, Andrew, had "sailed out of Newport" and was still at sea; she had come on her own into South Kingstown.[46] In 1783 Sarah Johnston explained to the Providence Town Council that her husband had gone to sea from Newport in 1776 "and hath not been since heard from." Johnston had moved from Newport to Little Compton and then to Providence, where for five years she had been trying to support herself.[47]

Just as often, seamen and their families moved together from place to place in search of prospects, replacing sea travel with an equally uncertain voyage on land. Town records reveal that councilmen questioned many a former sailor who had come looking for work or charity.[48] In 1764, when the South Kingstown Town Council tried to determine where transient Edmund Brown and his wife and child legally belonged, Brown told them that he had moved from Newfoundland to Boston to Newport, from which port he sailed on "sundry voyages," and finally to South Kingstown.[49] In 1785, John Carter told the Providence Town Council that he had been born in Africa, sold into slavery in Massachusetts, and earned his freedom by serving in the Continental Army during the Revolutionary War. Then he "went to sea and continued in that way ever since"; and now, at age 40, he lay sick in the workhouse after his last voyage. The council quickly ordered Carter to be sent back to Lancaster, Massachusetts, "as soon as indisposition will admit."[50] Nathan Tucker called himself a laborer when he appeared before the Cumberland Town Council and explained that he had learned the cooper's trade as an apprentice but had "followed" the sea for most of his life until his father died and he came into some property. But that property did not prevent him from falling into poverty and needing assistance from Cumberland, prompting the council there to order him removed to Smithfield.[51]

Unless poor transient seamen and their families moved frequently to avoid being forcibly removed by town council order, they usually found themselves back in their hometowns, whether or not they wanted to be there. Councilmen like those in Jamestown were anxious to situate needy transients within the borders of the responsible town before serious illness or other emergency froze them in their tracks as unwelcome dependents elsewhere. The only way desperate transients could avoid being unceremoniously returned home in the care of a town constable was to stay on the road almost continuously, taking work and charity here and there, and almost certainly hoping for better times.

When Primus Thompson arrived (via horse and chaise) in his hometown, one of the overseers of the poor put him in the care of Westerly inhabitant William Sweet Peckham. Until he was able to resume work, Thompson received support as one of "the poor of the town."[52]

Becoming one of those chargeable to the town was a solution of last resort. The town council or their agents—the overseers of the poor—determined all aspects of life for those people who could no longer support themselves. Town leaders decided where poor people would be boarded—usually with the townsperson who charged the lowest fees; this location could change yearly or even monthly, as the council received better offers. Leaders discussed the ailments of the poor in public meetings before authorizing medical treatment. They listed clothing supplied to the poor, down to the undergarments; when Sarah Whitman was reported as being "almost naked," the Exeter Town Council authorized one of the overseers to "procure two flannel shifts and a flannel petticoat" for her.[53] This was the fate that awaited destitute transients who finally made their way back home; and it was the fate that constantly threatened impoverished sea families who had remained in their home communities, eking out an existence on whatever money a seaman might send or bring home.

It is small wonder that struggling families tried to find alternatives other than public support. When mariner Stuckley Scranton of Warwick died, he left his widow, Hannah, with two small children "and no house to live in." Hannah Scranton resourcefully resisted poor relief and suggested to the town council that if they would provide her a "small house" where "wood and water was plenty," she would be able to support herself and her children "with her industry." The council, seeing a way to avoid a long-term welfare arrangement, promptly ordered a house to be built for Hannah Scranton and her children at the expense of the town.[54]

Freelove Tennant of Jamestown suggested another solution when she appealed to the town council for help because her seafaring husband had "left her with a family of children whereby she is at present utterly unable to support them." Following common practice of the day, the town council disrupted the family unit even further by binding out three of the Tennant children as indentured servants to three different masters in the town.[55] Public indenture of poor children was authorized by Rhode Island law and recommended by tradition.[56] It relieved the parents of the economic burdens of providing food, clothing, and medical care for the children, and it ensured that the children would receive a rudimentary education in reading and writing as well as training in some useful trade for the future. Having seen three of her children thus settled into indentures, Freelove Tennant then took up a position as caretaker for the poor of the town, receiving her rent free and £4 per week Rhode Island Old Tenor as her wage.[57] She had successfully avoided poor relief and translated her desperation into an opportunity to make an independent living.

Sarah Brickley of Middletown found a third solution to the poverty that dogged her when her husband's absence stretched into such permanency that she considered herself a widow. Brickley's husband, "a seafaring man" from Newport, had never returned from a voyage. Hoping to earn a living in another place, Brickley asked her town council for a signed certificate to present to the town council of Warwick—the surety all New England towns demanded before allowing a new person to settle in a community.[58] The Middletown council granted the certificate immediately.[59] Brickley's attempt to earn a living elsewhere may have been fruitless, but the alternative was for her to become one of Middletown's poor, with all its powerlessness and humiliation.

Seafaring's central irony was that it seemed to offer young men a measure of independence and a successful passage to adulthood. Yet while seafarers earned a living at sea, they and their families often became impoverished and dependent on land, the objects of town scrutiny and discipline. While sailors enjoyed a sense of community aboard ship,[60] they and their families often failed to become part of a community on land. While seafaring young men seemed fully adult at sea, they and their families were often treated as dependents and servants on land. Absent mariners were dead husbands and fathers in the eyes of town councils, who managed seafaring families. Other men ordered the lives of seamen's wives and children; other men doled out support when family resources shriveled.

The relationship between town leaders and seafaring families completed a cycle of dependency for many seamen. Seamen lived under a master at sea; they lived under a master on land. Seafaring was by no means a sure escape from poverty, as the town records of transience and poor support testify. Sailors may have regarded their work as virile, but that work reduced its practitioners to dependency all too frequently. Transient and impoverished seamen were hardly a good advertisement for the profitability of a life on the sea. When they were alone aboard ship, seafaring men may have viewed their physically demanding labor with masculine satisfaction, but this vision dissolved when seafarers returned to the society of wives, children, and fellow townspeople. From the point of view of home communities, seafaring stripped men of power more often than it endowed them with it.

LISA NORLING

4

Ahab's Wife
Women and the American Whaling Industry, 1820–1870

As in the preceding essay, Lisa Norling's study emphasizes the complex connections between maritime enterprise and shoreside community life. Rather than focusing on official town responses to the exigencies of seafaring, however, Norling instead examines the ways in which the dominant Victorian ideology of gender shaped both family adaptations and the social relations of work within a specific industry, the American whale fishery.

Feminist historians have pointed out that nineteenth-century gender categories, in particular the conceptual separation between a male, public world of work and a female, private world of home and family, have persisted in and compromised twentieth-century historical analyses. Norling builds on this insight in her challenge to the separateness of men's and women's "spheres" even in the context of seafaring, where a strict sexual division of labor had prevailed for centuries. Norling contends that the geographical split between sea and land did not necessarily correspond to any clear-cut differentiation between public and private or work and home. She argues that, in the American whaling community, men's and women's work interpenetrated in at least two crucial ways. First, related ideas linking manhood to providership and womanhood to dependency structured labor relations between shipowners and whalemen. Second, notions of female domestic responsibilities assured that women, whalemen's wives and mothers, would sustain their families and communities during men's absences and other stresses inherent in the industry. Norling's essay thus contributes to the growing body of scholarship uncovering the integral, yet contradictory roles played by women's labor and by the ideology of gendered spheres in nineteenth-century capitalist development.

THERE ARE very few women in Melville's novel *Moby Dick*. Captain Ahab did have a wife, but she never appears in person and is mentioned only twice: once to signify Ahab's warmer, softer side and once, by Ahab himself, in reference to his rejection of those qualities in his quest for the great white whale. Of course, most of the action takes place at sea, and very few women went to sea in the nineteenth century. So why remark on their absence from the book? I begin with *Moby Dick* because I think that where and how women appear, and do not appear, in the greatest whaling novel ever written is an accurate reflection of women's relationship with maritime culture of the nineteenth century and with most maritime history of the twentieth.

In both, attention has focused primarily on the ship itself, almost wholly a single-sex environment—though certainly not a genderless one.[1] Where women are mentioned, it is usually as the foil against which seamen and maritime culture in general asserted their aggressive masculinity and their alienation from land-based society as they "wandered" over "the trackless deep" on ships that were always called "she." In custom, song, and craft, women featured more prominently in maritime culture as objectified images than as flesh-and-blood persons.[2]

In fairness, it was (and is) harder to see maritime women than it was to see sailors themselves. Unlike Ahab, his wife did not look different from other women. She did not walk with a rolling gait; her face was not unusually weather-beaten; she did not talk or dress distinctively; nor could she tell heroic tales of the perils of the ocean, exotic foreign ports, or the hunt of leviathan beasts. Very few women spent much time aboard ship. Their connection to the sea was through men.

Nonetheless, real women as well as female imagery were important to the whaling industry. A strict division of labor by sex has characterized most European and American maritime industry for centuries. The hunting and processing of whales was no exception to the maritime rule, having been a strictly male activity from the earliest days of small boats launched from shore.[3] In the mid-nineteenth century, however, the social relations of work in the American whale fishery became gendered in a way that reflected the pervasive cultural ideology of separate spheres for men and women, along with its embedded assumptions about masculinity and femininity. In this essay I would like to turn our attention away from the ship itself to the broader community of which the ship was just a part, and examine how the notion of separate gendered spheres structured the American whaling industry through both a particular set of female images and the substance of women's work.

Women's involvement in the international whale fishery took a great many forms, ranging from their role in the marital alliances by which many shipowners amassed the capital necessary to launch the voyages[4] to the mediation by native women in the South Pacific between indigenous cultures and American and European whalemen.[5] My subject here, however, is the women in the American fishery's home region of southeastern New England, during the industry's peak years, 1820–1870: even more specifically, the female connections of what might be called the managerial class of career whalers. First, I consider what role images of women played in motivating men and how they affected the relationship between the shipowners and the mariners; then I turn to the women themselves and explore their direct and indirect contributions to the industry.

The American whaling community was perhaps more narrowly based geographically than most maritime industries; while whalers traveled from the United States into the far corners of the globe, nearly all of them hailed from southeastern New England. During the industry's heyday, the major American whaling ports were all located within a sixty-mile radius of Newport—from Provincetown, on the tip of Cape Cod in the east, to New London, Connecticut, in the west, and Sag Harbor, on Long Island, to the south. The American industry was also relatively specific in time: from the organization of sporadic shore whaling into a full-scale industry in the 1700s to the industry's decline at the end of the following century. At first the industry had centered on Nantucket, but by the 1830s Nantucket had passed the whale-oil torch to New Bedford, which boasted of both a deeper harbor and better connections. In 1846, when the size of the American fleet peaked with 736 vessels afloat, over 400 came from the greater New Bedford area. The boom was over by the 1870s, though, curtailed by the depopulation of whales, the discovery of petroleum, and the destruction of vessels in the Civil War. What whaling continued at all was from the West Coast; by 1884, the vessels out of San Francisco outnumbered all those sailing from eastern ports put together. By that time, most of the whale money in southeastern New England had been transferred into manufacturing and other ventures.[6]

As technological advances made whaling more expensive and more complicated, the highly responsible and lucrative officers' positions were generally reserved for a restricted pool of local men. A relatively small and homogeneous cadre of professional mariners developed: captains, mates, and young men essentially in officer training, who were mainly white, native-born, Protestant, and drawn from yeoman or artisanal roots in the coastal region of southeastern New England. This group might be considered maritime master craftsmen, specialists in the capturing and butchering of whales, who formed a stable core of the industrial workforce on which the managing owners and investors wholly depended. In contrast, the rest of the crew was filled out by other less well-connected young men with few economic alternatives—"greenhands" and other seamen marked by their diversity, nonlocal origins, youth, and propensity for desertion.[7] As profit margins shrank, the owners seemed to prefer inexperience and rapid turnover among the foremast hands.[8] But constantly changing crews with no allegience to the masters or to the enterprise only contributed to the risks inherent in the industry and further increased the owners' dependence on the officers.

As whaling voyages became more and more expensive in the midcentury period, stretching to three years and longer, the professional mariners at sea and the industry overall increasingly depended upon women to sustain maritime families and communities ashore. Indeed, the reliance of the male world of work upon the services and support provided by women within an ostensibly private home was particularly striking in the whaling communities. Yet, typically, the relationship was obscured in the gender ideology that cast men as autonomous, productive individuals and women as domestic dependents.[9]

We know that the majority of seamen were between the ages of 15 and 30.[10] For most, shipping out was part of their break from their natal families, a rite of passage toward male adulthood. For the group of professional mariners, though, continuing to go to sea was often linked to their eventual marriage and assumption of family responsibilities. Whaling represented one of the few ways to earn the cash they considered necessary to begin married life. Alonzo Taber of Mattapoisett, Massachusetts, wrote his brother in 1852: "if we do well in her [the vessel] this season I think I shall come home next winter and get married."[11] Ezra Goodnough recorded in his diary in 1847 (in appropriately nautical terms) that he looked forward to "getting spliced from the strength [profits] of this voyage."[12]

"Getting spliced" served to bind mariners more firmly to their home community, a connection that took on added significance given the extremely high rate of desertion in nineteenth-century whaling. Here the female image—or rather, memories of specific women—played an important part, as career whalemen's primary affective tie to their home communities was anchored in their spouses. Leonard Gifford, deep in the Pacific in 1851, explained to his fiancée, "had you not learned me to love you ... I might still have been the careless happy go luckey dog that I [was] for ... before I became acquainted with you ... all places were alike to me, and I felt that thear was as much happines for me on board of a ship . . . as I could find on my native land." He promised her that as soon as he returned to New Bedford, they would "have the silken cord wound around us, that binds two willing hearts in the holy bonds of matrimony."[13] Gifford and other mariners, like their land-based peers, privileged the marital relationship;[14] this emotional tie reinforced the economic and legal strings that pulled men back to the home port.

But marriage also served to send the mariner out to sea again. A man's financial needs only increased after his marriage; mariners, too, subscribed to the producer / provider ethic that linked their ability to provide for their families to their manhood.[15] During his first voyage after his marriage in 1845, after learning his wife had borne a son, Captain Samuel Braley reflected, "there are two beings whome I love dearer than self that are helpless as it were dependent on me for subsistence." Later, not having seen a whale in some time and feeling less sanguine about his responsibilities, he wrote glumly: "what a great fool I was to marry—if it was not for that Wife and her boy I would curse the whales and go cod-fishing."[16]

First mate Charles Peirce, forced to leave a New Bedford whaler midway through a Pacific voyage due to illness, was set ashore in Australia. He assured his wife, Eliza, "dear wife I have not forgotten you neither shal I . . . my family is what I am working for, trying to live for." By December he had improved enough to ship out on another whaler, though he promised Eliza, "dont think because I am sailing out of Sydney that I have forgotten that I am a Husband & Father. I am in hopes to be able to send you some Money from this Voyage, if I cant send for you [to come join me]." He sailed out of Australia off and on over the next three years, but his condition again took a turn for the worse. In early 1874 he reported, "my health is very poor, too bad to go to sea any more, but my dear and good wife, my mind has troubled me the most to think I have not been able to help you. sometimes . . . my brain is almost turned, when I look back and see how much better it would have been if I had not left home at all. . . . it was the fartherest from my thoughts, when I left you, for you to support yourself and the Children, all this time."[17]

Charles Peirce's tortured letters reveal especially clearly how important was the idea of women and children at home as the motivation for men's involvement with whaling—even when the idea did not necessarily correspond to reality. Women, though characterized as dependent in the dominant midcentury notion of family relationships, were forced to act independently in the absence of their husbands. Samuel Braley's wife, as it turned out, was back home quite competently running the farm she had just inherited. Many other seawives were not doing so well, of course, including Eliza Peirce, who was forced to rely on other family members for assistance. Regardless of specific circumstance or actual need, though, what is striking is the consistency with which the men referred to the idea of female dependency.

The association of femaleness with dependency and manhood with providership factored directly into the career mariners' relationship with their employers, the managing owners. To command the mariners' loyalty and, implicitly, their assumption of responsibility for the feminized ship, the owners offered assurances that the female dependents left at home would be protected and provided for, in a kind of exchange of obligation. Owner George Richmond tried to persuade Leonard Gifford to prolong his voyage by assuring him that the owners would protect the absent captain's interests in love as well as property. Referring to Gifford's fiancée, Richmond wrote, "That Young Lady up to the Corner . . . will be all the better for waiting another year. If you will agree to stay [in the Pacific] . . . Ezra & myself will see that no young fellows are allowed to trespass upon your grounds or pluck the blooming Flower but will keep everything 'all right' until you arrive."[18] Owner Matthew Howland similarly assured one of his captains, his distant relation Philip Howland, that "during thy absence thy Wife & family will be just as well cared for by us and thy friends as thee could do."[19]

The expectation of reciprocity was clearly articulated from the other side of the exchange as well. Captain Orrick Smalley wrote to his employers, Thomas Knowles & Co., after hearing of the outbreak of the Civil War, "I shall expect that you will advise my wife in regard to the safety of her money invested—the same as I shall endeavor to care for yours out here."[20] To the same owners, but from a different ship, second mate Henry Swain wrote in 1862, "I have just received a letter from my Wife wherein she states to me that the party that I left my affairs with . . . have not done as he should do by me for he has seen my Wife sick and in want . . . therefore I have Wrote to my Wife to call on you to receive from you what she may require to make herself comfortable." This was not "too great a favour" to ask, Swain felt, since, he informed Knowles, "we have now over 1150 [barrels] of Sperm [oil] and hope with good fortune to be soon Home."[21]

The managing owners were not always as accommodating as the whalemen wished: occasionally the mariners' expectations of reciprocity were demonstrated in the breach rather than in the observance. Accustomed to careful attention from Matthew Howland, Philip was considerably aggrieved several years later by the neglect he felt from his new employers, Thomas Knowles & Co. In September 1866, over two years out, he wrote bitterly to them, "you complain of my not writing. The fault is all your own. My family are only nine miles from you and the Mail Stage runs by the door every day, it would be very easy for you to ascertain the state of their health and mention it to me when you write. Capt. Cash, Capt. Coffin and others of my acquaintance are in the frequent receipt of news from their families by letters from their owners. . . . it seemed to me," he added pointedly, "that you cared little about us and that being the case I felt that I cared as little for you."[22]

Wives and mothers similarly referred to the exchange of male responsibilities in their negotiations with the owners for cash advances or other kinds of assistance. In so doing, they reinforced the image of female dependency by appealing for help on the grounds of need. In 1846, when John Codd was in the Pacific, his pregnant wife wrote to the shipowners, Charles and Henry Coffin of Nantucket: "Sir will you please advance me 50 dollars and charge the same to my Husband act John told me you would advance me two hundred pr year during his absence." A year later, Mrs. Codd wrote, "I . . . must say I do not feel that you have treated me well; My Husband did not think you would let his family suffer for the necessries of life, when he shipp'd in your employ. I am out of Food and Fuel, and unless you can do something for me must write by every Ship for him to return and take care of his family."[23]

Overall, in fact, any exchange of male responsibilities seems to have been more often rhetorical than actual. A survey of crew accounts kept by the managing shipowners shows that, in its most concrete form, the owners' concern for the seamen's families was quite limited. Whalemen were paid in fractional shares determined out of the net profit at the end of the voyage. Any cash or credits received before the final accounting were considered advances and deducted from the mariners' total earnings, usually with a steep interest charge tacked on. In other maritime industries where seamen were paid not in shares at the end of a voyage but in regular wages, arrangements could be made for the payment of installments of money to dependents. In the early U.S. Navy, for instance, seamen who were married could leave draw bills with the Navy agent that allotted one-half their pay to their wives in what the historian Christopher McKee refers to as "standard procedure."[24] In the whaling industry, the arrangements appear to have been more ad hoc, negotiated on an individual basis, and certainly less common overall.

Of the crew accounts for fourteen whaling voyages from the New Bedford customs district, twelve listed financial assistance to the relatives of one or more seamen. In all, 409 seamen were involved in the voyages, including those taken on in foreign ports: 60 officers (captains and mates); 94 petty officers in the steerage (boatsteerers, coopers, carpenters, shipkeepers, cooks, stewards); and 255 foremast hands. Twenty-five percent of the officers were charged for advances made to wives, and 7 percent for advances to parents. Among the steerage positions, only 3 percent were assessed for assistance to wives and 1 percent to parents. In the accounts with the foremast hands, there were no wives listed at all and just 4 parents (1.6 percent). The records of eight additional voyages, though less complete, show that advances were made to five officers' wives and two officers' parents, two steerage wives and two steerage parents, no foremast wives but six foremast parents.[25]

This evidence seems to bear out what we know about career patterns in the industry. The officers were older, on average, and more likely to have wives and families. The younger men in the forecastle were most often unmarried, and the men in the steerage fell in-between. Financial assistance was most commonly forthcoming to the wives of the top officers, the "master" whalemen on whom the shipowners relied. There was some assistance, but less, to the connections of the petty officers in the steerage, experienced men holding especially skilled positions in the crew and some of whom were on their way into the officers' ranks. The amount of assistance offered to the families of foremast hands was negligible. As predictable as these figures are, it is striking that no more than a quarter, then, of the officers' families, those connected to the career whalemen, actually received cash or credit during a voyage.

Some wives did receive regularly scheduled advances. Hannah Ashley, the wife of the first mate of the *Governor Troup* on its 1862–67 voyage, picked up $30 every two months from the agent.[26] The account for William Troy, second mate of the bark *Harvest*, in Swift & Allen's ledger book indicates that before he left in 1847, Troy arranged for the agents to pay $8 per month to a local merchant, to cover his wife's bills.[27] Orlando Houston's wife assured her husband, "the owners are very kind to me i have no troble in getting my money."[28]

Such arrangements, though, were made only with the families of the most trusted career whalemen. With an erratic market and the uneven success of the fishery, agents could not predict their profits or the eventual amount of a seaman's share. Consequently, they were often reluctant to supply funds on a regular basis. The climbing desertion rate undoubtedly discouraged them as well. The weighing of these kinds of concerns against the employers' dependence on their crews was reflected in Captain Smalley's assessment of his second mate: "I think it is a safe thing to advance his due . . . Mr Freeman is a good man & whaleman and I hope will continue the voyage. . . . he has some 60 or 80 dollars due him which I hope you will advance should his parents need it."[29]

More often than not, advances were paid out in irregular amounts at irregular intervals, in response to direct requests. The characteristically erratic timing and random amounts listed in the ledgers suggest that the advances did not represent the families' sole source of financial support. Phebe Cottle felt compelled to justify her request on the grounds of extreme hardship: "I am sorry to be obliged to again call for assistance but my rent has become due and my wood is out and I am in need of manny articles for my family that I cannot do without. I have tried to get along as sparingly as possible but mother is very sick and I am obliged to give up my work in some measure. . . . I want you should let me have 30 or 40 dollars and hope not to have to call again it is no pleasure to me I will assure you but my family is truly in need."[30] Other women simply did not bother to ask at all. "I hav not troubled mr Rodman nor dont think I shall," Emeline told William Parsons. Sylvia Leonard mentioned to John, three years after he had shipped out, "I have not seen the owners since you went away and do not feel as though I could go to them now."[31]

Ultimately it seems clear that the limited forms of paternalism and the language that cast females as dependents mattered less to the women than it did to the men, those at sea and those on land, as a means of cementing male relationships. The agents' dependence on the top-ranked officers was acknowledged in part through the agents' assumption of the male role of protector and provider during the mariners' absences. But that role turned out to be mostly rhetorical, of little substance from the women's perspective.[32]

Throughout American society by the mid-nineteenth century, recognition of a functional interdependence between husbands and wives was giving way to the notion that, while married couples were emotionally interdependent, wives were materially dependent on their husbands. Clearly, an image of female dependency structured labor relations within the industry. But, if these women had really been so dependent, the fishery could not have functioned at all. In fact, as whaling voyages stretched to three years and longer, the professional mariners increasingly depended on their wives and other women to sustain maritime family and community ashore. Rhythms of migrant labor were built into the industry's growth and expansion into distant seas. The men's repeated absences assumed the willingness and ability of those left on shore to do whatever was necessary: to care for the young, the sick, and the old; to oversee property, manage budgets, maintain households, and integrate the networks of kinship and neighborhood ties through which the larger community survived.

Women bore the primary responsibility for maintaining the families and communities on shore. What these women actually did on a daily basis varied a great deal. It depended on their marital and maternal status; their age and access to resources; and whether they found themselves in (or took themselves to) more rural or more urban settings. By the mid-nineteenth century, their responsibilities often took on the nature of cash management. Since whalemen were paid the bulk of their earnings in a lump sum at the end of a voyage, their wives often found themselves short of necessary cash during the men's absences. "I must have more money," Harriet Allen worried in New Bedford, while she borrowed small amounts of cash from her in-laws and friends in what appears to have been an informal deficit cash-flow system involving several households.[33]

Women in New Bedford or other urban centers earned money by accepting various kinds of piecework, especially sewing, or taking in boarders, or purveying many different kinds of goods in small shops.[34] Centre Street, part of the business district in Nantucket, even came to be known as "Petticoat Row" for its preponderance of female shopkeepers.[35] Many women in port communities certainly participated in other, less licit income-raising activities, but the women connected to the career whalemen appear to have remained well within the bounds of middle-class propriety.[36] "Sister Sally"'s letter to her seafaring brother suggests the range of respectable opportunities for female wage employment in the regional economy: "Sarah lives to home this summer," she wrote; "Mary is over here [in New Bedford] learning a trade . . . I still board to Charles & work in the shop." Perry Lawton informed a friend at sea of the whereabouts of the "girls" they knew: "Mary Ann Brownell keeps school down here and Hannah at the Sandford schoolhouse, Elizabeth keeps with her mother . . . Almeda King works at the tiverton four corners . . . your beloved Sarah C. Tripp is going next week to learn to be a tailoress."[37]

The whale fishery itself expanded the opportunities for women to use their needles and their housewifery skills. Eliza Stanton earned $27.17 sewing shirts for sailors over a three-year period for the New Bedford outfitters Cook & Snow. In 1837, the Ladies' Branch of the New Bedford Port Society for the Moral Improvement of Seamen opened a nonprofit clothing store for sailors, hiring as seamstresses seamen's wives and daughters at wages somewhat higher than average; it is not clear why the store closed a few years later. The demand for piecework certainly continued: Sarah Cory wrote her husband, "I have so much sewing all the time I dont hardly know what to do some times but they wont take no for an answer so I am obliged to do it."[38]

Taking in boarders tied or ran a close second to sewing in the ranking of women's income-producing possibilities. The practice ranged from the small-scale, informal, and occasional to large-scale commercial enterprise. Sylvia Sowle of New Bedford casually took in four ship's carpenters as boarders for a few months: "they are very good boards i like the buisness much beter than i expected to," she remarked.[39] In contrast, while Captain Silas Fisk commanded whalers in distant seas, his wife, Julia, ran a seaside resort–style boardinghouse that accommodated dozens of guests at a time.[40]

In rural areas, women like Hannah Blackmer of Acushnet, Mary Ann Braley of Rochester, Caroline Gifford of Dartmouth, and Caroline Omey of Westport typically kept farms going with their own labor and that of their children, other relatives, neighbors, and hired help. In addition to helping out on her parents-in-law's farmstead, Hannah Ashley gave piano lessons and utilized her considerable dressmaking skills for several local women.[41]

Abby Grinnell of rural Tiverton, Rhode Island, wrote a letter to her husband in 1845 that assured him the family and farm were doing well in his absence but also, with telling choice in possessive adjectives, reaffirmed his authority as father and head of household. "Your baby is fat and she grows like a weed," Abby told him. "Your little man Philip and Stephen go to school and they learn very fast. Your daughters remember their love to their respected father." Abby had equally good news about the farm:

> Our corn is very large and the barley is very good. We have thrashed . . . and we got sixty bushels. . . . Gideon's corn is not near so large as yours. . . . Your oxen have done very well this summer and they are fat enough for beef. The

carrot is as thick as white weed down below Gideon's corn and we want you to hom to be a pulling it. . . . I hope that you will be so lucky that you will come next spring and as much sooner as you are a mind to.[42]

As Abby's letter makes clear, with the husbands' repeated and prolonged absences, their wives had to step in and act on their behalf. Mariners at sea routinely relied upon their wives' ability to look after their interests. The records are full of instances in which wives settled debts, bought or sold property, paid taxes, and obtained insurance during their husbands' voyages. Unlike the reciprocity between shipowners and mariners, which was explicitly invoked more often than automatically acted upon, the agency of wives and other family members on the men's behalf was simply taken for granted.

Eliza Beetle, on Martha's Vineyard, frequently served as business agent for her husband. On one occasion, Henry wrote to her, "[The owners] hold my note for 200 dollars or a little over . . . to be paid when I get home," and he advised, "if you have the money to spare and pay it, it will stop interest [from accruing]." Off on another voyage, he instructed her, "I had so little time in New Bedford I could not get [my employment] agreement in writing. . . . Dont rest until you get it."[43] David Allen arranged for his wife, Harriet, to hold his power of attorney before he left in 1865. Perhaps he was inspired to do so because, during his previous voyage, Harriet had had to enlist the help of David's brothers when it was time to pay David's taxes, and when she made sure that the shipowners insured his share of the cargo.[44]

Other women acted on their own initiative, without specific instructions, though still on their husbands' and families' behalf. Caroline Gifford not only managed a farm, she also decided when to invest in land and how to dispose of funds in the bank. For example, she collected a note due her husband from the agent whose ship he commanded, and decided what to do with it: "There was about 5000 dollars due you at Philips after your voyage was settled . . . of what I didnt use, since you wrote about putting it in the Bank of Fall River . . . I told Philips I wanted about 800 put in your name & 800 in mine. I didnt know what better I could do [because you] cant put in but 1000 [per person] . . . write me if I shall put more in in the childrens names."[45]

Whether they worked for wages or by the piece in town, carefully managed a family budget, or kept a farm going in an outlying area, women did whatever they could—and had to—in support of their families. Most importantly, they cared for their children. As elsewhere in America at the time, being a wife was inextricably linked to motherhood, even here where the spacing between children corresponded more closely to the length of whaling voyages than to female biological rhythms. It was taken for granted that the mother bore the major responsibility for the children. She was, after all, the one left on shore with them.

Just as all the domestic manuals and magazines, sermons, and sentimental novels and poetry prescribed, many maritime mothers cherished and delighted in their children. Selina Coffin described her son as "a darling boy just as good as he can be," and Caroline Gifford reported proudly of her infant son, "he is the smartest & hansomest boy that I ever see."[46] But seawives found that the great social significance popularly ascribed to the role of mother in Victorian America could be a burden in the maritime context of virtual single parenthood.[47] Betsey King, for one, found her maternal responsibilities particularly heavy. In 1850, she told her husband that their youngest daughter, also named Betsey, was "a real little chatterbox." The harried mother confessed, "I get along very well when the other two are at school but when they come home it seems sometimes as though I should go crazy." Their son "is a very great talker and he loves to hector the other children." Not surprisingly, Mrs. King noted, "It is a task to bring up three children," and she added, "I feel the responsibility more and more every day . . . I do pray to my heavenly father that he would guide and direct [me] in the right path."[48] Myra Weeks was less willing to assume the properly humble and pious posture; nor did she acknowledge any delights in motherhood. She wrote somewhat acidly to her whaling husband in 1842, "I think it is rather lonesome to be shut up here day after day with 3 little children to take care of. I should be glad to know how you would like [it]."[49]

Myra's complaints notwithstanding, the records indicate that geographical mobility, extensive community interaction, and extraordinarily malleable household arrangements enabled maritime women to share the domestic responsibilities and tasks typically allotted to wives in mid-nineteenth-century America. In a common practice, new bride Susan Gifford remained a member of her parents' household after her husband shipped out. This did not mean that she stayed there, however. The first month John was gone, Susan spent only five days entirely at home. Her diary is filled with references to church services and Sabbath school concerts; sewing circles, literary meetings, and lectures at the Temperance Hall; picnics and parties, skating and sailing; weddings, births, and funerals; short trips to local shops and longer excursions to stores in New Bedford; innumerable calls on friends and relatives.[50] Her network was large: in that first month she mentioned by name thirty-eight individuals, twenty-seven women and eleven men. Susan wrote wistfully, "I have such a sense of loneliness come over me once in a while that I dont know what to do." She was lonely—but she was virtually never alone.[51]

Women with children of their own or greater responsibilities for the care of property remained home more often. But this did not mean less social interaction. Hannah Ashley lived with her husband's parents on their farm in a rural hamlet near New Bedford, where a regular stream of visitors flowed in and out of the farmhouse. Over a three-month period, Hannah mentioned forty-eight different individuals, ten men and thirty-eight women.[52]

Childbirth and care for the young, the sick, and the elderly were occasions for cooperative female endeavor, as women's labor shifted from household to household in response to need. When Hannah Ashley bore her only child, first a close female neighbor and then Hannah's sister-in-law came in to help care for the new mother and baby.[53] In January 1863, Harriet Allen paid a doctor $30.00 for a number of his visits to treat her and her two children over a period of time. She called in the doctor again when her two-year-old daughter fell seriously ill later that spring. It was not the doctor, however, but rather a series of female friends, relatives, and neighbors who came in and watched the sick child around the clock for several days.[54]

Shared work, then, daily brought women in and out of each other's homes. Indeed, mariners' wives seem to have been nearly as mobile and constantly in motion as were their seafaring men out on the vast oceans.[55] Many visits lasted not hours but days or weeks. A sense of the dynamic flow around the maritime community is conveyed in Nancy Child's chatty letter to her husband, John:

> Oliver and his folks are as well as comon I have ben over there and staid 4 weeks and worked for them I left bub [their young son] with Mother and he was contented enough . . . he looks so much like you that every one speaks of it. we have moved down into the shop where we used to live and Stephen lives where we did when you left and John B. Colman has taken there roomes.[56]

Some women simply moved in together, combining households with kin, friends, or neighbors. The Spooner family of New Bedford illustrates just how flexible and open-ended maritime households could be. All three Spooner sons, Gideon, Shubael, and Caleb Jr., went whaling. Gideon married in 1835 and seems to have brought his wife, Elizabeth, into his parents' home. In 1839, his sister Sophia married another whaleman, George Clark, who also moved in. Elizabeth, Sophia, and the two Spooner sisters who did not marry all lived together, caring for their children and the aging Spooner parents, while their men went to sea. Sophia died in 1845, during one of her husband's voyages; it appears that the other Spooner women raised her child until Clark came home, remarried, and moved into his new wife's parents' household, taking his young son with him. Shubael and Caleb Jr. left the household when they married, although they and their wives maintained close ties with the rest of the Spooners.[57]

The Spooner family expanded and contracted with the demographic rhythms of the whale fishery as well as the more common rhythms of birth, marriage, and death. This kind of flexibility and cooperative effort characterized maritime community life in general. Fluid and dense patterns of interaction between kin, friends, and neighbors linked households and wove together communities, enabling women to meet their assigned responsibilities of sustaining and renewing life under the extreme stresses of the whale fishery.[58]

The stresses could indeed be extreme. In 1856, first mate O. S. Cleveland wrote from the Pacific to his employers, Wilcox & Richmond, "I have written to my Father to apply to you for . . . two hundred dollars, to enable him to provide for my widowed sister, who lately lost her Husband in the Barque Undine." The *Undine*, owned by Thomas Knowles & Co., had left New Bedford on 28 October 1852. By 1856, the bark was presumed lost with all men on board. Knowles & Co. was not expected to provide for the men's families; the firm itself had suffered a tremendous financial loss (which was probably partially offset by marine insurance). Instead, the bereaved widows and other relatives turned to their own families for support. Cleveland's sister returned to her parents' household, and her brother asked his own employers for an advance with which to assist her.[59]

News of the tragic fate of the *Undine* traveled from the Indian Ocean to New Bedford, from household to household to office and back around the community, and then out to the Pacific. Sharing information about the men at sea formed an important component in the shoreside networks that sustained families during separation and loss. This kind of interaction also benefited the men at sea: the whalemen relied upon the women on shore to keep in touch with events and people at home and at sea. Two months out, Captain William Loring Taber wrote his wife, Susan, "I . . . hope you will write by every ship that comes around Cape Horn sperm whaling, & as soon as you receive this, please to write to me at Talcahuano, & at Paita."[60] William wanted to hear from her, of course, but he wanted to know about the others at home too: "How is father, & mother. . . . How does Mary Ann B. & Crandel get along, How is M. M. Barstow, is she married yet." William also asked for news of other seafaring men he knew: "I wish you to write me particularly about [brothers] Alonzo & Edwin, how they are getting along [at sea] & when they expect to come home, & if they were successful—Do you hear anything from Richard Barstow . . . where is David Dexter?"[61] None of Susan's answers have been located, but the correspondence from shore to ship routinely contained news of courtships and marriages, births and deaths, whereabouts, successes and failures. With their conversations, with their actions, and with their recording of both in letters then sent to sea, seawives mediated and maintained their husbands' family and community identities.

The mediating role played by maritime women also contributed to the smooth functioning of the fishery. Sweethearts and wives in particular served as intermediaries between the fraternity at sea and the management side of the industry on shore. With the unpredictable catch and variable prices, the agents needed as much information as possible to make decisions about selling cargo, how much insurance to buy, and so forth.[62] To add to their sources, they frequently turned to the mariners' families. During the *Hope*'s voyage under Leonard Gifford's command, the owners, Wilcox & Richmond, were in touch with the captain's mother, sister, and fiancée; they also wrote to the father of the first mate and the wife of the second mate for news. Mrs. Eliza Lewis, wife of the second mate, passed along what she had heard: "Sir I have Recieved the money you cent. . . . you Rote to Me to know About the ship and how they git a long he Rites me Word . . . to Give my self no uneasiness for all Things look promising for a prospours Voyge and a Lucky one. You may expect News when I git my letter from cros land. . . . they ware a doing well 5 month a gow."[63]

Captain William Loring Taber regularly enclosed news for the agent in letters to his wife. In one, he instructed Susan to "please write Mr. Thomas giving him the date, & Lattitude, & Longitude, health, & quantity of Oil, & bound South . . . I havent time to write [him]."[64] Mrs. J. E. Chase wrote with evident feeling to agents Swift & Allen, "My long patient waiting has been rewarded by two long letters from Capt Chase. . . . He has taken no oil since August and has seen whales but twenty eight times this voyage.... He keeps from five to twelve men on the lookout from daylight to dark. He is discouraged. I am sure I am. He will never come home at this rate. He received no letters from you."⁶⁵ In the communication with their husbands at sea and the whaling agents on shore, Mrs. Lewis, Mrs. Taber, Mrs. Chase, and all the others served as nodal points in a global information network.

The shipowners were willing to facilitate the flow of mail in both directions for the sake of industrial discipline as well as information. Almost two years after the *Milo* left New Bedford, the agent Robert Greaves wrote to Mrs. Cornelius Marchant, "Dear Madam.... All hands [are] well and in good spirits.... I have written you these few lines to reassure you on the subject of your letters to him." He also noted, "letters from home give men great satisfaction & keep them from listening to the many solicitations & overtures they receive from bad people [causing] them to run away & a happy contented crew will [illeg] make a better voyage than the contrary."⁶⁶

Women's contributions to the American whaling industry, then, were many. But in the whale fishery, as in so many other areas of production in nineteenth-century America, the fruits of women's labor were often unacknowledged, devalued, or obscured by their symbolic content. The gender ideology that focused on emotional bonds and portrayed women as domestic was integral to men's motivations—yet it also masked the substance of women's productive work.

Most mariners took along their wives' (or mothers', or sisters') handiwork in the form of clothing, bedding, special foods, medicines, and mementoes of home. Ruth Post asked her captain-husband: "do let me know if your butter and cheese and dried fruit turned out well." Samuel Braley told his wife that "Grandmother Douglas cotton stockings ware well, but then here is not more than half enough for the voyage; I wish you would send me a dozzen pair more." Braley's wife also made up some medicines for him. Samuel called her "my Apothicary," though later he appeared less than grateful when he wrote, "I have taken three Lobelia pills (large ones what great awkward things you and Kate made: they are enough to gag a horse)."⁶⁷

First mate Charles Peirce told his wife, "you spoke of my shirts, never mind the shirts, those will do at present." He was more grateful for the picture she sent, of her with the son he had not yet seen: "My darling Eliza I thank you a thousand times for such a handsome Boy ... your Picture you said was not a good one ... but the more I loock at it the better I like it . . . how I should like to kiss the original. you do loock so good, with the little fellow in your arms."[68]

Peirce clearly valued the emotional content of his wife's efforts over the practical. His attitude, shared by most of the men at sea, again served to obscure the substance of women's labor in stressing its affective associations. Braley requested more of Grandmother Douglas's socks because he viewed his wife's own work with such sentiment: "I cannot ware those that you knit; it seems sacralage: how much I prize evry thing that is the work of thy dear hands." In a similar vein, Jared Gardner wrote to the new wife he had left behind on Nantucket: "When I turn in [to sleep] and hol that camfiter on me that our sweet sister gave me I think of the patch work that she pointed out to me that was of your dress. It seams almost as though I can sea you with it on. . . . Pleas give my love to . . . that dear one who lade asside her own work and assisted in making my clothes for they are as well as hands can make them."[69]

The symbolic content of the clothing, food, and other comforts provided by the women was critical to sustaining (at both ends) intimate relationships over the miles and years of separation. In making concrete the ties of mariners to their families, the things themselves reaffirmed the responsibilities that in part sent these men to sea and thus reinforced their commitment to the industry.

The practical functions of the items were, of course, also important. In a small way, the things eased the discomforts of the voyage and encouraged the mariners to persist in their career. Perhaps more importantly, the items further distinguished the officers from the foremast hands in physical appearance, health, comfort, and their relationship to the industry. The clothing and bedding supplied by their female relatives, as well as the households the women maintained, may have helped the professional mariners avoid the web of indebtedness that characterized the exploitation of the men in the forecastle. The women's labor reduced the mariners' reliance on those suppliers of specialized goods and services colorfully known as "landsharks." The account books show that about 85 percent of the foremast hands saw much of their earnings siphoned directly off to the outfitters to pay debts incurred before the sailors had even left port. But just over a third of the officers were assessed such charges, mainly the younger (and still single) third and fourth mates, for generally smaller debts.[70]

Yet whalemen, like so many men of the period, did not consider women's work to be labor in a productive sense.[71] Work, especially heavy manual labor, was something many mariners emphatically did not want their wives to do. Charles Peirce, who had cavalierly dismissed his wife's concern for his shirts, also wrote to her, "you dont seem to say much about your health. I do hope you do not over work yourself, loocking out for every thing, both out doors & in. you know Eliza, I have always strickly forbidden you to work to[o] hard, and you know Wifey, thou hast Promised to honor, and obey thy Husband."⁷²

In April 1846, Henry Beetle was similarly motivated to write to his wife, Eliza, "You gave me a small description of a days work you done, I fear you will shorten your days. . . . I do not want my wife to work so hard. Is there no one you could get to cut your wood? . . . if I was with you I could help you do a few of the chores, but as I am not, I rather you would hire your wood cut." The following September, Henry wrote again: "I must say to you cut no more wood. . . . I hope I shall be able to support you and little sis without you doing such work." In fact, in every letter he wrote over the next year, Henry insisted that Eliza avoid cutting wood, even though he apologized, "I feel very sorry that I did not leave you better provided for but you must take the will for the deed."⁷³

We do not know how Eliza felt about chopping wood, nor about her husband's apologies. Other seawives, however, made their opinions quite clear. Even while their efforts were critical to sustaining the industry, they voiced their sense of deprivation or exploitation in the form of rather subversive complaints aimed not at the cultural system prescribing separate spheres for men and women but, instead, at the whale fishery itself.

Sweethearts and younger wives most often emphasized the emotional costs of separation. Sarah Pierce wrote Captain Elijah Chisole, "I want you dearest before you come home to make your mind up that you will never leave me again to go to sea. for I never could be happy with you at sea and I at home far from you that I love."⁷⁴ Wives who had seen their husbands leave again and again learned from experience to blame not seafaring but seafar*ers*. Libby Spooner observed sardonically, "Nehemiah talks of moving back to the farm I think he best wait till spring but he is a sailor and consequently very uneasy. I know something about it, they never stay set down in one place till they get so stiff and old they cannot get out of it."⁷⁵ Caroline Gifford wrote to Charles, "I am in hopes . . . that you will not have to go to sea again unless," she added pointedly, "you can enjoy yourself better on land." On one of Caroline's later letters, their daughter Eleanor penned an ambivalent postscript: "it seems a long time for a man to be away from his folks three or four years at a time. I send my love to you and hope you will prosper . . . for it seems as though you ought to stay at home a while and not be on the water all your days."[76]

It is difficult to tell just how much of an impact on the industry itself the women's complaints had. Some wives actively tried to persuade their husbands to give up whaling altogether. Myra Weeks told her husband, "I hope you will be blest with a short and prosperous voyage and then make up your mind to stay at home . . . I think that there must be some way to get a liveing without your always being away from your family and friends." Captain Edward Ashley wrote home to his parents from the Pacific, "I do not think I shall ever gow a whaleing again Caty [his wife, then sailing with him] says she will not let me." Nonetheless, Ashley made at least two more whaling voyages—and simply left Caty behind.[77]

But Ashley's brother, William, told his own wife, "I think some times if I ever get home again alive and well I never will leave you again. Oh what is the use to talk all I want is to see you awfully and I cant help it." After an absence of nearly two years, William concluded, "it does very well for single men to be goin [whaling] a life time but I do not think it is healthy for the maried ones."[78] Shortly thereafter, he requested his discharge and left the voyage halfway through it, returning to Hannah and the farm, where he settled down permanently.

Some captains, instead, chose to stick with whaling—and took with them, right onboard ship, their wives and all the comforts of home, at least all those comforts that would fit in the aftercabin.[79] It was ironic, certainly, but no coincidence that this happened when the doctrine of separate gendered spheres reached its zenith in American society. The intrepid captains' wives were actually pulled to sea, that most masculine place, by ideological prescription: because they felt so strongly that their most important function was to be at their husbands' side. But the captain's privilege of bringing a wife on the voyage, though it became more common after the 1840s or so, was generally restricted to the most favored, the most successful, or perhaps the most persuasive captains. Well after the eclipse of the New England whale fishery, the practice remained controversial and tolerated with considerable reluctance, as the price to pay to retain a good captain.

The majority of career whalemen continued to ply the sea for as long as they were physically able, leaving their wives behind by choice or necessity—despite their often fervent protestations during each voyage that *this* one would be their last. "I am determined that the ocion shall never seperate us again not as long as we can live in love & harmony with each other & no grate loss of property befalls us," Charles Weeks stated firmly. "Perhaps you will say that I roat you so before but would go again," he admitted, but added "you may be assured my dear if you ar ever blessed with the cite of your affectioned husband once more that he is determined never to be seperated from you untill death."[80]

William Loring Taber was stung when his wife doubted his intention to leave off whaling. "You wrote you wish you could think that this was the last time we should be seperated . . . [but] that Agents give successful captains such inducements that they cannot resist them, and you will not insure one of my ambition against their temptation." He protested, "my greatest ambition is to gain enough of this world's lucre to maintain my family through life, without ever having through necessity to deny them any necessary want." Three years and another voyage later, William reported to Susan, "I do not think any one can offer me inducements enough to leave my family again, unless I meet with misfortunes that would bring them to want, . . . if this voyage is well ended, I feel that I can stay at home. . . . I think a married man's place is at home with his family, and if he can stay, he ought to."[81] This time, he held to his word, returning a year later to give up commanding ships and managing them from shore instead.

William Loring Taber's letters to his wife, Susan, document both the power of the prevailing gender ideology defining men's and women's roles and the inevitable tension generated by those ideas in the maritime context. Both gendered imagery and the substance of women's work were crucial to the ways in which the industry was organized. The whale fishery relied upon a core of career mariners: this group was both sent to sea and kept tied to the industry and their hometowns in large part by the gender ideology that cast them as autonomous breadwinners and their female connections as domestic dependents. But, if we look more closely, we can see that these concepts about gender roles masked many of the ways in which the whale fishery was embedded in a community onshore, and thus misconstrued the real direction of dependency. In actuality, the men and the industry depended even more greatly on the work, productive and reproductive, performed by the women onshore to sustain their families *and* the fishery.

Parallel to the notions about manhood and the breadwinner's duties that sent men to sea, the notions about female domestic responsibilities recruited women to substitute for their husbands when necessary.[82] The radical separation of maritime men's and women's work actually brought about a trangression of gender roles as the home-based women were forced to substitute for their absent husbands. The women's ability to do so structurally enabled the men's absences, which in turn made possible the industry's extension into more distant seas. The women's willingness to do so testifies to the power of their ideas about marriage and family. Through sharing activities and concerns, the women onshore sustained a dense web of relationships that bound together a community extended over thousands of miles and years of separation, enabling it to survive the stresses particular to whaling. Though unacknowledged, this was perhaps women's most important contribution to the industry—indeed, the industry could not have functioned without it.

Melville's monumental novel *Moby Dick* remains one of the most detailed and most profoundly evocative descriptions we have of shipboard operation in nineteenth-century American whaling. But that depiction tells only half of the industry story. By shifting our focus to the perspective of Ahab's wife and her maritime sisters, we can see that casting off from shore did not mean casting off the functional interdependence of men's and women's work, even given their vast separation and shifting meanings. Nor did the whalemen's leaving home and this group of women behind mean abandoning the ideological interdependence of masculine and feminine, male and female, gender roles; rather, these roles underwent manipulation and shifts in meaning, too. Melville found in the whaling voyage a superb vehicle for his exploration of universal issues in human character. So too do we find in the American whale fishery a particularly compelling portrayal of the complexities, contradictions, pervasiveness, and significance of gender in nineteenth-century America.

HASKELL SPRINGER

5

The Captain's Wife at Sea

The group of women who draw Haskell Springer's attention, the wives of American sea captains, came from much the same communities as those Norling examines in the preceding essay. Springer, however, follows aboard ship the unusual women who sailed as companions to their sea-captain husbands, a practice that appears to have begun in the late eighteenth century and peaked in the late nineteenth or early twentieth. The women's experiences at sea differed dramatically from those of the early modern "female sailors bold." Springer's captains' wives lived the consequences of the transition in gender ideology described by Dugaw in the second essay of this volume: the emergence of binary concepts of sexual difference, which defined feminine delicacy and passivity in contrast to masculine strength and aggressiveness. Paradoxically, even as they broke with maritime tradition and went to sea, these women usually found their lives more closely approximating the prescribed strictures of separate male and female spheres than did the women remaining onshore.

Springer's contribution explores the intersection between the social history of seafaring and the burgeoning field of theory and criticism of women's autobiography; his analysis is sensitive to the ways historical experience and literary genre interact. Drawing on the journals of thirty-six women who went to sea between 1823 and 1913, Springer examines the parameters defining their experience, the nature of their subjectivity, and how the women negotiated both through their writing. What, he asks, did it mean to be a woman in the male-dominated, male-defined world of the nineteenth-century sailing vessel? To answer this question, Springer explores the language, form, narrative voice, and intended audience of the women's sea journals, listening closely both to their words and to their silences. He finds their constructed stories, and their lives, rife with contradictions that starkly reveal the ironies and tensions built into the dominant Victorian gender ideology—notions of femininity and masculinity that continue to influence us today.

> "Why, I 'member goin' a voyage with Cap'n Eaton, when I saved the ship, if anybody did,—it was allowed on all hands. Cap'n Eaton was n't hearty at that time, he was jist gettin' up from a fever,—it was when Marthy Ann was a baby, and I jist took her and went to sea and took care of him. I used to work the longitude for him and help him lay the ship's course when his head was bad,—and when we came on the coast, we were kept out of harbor beatin' about nearly three weeks, and all the ship's tacklin' was stiff with ice, and I tell you the men never would have stood it through and got the ship in, if it had n't been for me. I kept their mittens and stockings all the while a-dryin' at my stove in the cabin, and hot coffee all the while a-boilin' for 'em, or I believe they'd a-frozen their hands and feet, and never been able to work the ship in. That's the way *I* did."
>
> —Harriet Beecher Stowe, *The Pearl of Orr's Island,* Chap. 33

THERE WERE HUNDREDS. As students of American maritime history know, Stowe did not really invent her fictional Mrs. Eaton, though she did give her a colloquial voice. During most of the nineteenth century and the early part of the twentieth, unknown numbers of American women, the wives of sailing ship captains, accompanied their husbands on fishing, whaling, coasting, and deep sea commercial voyages for as much as twenty-five years of their lives together, on cruises lasting as long as five years each. Many took along some or all of their children, and almost all lived as the only adult female aboard a vessel crewed by many males. Some, victims like their husbands of shipwreck or disease, and others, victims of childbirth, never came home; but whether they returned or not, from their experiences at sea came diaries and journals.

Often giving their accounts resounding titles echoing with the pride of their accomplishment, adopting traditional genres normally the province of men (such as the log or ship's journal) and making creative use of their formulaic components, these women tried to capture and communicate their experiences of the nautical life. Their situations and their writing are inseparably but subtly linked; both their expression and their silences must be read if we are to understand the personal and the cultural stories in text, context, and subtext. In other words, the thirty-six personal documents read for this study, dating from 1823 to 1913, all but one belonging to the Victorian era, speak to us best when regarded as literary remains.[1] Though their subject matter tells us much about the writers' narrowly limited, simultaneously privileged and deprived lives at sea, their form, language, and concept of audience tell us more. First, these literary aspects of the journals newly reflect and illuminate those small places occupied by the women within their husbands' definitively male world of sailing vessels. Second, they show us that these women found their own, ambivalently gendered ways to record that complex experience, strategically creating on paper audience-conscious lives as protagonists of their narratives. Finally, their literary aspects reveal the journals to be not only records but also tools—devices by means of which the writers could occasionally modify their experience, and even transform it.

Whatever might appear on the page, the keeping of a personal record stems from some well-known motives, whether obvious to the writer or subconscious, common to men and women, on land or sea. Any diarylike document may be one or more of the following: an aid to memory, an expression of egotism, a family record for one's descendants, a weapon against boredom (a personal entertainment), a private history to be examined and thought upon in later years, an ongoing record of self-examination (religious or otherwise), a duty fulfilled, a result of established habit, an emotional safety valve, the record of a period of time thought to be unusual or particularly worth preserving, the product of a compulsive "itch to record."[2]

It is worth remembering, in addition, that the personal account has been the preeminent form of written expression among women. "The [diary or journal] has been an important outlet for women," says one critic, "partly because it is an analogue to their lives: emotional, fragmentary, interrupted, modest, not to be taken seriously, private, restricted, daily, trivial, formless, concerned with self, as endless as their tasks."[3] Though this list needs modification if it is to fit the journals under discussion, it is instructive in alerting us to the possible human meanings of even the mundane, uninspired account; we must not regard such a piece of writing as proof of the writer's unintelligence or lack of imagination. On the contrary, it makes more sense to read it as a correlative, though not objective, embodying the writer's sense of life as she is most forcibly receiving it. Her other emotions, dreams, imaginative life, may at that time live elsewhere. "Women, by their own account, do all they can to keep stable the lives of others in their care; they work so hard to see that as little as possible 'happens' that their writing obliges us to look deeper, to the very repetitive daily-ness that both literature and history have schooled us away from."[4]

No matter when or on what sort of vessel they sailed, special circumstances gave some captains' wives responsible shipboard roles ranging from traditional "women's work" to the highest command. If their children aboard were of school age, they taught the youngsters their lessons. Some wives also nursed sick and injured crewmen, and a few served as spiritual guides to the men—holding religious discussion and distributing Bibles. Others took sightings, some calculated the ship's position, and at least one held classes in navigation for members of the crew. On a few known occasions, because of the captain's illness or death, his wife even took control of the ship, bringing it to a temporary haven or safely navigating it to its destination.[5]

Most of the time, however, unlike Harriet Beecher Stowe's Mrs. Eaton, the real captain's wife was supererogatory. To everyone, including her husband, she was usually separated from the life of the ship except perhaps in leisure hours. Though this condition may have accorded with nineteenth-century concepts of separate spheres for men and women, a whole sphere of one's own proved a lonely one to many, another matter entirely from Virginia Woolf's wished-for room. Living on the same ship with dozens of other people, the wife was too often painfully isolated, because her sex and her elevated social position meant that except for her husband she was normally on speaking terms—and formal ones at that—with only the mates, steward, cook, and cabin boy. This disjunction was virtually inevitable and existed even when the woman (and her children too) were well regarded by the men, or when the ship's "old lady" really was old enough to behave in a motherly way to the seamen.

In addition, despite her best efforts, a woman aboard ship could not help but be in some respects an annoyance or a hindrance. The smaller the ship, the more likely her presence was to cause trouble: "The carpenter has put a long window In the forward part of the house so Mrs Hamblin can set down and look whats going on on deck, who goes over the bows, or to the Urine barrell," grumbled one Abram Briggs in his secret journal.[6] Or she could be resented just for having a pair of eyes whose observations might be reported to the captain in a way unfavorable to someone. An attempt merely to escape confinement and boredom below decks could bring on conflict and resentment, as it did to Lucy Smith in 1870 aboard the whaling bark *Nautilus:* "While looking over the stern of the ship watching the fish and the Boats that were then near the ship . . . I saw the Mates agreeable countenance turned towards me and heard the beautiful expression Damn you, look if you want to. . . . There is not much to be seen, and when the Boats are chasing fish I like to watch them, and think there is no harm in doing so but I never can do so without Mr Holmes cursing me."[7]

And should she be close to giving birth and her husband take her to some appropriate place, holding the ship for weeks in harbor, the lost time and money were sure to trouble some of the men aboard. Whalemen in particular, paid a percentage of the take rather than a salary, were likely to resent such an unprofitable delay, as did Abram Briggs: "When a Captain looks after the welfare of his wife more than the Interest of the voyage It is almost time to sell out, for we are playing a looseing game."[8]

It is no surprise, then, that the women's journals reflect their separateness, and also record occasional attempts to reduce the distance—psychic if not physical—from the crew. "I have sewed patch work that don't comprise no part of whaling," was the half-humorous comment by one wife, pointing to her lack of a role in the essential processes of her floating world.[9] Trying to integrate and ingratiate herself in the face of such difficulties, Elizabeth Morey, the lone woman on the *Phoenix,* reported, "I feel if I cannot help them I will let them know that I feel interested for them."[10] And rather pathetically, Margaret Fraser, on the famous clipper *Sea Witch* in 1852, recorded her unrealistic hopes while implying her fears of being inessential to the ship and its captain: "[I] have been making myself useful again to day helping to splice ropes; I am sure the work will soon get done, now that I have a hand in it. I know George will not be able to get along without me after this."[11]

Feeling their isolation and exclusion, and occasionally the antipathy of men such as Abram Briggs and "the Mate," some of the wives longed out loud, as it were, for other women. Passing close by another ship at sea, Eliza Williams, on the deck of the *Florida,* saw its captain's wife on deck and revealed her own feelings as she interpreted the other woman's using a telescope despite their proximity: "She was looking at me, I imagine, anxious with me to see a Woman; she had the glass up to her eyes, I could see."[12] Another whaling wife, less restrained, admitted "crying like a big baby" when she lost the chance to speak to a woman on another ship.[13]

The emotional consequences of their position in a world so male that even the ocean was masculine to those who spoke of it metaphorically are also evident in scattered comments about being a woman at sea or seeing another in the same situation. The anonymous wife on the bark *Clement,* bound from New Orleans to St. Petersburg, Russia, in 1838, revealed her emotion alliteratively when she wrote, "spoke Ship Triumph . . . , saw two women on board, so I am not the only female on this wide waste of waters."[14] Bethia Sears, sailing on the *Wild Ranger* in 1855, seems just as serious (and prey to an understandable though destructive self-image as she apparently accepts an old superstition): "We are making slow progress towards the line. Elisha says we are having hard luck—hope it is not because I am here."[15] Only Elizabeth Morey, on the whaler *Phoenix*, translated her separateness into humor: "crost the Line but see nothing of Old Neptune[.] I expect he saw A woman on Board and that fritened him away."[16]

One has to read very extensively, though, to find such comments revealing the need for other women, or conflict with seamen. The subjects commonly dominating the journals are few and immediate. Looking at them in terms of their frequency, one would say that as a group the documents are centered in personal physical experience (primarily the round of daily life) and that the writer's own emotions come second. Next in frequency is the writer's husband—as person and spouse but not as captain. Next is the realm of religion, a vital concern of many, followed by the husband again—as master of the ship and crew. The business of the voyage (whaling, trading, etc.); the life of the officers and crew; the outside world of events and places beyond ships and the sea; and the greater realm of ideas, issues, and perennial human questions complete the circle of journal subjects.

Such is the pattern of the journals as a group, but some few looked at separately present meaningfully different configurations. A number are virtually limited to husband, self, and religion, while just two of the thirty-six reach ideas and issues. Only one of the documents dwells largely in the realm of private emotion, imagination, or reflection—that one being the sole twentieth-century account. And differences occur, once again, relative to the type of vessel involved. On whaling ships the business of the voyage is at least mentioned frequently and is sometimes detailed at length because it was part of daily experience and concern. On merchant vessels, however, business was something that generally took place in ports when the writer was not aboard, and she usually ignored it—sometimes not even mentioning the nature of the cargo. Similarly, for reasons connected to differences in the ways in which crews were formed, and differences in the enterprises themselves, the whaling wives generally had more to say and seemed to be more concerned about the members of the crew and the life they led, whereas reading a few of the merchant ship journals might almost make one forget that there was a crew. In fact, many of the journals, for weeks at a time, show little more than do the official logs of voyages: weather; sea conditions; whales seen, chased, or caught; ships sighted or spoken; domestic work accomplished. Scarcely an explicit thought or emotion, much less one of interest, causes a ripple in the flat narrative and descriptive surface. Though on occasion even the dullest journalist may break out of deadened and deadening repetitiousness, more often (and perhaps more importantly) her form and content, read closely and placed in broad perspective, reveal a submerged emotional life.

Modern readers are almost sure to ask if the journals of these unusual women, in treating such subjects, are concerned at all with the social and religious construction of gender, particularly in terms of women's restricted sphere. Most of the wives seem not to have seriously considered the question of women's rights and limitations. Like Mrs. Follansbee on the ship *Logan*, who explained to her Chinese steward that in America "women had the same rights as a man had to express their opinions," they seem blind to the public dimensions of sexual politics.[17] Although several do mildly express or hint at consciousness of a woman's social limitations and disadvantages, only one of the thirty-six speaks of the issue itself. On the whaler *Merlin* in October 1869, reading a newspaper obtained from another ship, Harriet Allen comments: "From all I can gather, I think that women are decidedly making great progress towards equal rights in this age."[18] Her strongest statement, though, comes on May 21, 1871, after having dinner on the African island of Johanna with its prince: "I should have enjoyed the dinner very much if the ladies could have sat with us at table. The Prince says their religion will not allow it. Being a woman I felt insulted and degraded for their sakes. How I long for the power to take them away, to give them their birth right—freedom. And not only them but all miserable women slaves the world over." In the nineteenth-century journals, characterized by their focus on the personal and immediate, Harriet Allen stands out as the sole explicit feminist, or at least the only woman willing to express such ideas—while even she seems to have been intellectually unaware of her legal kinship to the "women slaves" she writes of.

Whatever subjects these women treated, of course, and whatever attitudes they expressed about themselves and their milieu, have to be understood in terms of the forms of presentation they used. Enough of them began with a preface, address, or explanation to make that rhetorical item noteworthy. Bethia Sears addressed her "dear Sisters," saying she intended to keep a journal, as they had requested, solely for them. Anne Brown of the *Agate* wrote that she kept hers for the sake of her female cousins at home.[19] Hannah Burgess began hers on land and alone, announcing on her first page: "Diary[.] The property of Mrs Wm H Burgess, Commenced the fifth of August, 1852. Written particularly for the amusement of her Husband, who is on the wide blue sea."[20] When she joined her husband aboard the clipper *Whirlwind* eighteen months later, he wrote log entries at the top of the page, and she entered personal comments below, clearly expecting he would read them. Enough such explicit remarks exist to show that the specific request of someone close was a motivating force for a number of the women.

The mere announcement of purpose, whether or not we read it as candid, tells us about some sources of the writer's endeavor—utility being an important one. Mary Lawrence, on the whaler *Addison* in 1856, addressing unacknowledged readers, perhaps disingenuously begins, "As this is my first experience in seafaring life, I have thought it advisable to attempt keeping a journal, not for the purpose of interesting anyone out of my own private family, but thinking it might be useful to myself or my child for future reference." The greatest consciousness of motive or intent, though, is expressed by Mrs. William Brewster of the *Tiger*, whose first page recognizes a variety of factors behind her journal keeping:

> I have thought best to keep some account of the time as it passes so should I live to return my friends can see what I have been doing, where we have been, and perhaps by reading *this* form some correct idea as regards my feelings whilst absent[.]
>
> It will also pass away many moments pleasantly and at some future period be a source of pleasure to my Husband and self to review these pages.
>
> I ardently hope that as the days pass away that I may so improve my time so a retrospective view will be agreeable to my feelings and I can say of the past, It has been properly spent[.][21]

Though no other writer was as explicit or as thorough in announcing her conscious purposes, Mrs. Brewster's statements fit most of the journals: they will inform family and friends, be a pleasant pastime, serve as enjoyable future reading, and be a ledger of the self—recording time "properly spent," not wasted.

The fact that about half of these journal keepers began with a title or title page, and that most commenced with the start of the voyage and ended when they returned home, indicates a consciousness that their being at sea was a matter of note, an extraordinary thing in others' eyes as well as in their own. The titles are revealingly formal, echoing first of all the traditional (read "male") usages of the sea (for example, "Journal of a Whaling voyage kept by John T. Peabody in ship Robin Hood of Mystic

Capt John McFindley Bound to the south seas in pursuit of Sperm and Right Whales Sailed from Mystic May the 25th 1858"):[22]

> A Journal of a Voyage to the Pacific Ocean To Obtain Sperm Oil, by Mrs. Almira B Almy[23]
>
> A Journal kept on board, Ship Lexington on her outward bound passage across the N Atlantic Ocean; Round the Cape of Good Hope, across the Indian Ocean; on the Coast of New Zealand; In 1853.
>
> Eliza Brock[24]

Another model for these representative titles might have been the published narratives, written almost exclusively by men, of long voyages of exploration. And it is tempting to imagine that some of the journal keepers might have seen still another source, an 1833 account of a famous exploring expedition: *Narrative of a Voyage to the Ethiopic and South Atlantic Ocean, Indian Ocean, Chinese Sea, North and South Pacific Ocean, in the Years 1829, 1830, 1831. By Abby Jane Morrell, Who Accompanied Her Husband, Capt. Benjamin Morrell, Jr., of the Schooner Antarctic*. No documentary evidence, however, supports that possibility. It is more likely that some of them had read, printed in local newspapers perhaps, the journal or letters written by a woman at sea, and that the printed account contributed to their sense of being noteworthy women whose experiences deserved a title resembling those in print.[25]

These were their Dickinsonian "letters to the world," or perhaps their memorials—and they generally took care with them. Eliza Brock's title, above, shows that she inserted it long after the journey and the writing had begun, and Mrs. Alonzo Follansbee's rewriting of her *Logan* journal, apparently expanding and smoothing the original after the voyage was over, is evidence of a similar regard for both the experience and its written record.[26] Mary Lawrence's title page carries the same sorts of messages, and goes further too:

> Journal of Whaling voyage of Ship Addison of New Bedford, Mass. Captain Samuel Lawrence. Written by Mrs. Samuel Lawrence (The Captain's best [underlined three times] "mate.") Vol. 1.[27]

The confidence and assertiveness of that punning title page help explain Mary Lawrence's ability to hold feelings of isolation at bay.

That the titles of these journals are intertextual—that they owe something to the formulaic beginnings of the logs and journals dutifully kept by captains and mates—is supported by the frequent appearance of loglike entries written by the women. The cut-and-dried midcentury journal of Mrs. Wanton Sherman and the idiosyncratic and extraordinarily personal diary of Dorothea Balano (1910–13), for example, are linked by their common records of latitude and longitude.[28] A log is a factual record of a voyage, written using accepted, traditional terminology. The fact that so many of the wives recorded at least some of this information, and copied established usage when they did so, is important because it tells us they conceived of their documents as expressive in a traditionally masculine mode.

For a few of the women the log data in their journals was apparently little more than imitative, but for others it was integrative. Sara Taber, of the whalers *Alice Frazier* and *Copia*, is the outstanding imitator.[29] In fact, she was an innocent plagiarist: many of her entries are virtually word-for-word copies from the loglike journal kept by her husband, Daniel. This copying might in part be explained by her weak writing skills but no doubt owes more to tradition and proprietary feelings—as do the other journals. First of all, the record of a sailing ship voyage traditionally documents progress by citing the appropriate geographical and meteorological evidence of movement and position. So, too, most travel journals kept on land find ways to indicate location. And, second, since many of the journalists participated in taking sights and making the calculations to determine position, it is understandable that they should record the results of their efforts in their own books. After all, some of them were, with their husbands, part owners of the vessels; their recording of data probably shows an appropriate proprietary concern. Some also recognized and prepared for the possibility of having to take charge of the ship in place of an ill (or dead) husband.[30] And, of course, such nautical, navigational immediacy helped make the writer feel more a part of the enterprise in which she too often saw herself as merely peripheral. To conclude an entry with the common nonsentence "So ends." was, for a woman, an integrational act.[31] It is reasonable to infer, in fact, that by means of her log notes she became something of a sea*man*. Thus, these journal entries should be read, and their contribution to the documents as a whole should be understood, in light of such personal considerations and traditional foundations.

In a few cases, at least, the log model proved emotionally useful to the journal writer in further ways. On whaling ships, for example, it was common practice to record whales chased and lost as well as those killed. Many ships had wooden or ivory stamps, carved to represent the different kinds of whales, which were inked and pressed to the page alongside an appropriate entry. Sometimes these included a representation of the tail of a whale disappearing beneath the water, which indicated a lost quarry. Describing a futile chase (8 August 1875), Sallie Smith of the bark *Ohio* made humorous reference to the practice by drawing a diagram of a disappearing tail and adding two appropriate words: "Our part."

Whether this is read as light humor, criticism, or sarcasm, literarily speaking it is another example of intertextuality — in this case of importing a stylistic convention from another context and knowingly playing off its original and official purpose for personal expression. In the case of Dorothea Balano, her diary at first shows no interest in logging the *R. W. Hopkins*'s official position, though she regularly took sights herself and compared her reckoning with her husband's. But as soon as she began a long-awaited, eagerly anticipated Christmas trip to Rio de Janeiro in 1911 (with a cargo of ice and apples), she recorded the ship's position almost every day, fretfully counting off miles, days, and degrees of latitude on the course to Rio. Only in that time of high anticipation did the public log find a place in the private diary.

That word, *public*, has been central to my discussion of the meanings of form in these journals. It is abundantly clear that although they were personal accounts, they were not private ones. While it is unlikely that any diary has ever been written with complete ignorance or disregard of its possibly being read by someone else, the remarkable fact that virtually all the records left by these seafaring women were written at least with the assumption that they would be read, and most often explicitly for the purpose of being read, by someone other than the writer, calls for an examination of audience and its effect on these particular texts. We should go back to the prefaces, title pages, and subject matter, thinking now of the writer's having audience in mind all along.

The anticipated audiences tacitly or overtly addressed range from husbands to parents, siblings, and children, and then to other relatives, friends, neighbors, and unknown readers. Several had still another audience — God; for, like many diarists of the previous two centuries in New England, some of these women were examining their lives from a Christian perspective, with the aim of improving their time in ways pleasing not only to themselves but also to their God.[32]

Those wives who wrote with the assumption of a divine observer not only said nothing unfit for the eyes of the Deity but recorded their strong sentiments and their actions in his cause. They lauded the Sabbath or lamented its nonobservance; they were distressed by oaths and sometimes campaigned against blasphemous language. Never addressing God directly, their sincerely pious prayers, affirmations of belief, and statements of personal striving occur with great regularity. Particularly important to these religious women was the sanctity of the Sabbath, a belief that caused personal conflicts. All the husbands of those on whaling ships conducted their Sundays at least as actively as advised by Captain Bildad in *Moby-Dick*: "Don't whale it too much a' Lord's days, men; but don't miss a fair chance either, that's rejecting Heaven's good gifts" (chap. 22). That tortuous, even hypocritical reasoning bothered most of the religious wives, two of whom reported approvingly of meeting captains who allowed no more work on the Sabbath than was essential for the safety and well-being of the ship. Once again the women were outsiders, this time impotently disapproving of a practice they acceded to from necessity.

It is possible, of course, that the pious comments were written mainly for public consumption, but their sincerity is convincing. When mindful of their extended audiences, the writers focused instead on the sorts of things one would tell friends and acquaintances about an unusual voyage to exotic places and about daily life under strange conditions. Some of them therefore recorded, at length, their experiences of alien customs, striking scenery, notable personages, and historically hallowed scenes. One such account of New Zealand ends, "I think I have said more than will interest," testifying to the writer's directly addressing her audience back home.[33] Sometimes copying passages from guidebooks, but most frequently responding freshly, the women commonly demonstrate a predictable political chauvinism, prudery, religious bigotry, and cultural blindness—although a few, including those with earlier experience of foreign parts, accept and enjoy rather than gape and criticize. Several of the journalists were so little concerned about other cultures, however, that their accounts skip over days spent in foreign ports and resume when the writer returns to her ship—as if to say, perhaps, that a journal records the "real" lived quotidian life of the ship, not its brief, uncharacteristic interruptions.

But the novelty of the nautical life—the presence of danger, excitement, fear, curiosity, joy, and other predictable emotions—frequently produced noticeable (if not notable) results as the journalists tried to express their feelings in adequate prose. That most often they failed to be more than stereotypically hyperbolic and sentimental should come as no surprise to anyone familiar with the popular literature and exhortational prose of the nineteenth century. Perhaps Mary Hayden Russell really did think she heard her son address her this way at the height of a brutal gale: "'Mother,' said he, 'try to compose yourself. Let us hope for the best. The hull of the ship seems, as far as I can find, to have not sustained any injury, but should it be otherwise, and this night is to prove our last, we will go trusting in the mercy of God.'"[34] Mrs. Russell's acquired notions as to what one ought to sound like at such a time, though, are more to the point when we think of her writing as public.

Similarly, notions of propriety ruled reports of pregnancy and birth. As might be expected, culturally dictated euphemism controls: "Mrs. D . . . is expecting the arrival of a little stranger."[35] But more than euphemism is revealed by the same writer's comments on assisting at the birth:

> Mrs. Davis was confined this afternoon and for the first time in my life I assisted the [?] Mrs Sherman, and Mrs. Carroll. Mrs Sherman acted as Doctor, and has instructed me in the Mysteries so that if I should ever be obliged to assist, I should be more capable of doing so. Mrs Davis has a nice large boy and was sick but a very short time not more than an hour and a half from the time she sent out it was all over with. (27 October 1870)

Her words "sick" and "it" to cover the entire birth process signal the Victorian attitudes accepted by virtually all bourgeois women of her time and place. Perhaps, given the restraint felt, the view of birthing as an illness to be gotten over permitted even this limited a narration of the process, for illnesses and their treatment are repeatedly dwelt on, while these women, unlike the later Dorothea Balano, who exclaims, "Glory be, I'm pregnant!" have virtually nothing to say of their own pregnancies and childbirth experiences. Only two of the five nineteenth-century journalists who were pregnant even allude guardedly to the fact, a detail that testifies once again to the power of the anticipated audience.

In the cases of Lucy Ann Crapo, Anne Brown, and Eliza Williams, not one word prepares the reader of the journal for the birth announcement. So observant of the conventions was Eliza Williams that her mention of her first shipboard birth is appended to details of a gale, meeting another ship, and accommodating four pigeons. There was nothing casual, as some have claimed, about such birth announcements; quite the contrary, the preceding silence and seemingly casual report of what was a deeply emotional event testify to the power of cultural norms over these women's pens. No such hindrance to emotionalism applied to death, however; and so, when some of those babies died, their mothers found sanctioned relief by grieving on the pages of their journals.

Copying poetry, sometimes writing verses of their own, alluding to the Bible and contemporary literature, using figurative language and multisyllabic diction (often incorrectly), a number of the writers tried to give to their productions a literary patina testifying to the writer's sophistication and awareness of audience. The attempt is obvious—and so, usually, is their failure. The exception (before Dorothea Balano) is Elizabeth Morey. Her mind, as Pamela Miller says, "is atypical. Fresh and untutored, it contains few of the more conventional effusions that lard the journals of most whaling wives."[36]

Barely literate as she was, she brought a freshness of response to her experiences that transcends audience-consciousness and makes them memorable. Vividly illuminating the lack of sensory reward with which she had been living, she describes a day in the Okhotsk Sea on a small island when the first taste of good water in a long time made her ecstatic: "and at last we came to A Beautiful stream of Water, I took of My Glove and Dipt My hand into the Running Stream, and took A good Draught and it was Dilicious to my taste, and I felt so happy that I began to sing Flow on Gentle Stream Flow on gentle River &c." (7 August 1854).

The verses she wrote to slaughtered whales are naive and funny enough to have come from Emmeline Grangerford of *Huckleberry Finn*:

> Lovely Mercy we do love thee,
> Now your Voige of life is Oer
> You was the first Discovered by me,
> I shall never Behold you more.

The first whale they killed she named, by extension, "Jonah." Why "Mercy" should have been chosen for the second is unclear, but as she goes on an ironic sort of appropriateness emerges from the list of whale names. Compare the names given by the whalemen themselves to the dangerous creatures they hunted (Timor Tom, New Zealand Jack, Mocha Dick) with the predominantly feminine and elevated onomastics of Mrs. Morey:

```
#3 The Sea Queen of Russia
 4  Queen Elizabeth
18  Queen Victoria           [monarchs of the sea]
 7  Fanny Fern               [The popular American author]
 5  Little Susan Darling
 9  Little Adda              [whales are anything but little]
```

17	Dodge	[the whales were no good at dodging harpoons, she said]
8	The Queen of Sheba	
24	King Solomon	
26	Bathsheba	[a royal and Biblical story here]
22	Napoleon Boneypart	[Right whales were hunted partly for their valuable baleen or whale*bone*]
23	Josaphene	[an appropriate consort to #22]

She named about thirty in all, thereby effectively transposing them from the prosaic male world of whaling to an imaginative context of her own.

Other kinds of transformations were called for, however, when the writer's husband, a recognized audience for her remarks, was also their subject. It would be more than extraordinary were a woman in that position to speak candidly of their relationship, even if others were not also figuratively looking over her shoulder. Although such conditions of audience tend to suppress certain kinds of emotion as well as whatever discord may have existed in the marital relationship, the strategies taken by journal entries may nevertheless illuminate as much as they conceal. To examine them, the journals can be divided into the large majority, which anticipate the husband as a future audience, and the few, which show evidence of having been read by him during the course of the voyage. In the latter case, the dynamics of the situation produced results absent in the other journals.

Bethia Sears, already quoted in reference to her intended audience and her self-image, had been married only one month when she sailed on the merchant-passenger ship *Wild Ranger* from Boston to San Francisco with her husband, Elisha, its captain. She appears, by her own comments, to have been a heavy and rather indolent person, given to aches and pains. Though she began her journal by addressing "solely" her sisters, her husband soon became a reader and contributor to her book. Less than a month out of Boston he writes, "Wife wishes me to fill up to day's log for her, as she is too warm or lazy to do so herself" (28 October 1855). Interestingly, and in contrast to the other journals, we learn as much about her attitudes toward the voyage from him as from her. Though it is she who tells about learning to box the compass, fears it will take her a long time to figure the ship's position, and complains how she suffers from the 92-degree heat, it is he who comments, on 4 November, about her relationship to others and her state of mind: she helps make the time pass quickly for officers and passengers as well as for herself, she seems to be happy and contented, and she thinks she's done the right thing by going to sea with him. He goes on, "Allow me to add that we have had light and head winds together with calms for the last eight days past and I must confess it is the worst luck I have ever had in the Atlantic. . . . I am most discouraged, if it was not for 'Wifey' I should be sick." Apparently also addressing Bethia's sisters, Elisha was in this case doing what the wives frequently did themselves in these journals: he was answering the probable fears of her relatives at home and also commenting on her importance to the captain. That Bethia herself didn't do so seems to be a measure of her self-absorption.

A contrasting marital picture and a different functioning of the journal entries are apparent in Margaret Fraser's account, written on the clipper *Sea Witch* four years after her marriage, but on her first voyage to sea. Six days after leaving New York, she is commenting on the happy Sunday spent in her husband's company as well as thinking of the loved ones left behind, when she adds an encomium:

> Ah! I love them as well as ever; but my heart acknowledges a dearer tie, that of a beloved husband. Oh! I have never known one half his tenderness and love until now. . . . All that kindness and affection can bestow, and gentleness and sympathy sweeten, have been mine since I left home, yes my dearest George, beloved husband; with you my mind is at rest, my hearts desire satisfied. (29 August 1852)

This early passage may be considered merely an example of rhetorical excess and "spontaneous overflow of powerful feelings," but succeeding comments suggest more complex sources and functions, as does this one, two weeks later:

> George has been reading in my journal and finds fault with my endearing mode of expression as regards himself, well! it is better I think that he should complain of a too great fondness than not enough; so I will retain it all; it may be called for one of these days, and I can then satisfy. (15 September 1852)

With her permission, apparently, her husband became an audience, and from at least this point on, every remark she made must be read as assuming his eyes over her shoulder. Given her knowledge that he will read what she is writing, Margaret Fraser's implication that George may soon want or need unambiguous evidence of her love for him resonates with possible meanings. Is she stating her awareness of the possibility that his problems as captain may make him need a fully supportive, loving wife, while reassuring him that she will be everything she can and should be to him at that time? Is she alerting him to her anticipations or fears and so hoping to shape his consciousness? Is she alluding to some situation, known only to husband and wife, which may produce future discord? Is she hinting at something specific in his behavior that troubles her? Or, knowing that George's "complaint" is affected, is she just archly defending herself?

Obviously, both motive and tone are obscure here, but as other remarks follow, her intent gets clearer. Only four days later she writes again about leaving a loving home in order to go on this voyage,

> with whom? One who is comparatively a stranger to me; for although we have been married better than four years; still his constant absence from home has left me no opportunity of studying his disposition; thoroughly. What little observations I have made has preponderated in his favor; I know he holds it in his power to make me very happy and contented, or on the contrary; most miserable; I have not the least fear of the result; in my confidence of his integrity. (19 September 1852)

And eleven days after that:

> George is very kind, so kind, and attentive, so solicitous for my comfort and recovery [from illness] that perhaps I should not make this remark, but I know that he is wholly unused to complainings and sickness, and I sometimes fear that he may get tired; and regret my being with him, still I believe he has a kinder heart than that, at least I have had every reason for thinking so. (30 September 1852)

By this time the reader sees that Mrs. Fraser's journal has a hidden agenda, that by expressing particular emotions in relation to her husband, Margaret hopes to influence his behavior toward her. Her "I have not the least fear of the result," is, because she says it, untrue. Writing always as though to herself and unspecified others, in such passages she is nevertheless covertly addressing George—as she was in the rope-splicing passage earlier quoted. That she had at the time unacknowledged reasons for doing so is revealed four months later:

> The misunderstandings that passed between us at the commencement of the voyage; have to my unspeakable joy disappeared, and I trust forever; we are becoming better acquainted with each other's dispositions and to bear and forbear, will henceforth I hope be our motto. (24 January 1853)

What "misunderstandings" might have caused her to use her journal as a means of saying things to her husband that she couldn't express face to face is never made clear, though clues to his personality may help explain the matter. George Fraser was apparently (like so many other ship captains) a strong, self-assertive man used to having his way. In relating to him, Margaret was, it seems, obedient and adaptive. For example, "As we have crossed the meridian 180 degrees, George tells me I must drop a day, and as I am in the habit of doing as he tells me; I therefore call this saturday" (29 January 1853). The statement functions both as a general assertion of fact and as a flattering remark from submissive wife to dominant husband.

George's cruel practical jokes on her and his behavior toward others may have had something to do with the trouble. As to the jokes, she merely reports them, suppressing her feelings about being their butt. Less restrained in her remarks on his behavior toward the crew, she may have seen in it some cause for apprehension: "To me he is ever kind and sympathizing; let him be to others as he may" (29 August 1852). "All hands watch him as narrowly as possible, and I am grieved to suppose that he is more feared than loved by them" (9 November 1852). This latter remark would not have been taken at all amiss, since George Fraser, like many of his brethren a "driver" who hit his sailors (and once got badly hurt in retaliation), no doubt felt that the crew's fear was a proper and useful emotion.

Given this evidence of George's personality, it is further revealing and symbolically apropos that he should invade Margaret's journal, not only by reading it, but by writing in it as well. On 16 November 1852, she expresses her gratification that for two days she has not heard George use any "bad language." She hopes he will stop completely, despite the force of habit. Writing across her paragraph, George obtrudes his opinion: "Humbug." Then, nearing the end of the voyage, for some reason, Margaret stops writing for a month. Following her entry for 24 April 1853 comes his for 20 May: "Margaret Youle is lazy, and does not write up her Journal." Her weak "You don't say so," two days later, is the extent of her resistance; then she resumes writing.

Margaret Fraser's journal is unique in this uninvited intrusion, though not in evidencing a dominant/submissive pattern of behavior of captain and wife. Most commonly, however, in all those journals addressed only to a future audience, both a more healthy respect for the husbands and characterization of the journey as a willingly fulfilled duty or act of love are evident. No doubt at least some of the writers were concerned to portray themselves and their marital relationship so as to please their anticipated audience of husband and others; their reiterated assertions of affection, respect, and devotion may therefore be advertisements for the protagonist self in addition to what they appear to be. But they are convincing nevertheless.

The traditional, supportive role of the wife who happily takes a "whither thou goest" attitude was, as several commentators have remarked, congenial to most of the women. Their assertions of such devotion to duty (even when they disliked being at sea and hoped for a short voyage) and their more frequent expressions of love are heartfelt—written, no doubt, with audiences somewhere in mind, but not invented for them. With great rhetorical variety, from bald statement to sentimental effusion, the wives were finding an expressive outlet for their emotions while also creating (as several said) the future opportunity to relive such satisfying feelings:

> It was a narrow escape for John [his boat was stoven by a whale], and it seems as if I could not be thankful enough to think that he is still spared, for I love him more than I can express, sometimes I am most afraid I love him too well.[37]

> It is true that for love the human heart will make almost any sacrifice, and it was this alone that prompted me to leave the scenes of my youth, the kind parents, and loved friends, to wander with my Husband, and with him share the joys and sorrows that fall to the lot of a Mariner.[38]

For the most part, the women who had good things to say about their husbands and their marital life said them; those who didn't stayed silent on that point and focused on matters less personal. Eliza Williams (*One Whaling Family*), for example, says nothing about arguments or even disagreements with her husband. In fact, she reports not one conversation with him. A few, though, give more realistically balanced views of their lives with their spouses. Harriet Swain, on the ship *Catawba* of Nantucket, was perhaps exemplifying the legendary independence and self-assurance of Nantucket women in making some unflattering comments about her husband in her otherwise traditional journal. "Obed," she says, "has finished his Vane . . . he thinks he has done great things, grows rather childish in his old age."[39] She was probably testy because two days earlier her husband had interfered with serious work that gave her a meaningful shipboard role: "Obed has finished his Jag knife and is now out of business so that he is very troublesome, interferes upon us very much as I am very busy instructing Jack, Mr May & Manuel in the Lunars."

Harriet Allen, the whaling wife most conscious of cultural limitations on women, is an interesting study because her comments about her husband vary according to whether she is at sea or ashore. She had been to sea in the late 1850s and had given birth to a son on the African island of Mahe. But she had waited at home with her two small children from 1860 to 1863 for David Allen to return from another voyage on the *Platina*. She anticipated his arrival in the late summer of 1863, but, "I have almost given D. up for this Fall. I am sorry for many reasons" (29 August). That oblique second sentence doesn't tell us much, but because Harriet's English is almost always unexceptionable (she had been a schoolteacher), when she trips over her syntax two days later we may feel justified in assuming that her emotions, hinted at above, are behind it: "The last day of Aug. and D. is not here. I think he will not come. If he can get more oil I would rather he would stay. If he had not written he was coming I would not have kept house if I had not expected him."

When David finally returns on 4 December 1863, she records his arrival matter-of-factly and follows in subsequent days with only a few comments of a personal nature, even about relations between the children and their stranger-father. On 13 December she says, "I never saw D. appear to be so happy. He is as easy as possible. I wish I could feel more like him." It is only much later that this inability to feel happy is explained—in an uncharacteristic outburst of emotion:

> I see how it will be. D. will go to sea, very likely this Fall. He thinks now, that he will not go without his family, but he will. He will not find ship owners willing to allow us all to go, and he will go for three years—and probably longer—and I shall remain at home just as I did this last voyage. . . . I see how it will be. (28 May 1864)

Convinced (as several entries reveal) that she will be forced to stay at home and contend, despite her bad health, with all the stresses of housekeeping and childrearing on an inadequate income while her husband is where she would like to be, she hints her dislike of male prerogatives—once by creating a sarcastic noun: "[I] thought we were going to the Light house, but the masculines concluded to fish a little more and come home" (4 July 1864).

On 24 May 1865 David does leave, on the *Sea Fox*, not to return until May 1867, when she once again makes little of his arrival. While he is gone she is sorry, but not longing for him; when he is home she is distant. Throughout the years without him and during the time he does stay at home, Harriet has nothing complimentary to say about David Allen, while she hints at his deficiencies. Her surviving entries stop on 2 July 1867, but after they resume on 23 June 1868, when she and her family are aboard the *Merlin* bound on an African whaling cruise, she makes no critical remarks. Rather (in her restrained way), she praises and relies on him: "I had confidence in the little ship and her Capt" (23 November 1869). Never expressing love for her husband, Harriet Allen nevertheless found satisfaction in her marriage—but only, it seems, when she and her family were at sea in their own special world: "It makes me homesick to think of going home. If it were not for school I should wish the voyage just commenced" (27 January 1872). Her diary testifies that in her case, the center of the marital relation was her husband's role in creating the possibility of contentment—by taking her to sea.

Harriet Allen's diary is unusual enough, among the documents left by the seagoing women, in the way it treats her husband, but Dorothea Balano's is truly extraordinary—unique in its candor as well as its clearheaded understanding of self and spouse, even when seen as the product of an early twentieth-century "New Woman" who had gone alone to Puerto Rico to teach school. Though she called it a diary, like so many journal keepers she said her writing had a purpose and an intended audience: "Here we are and here is my diary again for me to use as a relief valve when things go wrong or when something happens that should be recorded for explaining to my children the whims and waywardness of their roving parents" (14 May 1911). Intelligent, educated, culture loving, and independent-minded, Dorothea also had literary skill. Her diary, as has been the case with women for centuries, was the book she never authored, the story of a life she said she couldn't take the time to write.

Her husband, Fred, skipper and part owner of the schooner *R. W. Hopkins* of Port Clyde, Maine ("nee Herring Gut," Dorothea archly notes), son and grandson of down-east skippers, was an uneducated, close-fisted, unimaginative, and demanding man. That he was also handsome, strong, adventuresome, an excellent ship captain, and fascinated by her, helps explain her attraction to him.

In love with her husband ("without whom my life would be as vapid as that of [a] silly water nymph"), Dorothea nevertheless was distressed by his narrowness, crudity, and penuriousness, and his expectations of her as a sea captain's wife. She rebelled, sometimes to him and at times only to her diary: "Now I feel like a member of the crew. Washing, cleaning, sewing. What in hell do we have a steward for? What happens if I mutiny?" (14 May 1911). "Why did I marry?" she asks herself several times when her husband's demands and apparent lack of appreciation get her down. Her frequent passages concerning him, in which, addressing herself, she often comes to terms with his behavior and gets psychological control of him by seeing him as a boy, are mixtures of high emotion, affection, realism, and self-instruction. The voice is unique; none of the other wives was able to express herself so fully and so well:

> The loveliness of [the scene], buttressed by his success at the uneventful and quick turnaround, make my boy so exuberantly loving, despite his crippling rheumatism, that he holds me tight every time he sees me and boyishly, as though he had never been naughty, tells me he will always love me. Thank God for that, even though he's more in love with his good feelings of accomplishment, his ship and the sailing of it, than he is in love with anyone. I'm his audience, but I love to see him act. Never lose your reality, my girl, and enjoy him and his foibles. That may be wiser than being a moonstruck calf who might be a bit shaken when moods change such as might happen with a headwind. And make some chocolate ice cream. That will prolong the euphoria. (7 January 1912)

That was written in an accommodating mood. A few days later, her advice to herself is a response to necessity—not quite the same thing: "Concentrate on the wiles, my daughter. It's a better way than a frontal resistance to a six-foot, two-inch sea captain with the power of a Russian Czar over his ship kingdom" (12 January 1912). Sure enough, before much longer we see—and clearly, too, because the writer is not censoring herself—the virtually inevitable feeling of isolation experienced by her nineteenth-century predecessors come over this captain's wife as well: "I can't turn to anyone for understanding, let alone help, because all the creatures on board are completely and absolutely in his power" (20 January 1912). At this point, the captain's wife was experiencing and expressing the feelings of thousands of sailors, similarly helpless. But she knew she had signed on for a much longer cruise with this skipper than they had.

What is the difference, then, between the situation of the Victorian Margaret Fraser in 1856, using her journal in a wily fashion to influence an overbearing husband, and the New Woman, Dorothea Balano, in 1912, finding to her distress that she too must contend with the power and prerogatives of a husband-captain by means of the old womanly wiles? No difference at all, perhaps, but a textual one: the freedom and ability to vent her feelings and so let posterity, at least, know her situation. Despite the great shifts, during the intervening years, in the social construction of gender, the conditions of a seagoing life as the captain's wife seem to have been determining.

Dorothea Balano, Margaret Fraser, Mrs. Follansbee, and the others who went to sea shortly after being married—or who had had little time ashore with their seagoing husbands—went through the inevitable period of marital adjustment under unfavorable circumstances. Though their situation often called forth gallantry and special consideration, which they appreciated, it also forced on them a dependence, even a helplessness, which meant that the adjustments were hardly mutual in degree or kind. They had married men who spent their lives commanding others and expecting instant obedience, and then moved aboard a ship, where such behavior was not only sanctioned but considered essential to business and safety. It is no wonder, then, that some journals repeatedly express gratitude for a husband's kindness, or that Dorothea Balano, strongly independent as she was, should feel she was being treated like a member of the crew.

Fred Balano was a skipper when and where it was quite common to take one's wife to sea. He also sailed short voyages and did not have to spend much time away from his wife. Those factors no doubt made him less appreciative of his "best mate" aboard than were many of the earlier captains, especially the whalers. Dorothea's situation may, then, have been more difficult than most—but it was clearly not extraordinary. What is outstanding is the way she wrote about it; for, in the statements of her diary, we read the silences of dozens of other women, constrained, as we have seen, to speak less than the whole truth.

Nowhere are those silences more obvious than in sexual matters—in which Dorothea was astonishingly candid. She often describes and comments on her husband's desires and her refusals:

> Last night I was having a good sleep . . . when enters my goatish hubby, hell bent on what he calls, "A connection that will make you happy." I told him I was quite content with things as they were and rolled over away from him. . . . If he'd be a bit tender and loving, less abrupt, he might get somewhere. The brute doesn't have a snowball's chance in hell with me so long as he barges in and thinks with his genitals instead of his head. ([15?] February 1912, 119)

Not that Dorothea automatically rejects or even unwillingly resigns herself to Fred's desire. She recognizes and expresses the effects of her own sexuality as well, as she did one night when a woman guest was aboard ship: "Fred stayed primly away from me to avoid any noise that might betray his animal lusts when approaching me in bed. As I felt the oysters—or do I imagine it?—I finally told him to chuck his modesty and come to bed" ([15?] February 1912, 123).

The fact that she repeatedly addresses her children, "who read this in years to come," as she makes such comments, separates Dorothea from her predecessors, for whom the presence of an audience or potential audience meant the suppression of all personal sexual matters and the euphemistic handling of those involving others. Not one of the other writers had anything to say about her own sexual life, and only Lucy Smith commented on others: the first mate's venereal disease; an accusation of rape brought by an English captain and his wife against their steward, who allegedly attacked their five-year-old daughter.[40]

Silences, whether on sexual matters or not, are expressive. Though we can't always be sure of what they are saying, we can legitimately listen to them—remembering, perhaps, the remark of Eliza Williams's son who spent many childhood and adult years at sea: "Aboard ship is one place where you learn to control your emotions."[41] We have seen the power of modesty and propriety to skew a personal account. We can also infer the desire of the writer to create a certain prose reality—to draw for herself and her eventual readers a picture of life that accords with her investment of self in that life. The central figure of such a reality is the shipboard wife herself, characterized by her written words and reported actions, created by the writer in response to any number of personal and societal imperatives. In her silences we may also read an accommodating and self-conscious personality, limited emotional freedom and intellectual strength, innate restraint, avoidance of conflict, possible lack of imagination, limited interest in or understanding of certain matters, and a self controlled by the quotidian—bearing the weight of the seemingly endless repetition of daily trivia. Silence also testifies to itself. For some women it was the silence of an endless and omnipresent ocean, the silence of hours of sewing alone or reading alone, or thinking alone in the cabin of an otherwise busy ship, the silence of long, hot calms, and of seasick days spent wedged into a soft nook on a ship plunging so wildly that even sewing and reading (much less writing) were impossible.

The reading of omissions, however, only goes so far before we are brought back to what *is* said in response to experience. The shipboard physical conditions that contributed to journalistic silence help to explain why most of the novelty of the sea and ship wore off before long, and why initially high spirits sank. It took eight months at sea to change its "peculiar charm" to "dull monotony" for Sarah Cole, whaling on the *Vigilant*, but only one month for the anonymous wife on the *Clement* to say allusively, "I have got almost enough of the sea, and the sound of many waters has not that charm upon me it once had" (4 July 1838).[42] Though all the writers appear to have gone willingly to sea and a few even to have persuaded reluctant husbands to take them along, some of the whaling wives found the conditions too trying and left their spouses in midvoyage to return home on another ship. Most of the women, though, came home in the way they anticipated. And in general, once home, they stayed there, either with their husbands or alone.

Some at sea had felt as had Mrs. Swain, who missed the "blessings and comforts of the land" so much that she was moved to "hope we may get sufficient this voyage to bid a dieu to Sea life" (22 September 1854). Others, though (such as Harriet Allen), stayed home reluctantly, having found their shipboard experience particularly appealing. A major source of such appeal was the magnificance of the sea as witnessed from aboard ship: "As I gaze on Old Ocean's heaving bosom I feel to exclaim, in the language of Holy Writ 'Wonderful are thy works' " (Hannah Burgess, 26 February 1854). Even storms at sea, which convinced some of the wives to end their seagoing careers, had quite the opposite effect on a few women of strong temperament. Harriet Allen responded to a storm so fierce that it shredded sails and forced her husband to cut away part of the foremast: "The strange wild excitement, even fascination, of the scene, banished fear" (23 November 1869). The next day she commented that although glad for good weather, she was not sorry to have gone through the hurricane. "It is a thing to remember always—I feel that I should have *lost much* had we escaped it." Mary Lawrence agreed, expressing herself as strongly as she could: "It sometimes seems impossible that we can live through it, but our gallant ship rides along fearlessly. It is grand beyond anything I ever witnessed, sublimity itself" (27 November 1856).

While such response to danger at sea is not typical, neither is it unique. Whatever its source, sexual or otherwise, it complements remarks asserting that their voyages to sea were at the center of some women's emotional lives:

> Every body anxious to get home—excepting myself.... I know this kind of life is forever one for me. This is my home I have no other. I want to see my friends but I do not feel that I am going *home*. (Harriet Allen, 12 April 1872)

Once again, Dorothea Balano's words are memorable:

When I sailed down the Hudson I did not know why I felt so good but now I know, from my Maine experience, that I felt like a salmon, an alewife, or a smelt, heading for my natural habitat, the open sea. (9 June 1912)

Natural habitat or not, the special factor in the lives of the seagoing women is that while they did not choose to be born into the disenfranchised and dependent place assigned to them in American society, they did themselves choose to live aboard ship. That in so doing they put themselves in a world more thoroughly and dominantly masculine then the one they had left is, in this light, beside the point. Though they worried about their decision, frequently felt the need to explain their motives (at least those that could be voiced) to dubious friends and relatives, and sometimes fought determined family opposition, the wives who went to sea exercised one of the very few real options they had.[43] Maybe they were jumping from the frying pan into a cold douche, as Dorothea Balano put it in another context, but there was great satisfaction in the doing: "I expect my friends feel anxious about me and I wish they could know how contented I am. I believe this is the place for me" (Lydia Beebe, 12 December 1863).

Perhaps, all in all, the story of these women and their journals is one of repeated contradictions. Freedom from the shore meant confinement at sea; achieving traditional ends required using nontraditional means; the personal became public, deep emotion produced silence. While all around them was in motion, they sat; while everyone else worked, they watched. Though consorting with kings and queens in exotic parts, they sewed overalls on deck. And in telling their own unusual stories of female experience, they frequently used the common, restrained, and traditional expressive forms supplied by men. But to say all this is to say no more, really, than that they were, in the ways we see all too clearly now, the second sex. How ironically apropos of them was George Sand's remark, "Writing a journal means that facing your ocean you are afraid to swim across it, so you attempt to drink it drop by drop."[44] The journal-writing wife was facing *her husband's* ocean. But while she was, of necessity, drinking it in gulps, she was all the while converting it, drop by drop, in the ink of her pen, to *hers*.

MARGARET S. CREIGHTON

6

Davy Jones' Locker Room
Gender and the American Whaleman, 1830–1870

The focus of the next three contributions shifts from maritime women to seafaring men, in particular to the variability and specificity with which different groups of seamen defined and experienced masculinity. Margaret Creighton argues here that the nineteenth-century American sailing ship not only reflected shoreside attitudes toward gender but that it was an important site for the construction and strengthening of masculine identities. Drawing on ship logs and sailors' diaries from the nineteenth-century American whale fishery, Creighton thus significantly extends our understanding of the male side of the picture begun in the earlier essay by Norling.

Creighton's study reveals the wide range in gender identities of whalemen, even within the group of white, native-born men on which she focuses. She examines how a sailor's age, class background, and shipboard rank helped determine how these men expressed and experienced their manhood. Important to Creighton's analysis is the material culture of the deepwater vessel, particularly the ways in which "women" as objects, as physical space, and as nautical nomenclature appeared in the male-dominated environment. She finds that the absence of flesh-and-blood female referents at sea did not make gender an irrelevant category in the occupational subculture of seafaring. To the contrary, Creighton (as do Bolster and Tabili in the next two essays) documents how dominant land-based gender norms were reinscribed and manipulated onboard ship in ways that reflected or reinforced certain social relations of work within the maritime industries.

IT HAS BEEN OVER twenty years since women's historians redirected the course of American social history, and over half that long since scholars began looking at gender as a decisive component in human experience. Scholars working in certain fields, however, have been slow to take up the study of women and to apply the lens of gender to their subjects. Historians of the American West, the Civil War, and the American maritime enterprise, in particular, resisted the trends in the discipline as a whole, and for a long time represented their subjects as exclusively male enterprises, made tragic or glorious by combat or conflict.

But things have begun to change. Historians of the West have recently overturned our understanding of the region, noting how women of diverse backgrounds played vital parts in resisting and sustaining settlement and conquest. And recent scholarship on the Civil War has not only highlighted women's decisive roles in the military effort and the war's outcome but has also described the part that gender played in political discourse, as well as the way that the war influenced the construction of womanhood and masculinity.[1]

American maritime historians have moved more slowly. They have continued to define the ocean as a male domain and to populate sailing ships with an unvaryingly single sex. It is, of course, difficult to dispute the maleness of American sailing vessels, if by that we mean the preponderance of men aboard ship. It is much easier to challenge the notion that because sailors were mostly men, they were permanently and naturally masculine in the very same manner. Men are gendered individuals, who learn different ways of acquiring manhood and of wielding social power. They are schooled to be "men" by parents and peers and in social and economic institutions (like sailing ships). Their conduct and demeanor vary from time to time, from place to place, from culture to culture.[2]

To hear most maritime historians tell it, though, American sailors were cast from the same hard and timeless mold. Scholars writing from the late days of merchant sail and whaling into the recent past have depicted sailors as universally tough and thick-skinned men who enthusiastically turned their backs on domesticity and the soft comforts of shore life. Numerous accounts and studies have described sailors' distaste for quietude, harmony, amity—domestic and "female" virtues[3]—and their eagerness to enter the whirling fracas of a deepwater war zone. In books with titles like *The War with Cape Horn*, these chroniclers have claimed that mariners, once they are rid of the "distracting land," and once they are liberated to "live a man's life," go to battle.[4] Whalemen, according to Alexander Starbuck, sailed in "one continual round of hairbreadth escapes," in which "no shirk could . . . indulge his shirking." Clipper ship sailors, claimed Robert Carse, constantly challenged "storms, the sea, anything which might oppose them." Deepwater seamen, agreed Alan Villiers, were "habitually tried searchingly and savagely by the life they led and the fight they fought in a manner unknown in other fields, save active war. They fought with their beautiful ships against all odds and they generally won."[5]

The portrayal of seafaring as a combat engagement, and sailors as warriors opposed to the tame female style of the shore, reflects in part middle-class gender ideals of the late nineteenth and early twentieth centuries, to which these historians were clearly attached. These ideals stressed the "natural" polarities of male and female and celebrated a rugged, physical masculinity.[6] But is the portrayal mostly scholarly imposition or does it also reflect to some degree sailors' self-image and behavior? And if sailors espoused "toughness," which sailors did so, and why?

Literary critics, it should be said, have been addressing a related set of questions for some time. A number of scholars have used a gender analysis to evaluate nineteenth-century American maritime fiction, especially that of Herman Melville. Melville critics have identified the ways that the author's sailors diverge from or sustain the "iron men" characterization and the extent to which they are antiwoman or antidomestic.[7] This criticism prompts us to a further consideration of the ways in which literary representations are borne out in historical accounts.

The study here, which applies the lens of gender to the records left by nineteenth-century whalemen, is grounded in the experience of men in the American fishery in the mid-1800s. Evidence examined includes correspondence between shipowners and masters, letters between women at home and men at sea, but most importantly nearly two hundred ships' logs and journals. The men who wrote them were white northeastern Americans who sailed on whaling voyages lasting from two to five years. Approximately 20 percent of these men, whom we shall designate as "middle-class" seamen, described themselves as individuals of "refinement" or "talent" or "discernment" and were clearly men of some wealth and education. Most of these men lived before the mast, in the forecastle, as inexperienced seamen. The majority of mariners described here, though, were men who had come to the sea from farming or fishing communities or from work in mills or workshops, or from the ranks of the unemployed. These men also inhabited the forecastle of the whaling ship, although some served as skilled seamen and as lesser officers, and lived aft in the vessel.

The records left by these mariners yield a rich amount of information about gender identity and behavior. They indicate what mariners meant by "manhood" and how seafaring fit into notions of proper masculinity.

They open a window onto the nature of social relations between women at home and men at sea. They also describe sailor culture and the social and material space of the ship and provide evidence about the place of women, both real and fictive, in seafaring society.

The evidence studied here suggests that, contrary to many historical accounts, nineteenth-century whalemen did not embrace a single masculine self-image or social style.[8] Furthermore, the sailing ship was hardly a "hisland" but was instead a highly heterosocial space.[9] At the same time, however, the sea / shore, male / female dichotomy was not purely popular stereotype. Records show that, depending on their age, class, and rank, some whalemen did relish confrontational toughness and oceanic fury. And some sailors did indeed take part in a shipboard society that prohibited women and condemned womanliness. Mariners became "men" at sea, therefore, but in more ways than one.

I

Like most accounts of American seafaring, traditional histories of the American whale fishery equate the whaling voyage with an endless round of contests. And nineteenth-century whalemen, particularly those who hailed from working backgrounds ashore, lend credit to that depiction. They viewed the whales that they hunted as "monsters of the deep," which made the chase a bloody battle and themselves valorous champions. "The noble whale," explained one mariner in 1847, "is the game worth killing and which makes a man proud to look upon, to feel that he can conquer the King of the Seas." Whalemen saw the ocean setting, too, as a challenge of formidable dimensions. Waves that could be "mountains high" certified the men who ascended them as peculiarly intrepid. Cape Horn, with its cross winds, currents, and violent weather, was a favorite testing ground for mariners, and it allowed the seamen who rounded it to compare their daring with the alleged temerity of landsmen. Sailor George Blanchard put the matter into verse:

> [The wind] increased at night untill it blew a gale
> And though 'twas not much to a sailor's mind
> A landsman would have looked a little pale
> For sailors are in fact a different kind.[10]

Middle-class seamen, too, reveled in ocean turbulence, but for a different reason: they looked for the "sublime" at sea. While their counterparts ashore flocked to Niagara Falls, to the Catskills, or to the White Mountains, they sought exhilaration through a firsthand confrontation with the infinite ocean.[11] The more violent the weather and the more stormy the ocean, the happier these men were, for they thus stood face-to-face with the awful but grand divinity. When whaleman Robert Weir's ship struggled through a frenzied sea in the South Atlantic in 1855, he was thrilled and comforted by the scene around him. He tried to be on deck as much as he could, to "hear the Allmighties voice in the storm." "It makes us feel," he said, "that we are actually in the great presence of the Omnipotent." Likewise, when he beheld his first big whale, he said it was "a blessing that I could behold a mighty work of God."[12]

For all the attention that mariners of every background gave to pelagic fury, though, they also appreciated the more pacific dimensions of seafaring. Unlike later historians, in other words, these men acknowledged that the deep sea has a tranquil side. They readily noted that ocean weather went beyond hurricanes, gales, and typhoons, and that a sailing voyage could not be reduced to the dramatic rounding of the two Capes. They recognized the place that soft fogs, warm calms, light airs, and even gentle breezes played in their seafaring experience.

Some mariners contemplated the land-based fallacies of "dramatic" seafaring, and scientifically dismantled tumultuous depictions of the ocean. Orson Shattuck, a greenhand aboard the *Frances* in 1851, made it plain to the readers of his diary that they should discount any depiction of sailing that overstated the frenzy of the sea. "I will state here," he noted, "that when people on shore read or hear about the waves being like mountains they may put it down as figurative language for they never are except in shape: they are never more than twenty-five or thirty feet in height." Another sailor agreed. "Oh these authers," he exclaimed, "their stories of Old Neptune's Home are 'all in my eye.' "[13]

While these particular mariners expressed disappointment at the ocean's subdued nature, other men rejoiced in the pacificity of the sea. Dead calms had few enthusiasts, of course, but whalemen took deep delight in sailing through relatively still, serene, and untroubled expanses. They relished the quiet beauty of a sunrise or sunset, for example, and they appreciated the soft, eerie beauty of moonlight on the water.[14] And they were not unaware of the gendered implications of such appreciation. As he was leaving the Pacific Ocean in December 1845, veteran George Blanchard exclaimed upon the (feminine) wonders of that sea. "It *is* a lovely ocean," he said. "It is the calm 'Summer's Sea' of a young Lady's

Album to a T. It is a genuine personification of aqueous perfection; so *tame* is it, that old women might sail upon it, with the help of a few mariners—in short the Pacific is pleasanter, with 'all hands ahoy,' than the Atlantic, with two watches in, and Duff for dinner."[15]

Even the whale, it seems, which was the ultimate signifier of confrontational toughness, was occasionally valued for other attributes. Although it would be well over a century before whales would be redefined as gentle giants, as acrobatic playmates, or as singers of dreamy songs, whalemen sometimes recognized and appreciated their unobtrusive beauty. Seaman Samuel Chase, for instance, challenged the whole continent of America to produce a scene as sublimely beautiful as a pod of whales spouting on a glassy, calm sea. The ocean, he said, appeared like a "forest of ceders, such a multitude of spouts were continualy heaving up into the air." It was, he claimed, "beautifully diversified."[16]

Whalemen not only enjoyed the ease of calm weather and docile whales; they also appreciated the passivity that a sailing life sometimes afforded. When warm winds moved a vessel smoothly along and mates eased up on busy work, mariners claimed they experienced a life of near loafing. Relinquishing the aggressive and combative aspects of whaling was no hardship for Edwin Pulver, who was so pleased with passive seamanship that he put his sentiments into verse:

> Very Good times we have indeed
> Nothing to do but sleep and feed
> But sleep is the best I think of the two
> For there's No Exertion to go through
> But in eating we have to use our paws
> To pass the grub into our jaws
> And when A man Eats a great deal
> It will make him rather tired feel.[17]

Whalemen not only took pleasure in relaxed pastimes like viewing a still sea or calmly sleeping, but they also sometimes practiced and enjoyed close friendliness with one another. Maritime historians have frequently stressed accounts of sailors' social conflicts, of standoffs between men, and of harsh violence. These diaries reveal the unhappy realities of such depictions. But they also describe the cooperative sociability of the sailing ship, particularly among men of the same rank. Sailors learned the importance of fraternity early on in the voyage. The King Neptune Ceremony, which on some whaling ships symbolically transformed first-time seamen into experienced hands, awarded and celebrated brotherly caring and the acquisition of seafaring skills. It did not test physical daring and individual assertiveness. Sailors who decided to tough out the ritual or to stand up to Neptune and his court were, in fact, more harshly treated.[18]

Epitomizing whaling fraternity was something called the "gam." Gams were meetings between whaling ships at sea, in which a captain and whaleboat's crew from one vessel were exchanged with those of another. During a gam, officers socialized with each other and sailors often traded gifts and sang and danced together. William Abbe, a sailor aboard the *Atkins Adams,* described a gam in 1858 as a scene of delicious, harmonious pleasure: "The three barks lay nearly in a triangle—on a quiet sea—in nearly a dead calm—while the moon . . . shed a brilliant light over the ocean—and shone with elfish gleam on the white sails. . . . We could see in the distance two other ships gamming—and amidst this scene of quiet beauty—beneath the moon— . . . we danced away."[19] Whaleman Silliman Ives brought gender more explicitly into his account of gamming: "Talk about a 'sewing society' or a 'tea party' why it can't begin to compare with a whaleman's gam. Everyone gets up their 'fantackle' and then they go at it and the way small talk suffers is a caution. All the news that has lately been heard, and considerably more that is manufactured on the spur of the moment is exchanged. . . . And so the many tongues wag merrily."[20]

The fact that whaling represented the spectrum of social experience from battlegrounds to parlors and that men appreciated the variety of such a life is underscored by the advertisements recruiters used to bring men into the fishery. Whaling was billed in posters and by word of mouth as an assertive adventure replete with whale attacks, ferocious cannibals, and oceanic cyclones. But it was also billed as "easy times."[21] And whalemen explained that they were drawn to seafaring by that promise. Edwin Pulver described his crew as men who hoped to prosper "with very little effort." Another whaleman had a "moral antipathy" to hard work. The ubiquitous Charles Nordhoff claimed that men who went by the dozens into shipping offices were those who looked forward to an "easy berth."[22]

Whalemen, then, celebrated surviving whaling's harsh dangers but also relished a calm life that lacked struggle. Their attitudes call into question not only stereotypes of the assertive sailor, so popular with twentieth-century maritime historians, but also more recent depictions of turn-of-the-century masculinity. Scholars, who agree that a martial type of manhood dominated gender ideals in the early 1900s, also argue that a rising minority of men embraced a more tranquil masculinity and revealed "feminine" domestic sensibilities.[23] Their assertion that these sensitive men were a "new" sort may deserve modification in the light of sailor evidence from an earlier period.

But nineteenth-century seamen may have been unique in their willingness to express their softer sides, for reasons having to do with their distance from home and from women. Historians have suggested that nineteenth-century American men diversified their ideals and behavior, entertaining more "feminine" attributes, when female and male occupational worlds were most distinct. When women closed in on male domains, however, men tightened up and suppressed sentimentality and domesticity. Scholars have associated the rise of the ideal of strenuousness in the late 1800s, for example, with the fact that the occupational spheres of women and men were breaking down. As the twentieth century approached, white women increasingly entered the male public worlds of business and the professions, and made a higher profile for themselves in social and political reform. A rigidification of the lines of manhood served as a way to stave off a loss of power as women took on so-called men's work and encroached on their workspaces. "When changes in the workplace caused men to feel uncertain of their manhood," Anthony Rotundo has argued, "their primary response was to seek new forms of reassurance about it." This reassurance came in a cult of wilderness, of athletic prowess, and of warmaking, all to some degree off-limits to women.[24]

American whalemen working in the mid-1800s hardly had to be concerned with female intrusion into their spheres. With a few exceptions, sailing ships were male bastions, and American women were more than half a world away.

II

To argue that whalemen sometimes delighted in gossip, sociability, and passive sailorizing—"feminine" pleasures—is not the same as to claim that they welcomed women or tokens of women in their environs. Indeed, as has just been suggested, their flexible social styles and interests may have rested on a clear separation of the sexes.

Whalemen, though, had different ways of dealing with women depending on their age, rank, and social background. Men who lived before the mast, many of whom were new to the sea, shaped a gender culture that was in some ways distinct from that established by ships' officers, who were often married or engaged men, and who were necessarily tied to the capitalist interests of shipowners.

Whalemen who were inexperienced greenhands lived in the legendary forecastle in the very bow of the whaleship. Most of these foremast hands, (white northeastern men in this sample) were young, in their late teens and early twenties.[25] They thus had joined the sailing ship and the forecastle at an important social and physical juncture in their lives. Having left the domestic arena only recently, they were about to be educated in how to relate to their homes and to the women who inhabited them.

One of the first things a greenhand learned was that seafaring society placed a high premium on male-centered fellowship. As he entered the forecastle for the first time, he went through a desensitizing process that simultaneously separated him from women ashore and redirected his attachment to the men around him. This was not necessarily an easy process. Aboard the bark *Java*, the stress of the first two weeks under sail provoked a number of young men to tears. Men who were seasick, noted a veteran sailor, could be seen "leaning over the rail and some down below with a bucket heaving up all the Salt junk and potatoes they had ate for a week before." They were, reported this observer, "a wishing themselfes to home with their mamys."[26] Other seamen who fell ill wished in private that they, too, could feel the caring ministrations of a mother or sister. Marshall Keith explained in a note at the end of his journal that "the first thing that rushes into the recollections of a sailor that is smitten with disease at sea is his Mother. She clings to his memory and affections in the Midst of all the forgetfulness and hardihood induced by a roving life." Orson Shattuck, afflicted with a sore hand, ardently wished that he "was at home under the care of Betsey, Julia or Mandana." Yet as much as Keith and Shattuck expressed a need for caring female attention, they acknowledged the pressures to conform to a more "manly" standard of behavior. Keith spoke of the "hardihood" that was produced by seafaring, and Shattuck would not let his indulgence get the better of him. "But I must stop this," he cautioned himself, "for I can hardly hide the tears from the rough men around me."[27]

Those "rough men" could be unforgiving sorts. Sailors aboard the *Sunbeam*, for instance, targeted a young sailor named Smith for "innumerable practical jokes." Smith's greatest sin, it seems, was displaying his affection for his elderly grandmother, and his greatest mistake was being found at it. He "was discovered sitting upon his chest bathed in tears . . . weeping excessively" over a bed quilt that his aged grandmother had given him.[28]

While filial affection was proscribed with regard to a sailor's biological family, it was, when applied to a forecastle family, fully necessary. Sailors sometimes underscored the importance of a distinct seafaring family with the King Neptune Ceremony. Veteran sailors, dressed up as the God of the Seas and his attendants, initiated neophyte seamen as sons and brothers of the sea. Father Neptune stripped his sailors of their ways of seeing with blindfolds, then gave birth to them by dunking them, initiated them into manhood by shaving them, and finally baptized them as his "children." Then he advised them to be protective and generous toward each other.[29]

The Neptune ritual is significant, not only for its attempt to sever men from their biological attachments ashore, but also for its attempt to provide a substitute family. Sometimes sailors learned the lessons of fraternity and seafaring family well. Forecastle hand Stephen Curtis described how his shipmates transferred filial allegiance from shore to sea. His fellow mariners aboard the *Mercury* in 1842 took "great pride" in their ship. It was, he said, their "father, mother, brother and sister, in fact [their] very life."[30] It is likely that one of the threats sailor culture posed to middle-class female reformers ashore—in addition to allegedly profane living—was that they not only removed themselves from the female-centered family ashore, but they created it anew, by themselves, at sea. To women who located the source of their own power and autonomy within the domestic institution, such an act would have been singularly disconcerting.[31]

Foremast hands called on their shipmates not only to distance themselves emotionally from female family members but also to disengage from particular sweethearts as well. They honored "women" as a set of romantic and sexual types even as they removed themselves from females of flesh and blood.[32] They devoted no small amount of recreational space to talking about women, singing about women, even sketching and scrimshawing women. But the women they depicted were invariably stereotypes, commonly the whore or the loyal wife or sweetheart.[33]

Using these familiar typologies, sailors objectified women with regard to the whaling ship as well. A ship might be a domestic sort, according to one mariner, because "like a lady's work box she contains a good collection of *pins, needles, thimbles, hooks,* and *eyes.* For housekeepers she had *beds* with *sheets* and other *coverings,* a variety of *plates* and a great deal of *service.*"[34] Or she could be a woman a mariner might possess in sexual terms. Seamen could, they said, "ride" her, overhaul her, and even have her "bottom" scraped.[35]

At the same time that women became wooden generalities, they were made into property to be shared. It was not unusual for whalemen to exchange or purchase love letters from each other, thus making the most intimate and private exchanges public and rendering the letter writer commonly accessible.[36]

The forecastle as a material space furthered the removal of sailors from domestic life. The forecastle was an undifferentiated, undecorated, barely furnished public arena—as unhomelike as possible—where men slept, ate, entertained, and passed leisure time together. This is not to say that "women" and domestic tokens were not permitted some material space forward, but it is not easy to find them. They essentially remained under wraps, deep within wooden sea chests. There sailors carried female keepsakes, letters from home, photographs, and perhaps even a Bible. There they also locked up their "ditty boxes," which held domestic apparatus: needles, buttons, thread, and thimbles.[37]

Sailors literally lifted the lid on women once a week. On Sundays, foremast hands opened these chests in a ritual they termed the "sailor's pleasure." They took out their "longtogs"—their shore clothes—and their photographs and letters, and they "trimmed" (organized) their ditty boxes. After an hour or two of centering their thoughts on women and home, they tidied these materials up again and returned to the attention of their shipmates.[38]

The disassociation of forecastle sailors from women—actual and symbolic—raises the question of whether seamen simultaneously took sexual and romantic partners among their shipmates. If sailors found "family" aboard ship and claimed their self-sufficiency from shore in that regard, why might they not also find lovers or sweethearts? While it may be assumed that some did, evidence concerning sexual contact between men is frustratingly paltry.[39] Most evidence in the literature reviewed here arises from sodomy "crimes" committed on an unwilling partner, which tells us little about mutual involvement. Moreover, some of these alleged acts involved other crimes, such as threats of poisoning and armed violence, making it difficult to interpret the sexual element.[40] We will probably never know the extent of same-sex relationships at sea, but further research may help us understand how they fit into shipboard culture.

We do have more evidence, albeit not a great deal, on male-centered "romances." Some middle-class men before the mast—like Victorians ashore—carried with them a special fondness for male intimates.[41] They searched for and sometimes found men whom they found physically appealing and men with whom they might share their deepest, most personal thoughts. Elias Trotter was such a sailor. Trotter, who sailed aboard the *Illinois* in 1845, relied on gams to meet men of his sort. At the end of November 1845 he found a sailor, Charles Wheeler, who "drew [his] attention" for his "manly beauty, activity, and intelligence." They carried on secret conversations for the course of the gam, but then "had to part." As Wheeler's ship sailed astern, Trotter realized that "in all probability they would never meet again." On his own ship, though, he did discover one man who could be his soulmate. He was a sailor named Longworth, a man of "sensitiveness and discernment." In the night watches and on lookout, Trotter tightened his friendship with this man. But he discovered there were limits to their closeness, for privacy was impossible: "It is not natural," Trotter complained, "so many beings imprisoned in a small compass and living with the eyes of each continually fixed upon another."[42] Trotter came up against what other "romantic" sailors must also have encountered. He was following forecastle dictates by distancing himself from women ashore, but by substituting male for female intimacy he had violated the collective ethos before the mast. In an arena that stressed sailors' general camaraderie and enforced this fellowship with a lack of private space, sailor romances were highly problematic.[43]

The gender culture and material space of the forecastle served three constituencies: owners, officers, and sailors themselves. Shipowners and captains benefited in several ways by the setup of the forecastle. Housing sailors together in the forward part of the vessel with few amenities and without privacy was certainly an inexpensive way to accommodate men (separate parlors and pantries cost money), and owners were nothing if not cost-conscious with regard to labor. Since the eighteenth century, in fact, owners had been privileging masters over sailors with disparate pay scales.[44] The open design of the forecastle also provided the master with a good means of surveillance and control. Even though the foremast cabin was generally off-limits to the captain himself, the lack of privacy meant that any untoward behavior was immediately obvious and often went reported to officers. By placing foremast hands in undifferentiated circumstances, by forcing them into the public eye, and by reducing the degree of home comforts they might enjoy, owners and masters rewarded and empowered officers. At the same time, they distanced themselves from their employees.

If forecastle space was determined by owners and captains, forecastle society was another matter: this was a direct reflection of the needs of sailors themselves. The fraternal camaradarie of the forecastle not only facilitated gender indoctrination, as we have discussed, but facilitated the political unity of the forecastle. Men who learned to live together and who shared hardship could stand up together against the dictates of the officers. They acted in concert to demand an improvement in living conditions, to resist ship discipline, and as a gesture of defiance against officers' "genteel" attachment to home and family. Many of the foremast hands in this study hailed from working-class backgrounds, and thus harsh conditions at sea not only exacerbated class antagonism but also encouraged fraternity as an expression of gender conflict.[45]

Ultimately, however, one of the crucial determinants of social behavior and identity before the mast was the work and life of whaling itself. Shipboard labor demanded utter collaboration. An unwillingness to watch out for a shipmate when a man was high over a ship's deck in a storm or in a boat on the back of a whale meant certain disaster. Sailors' fraternity within the forecastle must also be seen in this context.

As much as sailors are conventionally dismissed as social renegades and cultural aliens, the construction of fraternity before the mast was not so different from rites of passage on the American mainland. Like youths ashore who used pranks and vicious taunting to rid each other (and themselves) of maternal attachment, these seamen employed public ridicule to cure shipmates of their homesickness.[46] And when they substituted male nurturance for female care, they also paralleled shore practices. Mark Carnes, who has studied fraternal societies in the nineteenth century, claims the prevalence of land-based rituals, which "succeed[ed] in eradicating the emotional and ideological attachments of men to their mothers . . . [by appropriating] some of the tasks formerly associated with maternal nurture."[47]

III

In many ways, whaling officers established a gender culture aboard ship that was distinctly different from that of men before the mast. Ships' officers (mates and the shipmaster) lived in the aftercabin, a space in the stern of the vessel that accommodated several smaller cabins. In its layout and decorations, it was not unlike a middle-class home. The officers' cabins were frequently organized around a central dining area and were close to the ship's kitchen (galley) and a pantry, where provisions, crockery, and utensils were stored. Within this complex, the captain himself had a private stateroom and toilet area and an office / sitting room furnished with a parlor sofa. On larger vessels, these cabins might be furnished with bird's-eye maple or mahogany furniture, carpets, and possibly even a piano. While they remained in port, shipmasters sometimes displayed wall hangings and pictures.[48]

Officers on these deepwater ships had homelike attendants to go with their homelike quarters. Stewards, cooks—and, very often, cabin boys—performed the wifely tasks of cooking and housekeeping. They did laundry, they swept, they bought groceries when in port, and they prepared and served food. Unlike sailors forward or officers aft, these service workers slept in at night and did not usually participate in sailing the vessel.

It was within these relatively homey aftercabins that officers took time off duty to focus their attentions on women they left ashore. Within the privacy of their cabins, they opened their diaries to write journals addressed to their wives or sweethearts, and they composed letters of love and domestic concern. They also brought out their miniatures and focused their thoughts away to the mainland. "Here I set," commented Benjamin Boodry, mate of the *Arnolda*, "the door shut and my whole family of Daguerreotypes around me and my Accordion in my hand and try to imagine myself in old Mattapoisett."[49] In the privacy of their cabins, officers also opened their hearts to their companions across the ocean's expanse, and, giving way to their lonely misery, they cried. Edmund Jennings locked himself in his room on Thanksgiving Day in 1877 and had a "crying spell." "I wondered," he wrote, "if they missed my place at the Table. Or if they thought of me. . . . May God bless and keep you all." Marshall Keith, mate of the *Cape Horn Pigeon*, wrote that he had "cryed all the afternoon" after his shipmaster had lectured him about loving his wife too much. "He went so far as to tell me you were in my mind most of the time," Keith lamented.[50]

Officers carried themselves homeward, not only in thoughts and actions and with tears, but also with one of the most evocative senses of all: taste. They brought aboard condiments and preserved foods made by loving hands in home kitchens. Edmund Jennings packed "Aunt Dyer's cake" to sail with him; Samuel Braley carried his mother-in-law's quince and his wife's cranberries. Other mariners opened "home cakes," which were alcohol-preserved sweets that were scheduled to be eaten on special days: a wife's birthday, a couple's anniversary.[51]

Men of the aftercabin thus spent much of their off-duty time in relative isolation, reinforcing shoreside intimacies. They did not completely confine practices that celebrated women and family to the privacy of cabins, however. One of the time-honored traditions of the afterguard was the "Saturday night" ritual. On this occasion, master and mates together saluted special women at home. Bringing out whiskey punches, grog, or rum, they raised a glass in toast to wives and sweethearts. This was, said one mariner, "an old established custom." Another acknowledged the importance of the occasion while at the same time lamenting the mode of celebration on his ship. "This is Saturday night at sea," wrote John Jones, "the night in which sailors of olden times used to drink to the health of sweet hearts and wives. Them was the times wee read of, times past and gone, now, instead of the can of grog wee have a filter full of cold water on the table the look of which makes a fellow shiver . . . forgeting wives and everything else."[52]

The aftercabin not only housed men who had the privacy to enjoy homeward reflections and who practiced domestic rituals, but it also served as the site of pietistic—"female"—activities. Some shipmasters were enthusiastic evangelists and organized prayer meetings, Sunday schools, and hymn sings. From the afterdeck they produced temperance pledges and New Testaments, and they fervently solicited compliance with Christian precepts from the men around them.[53]

Whaling captains sometimes carried their commitment to "female" agendas and to women themselves even further: they sometimes sailed with their wives and families. Indeed, it seems that increasing numbers did so in the nineteenth century. By 1853, according to one industry newspaper, nearly 20 percent of whaling captains sailed with their spouses.[54]

To a degree, then, the aftercabin of the whaling vessel accommodated women and their traditional concerns and, relative to the forecastle, was noticeably domesticated. The aftercabin took the shape that it did at this time for several reasons. Shipowners, officers themselves, and women ashore all had a hand in making the stern of the ship relatively amenable to female interests. Owners, first of all, had their vessels built not only to ensure a profit margin but also to support the social conventions of the day. These conventions embraced the gender division of labor—men worked at sea, women at home—and also the complementarity of male and female worlds.[55] In other words, the life of a civilized workingman was incomplete without residence in the home.[56] When they built homelike aftercabins, then, owners honored the shipmaster's need for his domestic *and* working domain.

The cultural configuration of the aftercabin was as much determined by resident officers as by owners, of course. The journals of these officers speak to the heartfelt intimacy that existed between lovers and spouses.[57] Many shipmasters pointedly explained to their private diaries that their voyages were not expressions of estrangement but rather signs of affection and devotion. "I often ask myself the question," noted Captain Samuel Braley to himself, "for what are you toiling? I want to leave just enough to pay the sexton that places the last sod on the grave of my wife after she has been well supported through life." Marshall Keith was as "homesick as a dog" and plotted, from the very first day that he shipped as a mate aboard the *Cape Horn Pigeon,* that he would jump ship to rejoin his wife, Sarah. But when he heard she was pregnant, he thought it "my duty to go the voyage to get something to support it and my little darling."[58]

Leavetaking for such men could be poignantly painful. "Talk about dieing," lamented Samuel Braley, "I hope that I shall never suffer any keener pangs than those that now pierce my heart. This is a parting such as [presses] the life from out young hearts." Mate Edward Jenney was "desolate," "miserable," "sad and lonely." "Oh God," he wrote in his journal, "I am near crazy." Captain Henry Beetle wrote to his wife that leaving her was "like parting soul from the body."[59]

Shipmasters who suffered from homesickness and lovesickness often asked their owners to let them take their spouses to sea. And then they confronted the fact that while owners were all too willing to honor them with domestic furnishings and wifely servants, most would not readily permit the woman of flesh and blood aboard. "We unanimously believe," wrote Jonathan Bourne to a shipmaster's wife whose husband had invited her to join him, "[that] a whaling voyage is wholly unsuitable for a female to encounter."[60] Owners offered a number of reasons to explain their reluctance to ship women. Women tended to become pregnant. "Your wife like all *females,*" remarked the agency of Swift and Allen to Captain Josiah Chase, "is much more likely to get sick at sea than any man, under ordinary circumstances, and extraordinary ones are about sure to raise soon after she meets you the like of which in two instances caused our ships to leave good whaling grounds in the midst of a season."[61] Women also seemed to interfere with the whale hunt. As Lisa Norling has explained in a recent essay, some owners feared that women would bring reformist agendas, such as Sabbatarianism, to sea and thus interfere with masters' round-the-clock search for whales. They might also make a captain "unduly" cautious, or they might encourage a captain to give his whaling life over to gamming, and gamming—which distracted sailors from work—owners did not like.[62]

The most important consideration, though, according to whaling agents Swift and Allen, was that women cost money. "The owners of our ships have suffered to the extent of $20,000 by having the Captain's wife on board," they remarked in 1861. Some whaling masters made it clear to owners, however, that they would lose more money if the merchants did not comply with their wishes. Every time a master returned home to see his family, as he would insist on doing, he took perhaps a half a year to do so. Why not ship a family and save all the time and money spent on sailing a man home? Owners saw the logic in this, too, and permitted women and families aboard, at the same time insisting on lengthy voyages. "Now that you have your family with you," asserted Smith and Allen, "it cannot be considered unreasonable in us to ask for a continuation of your voyage even if you should have a streak or two of success."[63] Whaling wives could sometimes assist the profit margin at the same time that they provided their husbands with the company and love that they wanted.

Ship's officers, then, while distancing themselves from home by as much as a hemisphere, frequently did their best to keep connections strong. With the assistance of women ashore and their owner-employers, they created a shipboard space that expressed domestic allegiances, and they carved out social time for dwelling on family and lovers. Furthermore, they sometimes defied prescribed gender divisions by bringing their spouses aboard.

Owners and shipmasters were instrumental architects of the aftercabin, but women were also responsible for its domestic dimensions. Evangelical reform was one of the few public activities open to middle-class women in the 1800s, and sailors and their ships were a favorite target of women reformers and their minister compatriots. Such national agencies as the American Seamen's Friend Society, founded in 1825, or—more specific to whaling—the New Bedford Port Society, established in 1830, sponsored sailor "homes" in port. In these domiciles, wandering men could reacquaint themselves with domestic virtues such as neatness, temperance, and providence, and learn to save their money "to comfort the heart of some loved mother." These societies also tried to work through the shipmaster to reform sailors. They sent him aboard with testaments, religious tracts, and enlightening reading such as the *Sailor's Magazine*. In their newsletters and at their meetings, they congratulated what they claimed were the growing number of masters who shared their concerns.[64]

Women as reformers may had a hand in shaping aftercabin society, and so did women as wives and sweethearts. They prepared at home the cakes and preserves that men relished at sea. They gathered their families together and sat for daguerreotypists, to send their spouses or brothers or lovers visual reminders of themselves. They mailed letters to sea by the dozens, hoping that at least a few would reach their mark. And some women went to sea of their own initiative, demanding companionship in a marriage, insisting on being a helpmate, and perhaps hoping to exert a measure of influence over their husbands' lives and a measure of control over their own.

As distinct as the aftercabin was from the forecastle with regard to women, it may go too far to say that whaling officers were unequivocably friendly to females. Reconsider, for instance, some of the facts of the case: 20 percent of sea captains sailed with their spouses in the late 1800s, but that means that 80 percent did not. Men bemoaned long absences from home, even as they lengthened the distance between ship and shore. Men regularly made toasts to wives and sweethearts, but they reserved their respect for Saturday night.

There were some important continuities, clearly, between the ways that the young forecastle hand and the first mate or the shipmaster related to women, real or imagined. The officer may have been an older man, the owner of property, and, unlike the greenhand, married. But they both had learned how to limit the power and, most importantly, the presence of women. The foremast hand tucked her away in his sea chest or made her his love object in a chantey. The officer gave her more room aboard ship, and even asked her aboard on occasion, but her presence was carefully circumscribed. She was limited to a small area of the deck, and frequently spent days below. She did not usually contribute to the productive work of the ship, and she was not needed for housekeeping and cooking. Those jobs, as we have seen, were already assigned to men. She may have established for herself a positive and autonomous self-image (Haskell Springer discusses this in this volume), but socially and spatially she was decidedly confined.

The nineteenth-century sailor was no simple man. He saw himself as a ferocious hunter of the leviathan one day; a happy shirker of work the next. He liked the sea for its wild trials and luxuriated in its tame beauty. Depending on how old he was, and his rank and class, he participated in a culture at sea that ranged from a celebration of home and its women to a thorough disavowal of them. And to some degree, all sailors practiced the objectification of women. As they moved from life before the mast to life as an officer, their view of women changed, but it mainly shifted from that of common to private property.

Maritime historians have carried on a debate for some time as to whether sailors shaped a distinctive culture at sea and whether they differed from landsmen by virtue of their deepwater work. These men may have demonstrated a unique range of masculine styles, given as they were to enjoying the merits of both tranquil and rugged work, but when it came to their relations with women, there is little to suggest they were unlike men at home. Studies of American men from different backgrounds show that men were universally conversant with putting women in their "place."[65] When whalemen sailed home, three to four or five years after first weighing anchor, then, they carried with them skills and social practices that were probably translatable to circumstances ashore.

The whalemen described here lived at the very edge of the age of sail. Thirty or so years later, in the early decades of the twentieth century, whaling would be seriously diminished as a profitable industry; when a man did engage in a whale hunt, he would likely do so from a steam vessel. In other shipping industries as well, steam power would supplant sail on most ocean-going voyages.

The industrialization of shipping and the shift from sail to steam would certainly have serious consequences for a mariner's sense of manhood and for relations between the seafaring sexes. Even as it was becoming more important for men to define themselves in terms of combative, strenuous, and daring labor, for instance, it became less possible to do so at sea. In part, this had to do with the feminization of steam relative to sail. Whatever its demands—and certainly, stoking engines was no leisurely task—steamship work was defined as less physically challenging and thus less masculine than sail.[66] The growing division between capital and labor in shipping also meant that breadwinning, occupational mobility, and aspirations to independence, all traditionally critical to the concept of manhood, were increasingly problematic. Furthermore, at the same time that women ashore expanded their social and political parameters, the domain of men at sea was reduced. Steam travel lessened the time sailors spent by themselves at sea and increased their days ashore in mixed company.

But the story of the industrialization of whaling and shipping may not be simply reduced to the decline of male bastions. The fraternity that was so effectively established at sea in the nineteenth century was to some degree reestablished ashore later on. The rise of seamen's unions in the first decades of the 1900s—challenging the privilege of capital *and* the incursions of women—meant that fraternal solidarity remained a potent force in sailors' lives for some time.[67] And certainly many would argue that today, at the turn of the twenty-first century, seafaring—no matter the size of the ship, the scope of the voyage, or the nature of the service—remains a man's world.

W. JEFFREY BOLSTER

7

"Every Inch a Man"

Gender in the Lives of African American Seamen, 1800–1860

Few scholars have written about white sailors as gendered individuals, and even fewer have focused on masculinity and seamen of color. W. Jeffrey Bolster thus addresses an important gap in the historical literature with his consideration of African American seamen in the early national and antebellum periods. By placing race at the center of his analysis, Bolster greatly complicates and enriches our understanding of the mutability of masculinity in the mostly male maritime subculture and in working-class occupational subcultures more generally.

Black seamen, Bolster argues, found in maritime employment a means to a "potent" and distinctive male identity in three key ways. Like white sailors, they were able to build masculine reputations on qualities prized among common seamen: worldliness, fearlessness, pugilistic ability, specialized occupational skills, and a camaraderie based as much on collective leisure activities as on their highly collaborative work. Black seamen also shared in the class-based foredeck assertion of manly egalitarianism that, for a time, mitigated against race-based divisions. For some African American men, too, seafaring was one of the few jobs in a highly race- and gender-stratified labor market to offer sufficient remuneration for them to achieve a measure of respectable family providership—a consequence of this occupation for male gender identity quite different from its implications for most white maritime workers.

Bolster also emphasizes the historic specificity of the expressions of manhood represented in seafaring for blacks and whites alike. He suggests that its gendered meanings shifted dramatically with the degradation of maritime work over the course of the nineteenth century. Bolster's work thereby underscores both the interlocking of race, class, and gender categories in the construction of male occupational identities and the fluidity of those categories in the context of economic and political change, themes with significant parallels in the following essay by Laura Tabili.

"THOSE BEAUTIFUL VESSELS, robed in white, and so delightful to the eyes of freemen," remembered Frederick Douglass of the sailing ships he saw daily during his boyhood along the Chesapeake Bay, "were to me so many shrouded ghosts." Douglass contrasted the ships, "loosed from [their] moorings, and free," with his own condition—"fast in my chains, and . . . a slave!" And he swore, as he later recollected, "This very bay shall yet bear me into freedom."[1]

As it turned out, Douglass employed a seafaring subterfuge instead of a ship to escape his chains. Rigging himself out in "a red shirt and tarpaulin hat and black cravat, tied in sailor fashion, carelessly and loosely about my neck," he borrowed a seaman's protection certificate from a bona fide black sailor and brazenly struck out for Philadelphia by train. He succeeded that September day in 1838 largely because free black seamen were then so common as to cause few second looks.[2]

Frederick Douglass never went to sea. Yet as a skilled ship caulker he worked on the wharves in Baltimore (and later did odd jobs in New Bedford, Massachusetts) shoulder to shoulder with black and white sailors and, in his own words, "knew a ship from stem to stern, and from keelson to crosstrees, and could talk sailor like an 'old salt.'" No stranger to waterfront tales of hardship, brutality, and deprivation at sea, Douglass nonetheless persisted in his metaphorical view of ships as "freedom's swift-winged angels" because, unlike the white men who spoke movingly of the "slavery" aboard ship, he knew real slavery firsthand.[3]

Whether ex-slave, like Frederick Douglass, or freeborn, all northern black men recognized seafaring as one of the few jobs readily available to them in the racially restricted and highly gendered employment market of the late eighteenth and early nineteenth centuries. Blacks then consistently signed aboard ship in disproportionately large numbers relative to their strength in the northern states' populations as a whole. African American men filled between 17 percent and 22 percent of Philadelphia's seafaring jobs between 1800 and 1820, when blacks (both men *and* women) in the Pennsylvania–Delaware–New Jersey area were only 5 percent of the population. During those years, black men occupied approximately 20 percent of the available berths in Providence, Rhode Island, when blacks constituted only 8.5 percent of that city's population and only 4 percent of the state's. Similar figures reflect a higher proportion of black seamen than black residents in New York, Connecticut, and Massachusetts. In a petition to the Massachusetts legislature in 1788, African American sailors from Boston stressed the importance of the occupation for men of their race by arguing that shipping-out provided one calling in which "thay might get a hanceum livehud for themselves and theres" (table 7.1).[4]

Most black seamen's lives unfolded differently from those of other northern black workers precisely because of the specialized nature of seafaring, an occupation with significant psychological and social ramifications for its workers. This essay is attentive to those differences, especially to the gendered nature of seafaring work and to the unique appeal for black workers of the Atlantic maritime culture then prevalent aboard American ships.[5]

Maritime work and maritime culture offered men of color significant ways to certify their manhood not readily available ashore. The routine and extraordinary challenges posed by unsettled weather, capricious officers, and failed rigging led to the bold actions and daring exploits from which masculine reputations could be constructed. Mobility and worldliness, dimensions of a manly reputation often denied to other black males, were likewise important components of many black sailors' identities. The personal reputations important to many black men, however, hinged even more on the gregarious male socializing often associated with alcohol and storytelling. By no means unique to maritime work, those forms of boisterous and exclusively male relationships flowed naturally from the collective nature of seafaring, and from the drinking and yarn spinning fundamental to maritime culture. Many men of color in the early nineteenth century thus found that the conditions of maritime work boosted their masculine reputations.

Atlantic maritime culture also promoted an equality of the oppressed, an assertive foredeck egalitarianism that to some degree diminished the divisiveness of color. In stridently professing their equality as men, black and white seamen questioned the salience of race. But seafaring meant even more to black men. The earnings from shipboard employment, meager as they were, provided a degree of economic self-sufficiency in an era when patriarchal norms stressed men's breadwinning role. Male dignity and respectability in northern free black communities often were advanced by men's ability to earn a "livehud for themselves and theres." In light of nineteenth-century African American definitions of manliness, which included equality, reputation, and respectable providership, it comes as no surprise that during the 1830s a white wharfinger like James Kelly would write, "In the presence of the sailor the Negro feels as a man."[6]

Equality, reputation, and respectability were not mutually exclusive components of black manliness. Even reputation and respectability, frequently associated with specific stages of life, were not opposing values in the black community as much as distinct ways of embodying and expressing masculinity. Young men often strove for a gregarious, peer-based reputation; older men, for the respectability that came with providership and a family. Homosexuals may have further complicated the definitions and meanings of manhood for African American seafaring men, but a paucity of data precludes examination of this dimension of masculinity.

Historians, like the train conductor who let Douglass slip by, have usually been blind to African American sailors. Maritime historians have ignored the fact that foredeck gangs were substantially integrated, more so than most early-nineteenth-century labor forces.[7] Historians of black labor have neglected the tensions internalized by large numbers of black men laboring in a predominantly white workplace.[8] Even more surprising, given Herbert Aptheker's observation more than forty years ago that "maritime occupations were among the most important followed by Negroes," has been the neglect of black sailors by scholars of northern African American communities. That oversight has implicitly reinforced the conventional notion that sailors were beyond the pale, rather than the more accurate recognition that seafaring was inextricably entwined in the family life, community structure, and sense of male self of northern blacks in the early Republic.[9]

The few histories of black sailors have focused on the aggregate rather than the individual, on wholesale data—such as James Barker Farr's point that in the 1850s "6,000 black men were serving in the American merchant marine"—rather than on the processes through which such men's sea experience changed, and the meanings that seafaring held for them.[10] Simply knowing that black men were part of ships' crews prompts questions about their commitment to seafaring, about their prestige in the black community, and about how their lives and careers may have differed from those of their white counterparts. It also generates investigation into the gendered identity of nineteenth-century black seafaring men. Probing what it meant "to be a man" for black seamen in the age of sail reveals an important workplace dialectic between social prescription and self-representation, which shaped black sailors' lives. Moreover, exploring those men's racial, class, and gendered identities reveals how interlocked they were. Black sailors alternately fused those identities or played off one

Table 7.1
Allotment of Berths by Race

Year	% of Population African American	% of Males African American	% of Berths Held by African Americans	% of Berths Held by Whites	All Berths
		Providence			
1800	8.6	—	—	—	—
1803–1804	—	—	22.0	78.0	723
1807	—	—	23.0	77.0	381
1808	—	—	15.5	84.5	245
1810	8.6	—	21.5	78.5	683
1816	—	—	21.6	78.4	333
1818	—	—	18.7	81.3	609
1820	8.2	6.7	23.0	77.0	456
1822	—	—	19.0	81.0	788
1825	—	—	23.8	76.2	554
1829	—	—	23.3	76.7	459
1830	3.3	2.7	18.0	82.0	396
1832	—	—	22.5	77.5	517
1834	—	—	29.0	71.0	543
1836	—	—	30.5	69.5	246
1839	—	—	20.0	80.0	440
1840	5.6	4.8	16.0	84.0	361
1844	—	—	11.4	88.6	369
1846	—	—	15.0	85.0	342
1850	2.0	1.9	7.5	92.5	200
1853	—	—	11.0	89.0	277
1856	—	—	9.0	91.0	242
		New York			
1800	10.5	—	—	—	—
1803–1806	—	—	17.1	82.9	561
1810	10.2	—	—	—	—
1818–1819	—	—	17.4	82.6	688
1820	8.6	7.0	—	—	—
1825	—	—	18.2	81.8	734
1830	7.0	6.3	—	—	—
1835	—	—	13.8	86.2	523
1840	5.2	4.6	8.3	91.7	1407

Table 7.1
Continued

Year	% of Population African American	% of Males African American	% of Berths Held by African Americans	% of Berths Held by Whites	All Berths
1846	—	—	6.9	93.1	686
1850	2.7	2.4	—	—	—
1856	—	—	7.6	92.4	499
1860	1.5	1.3	—	—	—
Philadelphia					
1800	10.3	—	—	—	—
1803	—	—	17.4	82.6	811
1810	11.8	—	22.4	77.6	1047
1820	11.8	10.3	18.4	81.6	1026
1825	—	—	19.5	80.5	1083
1830	8.3	7.5	17.0	83.0	862
1838	—	—	16.6	83.3	946
1840	7.7	6.2	15.4	84.6	643
1846	—	—	18.0	82.0	1039
1850	4.8	4.3	13.2	86.8	1127
1853	—	—	17.0	83.0	1029
1860	3.9	3.4	—	—	—

Sources: Providence Crew Lists, U.S. Customs House Papers, Providence, R.I., RG 28 (Manuscript Collection, Rhode Island Historical Society, Providence); New York and Philadelphia Crew Lists, Records of the U.S. Customs Service, RG 36 (National Archives); U.S. Census Office, *Return of the Whole Number of Persons within the Several Districts of the United States, According to an Act Providing for the Second Census or Enumeration of the Inhabitants of the United States* ([Washington], 1800), 26, 27, 35; U.S. Census Office, *Aggregate Amount of Each Description of Persons within the United States of America, and the Territories Thereof, Agreeably to Actual Enumeration Made According to Law, in the Year 1810* [Washington, 1811], 23, 28, 51; U.S. Census Office, *Census for 1820, Published by Authority of an Act of Congress under the Direction of the Secretary of State* (Washington, 1821), 8, 13, 20; U.S. Census Office, *Fifth Census; or, Enumeration of the Inhabitants of the United States, Corrected at the Department of State, 1830* (Washington, 1832), 24–25, 54–55, 66–67; U.S. Census Office, *Sixth Census; or, Enumeration of the Inhabitants of the United States, As Corrected at the Department of State in 1840* (Washington, 1841), 54–55, 122–23, 156–57; J. D. B. DeBow, *Statistical View of the United States, Embracing Its Territory, Population—White, Free Colored, and Slave—Moral and Social Condition, Industry, Property, and Revenue; The Detailed Statistics of Cities, Towns, and Counties; Being a Compendium of the Seventh Census* (Washington, 1854), 278, 296; Joseph C. G. Kennedy, *Population of the United States in 1860, Compiled from the Original Returns of the Eighth Census* (Washington, 1864), 337, 432, 444.

against the other in response to cultural pressures (both white and black) to be docile, supermasculine, comradely, or respectable.[11]

Between the seventeenth and the late nineteenth centuries, black men worked aboard all sorts of vessels as sailors, stewards, and cooks, and occasionally as officers or petty officers. Slaves were forcibly packed off to sea by masters eager for their wages; runaways gravitated toward ships to make good their escape from bondage; freemen recognized an occupation in which they would receive the same wages as similarly skilled white men and in which they might escape the strictures of white society ashore, as well as the taunts that undermined their manly self-worth. Observers along the wharves and aboard ship during the years of the early Republic saw a variety of African American mariners—greenhands and old salts, casual laborers and committed professionals, adventuresome rakes and responsible providers. Contemporaries recognized the ambiguities and multiple realities of blacks' seafaring experience. Scholars should do the same and should resist the attempt to reconstruct that experience in entirely consistent terms. As seafarers, African American men experienced relative racial toleration as well as racial friction; they embraced the quintessential American appeal of economic mobility through seafaring wages, yet they expressed the opposition to shoreside norms common to many sailors; they felt the lure of the sea and the appeal of what many considered a manly life, along with the subjugation, tyranny, and iron discipline prevalent in life under sail.

Masculine equality among black and white men aboard ship corresponded with the hierarchical and collective structure of seafaring work, in part because hidebound seafaring customs originally evolved without the complication of race. Neither officers nor men were race-blind, but all labored in a workplace where duties had been largely defined before many blacks went to sea. In the early eighteenth century, for instance, no shipboard roles were reserved for blacks, with the partial exception of warships' musicians. Blacks were often favored for that billet, but even it was open to both black and white men. So, too, with jobs as able and ordinary seaman, cook, steward, and pilot. To comprehend the resonance of black sailors' assertions of manly equality, we need to examine the maritime workplace and Atlantic maritime culture.

Since the age of the Roman Empire, Atlantic and Mediterranean seamen had been shaped by historically developed cultural forms aboard ship

Anonymous Revolutionary War sailor by an unknown artist. Oil, c. 1780. Proudly conveying a splendid sense of self, this sailor (probably a privateersman) drew on his sartorial splendor and sword to construct a reputation as the dignified equal of any man.
Photo courtesy of Alexander McBurney, Kingston, R.I.

that endowed them with distinctive attitudes and perceptions. In common parlance, these forms evolved as the traditions or usages of the sea. Samuel Taylor Coleridge acknowledged the generation of a distinctive maritime culture by sailors who were

> Crowded in the rank and narrow ship, —
> Housed on the wild sea with wild usages.[12]

Following the work of Charles Valentine and Eric Wolf, it is appropriate to regard men socialized in those shipboard usages as at least bicultural, as having simultaneously available two or more distinct yet intertwined cultural systems or resources, based on their origins and on their international occupation.[13] Individuals belonging to bounded ethnic or occupational groups often have multiple, sometimes conflicting allegiances and play multiple roles. Nineteenth-century black American seamen daily lived that multiplicity, maneuvering through white and black societies ashore and through an all-male maritime society afloat. When under way in the company of other seamen, sailors' behavior was largely conditioned by their Atlantic maritime culture.

Seafarers' culture, as Marcus Rediker has vividly shown for the eighteenth century, included strong egalitarian impulses. That egalitarianism frequently confounded shoreside racial etiquette. Three white sailors from the American brig *Neptune*, after being befriended in 1787 by a black Georgian named Charles, "thanked him, [and] shook him by the hand" — a gesture unthinkable to the mass of white Georgians. During the War of 1812, the crew of an American warship, invited to a theatrical performance in New York City honoring their bravery in battle, "marched *together* into the pit, and nearly one half of them were negroes." Forecastle culture evolved in shipboard populations recruited by merchants with more of an eye to muscle than complexion. While by no means either color-blind or without internal frictions, Atlantic maritime culture created its own institutions and its own stratifications, which could work to the relative advantage of black men. One observer summed it up by writing, "The good will of 'old salts' to negroes is proverbial."[14]

The written laws associated with Atlantic maritime culture stretched back to medieval codes, including Barcelona's thirteenth-century Consolato del mare, and to the Rolls of Oleron, the basis of maritime common law in the North Sea and in the Atlantic Ocean. For centuries these codes served foremost to protect the property of owners and shippers. The legal emphasis was not on seamen's rights but on their restriction and punishment.¹⁵ This is not to say that sailors succumbed without resistance to a hegemony imposed by merchant capitalism. They did not. It is to say that shipboard life and Atlantic maritime culture revolved around the concept of order—no matter how contested that order may have been. Today our language retains the word "shipshape" to connote compulsive orderliness. We acknowledge that a teacher, an executive, or a coach who runs "a taut ship" is not one with whom to trifle.

The seagoing workplace in which early-nineteenth-century black Americans found themselves gave priority to a shipboard order that was maintained through a precise "distinction of role and status." As Greg Dening points out, "In the total institution of a ship, persons were owed little. Role and rule were owed everything. . . . all was depersonalized."¹⁶ The articles that each man signed indicated his position (mate, second mate, carpenter, cook, seaman, ordinary seaman, boy), almost immutably fixing his status on board. Boundary maintenance—between officers and men, between larboard and starboard watches, between idlers and watch standers, between skilled hands and greenhands—was the essence of life aboard ship, for boundaries delineated privileges, perquisites, and punishments. Though formal boundaries could flex to accommodate human relationships, they never entirely broke down, and they essentially defined the social combinations and conflicts at the heart of seafaring life. Racial boundaries certainly existed, but they were often secondary to those established by the institution of the ship. Sailors frequently identified manly equality by role as much as by race.

For a black man before the mast, then, and even for many cooks and stewards, the ship provided a unique workplace where his color might be less a determinant of his daily life and duties than elsewhere. The power of the Atlantic maritime culture to offset racist norms was nowhere better dramatized than by a visitor's observation in New Orleans around 1800 that quadroon naval officers aboard ship might "give twenty lashes with the end of a rope to white sailors, but ashore they dare not even look them in the face." New Bedford whaling ships—dirty, dangerous, isolated, and one of the few places where black men might sail as officers—also upset established racial hierarchy. Young Frank T. Bullen found himself questioned by a black man moments after joining the *Cachelot* in 1875.

> I said "yes" very curtly, for I hardly liked his patronizing air; but he snapped me up short with "yes, *sir*, when yew speak to me, yew blank limejuicer. I'se de fourf mate ob dis yar ship, en my name's Mistah Jones, 'n yew jest freeze

on to dat ar, ef yew want ter lib long 'n die happy. See, sonny." I *saw*, and answered promptly, "I beg your pardon, sir, I didn't know."[17]

Less compelling in their drama, but no less indicative of the fact that a seaman's billet meant more than his race when it came to pay and privileges, were the innumerable Yankee ships on which black men before the mast ranked higher and earned more than white co-workers. The best-paid sailor aboard the Rhode Island brig *Mary* sailing to Cuba in 1819 was Cato Burrill, a black veteran of twenty-five years at sea. Sixteen years later, when the *Panther* cleared for the East Indies, only one black man was aboard. Paid the same as the white sailors, he earned three times as much as the white "boys" and would not have deigned to stoop to their menial and unskilled tasks. Seafarers' vernacular categorized crew members as "men" or "boys" not by race, as was the case in the nineteenth-century South, but by skill and time at sea. The historical precedent arising from black seamen's experiences and their shipmates' respect contributed to Herman Melville's introduction of a manly black as the archetypal "Handsome Sailor" in *Billy Budd*. "The center of a company of his shipmates," he was "on every suitable occasion always foremost."[18]

This is not to suggest that all white Americans' racial prejudice disappeared, or that they welcomed blacks as men, when they stepped over a ship's rail. Duncan McClellan, late supernumerary of the bark *Triton,* said of a shipmate in 1840: "Mr. Hansen was the most unpopular person on board, both with the officers and men, more so than the nigger cook." Prejudice, the implication is clear, remained the norm among seamen as among other white Americans. When festering in a captain well beyond the law, it could be deadly.[19]

Institutional barriers, some carried over from shore, likewise restricted the nature of equality aboard ship. One of the most integrated and tolerant industries in the nation, shipping still reflected the vindictive prejudice of American society in periods of economic difficulties. During the embargo, in Thomas Jefferson's second term, the proportion of integrated crews in Rhode Island dropped from three-quarters to one-half, and the number of available berths going to men of color fell from 22 percent to 15.5 percent. Overt discrimination along the Providence waterfront began as soon as the embargo's restrictions took effect.[20]

Even in good years, well-defined limits established what a black man might do aboard American ships. With the extraordinary exception of Captain Paul Cuffe and a few other notable individuals, African Americans in the maritime labor pool had little chance of advancement outside of whaling ships and small coasters. Black men's occupational mobility in merchant ships was all lateral at best, between cook and steward and seaman. Among a sample of thirty-five hundred crews outward bound from Providence, Philadelphia, and New York between 1803 and 1856, only three had a nonwhite officer. George Henry, an ex-slave seaman who escaped to Providence after years of commanding a coasting schooner in his native Virginia, curtly recalled in his autobiography, "I found prejudice so great in the North that I was forced to come down from my high position as captain, and take my whitewash brush and wheelbarrow and get my living in that way." The prestige and the honorific "Captain" associated with command were still too important in northern seaports to bestow on a black man.[21]

Despite the institutionalized obstacles to advancement, young black men vainly aspired to officers' billets and sought the training necessary. Noah Brown attended a school in Providence whose Quaker teacher "was celebrated for teaching the Mariner's art." In the late 1820s, the New York African Free School added navigation to its curriculum. A Scots traveler to the New World, who in 1833 published *Men and Manners in America*, did not miss the incongruity of a society that taught navigation to a class of men and then frequently relegated them to the galley aboard ship.[22] Black sailors remained painfully aware of the very real limitations to equality in the maritime workplace. But overtly racist actions by other sailors were often subordinated to the requirements of shipboard order, and the unprecedented toleration that existed at sea afforded black men a virtually unknown degree of manly equality with white co-workers.

Even within its limitations, ships' rough-hewn forecastle culture promoted workplace equality. Northern blacks had traditionally been barred from trades, and even road crews occasionally demanded segregated gangs for different tasks. Blacks ashore were regularly subject to insults and invective. "If you were well dressed they would insult you for that, and if you were ragged you would surely be insulted for being so; be as peaceable as you could there was no shield for you," recalled William J. Brown in his memoirs.[23]

The pervasive prejudice encountered in the shoreside workplace and on the street, and embodied by the government in its naval manning regulations, seems to have been ameliorated offshore. Despite the order of Secretary of the Navy Benjamin Stoddert in 1798 that black and mulatto men were not to be enlisted aboard ship, many were. Surgeon Usher

Parsons wrote of his service on the *Java* in 1816 that "the white and Negro seamen messed together. About one in six or eight were Negroes." Parsons also noted that on the *Guerriere* three years later, "There seemed to have been an entire absence of prejudice against the blacks as shipmates among the crew." Others too noted a rare racial toleration found off-soundings. It could get under the skin of a proslavery Kentuckian like J. Ross Browne, who found himself before the mast in a Yankee whaler. "It was . . . particularly galling to my feelings," Ross said, "to be compelled to live in the forecastle with a brutal negro, who, conscious that he was upon an equality with the sailors, presumed upon his equality to a degree that was insufferable."

Personal grudges like the one this "Kentucky dandy" held against his black shipmate soured the peace in many shipboard societies. But the evidence indicates that black and white sailors fraternized easily early in the century. James Kelly, in his *Voyage to Jamaica*, recorded that in the 1820s and 1830s, "Sailors and Negroes are ever on the most amicable terms. This is evidenced in their dealings, and in the mutual confidence and familiarity that never subsist between the slaves and the resident whites. There is a feeling of interdependence in their intercourse with the sailor. . . . In the presence of the sailor the Negro feels as a man."[24]

Black sailors must have appreciated the toleration extended them by white shipmates in their narrow wooden worlds, where food, danger, and duty were equally shared. They probably appreciated even more the chance to sail as part of all-black crews, whose forecastle life would reflect norms and behavior of their own making. In 1803 more than a quarter of the black men who sailed from Providence did so in ships where only the officers were white, and many other black sailors made voyages from New York and Philadelphia to the Caribbean, to Europe, and to the coast of Africa with a black majority before the mast (table 7.2). These all-black crews probably fostered even more reputation building among men of color than did voyages that black men made with whites.[25]

The fact that few black sailors kept journals precludes us from examining firsthand the social dynamic aboard predominantly black ships. But crew lists such as the one left by the brig *John Josiah Arnold*, which sailed for Spain in 1803 with a white master and mate, and five black men before the mast, speak eloquently enough. Those black sailors lived in the forecastle, a part of the ship reserved for them alone by custom and practice as ancient as the common law. No officer (on the *John Josiah Arnold*, no white man) concerned for his physical well-being or for the effectiveness of his

Table 7.2

African American Seamen Working in Ships with All-African American Crews

	Providence			New York	
Year	African American Seamen Sampled	% of African American Seamen Working in All-African American Crews	Year	African American Seamen Sampled	% of African American Seamen Working in All-African American Crews
1803–1804	160	27	1803–1806	96	9.3
1820	105	9	1818–1819	120	15.8
1830	71	18	1825	133	7.5
1836	75	41	1835	72	22.2
1839	89	20	1840	117	7.6
1840	58	7	1846	47	0
1853	30	0	1856	38	10.5
1856	22	0			

Sources: Providence Crew Lists, U.S. Customs House Papers, Providence, R.I., RG 28 (Manuscript Collection, Rhode Island Historical Society, Providence); New York Crew Lists, Records of the U.S. Customs Service, RG 36 (National Archives).

authority would dare trespass in the men's domain without fair warning. The officers likewise kept their distance during the dogwatch, the leisurely two hours at the end of the day when the men gathered around the forebitts to smoke or sing, to yarn or just chat. Officers and men, in this case whites and blacks, each maintained their own sphere in their tightly ordered world afloat. Aboard the *Arnold* a black man controlled the cooking, an important post with immediate repercussions for sailors who wanted to dry their socks or light their pipes at his hearth, and unless the captain regularly stood a watch, a black man also had charge of the deck at times—making him an officer de facto if not de jure.[26]

Black sailors on ships with a black majority before the mast, such as the *John Josiah Arnold*, had found a more congenial workplace than many of their brethren ashore. Sailors, black or white, had to create a pattern of existence as satisfying as possible under the constraints of their ship's demands for labor and its restraints on personal freedom. Black men who signed aboard ships with an entirely black crew were conscious of the opportunity (even within the inevitable hierarchy of the ship) to mold their own forecastle social life from the camaraderie of an isolated, masculine, and African American world. It is probable that many black men chose seafaring precisely for this sociability in the workplace. When the number of all-black crews declined at midcentury, individual black sailors became increasingly isolated in the midst of otherwise white forecastle worlds. As late as 1839, however, a fifth of the black men sailing out of Providence did so in predominantly black crews.

Defining themselves as men was important to black seamen and landsmen alike, in part because manliness asserted their God-given equality with whites. The transformation of a slave named Caeser provides a case in point. In 1781 John Isham, of Colchester, Connecticut, manumitted the enslaved Caeser, an action common among northern slaveholders affected by the philosophies of libertarianism and natural law during the Revolutionary era. Caeser responded to freedom as did many other recently manumitted black Americans of his generation. He immediately began to act like a free man, and to define himself as one. He joined the Continental army, and he married eighteen days after Isham manumitted him. Most tellingly, Caeser took a new surname. Henceforth he represented himself to the world as Caeser Beman. For him, the end of chattel slavery meant that he would "be [a] man." Conscious of his manhood, Caeser Beman used it not only to define himself against women but to represent himself as the dignified equal of any man.[27]

By the antebellum era, black American men commonly asserted equality based on manliness. Abolitionist William Wells Brown addressed a New England convention of blacks in 1859 by saying, "We must take a manly stand, bid defiance to the Fugitive Slave Law, Dred Scott Decision, and everything that shall attempt to fashion fetters upon us." William P. Powell, an ex-sailor known throughout the Atlantic world as keeper of the Coloured Sailors' Boarding House in New York City, referred to race-blind equality at sea when he wrote, "There is not that nice distinction made in the whaling as there is in the naval and merchant services; a coloured man is only known and looked upon as a MAN, and is promoted in rank according to his ability and skill to perform the same duties as the white man." Powell often used "man" to affirm blacks' skill and equality. Introducing Mr. Charles Flowers to William Lloyd Garrison by letter in 1853, Powell wrote, "Though one of the Sons of *Neptune* he is every inch a *man* and entitled to be respected as such wherever he may go."[28]

Black seamen like Powell linked assertions of equality with a clearly defined gender identity. They saw manliness as common ground among all men, even though education, wealth, and status were denied to blacks by white-dominated society. More importantly, black men oppressed by almost insurmountable burdens fell back on claims of manhood—rather than appeals to a common humanity—because the canons of nineteenth-century masculinity invested manhood with a special dignity. Referring to manliness and to workers' manly bearing, historian David Montgomery noted, "Few words enjoyed more popularity in the nineteenth century than this honorific, with all its connotations of dignity, respectability, defiant egalitarianism, and patriarchal male supremacy." The irony is that manliness did not mean the same thing to white and black Americans, or to white and black seamen. And manliness was far from a God-given constant. Historian E. Anthony Rotundo reminds us that "ideals of masculinity and femininity are cultural constructs, . . . they have a history, . . . and they develop and change like any other products of the human imagination."[29]

If equality was the most important trait a black male might assert in the white-dominated social world, reputation was crucial to most men within the black community. The specific kind of manliness associated with a robust calling, the prestige conferred on the traveler, the sea's own ineluctable charm, and the sense of belonging to a small community all combined to draw black men into the maritime labor market. Like white men, blacks were "captivated with the tough stories of the elder seamen, and seduced as well by the natural desire of seeing foreign countries." They built manly reputations in part through mobility and worldliness. John Malvin, a freeborn Virginia black man who became cook and ultimately captain of Great Lakes coasting schooners, recalled his wanderlust. "In the year 1827 a spirit of adventure, natural to most young men, took possession of me and I concluded to leave Virginia."[30]

Some black men cultivated an important occupational identity through repeated voyaging. Restricted from plying artisan trades ashore in the northern states, black sailors proudly picked up marlinespike and serving mallet instead. A decided hierarchy existed among Jack Tars, ranging from the "landsman" to the ordinary sailor who could "hand, reef, and steer," to the skilled able-bodied seaman (AB) who could turn in an eye splice, set up a dead-eye, or send down a yard. Chief mates prized "old salts" who had mastered tools and skills essential to maintaining the tautness and integrity of their ships' rigging. Only racist exclusivity kept such men from advancing, a point acknowledged years later by schooner captain Fred Balano's wife. Referring to a black man in their crew, she confided to her diary, "As Fred says, Dawson would be a captain if he were white." Dawson and other seamen of color did not advance to be officers, but neither were they restricted exclusively to dirty or heavy labor aboard ship. They had access to the arts and skills of the sailor, and to the manly pride that these entailed.[31]

Acculturation to the world of the ship also conferred on professional black seamen, as it did on their white shipmates, a distinctive identity separate from that of common laborers. Seamen boasted to provincial acquaintances of their worldly travels and exotic encounters; they took a fierce pride in their technical competence; they cultivated a fatalistic stoicism in the face of frequent danger; and they valued pugilism and pluck, traits that stood them in good stead in both their rough-and-tumble waterfront world and their routine defiance of ships' officers.[32]

Many African American seamen defined manliness through reputations based on bold exploits and toughness. An exceptionally perceptive critic of shipboard sociology commented in the 1830s on this variant of sailors' masculinity. "An overstrained sense of manliness is the characteristic of seafaring men, or rather, of life on board ship," reported Richard Henry Dana. "This often gives an appearance of want of feeling, and even of cruelty. From this, if a man comes within an ace of breaking his neck and escapes, it is made a joke of; and no notice must be taken of a bruise or cut; and any expression of pity, or any show of attention, would look sisterly, and unbecoming a man who has to face the rough and tumble of such a life." A generation earlier, Benjamin Franklin observed the same phenomena during one of his many transatlantic voyages. "Our seafaring people are brave," he noted, "being cowards in only one sense, that of *fearing* to be *thought afraid*." In 1807 a black sea cook named Stephen Revel "expressed the first idea" to his shipmates of recapturing their vessel from the French privateersmen who had overwhelmed them. They succeeded, and an American judge subsequently referred to Revel's "spirited conduct." It is probable that Revel, or his black shipmates, long regaled others with the tale as they treated friends in dramshops with their salvage money.[33]

Seafaring provided a venue to many black men for demonstrating feats of strength, skill, and bravery, all of which contributed to a man's reputation with his peers. A slave named George, "a bold, ambitious, adventurous fellow," responded with all hands aboard the *Dudley* at their captain's summons to assist in fending off another vessel. Warned to avoid danger, George nonetheless took up a position outboard of the *Dudley*'s bulwarks as the *Neptune* approached. His bold reputation-seeking came at a price: as the two vessels collided, they crushed his leg.[34]

Manly sports like boxing, along with workplace bravery, contributed to sailors' reputations. Long before that bloody sport found national favor in the United States, English-style bareknuckle boxing became popular among American seamen, who learned it from British tars. Black men gravitated to the prize ring for both economic and psychological reasons, and a substantial number of African American sailors went ashore in England to become professional boxers during the early nineteenth century.[35] During the War of 1812, the most awe-inspiring American in England was former seaman Tom Molineaux, the Virginia-born "tremendous man of colour" who had recently contended for the national bareknuckle championship. Meanwhile, about 6,560 American sailors (including 1,174 African Americans) languished as prisoners of war in Dartmoor Prison on the windswept Devonshire moor. Head and shoulders above them towered a "stout black" privateersman named Richard Crafus—known to Dartmoor as King Dick. Herculean and skilled, Crafus taught boxing to imprisoned American sailors. Blacks and whites alike flocked to his academy.[36]

The boxing ring attracted black sailors like Crafus and Molineaux because bareknuckle boxing offered men otherwise on the social and economic periphery a chance to compete man-to-man and a chance to build their reputations.[37] It provided a forum for self assertion and achieving status, as well as a chance to earn money. But while black and white sailors found common ground in the boxing ring, it is by no means clear that the underlying rules and meanings that black sailors attributed to rough sports were identical with those of white men. As seamen, their experiences conditioned them to fight; as African American seamen their experiences invested that manly scrapping with layers of meaning and with forms distinctly their own. Black sailors, for instance, competed in rough play and real fights by butting heads. Whites generally did not. Head butting warrants attention as distinctly black behavior within the manly waterfront world of personal challenge and provocative self-assertion. On boxing and butting were reputations built.[38]

Battling a black overseer, slave William Grimes "let him have it in old

Virginia style, (which generally consists of gouging, biting, and butting.) I drove my head against him," remembered Grimes, "until he could scarcely stand or go." On board the *Alert* in 1836 the black steward "enraged the mate, who called him a 'black soger'; and at it they went, clenching, striking, and rolling over and over," recollected a white sailor. "The darkey tried to butt him, but the mate got him down."[39]

Black and white seamen tarrying ashore in Guadeloupe in 1787 watched a Sunday gathering of slaves on holiday. The males, according to one sailor, regarded butting as a "favorite amusement . . . for which purpose their wooly hair is suffered to grow on the top of their heads, whilst that from behind is cut away, and frizzled in amongst that left on top, which forms a kind of cushion, or firm tuft of hair." To "African" music, "the opposing combatants dance with careless gaiety, frequently exchanging smiles, and significantly nodding their heads at each other," until they separate and advance toward each other, "when if as by mutual impulse, both dart forward, head against head, like two rams!" Intent on reputation, a free seaman of color from Philadelphia named Tom Grace challenged the local champion, swearing to onlookers that he would "capsize one of these fellows in a crack." Grace's actions matched his big talk. His white shipmates, however, remained spectators on the sidelines at this arena of manly black style and assertiveness. Originating in the Congo, head butting was an important part of the martial repertoire of African Americans. It reaffirmed diasporic connections among many reputation seekers, including sailors, slaves, and non-English-speaking blacks.[40]

African Americans' masculine reputations often depended on more than bravery and personal pluck. Choices that seamen made about shoreside housing reflected how they wished to be known as men, too. According to the *Sailor's Magazine,* of the twenty-two hundred African American seamen sailing out of New York in 1846, only one hundred sailors, or less than five percent, lived with their families. Four hundred more boarded at William Powell's Globe Hotel, commonly known as the Coloured Sailors' Boarding House—a staunchly Christian, temperance, and abolitionist house. Another one hundred boarded "at that earthly pandemonium, the Five Points"—a notorious crime and vice district. The remaining sixteen hundred found quarters at sixteen other black sailors' boardinghouses, "every one of which is anti-temperance" and managed by landlords "hostile to reform." About three-quarters of these sailors obviously voted for a good time—for barrooms, music, and the kind of "Boarding houses for colored seamen" where, according to one reformer, "the rear of the building is rented for bad women."[41]

Most black seafaring men did not embrace the "bourgeois interior" of domestic virtues and respectability that William P. Powell cultivated in the Coloured Sailors' Boarding House. Coming ashore in whatever port, they headed for places like the west end of Olney Street, in Providence. "Here were a number of houses built and owned by white men," wrote William Brown, "and rented to anyone, white or colored, who wanted to hire one or more rooms, rent payable weekly." More respectable landlords in Providence, he pointed out, collected quarterly. "Some of these places had barrooms, where liquors were dealt out, and places where they sold cakes, pies, doughnuts, &c. These they called cooky stands. In some houses dancing and fiddling was the order of the day." Brown recognized that "this street had a correspondence with all the sailor boarding houses in town, and was sustained by their patronage."[42] He fully understood how black sailors streaming ashore in Providence defined themselves as men through reputations built on their worldliness, bravery, and skill at sea, complemented by their liberality ashore. He knew, especially among the young men, that working too hard and valuing money too much detracted from a man's reputation among fellows who valued treating and camaraderie. On the other hand, Brown recognized that his father—well-respected in Providence's black community—had supported a family on a seafarer's income.

If the social organization of seafaring provided black men a professed equality of sorts with white workers, in addition to an unruly and convivial ground for enhancing one's reputation, seafaring wages were a strong drawing card for African American men seeking respectability in the black community ashore. Providership defined one channel to nineteenth-century respectability. Although shipboard wages declined with the resumption of peace in 1815, they generally equaled or exceeded those paid shorebound laborers through the 1850s.[43] Ships provided room and board too, an important consideration for poor laborers who sought to minimize household expenses. The irregularity of sailors' work was nothing new to black men: a job that promised to last several months remained an almost unheard-of luxury in the black community.

Black sailors generally received pay equal to that of whites in the same position—yet another dimension of shipboard equality that may have contributed to black sailors' pride. It certainly facilitated their role as providers for families ashore. Aboard the brig *John* in 1806, each of the seamen—one black, one white, one mulatto—earned $18 per month, while the white cook and ordinary seaman earned only $14. Lays (that is, shares) on the whaling ship *Bowditch*, whose complement in 1843 was about two-thirds black, were assigned by berth regardless of race: 1/185 for greenhands, and 1/150 for seamen. A man motivated to resist the temptation of substantial advances in foreign ports could be paid off handsomely at the end of a voyage. "My entire savings up to the period of my return from this voyage," remembered Moses Grandy of his trip to the East Indies aboard the ship *James Murray*, "amounted to $300. I sent it to Virginia and bought my wife." Men with less compelling reasons to save could also do so. The black cook and black steward of the ship *Lion* stepped ashore after twenty-two months around the world with $254 and $280 respectively, each having been paid as well as the best white sailors aboard.[44]

A lucky few parlayed maritime work into a good subsistence, contributing not only to their financial security but also to their masculine identity as providers. Born in Africa, Venture Smith was sold as a child to a slaveowner on Fishers Island, New York. He later earned his freedom and that of his family, made a profitable cruise on a whaler in the 1770s, and ended his days as a landowner in Haddam, Connecticut—in great part due to the success of his small-boat freighting ventures between Rhode Island, eastern Connecticut, and Long Island. Smith more than fulfilled society's expectation that, as a man, he should provide for his family.[45]

African American Yankees more typical than Smith also sought a livelihood on the water. Providence-born Noah Brown was fortunate to survive a romantic career on coasters and transatlantic ships, including British impressment and prison, Spanish capture, and service under fire in the War of 1812. Elisha Carder, born in Warwick, Rhode Island, in 1779 was like Melville's heroic Bulkington: "the land seemed scorching to his feet." Carder shipped out of Providence as sailor or steward on international voyages seven times in the six years following 1803, with barely a respite ashore.[46]

These black Rhode Islanders sailed in part because they knew their prospects ashore were not very flattering. Noah Brown's son William recalled their plight. "To drive carriage, carry a market basket after the boss, and brush his boots, or saw wood and run errands, was as high as a colored man could rise." Limited to odd jobs and farm labor, Rhode Island's African Americans naturally gravitated to the maritime labor force in the early nineteenth century as Narragansett Bay agriculture declined and shipping expanded. Blacks outside New England made similar moves. Those from the upper south flocked to Philadelphia to search for jobs on the ships that provided the single largest employment for black and mulatto men in the region.[47]

A substantial case can be made in retrospect that seafaring was a pillar of support for the aspiring black "middle class," for those respectable blacks who owned property and who were determined to improve their situation. When the Providence African Union Society (the city's first black benevolent group) drafted its bylaws at the turn of the century, it acknowledged seafaring's importance to eminent black citizens by agreeing to a common sacrifice: members covenanted not to serve on slavers, despite those ships' prominence in the Newport and Bristol fleets. Other African American mutual aid and fraternal organizations recognized the prominence of seafaring in their members' lives, along with its ever-present dangers. The African Marine Fund incorporated itself in New York City in 1810 "For The Relief Of The Distressed Orphans, And Poor Members Of This Fund." Seafaring was the sole occupation specifically mentioned in the constitution of the Brotherly Union Society, founded in Philadelphia in April 1823. That organization maintained moral standards not usually associated with seamen, reinforcing the point that many black men seeking respectability were then shipping out. The Brotherly Union Society expelled members for "fraudulent, base or immoral conduct" or for "gambling, tippling in shops, or spending time in brothels."[48]

Paul Cuffe, a Massachusetts merchant and shipmaster, and James Forten, a Philadelphia sailmaker with sea experience and a patented device for handling sails, best exemplify the financial success and respectability of black Americans in maritime enterprise. Elleanor Eldridge, a Rhode Island seamstress and weaver whose prowess at the loom earned her modest wealth and property, was another exemplar of the tiny black "middle class": she had been engaged to a man lost at sea. Yet an important question remains unanswered. To what extent did the "better sort" of black citizens look to the sea and ships as an avenue of advancement, and as an acceptable place for a respectable man? It is fair to say that many an enterprising black man shipped out in the early and mid–nineteenth century; it is probably fair to say as well that seafaring never attained the status of barbering or other dignified professions in the black community ashore. Henry Highland Garnet, a respected black preacher and abolitionist who had been to sea as a boy, castigated seafaring in 1852. Writing from Jamaica, Garnet asserted that "West Indian towns are generally notorious for immorality, and the reason is they are usually seaports."[49]

Maintaining their respectability was generally the concern of older or married men. But even unmarried young men from the black community occasionally made an effort not to let seafaring's occupational hazards blemish their character. When Jesse Almy, a twenty-three-year-old unmarried man, applied for his Seaman's Protection Certificate in Providence in 1809, he simultaneously requested a letter from his Baptist parish "to any sister church for transient membership."[50]

Older men often had little choice but maritime employment as a means to establish households and raise families. William J. Brown noted that his father was married in Cranston in 1805, "and commenced keeping house in that town, but being engaged in a seafaring life he removed to Providence and rented a house of Dr. Pardon Bowen." Noah Brown continued to ship out on deepwater voyages for another decade. The "Return of Coloured Persons Being Housekeepers," compiled in Providence in 1822, listed a number of black sailors, including Fortune Dyer, whose wife and child profited by a boarder's company in his absence. By the time the Providence City Directory was published in 1832, one-quarter of the heads of African American households were mariners. These Rhode Island sailors were by no means anomalies: city directories for seaports from Portland, Maine, to Baltimore consistently listed seafaring in the three or four most common occupations for black men. A free black sailor on a cotton ship told runaway slave Charles Ball in Savannah "that his home was in New-York; that he had a wife and several children there, but that he followed the sea for a livelihood, and knew no other mode of life." An African American named Charles Williams testified in 1830 that his "permanent residence is in New York where he has a family, has been a seafaring man off and on for twenty-two years."[51]

With few other jobs at their disposal, black men found they had to persist at seafaring, especially if they wished to support families. Blacks aged in the forecastle watching white youngsters parade through (table 7.3). In fact, a preponderance of "old salts" in the early Republic's fleet were black men with no better place to go, seamen like Prince Brown, who in his mid-forties, during the era of neutral trade, made at least six voyages out of Providence.[52]

Black and mulatto seafaring men who took seriously their masculine role as providers lived with the constant tension of separation from their families. Seafaring provided bittersweet support at best for a family. Samuel Crawford's private entrepreneurial venture of four barrels of potatoes aboard the brig *John*, when added to his wages, put him far ahead of

Table 7.3
Seamen's Ages

	1803		1820	1830		1850	
Ages	African American	White	African American	African American	White	African American	White
Philadelphia							
To 19	10.8%	18.0%	3.8%	8.9%	20.1%	5.7%	—
20–29	62.5	62.8	46.7	47.9	45.4	37.5	—
30–39	20.0	16.2	29.1	30.2	24.2	30.7	—
40–49	5.0	2.3	16.5	7.5	8.3	20.4	—
50+	1.7	.7	3.9	5.5	2.0	5.7	—
	100.0%	100.0%	100.0%	100.0%	100.0%	100.0%	
N	120	513	182	146	566	88	—
Providence							
To 19	15.0%	30.0%	—	11.0%	22.5%	—	22.0%
20–29	62.0	54.5	—	41.0	55.5	60.0	53.0
30–39	17.0	12.0	—	35.0	16.0	33.0	19.5
40–49	6.0	3.0	—	11.0	5.0	7.0	5.0
50+	—	.5	—	2.0	1.0	—	.5
	100.0%	100.0%		100.0%	100.0%	100.0%	100.0%
N	48	167	—	46	157	15	153

Sources: Providence Crew Lists, U.S. Customs House Papers, Providence, R.I., RG 28 (Manuscript Collection, Rhode Island Historical Society, Providence); Philadelphia Crew Lists, Records of the U.S. Customs Service, RG 36 (National Archives).

intermittent day labor ashore. So Crawford spent only a few days at home with his wife after a five-and-a-half-month trip to Europe aboard the *Columbia* before sailing to Havana aboard the *John* in 1806. Money Vose, an African-born seaman who sailed out of Massachusetts from the late eighteenth century until he was impressed by the British in 1813, married the widow Gardner in 1799. He supported her two children, along with those he subsequently fathered. "By industry a humble home was provided," related his stepdaughter, "for my mother and her younger children."[53]

Black men of the next generation were likewise forced financially to leave their wives alone on shore. John Gardner, who acknowledged in 1831 that he "follows the sea mostly," came to resent his calling. Until age 32,

Table 7.4
Persistence at Sea
(Men Making at Least Three Voyages from Providence in Seven Years)

N = Men Sailing in First Year / Men Still Sailing Seven Years Later

Years	African American		White	
	N	%	N	%
1803–1810	48 / 10	21	167 / 43	26
1830–1837	45 / 11	24	156 / 27	17
1850–1856	15 / 1	7	153 / 19	12

Source: Providence Crew Lists, U.S. Customs House Papers, Providence, R.I., RG 28 (Manuscript Collection, Rhode Island Historical Society, Providence).

Gardner lived with his mother and sisters by the Canal Basin in Providence while ashore. Then after a two-year courtship punctuated by voyaging, he married Mary Ann Elizabeth Stewart in a Presbyterian service at her father's house. She contributed to the household they established on Olney Lane by doing laundry for the steamboats and taking in sewing and washing from other black people in the Hardscrabble neighborhood. Always pressed financially, however, Gardner spent time in jail for debt and reluctantly shipped out again in 1835. During that absence, three drunken white men gang-raped his wife.[54]

White sailors rarely had families to be threatened ashore in their absence, as Nathaniel Ames indicated in his *Nautical Reminiscences.* "I do not know that I ever sailed in an American ship," he recalled, "with an individual before the mast that was a married man with the exception of one Negro cook of Boston." The fact that New England's black mariners had families ashore made them more likely than footloose white deckhands to ship out of a home port regularly, and to keep returning there (table 7.4). It also meant that maritime tragedies struck directly at the black community struggling for stability and respectability on shore. Betsy Watson of Providence lost several husbands to the sea around the turn of the century; by 1822 she had married a fourth time—to seaman Henry Gray.[55]

Seafaring, then, meant something very different for black men and white men in the early nineteenth century. White sailors—whether gentlemen's sons inspired to dare "an insight into the mysteries of a sailor's life," or ambitious boys eager to gain a command, or "rebels who left the land in flight and fear"—were geographically mobile, unmarried, and unlikely to stick with the sea unless promoted. Black sailors were older than their white shipmates; more rooted in their home ports; more likely to be married; more likely to persist in going to sea; and more likely to define themselves with dignity as respectable men because seafaring enabled them to be providers. (See tables 7.3 and 7.4).[56]

Despite African American sailors' assertions of manly equality, bold reputations, and respectable providership, as the nineteenth century progressed they were increasingly relegated to jobs as cooks or stewards—the "feminine" jobs aboard ship with potential problems for a man of any race. Cooks' power over the larder could lead to either favoritism or antipathy with men in the forecastle, but stewards—the cabin servants—were easy scapegoats and were frequently perceived by sailors as captains' flunkies. The log kept by Amos Jenckes aboard the ship *Resource* on the ceremonial occasion of crossing the equator recorded a common sentiment: "and as the Ship Steward was by no means liked of, he was the last brought up and handled more rough than any of the rest."[57] Such billets' separation from the rest of the crew—in bunking, in duties, and in gender associations with the job—reflected and reinforced black men's distinctiveness. Cooks and stewards were not always bona fide sailors with the skill to steer a ship and maintain its rigging, and in the antebellum years fewer black men were initiated into the mysteries of the sailor's art. White workers' hegemony over shore-based crafts slowly extended to shipboard ones as well.

White sailors probably regarded cooking and domestic service as more feminine than real sailors' work, characterized by physical danger, elemental challenge, and technical skill. Echoing the paternalistic norms of the larger society, a captain's son aboard the brig *Palestine* in 1832 referred to "our Steward—alias Kitchen Maid" gleefully, because he was "a black *man!*" A seaport newspaper in Wilmington, North Carolina, claimed (erroneously) in 1831 that "In nine cases out of ten, no white sailor can be employed as cook or steward."[58] That editor implicitly linked race with gender in a myopic and self-serving fashion, as did many white men in nineteenth-century America. As historian David Roediger points out, "The expectation by workers of service from nonwhite workers was far from confined to domestic labor. The rituals of white working-class manliness, performed at sites as various as barber shops, bars, and brothels, often included service by African-American workers." What is of interest here, however, is not whether black men discharged the duties of sailors, or whether white men sailed as cooks (each did, of course), but how black sailors and black women perceived sex roles in light of prevailing ideologies and seafaring work.[59]

Many black sea cooks and stewards, along with foredeck hands, shipped out voyage after voyage to fulfill respectable masculine roles as providers. Cooks and stewards paradoxically assumed the most feminine roles aboard white-dominated ships to maintain their masculinity in the black community. Recognizing this, black men and women maneuvered around the prescriptions of white society to validate themselves from their own perspectives.

The diaries of a mulatto ship's steward named Charles Benson, who sailed out of Salem and Boston from the late 1850s until his death at sea in 1881, reveal how one "Kitchen Maid" took seriously his duties as a husband and father. Writing to his wife in 1862, a homesick Benson complained, "What a miserable life a sea fareing life is. I will stop it if I live & that soon. (that is if I get anything to do on shore) you & the children must have things to eat drink & were [wear] & I must get it some were [somewhere] if not on land, on the sea." Sixteen years later, his tune had not changed much. "How can I ern my bread without it on the Mighty Deep."[60]

Still at sea in 1880, Charles Benson defined himself through his occupation by some of Victorian society's masculine virtues: stoicism, prestige, and profit. "Was there any comfort any time, any where at sea? I cannot really say I ever did. it is the excitement, danger, and money that a sea life Brings, that keeps me at sea. Nothing else. 226 days from home."[61] Benson did not envision himself as maid or servant. He took pride in his work and in the images of himself he constructed because of it. As steward he was the captain's servant. But he was also the ship's barber and doctor, as well as the individual responsible for all of the stores and provisions on voyages to East Africa, which averaged nine months in length. Most importantly, he was a respectable provider for his family and a man respected ashore because of his steady work.

Other black stewards also took seriously their roles as providers. Jesse Scott, formerly a slave to General Robert E. Lee, and by 1868 cook and steward aboard the brig *Charles Albert* of Baltimore, opened a bank account between voyages. He made it "subject to the order of my children Letty & James Scott." The keeper of the Coloured Sailors' Boarding House in New York reported in 1864 that his boarders "save their money, sending their parents and families, through our agency, more than half of their earnings."[62]

Whether in a dramshop or a temperance boardinghouse ashore, or whether stowing headsails or stewing salt beef at sea, African American seafaring men commonly linked their work and their gender identity as men. A means to male sociability and expressiveness, as well as to earnings absolutely necessary for the continuity of black households ashore, seafaring provided an arena in which black workingmen could establish reputations and respectability. Bending institutional and social dimensions of the occupation to their own ends, black sailors maneuvered around some of white society's restrictions on them as workers and men. In those ways, and through the defiant egalitarianism with which a black seaman could "presume upon his equality" in the presence of white shipmates, the African American sailor felt "like a man" in the maritime world.

But black sailors' fortunes took a decided turn for the worse in the 1840s, along with those of other northern black workers. The consolidation of "whiteness" as a working-class value in antebellum America, persuasively argued by David Roediger, affected workers' gender definitions and class alignments. On both fronts, black sailors lost ground, as evidenced in the assignment of more black men to the cook's camboose or steward's berth. More telling, perhaps, was the growing assumption among white sailors that those billets naturally *belonged* to men of color. No such assumptions had characterized the late-eighteenth-century maritime world.[63]

This shift reflected changes in the nature of seafaring itself. Once New England's economic mainstay, shipping declined in relative importance as industrialization caught Yankee entrepreneurs' imaginations and their investment capital. As one successful shipmaster had put it earlier in the century, working at sea then appeared to be "the most sure and direct means of arriving at independence." Consequently, in the early national years it entailed a certain degree of social acceptability. Elmo P. Hohman exaggerated when he wrote that early-nineteenth-century crews were "drawn from the best stock of New England, and could look forward to becoming officers and owners."[64] The Federalist *aristoi* who constituted "the best stock of New England" would have resented the inference that their ranks spawned common sailors, and most seamen actually came from the laboring population. Yet in the early national period, seafaring did offer the possibility of prestige and promotion to white men who could withstand its rigors and of regular, even tolerant, employment to black men. Seafaring employment provided a rare opportunity for black men to be providers and to fulfill culturally sanctioned roles as good husbands and fathers. Seafaring also extended opportunities to establish manly reputations in the eyes of both peers and the women whom sailors wished to impress. Northern men shipped out in large numbers, including the talented and ambitious from each race.[65]

By midcentury, however, mariners experienced "the lowest degradation of [free] labor" in American history.[66] Describing themselves as "vassals" or "slaves of the lowest cast," white seamen typically moaned, "And now I ask what slave at the south suffers more hardships or feels more keenly the bitterness of oppression than the poor care worne sailor." Uncontrollable captains like Frank Thompson, master of the brig *Pilgrim* on a voyage from Boston to California in 1834, drove the point home. Seizing up two white men by their wrists to the main rigging, he laid on the stripes with a rope's end and screamed:

> You see your condition! . . . I'll make you toe the mark, every soul of you, or I'll flog you all, fore and aft, from the boy up! You've got a driver over you. Yes, a *slave-driver—a nigger-driver!* I'll see who'll tell me he isn't a *nigger* slave![67]

Shipboard institutions thus posed a dramatic conflict with the "equality" and "independence" that white American men had come to expect from mid-nineteenth-century democratic rhetoric. Under such circumstances and in light of black Americans' traditional seafaring, it seems as though America's most degraded caste of workers—black ones—might have shouldered more and more of the merchant fleet's burdens as those burdens became increasingly onerous to white Americans. Ironically, they did not. With Irishmen and other white foreigners "willing to submit to oppressive and despotic treatment," blacks' seagoing tradition seemed to count for little when it came to hiring time. Midcentury discrimination extended not only to new occupations in the expanding economy but also to carryovers from the past such as seafaring.[68]

Although black men would continue to work on American ships, the circumstances of their individual sea experiences began to change after 1840. Fewer black men were found in many ships as time passed, and in New York and New England, fewer all-black crews existed to provide the workplace sociability that had been so important to the previous generation (table 7.5).[69] And black men throughout the north were increasingly relegated to jobs as cooks or stewards.

Table 7.5
Crews with African American Majorities

	Providence		New York	
Year	Crews Sampled	% of Crews with an African American Majority	Crews Sampled	% of Crews with an African American Majority
1803–1810	98	19.0	71[a]	8.5
1807	61	14.5	—	—
1808	29	6.4	—	—
1810	105	15.5	—	—
1816	52	15.5	—	—
1818	91	11.0	104[b]	5.8
1820	72	16.7	—	—
1822	121	7.5	—	—
1825	92	15.2	106	9.4
1829	82	13.4	—	—
1830	74	5.5	—	—
1832	87	15.0	—	—
1834	102	21.5	—	—
1835	—	—	60	5.0
1836	49	26.5	—	—
1839	84	13.1	—	—
1840	75	8.1	125	2.4
1844	58	8.6	—	—
1846	61	10.0	114	.9
1850	45	2.2	94	7.4
1853	68	8.9	—	—
1856	57	5.3	59	4.3

Sources: Providence Crew Lists, U.S. Customs House Papers, Providence, R.I., RG 28 (Manuscript Collection, Rhode Island Historical Society, Providence); New York Crew Lists, Records of the U.S. Customs Service, RG 36 (National Archives).
[a] 1803–1806
[b] 1818–1819

The degradation of the industry (including declining wages and increasing brutality) likewise worked against black family formation ashore. With conditions making it tougher to support a family through seafaring, black mariners increasingly became rootless and casual laborers. No longer did a large number of black sailors aboard Providence-based ships have Rhode Island birthplaces, nor return to Providence as home port—a pattern repeated in Boston and New York. Even in Baltimore, where many black men continued to find work aboard ship, few used that work to support families ashore. By midcentury, then, the changing nature of the maritime labor market conspired against black men who wished to be respectable masculine providers.

The most striking thing about the Rhode Island fleet in the 1850s was that black *sailors*—the real seamen who persisted in shipping out time and time again—had disappeared. Throughout the 1850s the black men aboard Rhode Island ships were all casual laborers, men who made one or two voyages at most. The prominent group of black mariners who considered themselves professionals, the "old salts" in the two generations that had included Cato Burrill and Prince Brown, were gone (see table 7.4).

Though seafaring still provided casual employment to black men with limited options in every seaport, and lifetime work for individuals like Charles Benson, the black man's position declined in the world of the ship by midcentury. A new constellation of relationships between race, class, and gender among American seafarers led white sailors increasingly to redefine blacks in feminine roles. Of course, blacks had long since learned to live with white prescription, and they armored themselves from these assaults. They recognized the actual whitening of the maritime labor force as substantially more threatening than white folks' talk. That sociological change sapped the economic vitality of the black community and removed an important institutional prop from African American men's standard of masculine behavior. By midcentury, seafaring was no longer a bastion of black professionalism, a bulwark of the tiny black "middle class," or as much of a means as it once had been to potent male identities.

LAURA TABILI

8

"A Maritime Race"
Masculinity and the Racial Division of Labor in British Merchant Ships, 1900–1939

Laura Tabili continues the exploration, begun in the preceding essay, of the ways gender, race, and class intersected in the shaping of Anglo-American maritime work. Unlike Rediker for the early 1700s or Bolster for the early 1800s, however, Tabili finds little evidence by the early 1900s of either a radical foredeck egalitarianism or unusually open opportunities in maritime work for black men. Instead, she argues, in the British steam-powered merchant marine, shipowners manipulated and conflated race and gender stereotypes to legitimate the degradation they imposed in both wages and workplace conditions. Faced with rapid technological change and rising foreign competition, employers defined certain shipboard jobs as unskilled and feminized, and they assigned them to men whom they deemed as "naturally" fitting the positions by virtue of their race. The redefinition of work and skill accompanying the shift from sail to steam (examined from a different angle by Lillian Nayder in the next essay) was thus at the same time gendered, racialized, and politicized.

Tabili suggests that socially constructed divisions of race and gender were lifted from land-based experience, domestic and colonial, and applied to the division of shipboard labor in ways that undercut potential working-class solidarity and maintained male ruling-class domination. She graphically depicts the connections between labor practices and relations in the British steam-powered merchant marine and large-scale developments in the international political economy. Merchant shipping had from the beginning formed the circulatory system of the British global empire; in the twentieth century, it was both deeply implicated in and a reflection of British imperial and industrial decline.

ON 12 NOVEMBER 1928, the decrepit Lamport and Holt steamship *Vestris*, two days out from Hoboken enroute to Barbados, sank in the Atlantic Ocean, 240 miles from Sandy Hook, "in a sea that would not have endangered a well-formed vessel." Of the 112 lives lost, 68 were passengers, including "most of the women and all of the children," and 44 were crew members, among them "Negro stokers [who] were tied in the below deck of the ship as she plunged to the bottom of the sea."[1] In the aftermath of the tragedy, the press and the company's attorney sought to blame Black crewmen for the loss of life and property, impugning their manhood with charges of cowardice and emotional instability. They promoted the scenario of "panic-stricken" Black seamen, "impossible to handle," pushing their way to the lifeboats ahead of the passengers. In contrast, the white engineers reportly "struggled to replace the Negro firemen... manfully."[2] Survivors complained of "phlegmatic slowness and inexperience" among "the motley crew of the vessel—white, yellow and negro" and of "downright cowardice, panic, desertion and brutal neglect of the passengers."[3] In the insurance investigation to fix responsibility for the wreck, the company's legal counsel stated that "coloured members... showed some excitement, which is their nature."[4]

In contrast, another survivor, Edward Miles Walcott of Georgetown, British Guiana, praised the conduct of "coloured men aboard who behaved better than most of the white men."[5] The Barbadian quartermaster, Lionel Lickorish, praised as a "heroic little negro," had saved over twenty lives.[6] Writing in the labor periodical the *Negro Worker*, labor activist J. W. Ford reported that Black stokers had shoveled coal for hours in chest-high water attempting to save the badly listing vessel. He deplored the racially segregated mess halls and sleeping quarters that had prevailed aboard the sunken ship, adding that while all the food served aboard had been "rotten," the most "inferior food" was served to the Black stokehold crew. Black stokers on the SS *Vestris* were paid $30 per month, while white seamen on the same ship earned $45: either wage, Ford alleged, was far from sufficient to ensure a "decent living standard."[7]

The outlines of this episode, of economic exploitation reinforced by race discrimination and its justification through a rhetoric of race- and class-specific incapacity, illustrate the divisions and antagonisms of industrial society reproduced aboard British merchant ships. What is less apparent is the gendered aspect of these divisions and the rhetoric that justified them. Understanding how assumptions about gender structured shipboard relations can illuminate the connections between the racial division of labor and racial hierarchies aboard ship and the multiple inequalities, including class, race, gender, age, skill, and region, undergirding Britain's global empire—an empire whose might was sustained by Black and white merchant seamen.

In early-twentieth-century Britain and the empire, the population called "black" or "coloured" was culturally heterogeneous, including West Africans, Indians and Malays, people from the Caribbean, and "Arabs" from the Eastern Mediterranean, the Arabian Peninsula, and East Africa. Their sole apparent common characteristic was neither physiological nor cultural: they were united by a political and historical relationship of colonial subordination. In the course of the nineteenth century, Britain had become the most powerful country in the world, dominating an empire that encompassed India, Canada, Australia and New Zealand, and much of Africa, Southeast Asia, the Middle East, and the Caribbean. Britain's global expansion was driven first by commercial and later by industrial capitalism, supported by the world's most powerful merchant fleet. Due to the industry's historically critical role in national prosperity, the shipping industry and the national interest were closely identified in economic, political, and cultural terms.[8] Examining shipboard relations in this industry can tell us much about race, gender, and class dynamics in Britain and its global empire.

Anglo-American maritime historians have promoted a view of shipboard social relations stressing rank-and-file harmony and solidarity in coping with and subverting the oppressive and inhumane working conditions for which the shipping industry was notorious. Aboard merchant ships, they argue, an all-male subculture of resistance, camaraderie, and "rough-hewn equality" prevailed, uncomplicated by social stratification: racial, cultural, and gender barriers and conflicts were left ashore. Shipowners themselves accepted a version of this view, celebrating "the glorious comradeship of the sea, which unites all true seamen in blood brotherhood, Norwegian and Swede, Dane and Dago, and even him from nowhere in the East."[9] The view that maritime culture developed in isolation "beyond all normal experience" has been assailed, rightly, for its technological determinism: shipboard "relationships were social artefacts created by men and not by ships."[10]

By the late nineteenth century, as the *Vestris* incident suggests, "rough-hewn equality" was dissipating in American ships, and it was absent if it had ever existed in British ones.[11] Shipboard relations in the British mercantile marine bore the imprint of the empire to which the industry was integral: a racial division of labor and a racial hierarchy took shape aboard British merchant ships, structured by imperial economic imperatives and racial inequalities and by domestic class and gender relations.

This division of labor and hierarchy reflected a set of practices and a system of symbols through which ruling-class white men in Britain and in the colonies distinguished themselves from and justified their power over women, colonized people, and other subordinates. Middle-class men saw themselves as cerebral, as capable of abstract understanding and self-control. In contrast, they depicted women, children, working people, and colonized people as unstable and mentally incapable, physical and emotional, visceral and tactile, bestial and "closer to nature." Indeed, they understood their world through a series of interchangeable polarities: man/woman, lady/woman, white/black, familiar/foreign, home/empire, colonizer/colonized, middle class/working class, control/chaos, clean/dirty, intellect/sensuality, culture/nature, civilization/savagery, intelligence/emotion, rationality/sensuality, self/Other, subject/object. These dichotomies and the subordination they rationalized were "naturalized," by depicting them as innate or natural, and they were also assigned unequal value, implying good/evil, superiority/inferiority, so that ruling-class white men always appeared superior.[12] The ideal of masculinity itself had evolved historically, from Christian and "contemplative" in the 1850s to what scholars call "imperial manhood" by the end of the century, a more "active" ideal that embodied "genetic virility," racism, chauvinism, and imperialism.[13] Exposing the process of dichotomizing, naturalizing, and hierarchizing can help us to make sense of the explanations for the *Vestris* disaster and of the shipboard hierarchies of race, skill, and gender which this tragedy brought to light.

While we have learned much more in recent years about the use of gender to reinforce and justify inequalities between men and women in the workplace and in the society at large, there has been little attention to gender distinctions in the all-male workplace—to how levels of skill, by which workingmen have measured their manhood, for example, might have affected definitions of masculinity. Our grasp of the multiple meanings and uses of race is also in its infancy. Understanding the gendered construction of racial differences can explain the division of labor and attendant redefinitions of skill and status aboard British ships, and can enhance our understanding of how race and gender as well as class fissured modern British society both ashore and aboard ship.

"Skill" itself has been defined historically as a masculine attribute involving mastery of technology, control of metal and machines, physical strength, autonomy, and empowerment. In addition, skill has implied wages adequate to keep one's wife out of the paid workforce and in the home performing personal service. Men who do "women's" work, conversely, may be seen as weak, effeminate, or even homosexual. Since in the process of technological innovation "all jobs are becoming more like women's jobs," workingmen may feel emasculated as well as economically threatened by apparent deskilling. Scholars have reasoned, indeed, that rather than eliminating skill, technological innovation continually demands new types of skills, yet these new skills may go unrecognized because "the definition of skill is highly political."[14] A distinctly political and racialized redefinition of skill and masculinity accompanied the technological innovations in Britain's late-nineteenth-century maritime industry.

Recent attention to the economic interdependence and other links between wives and families on shore and men at sea has undermined the notion of seafaring as the quintessential masculine occupation, in an industry in which women took no part. The division of labor between men and women occurred before a ship set sail, but the work of both sustained the industry, and maritime wages conferred benefits in shore communities.[15]

But a gendered division of labor prevailed aboard ship as well. The survival of the shipboard world as a "total institution" required that women's work of reproducing the workforce—cooking, cleaning, and personal service—proceed onboard.[16] In earlier days this "women's work" was performed by cabin boys, apprentices, or disabled older men, or shared out among the crew, but in the early twentieth century much of it was assigned to Black men from the colonized empire, principally South Asians, East and West Africans, Arabs, and men from the Caribbean.[17] Black men were also assigned shipboard jobs considered menial, unskilled, or low in status, such as stoking, while high-status jobs such as engineering were reserved for white men. Black men's assignment to shipboard women's work and their relegation to unskilled work were not parallel processes but part of the same process. The gendering of work and the gendering of skill mutually reinforced and were built into the racializing of work and the racializing of skill.

As the wreck of the *Vestris* suggests, employers reconstituted imperial social relations aboard ship, infusing domestic class and gender definitions with racial content imported from the colonies. Not only were Black men feminized and assigned women's work, but they were also depicted as bestial, infantile, subhuman, and exotic in order to justify their relegation to unskilled work. Black seamen's relegation to women's work and imputedly unskilled labor could be dismissed glibly as a consequence of their low status or their alleged inexperience in seafaring. But the skills and relative status of shipboard tasks were subject to negotiation and redefinition. Stoking, for example, was scorned as unskilled, yet when white men did it they were paid more than white deckhands, and "skilled seamen acquainted with steam" were a valuable and scarce resource.[18] Shipowners, moreover, apparently felt a need to justify employing underpayable colonized labor by denouncing white sailors too as unfit, incompetent, unmanly. Rather than privileging white sailors over Black ones, these practices enabled employers to reproduce, preserve, and even intensify aboard ship the hierarchies that kept British workers disunited ashore. Indeed, at sea as on land, employers' rhetoric blurred the distinctions among women, colonized people, workers, children, animals, and other subordinates, stressing instead their common unlikeness to ruling-class white men. Colonized men were described in feminine terms, as "effete" and "unmanly," "sedentary . . . delicate . . . languid," "enervated," and "childish."[19] Women and workingmen, Black and white, thus had much in common—both structural subordination to British ruling-class men and culturally dominant images of unlikeness to them.

Rather than seeing race, class, and gender as independent or overlapping categories, then, it might be more useful to see them as dynamics that flow from the same power structure, ordering or positioning people in various ways in relation to power and wealth and to one another. Then it is possible to understand how and why racial and gender assumptions worked together, reinforced by infantilization and bestialization, to define Black sailors as unskilled and to relegate them to menial, unpleasant, and "unmanly" labor.

The racially segmented shipboard labor system took shape in the late nineteenth century, as the technology, the work process, and the structure of Britain's once-unrivaled merchant marine responded to foreign competition. A global industry with a multiracial workforce drawn from all parts of the empire, merchant shipping was deeply implicated in imperial as well as industrial decline.[20] Britain's nineteenth-century domination of the global economy rested on the twin pillars of industry and empire, and could only falter as other industrializing powers developed merchant navies to compete for Britain's historically disproportionate share of world markets.[21] The maintenance of profits—indeed, the shipping industry's very survival—demanded wage cuts and technological innovation.

With the repeal of the Navigation Acts in 1849, employers began to hire men of any race or nationality who would accept lower wages than British seamen. In the words of shipowner Thomas Brassey, M.P., written in 1877, "Foreign seamen keep wages down."[22] Employers and their allies viewed

British seamen's solidarity and resistance with little sympathy, denouncing "the utter absence of discipline on board the British merchant vessel . . . the drunkenness, disobedience, and insolence of their crews," whose "refractory," "mutinous," and "intemperate" behavior, they lamented, forced them to resort to foreign labor.[23] Comparing British seamen unfavorably with "the seamen belonging to the Danish, Swedish, French and North German vessel," they complained, "The wages paid in England are higher than those of most other countries, and the value the British seaman gives in return is as a rule less."[24]

Heightened militancy itself was British seamen's response to the deteriorating working conditions common to many British industries facing foreign competition in the late nineteenth century. It was part of the broader working-class awakening embodied in the "New Unionism" of the 1880s. Joseph Havelock Wilson, president of the National Sailors' and Firemen's Union, Britain's major maritime union, complained that employers, seeking a "more docile" workforce, employed a succession of non-British seamen, including "Norwegians . . . Germans, Dutchmen, Greeks, Spaniards and Turks."[25]

But by the early twentieth century, the NSFU had successfully organized most European seamen, and employers next sought cheap labor in the colonies.[26] Wilson commented perceptively in 1911:

> At one time the European foreigner was sufficiently docile to play off against the Britisher. But now, seemingly, all European seafarers are a "drunken," "unsteady," "inefficient" lot, and the long-suffering shipowner turns reluctantly to the ASIATICS! But already history again begins to repeat itself. The Chinese are no longer all docility. They too are "becoming demoralized, insubordinate and defiant." Of course they are. Because . . . the conditions of employment aboardship are insufferable.[27]

Employers ultimately resorted to seamen from India and other British colonies because of a preexisting contract labor system—Asiatic or "lascar" articles of agreement (work contracts)—that inhibited their organization by British unions.

Lascar seamen served on special two-year labor contracts first codified in 1834, although the institution was much older. Like the term *coolie*, *lascar* denoted both race and occupational status, and, in the mouths of the British, was somewhat pejorative.[28] Gangs or crews of kinsmen or co-villagers were recruited, often from rural areas in India and elsewhere, by a headman or broker called a *serang*.[29] Black seamen had worked on

British ships since well before the technological innovations of the 1870s, and Indian seamen since the seventeenth century, for seafaring was a traditional occupation in India and West Africa. The East India Company charter of 1823 specified pay scales for both Indian and Caribbean seamen, and "men of colour" had constituted a significant though unmeasured proportion of the workforce from at least the mid-nineteenth century.[30]

Employers' bargaining position with lascars and other colonized workers was enhanced by British colonial governments' interest in keeping colonized populations unorganized and politically and economically subordinate.[31] In the twentieth century, employers extended Asiatic articles beyond South Asia to new sections of the workforce. With British government sanction, special articles were imposed on Adenese in 1903, on Somalis and men from Port Said in 1918, on some "white natives of India" in 1923, on Goans in 1925, on men from the Red Sea ports and, with modifications, on Chinese seamen and West Africans in the 1920s.[32] From 1901 until World War II, the relative numbers of men bound by Asiatic articles grew steadily at the expense of unionized white and Black British seamen—from less than a fifth (18.5 percent) in 1901 to more than a quarter (26 percent) in the late 1930s.[33]

By the early twentieth century, British maritime employers had created a dual labor system in which some fifty thousand of their total labor force of two hundred thousand were contract laborers (table 8.1). Hired in colonial ports at colonial wage levels and exempt from state or union-sanctioned protections, men bound by lascar or Asiatic articles were paid one-third to one-fifth as much as white or Black seamen who operated in a nominally free labor market.[34] Lascar seamen also labored under inferior working and contractual conditions and were given cramped living space and inferior food.

For their own protection, unionized seamen were required to sign new articles of agreement for each ship, but two-year Asiatic labor contracts precluded this. Employers could legally abridge this contract any time after the first three months, while crewmen had no legal grounds for quitting and no procedure for recovering wages due.[35] In 1913–14, employers were required to provide 120 cubic feet of shipboard space for each European seaman, while lascars were allotted 72 cubic feet per man.[36] When requirements were upgraded, the differential remained. In 1959, the Elder Dempster Company reported that an incentive for the "Africanisation" of their crews was the need to upgrade facilities if white crews were retained.[37] As shipowner Charles Ainsworth explained, "The food and

Table 8.1

Seamen Employed in British Ships

Year	British	Foreign	Lascars	Total
1901	136,010 (.68)	28,073 (.14)	37,392 (.19)	201,475
1910	179,422 (.72)	27,117 (.11)	43,934 (.18)	250,473
1920	175,239 (.73)	14,760 (.06)	50,227 (.21)	240,226
1925	164,117 (.71)	11,869 (.05)	54,969 (.24)	230,955
1930	160,410 (.68)	18,899 (.08)	56,416 (.24)	235,725
1933	125,599 (.68)	11,089 (.06)	49,080 (.27)	185,768
1936	130,830 (.70)	7,830 (.04)	47,310 (.25)	185,970
1937	133,110 (.70)	8,720 (.05)	48,660 (.26)	190,690
1938	131,885 (.69)	9,790 (.05)	50,700 (.26)	192,375

Sources: Figures through 1935 are taken from the Board of Trade Papers, MT9/2737 M.4541; those for 1936–38 are from C. B. A. Behrens, *Merchant Shipping and the Demands of War* (London: HMSO, Longmans, 1955), 157. A census of the men employed on a given day each year (a somewhat smaller figure) was also published in the Board of Trade Parliamentary Command Papers each year until 1935, and for the years 1936–38 in a separate publication, Board of Trade, *Census of Seamen* (London: HMSO, 1937, 1938, 1939). Because of changes in the method of computation in the years 1901–33, as well as in ways of documenting British citizenship, the category "Foreign" included alien seamen, white and black, as well as many black seamen who were British subjects but undocumented, while the category "British" included some documented black British subjects. Hence the difficulty of estimating the numbers of black seamen on standard articles.

wages required to maintain one British seaman equal the needs of six or more Chinese; moreover, native crews work longer hours and can eat and sleep anywhere."[38] Asiatic articles also exempted employers from British social wage provisions such as unemployment insurance and pensions.[39] For all these reasons, Black seamen were more cheaply and flexibly deployed.

In addition to these contract laborers, several thousand Black seamen served in the British merchant marine under terms similar to those of white seamen, but they were confined to the least desirable jobs.[40] For as foreign competition intensified from 1870 onward, tramp ships, which plied from port to port in search of odd cargoes, formed an increasing proportion of the British merchant fleet. They were an unreliable source of employment, and voyages could last months and even years. Tramps were thus undesirable to a man with a family or other commitments in port.

They also paid poorly due to the industry's sensitivity to foreign competition, as well as its domination by smaller, economically vulnerable firms. Unable to sign lascars for voyages of indefinite duration, tramps offered employment to Black seamen on union-mandated articles, but often paid them less than white seamen and relegated them to the worst jobs. Liverpool investigator David Caradog Jones reported in 1932, "Negro Firemen and greasers are very frequently employed in the West African trade, as their wages are less than those of white men." Employers were required to repatriate U.K.-domiciled seamen at their own expense if their voyages terminated abroad, for instance, but these stipulations did not apply to non–U.K.-domiciled seamen, foreign, or "coloured" seamen, even those on European articles.[41]

By the 1920s, Black seamen on standard articles most often found work on cargo ships, especially the "dirty little tramps," rather than in liners, which had shorter, regularly scheduled runs and paid the highest wages.[42] Black seamen stoked the furnaces of the now old-fashioned coal-fired steamships, rather than staffing the deck crews, which were more visible and enjoyed more pleasant working conditions.[43] When cleaner oil-powered ships were introduced, "The fireman ceases to be a laborer and becomes little more than a watchman"; these jobs were given to white sailors.[44] Even after World War II, reported Black seaman Hermon McKay to historian Tony Lane, many of the most desirable jobs, such as the steady jobs on Shell's oil tankers, were closed to Black men: "On those it's mostly company's men and it's mostly white."[45]

In the same years, as employers cut wages by hiring increasing numbers of colonized men, European competition was forcing technological innovation on British shipowners, as on their fellow industrialists on land.[46] The late-nineteenth-century transition from sailing to steamships involved new shipboard tasks and a new working environment—intensified supervision and deskilling that some seafarers experienced as an emasculating loss of control.[47] These transformations were accompanied by a new division of labor and a gendered and racialized redefinition of skill and status aboard ship.

The workforce of a steamship was divided into three distinct crews: sailors on deck, firemen below stoking the steam boilers that powered the ship, and, in passenger liners, stewards in the catering and housekeeping crew. Up to 50 percent of crewmen were now engaged in jobs not traditionally found on sailing ships—stoking, engineering, and catering.[48] Even deck crews' work had changed: complained "an old-time sailor" in 1917,

"The sailor's tools of trade are paintbrushes, squeegees, and wads of cotton waste. They know nothing of the seaman's art."[49] Although shipowners debated whether steamships attracted an improved "new race of seamen" or "injured seamanship," many deprecated these new shipboard tasks as less than proper seafaring.[50] In 1939, shipowner R. H. Thornton ridiculed the "romantic allusions to the great days of sail." He ruled merchant "firemen, greasers, oilers, engineers' helpers, cooks, scullions or stewards" out of the category "sailors," and argued that "even the sailors should rather be called deckhands [since] a high percentage of our able seamen have no such relationship with their craft as is found in a truly hereditary trade." He dismissed stokers as "the lowest ranks of unskilled labour."[51]

Stoking a steam engine with coal was indeed heavy, hot, dirty work. Yet it was also extraordinarily demanding of both skill and endurance, and white stokers could sometimes command more pay than deck sailors—especially in the tropics.[52] On large ships, the fireroom, "hotter than hell or Panama," might have twenty boilers with three or four fires apiece. At each boiler worked a fireman, responsible for throwing coal on the fires and for "slicing" them with a hundred-pound iron bar to keep them burning:[53]

> If full pressure of steam is to be maintained, [he] will need both skill and experience to keep his fires burning with a nice, even intensity over the whole grate area. He will need good coal too and nothing will break his heart so effectively as a run of ill-burning, heavily clinkering stuff, which must be raked and sliced continuously if it is not to stifle its own combustion.

For every three firemen, the "stokehold watch" carried two coal trimmers:

> The latter trim the coal in the main bunkers so that a regular flow is maintained through the exits on the level of the stokehold floor, thus providing a constant supply within reach of the fireman's shovel.[54]

In less efficient ships, coal passers supplied coal to the firemen by the wheelbarrowful: "you had to go as fast as you could to keep up with the firemen, because if the fireman needed to make a pitch and there was no coal you were fired." The pace of work, thus the speed of the ship, was maintained by the "leading hand" in the department:

> The fireman would often pass out from exhaustion and the heat, and the leading hand would go over to him and give him a kick, to see whether he was . . . just faking it.[55]

The work of the stewards varied according to the size and type of ship. On cargo steamers, which carried no passengers, a single steward, supported only by the cook, a mess boy, and an assistant for the officers' mess, was responsible for keeping crews fed, clothed, and fit to work. He ordered food and other supplies; kept accounts; supervised his subordinates in their cooking, cleaning, and other work; and provided personal service to the captain. Although in some respects demeaned as "women's work," these tasks entailed heavy responsibility and also, as feminist as well as maritime historians have emphasized, a degree of power inherent in the control and distribution of food and other supplies such as soap and cigarettes.[56] On passenger liners, in contrast, stewards' and catering crews could outnumber all other ranks combined, subordinate to one managerial chief steward.[57] Their work consisted mainly of housekeeping and personal service: cleaning decks and cabins, preparing and serving food and washing up afterwards, and attending to the personal needs of passengers and crew alike. Although defined as unskilled, the stewards' department could comprise myriad specialized service workers, including "stewardesses, butchers, bakers, cooks, bath attendants, masseurs, barbers, manicurists, printers, tailors, librarians, professional musicians and interpreters."[58]

In the eyes of employers and perhaps of the men themselves, each of these jobs carried a race- and gender-specific status, based on its definition as manly or menial, skilled or unskilled. Stewards' jobs were deprecated as "women's work," and stoking "is not seafaring . . . it is arduous, dirty and hot . . . with no sea-going traditions to support it."[59] These jobs were also typecast along racial lines, and Black seamen more often filled them while white men dominated deck crews.[60] The Blue Funnel lines put Chinese in catering and stokehold crews and white men on deck; the Palm Line used Nigerian catering departments, "Somali" firemen, and white deck crews.[61] Goans, although Portuguese rather than British subjects, had a longstanding monopoly of saloon crews.[62] Cunard refused to hire Black men for the highly visible deck crews of their passenger liners until Black seamen "fought for" and won access in the mid-twentieth century. "In Lamport's," reported Hermon McKay, "they'd only allow colour in the galley."[63]

Apologists for the industry alleged that Black men only filled the jobs that white seamen refused, while critics charged that employers used Black seamen to undercut white seamen's wages and working conditions.[64] Both were correct. It was precisely in the stokehold and in the tropics, for example, where white men demanded extra pay due to the heavy work and the unaccustomed, "unhealthy" climate, that Black men had the firmest foothold.⁶⁵ For it would be an error to see in these arrangements a division of labor that simply benefited white sailors at Black seamen's expense.

Employers mobilized a rhetoric of race, class, gender, and skill to devalue Black as well as white seamen's labor and to justify racist practices that kept them all disunited and vulnerable. Employers manipulated race and gender stereotypes to characterize Black and white seamen alike as less than men. Black men were depicted as irrational, emotional, cowardly, effeminate, weak, childlike, hypersexual, physically less "efficient," mentally immature, culturally exotic and backward. These images were used to justify low wages; stringent labor discipline; and inferior quarters, food, and other amenities.⁶⁶ Conversely, white men were depicted as unruly and undisciplined, deficient in the qualities that defined middle-class masculinity: strength and "pluck," independence, self-reliance, "generosity and chivalry, courage, and individualism."⁶⁷ Working-class white men's alleged deviation from this class-based ideal justified their replacement with Black men, as well as employers' resistance to wage raises for both.

Shipboard racial and cultural divisions were merely an extension of the rigid class distinctions between officers and men: "To them you were even less than the ordinary crew members who were white."⁶⁸ The imputed barbarism of the lower ranks, both Black and white, justified a host of petty distinctions between officers and the rank and file. In many ships officers got more and better quality soap, better quality food, more expensive cigarettes, an unlimited beer ration, and superior living accommodations at sea. The officers' bar was not only separate from that of the regular seamen but featured more comfortable and more attractive furnishings.⁶⁹

Similarly, employers routinely practiced segregation and fomented ill feeling among different departments aboard ship, reinforced by race segregation. Status and interdepartmental rivalries were intensified through the use of culturally or racially homogeneous departments and white officers, or supervisors recruited from different cultural groups than their subordinates.⁷⁰ Although all were paid much less than white seamen, imputed natural attributes justified typecasting certain nationalities or "races" into certain jobs. In the 1920s, lascar deck crews were commonly composed of Hindus from Bombay and other ports in Western India, and stokehold crews of Muslims from Bombay and Konkanis. By the 1940s, however, employers were recruiting cheaper labor from Eastern Indian ports, showing that rigid notions of appropriate work were flexible when profits were at stake. Punjabis and Pathans employed by the Peninsular and Oriental lines, for instance, were hired precisely because of their unfamiliarity with the work and its traditions, in an effort to undercut other Indian seamen.[71] Many West Africans entered the seafaring workforce at age 13 or so, possibly reinforcing their image as less than men, easily bullied, and logical replacements for cabin boys and apprentices.[72]

National Maritime Board regulations, by exempting all-Black crews from equal pay, rewarded race segregation and discouraged mixing "coloured" and white seamen in the same department. But then, these regulations themselves were formulated with employers' participation.[73] Race segregation enjoyed the endorsement of self-styled experts. Adam Kirkaldy deplored the "mixing in common quarters of men of very different habits and nationalities."[74] Employers, conversely, asserted smugly that crews so divided were "more amenable to discipline" and "easier for the masters and officers to . . . control."[75]

State- and union-sanctioned agreements provided a larger number of Black men to do the same job as a smaller white crew, on the pretext that Black men were less "efficient" or physically inferior, thus tying lower wages to imputed differences in competence and skill.[76] On some ships, Black crewmen routinely received inferior or leftover food, watered beer, cheaper cigarettes, and substandard accommodations compared with white crew members.[77] Such practices, accompanied by continual references to Black men's alleged "excitability" and "fatalism" and liner officers' habit of summoning crewmen by clapping their hands, suggest that Black seafarers were treated as beasts as much as men.[78]

Somewhat contradictorily, shipowners extolled Black seamen's sobriety, docility, diligence, and obedience, characteristics reminiscent of appropriate feminine behavior.[79] A common theme was the Black seaman's imputed tractability in comparison with the fractious freeborn—and unionized—Englishman: "Stokehold staffs recruited from Malta, the Punjab, British Somaliland and other British possessions . . . are better firemen and do not get drunk. The British fireman has never been satisfactory and never will be."[80] Thus, Black seamen were depicted simultaneously as inferior to and superior to white seamen; racial attributes were so defined as to justify penalizing both Black and white men as inadequate. As the reportage on the SS *Vestris* suggests, the boundaries between these dichotomized categories were fluid rather than fixed.

For white seamen were stigmatized with a different set of stereotypes that marked the boundaries between middle-class and working-class masculinity. If sobriety, discipline, and orderliness defined middle-class manhood, working-class masculinity was allegedly characterized by rebelliousness, drunkenness, indiscipline, and lack of control—manifested in "drinking and fighting," "swaggering and brawling."[81] Thornton commented, "If two new ships of identical amenity and space were occupied, one by an average British and the other by a Norwegian or Swedish crew, the latter would contrive to create and retain an atmosphere of modest but homely comfort, while the former might well degenerate into an unattractive squalor.... British seamen in short possess all the virtues and defects of their race."[82] And in 1919, a shipowner compelled to replace his Chinese crew with a British one complained that work which his Chinese crews completed in two days took the British crew three and one-half, commenting dolefully, "the British firemen do not seem to worry about steam as the Chinamen used to."[83]

As these examples illustrate, employers' rationales, like the inequalities they explained and helped to perpetuate, were riddled with internal contradictions and inconsistencies and were frustratingly elusive if taken at face value. Yet their appearance in the historical record cannot be ignored, for employers used them to legitimate and to "naturalize" exploitative relations of race, class, and gender. Far from a product of shipboard labor relations or maritime technology alone, their vocabulary derived credibility from class and gender relations in the mother country, as well as from colonial racial myths.

In Britain and in the colonies, women and colonized people performed roles involving "subordination, physical closeness and servicing of personal needs," products of what one scholar has called the "sexualization" of views of colonized people and a converse "exoticization" of Western views of sexuality. Women were depicted as mentally and physically frail; they allegedly "lacked . . . stability or assertiveness," while unreliable or irrational behavior was seen as the norm for "natives," innate characteristics that prevented them from attaining white men's levels of "achievement . . . or creative activity."[84] In the writings of Victorian men, indeed, women were symbolically interchangeable with animals, Black slaves, and the natural world. All were seen as dangerous, inferior, dirty and polluting, and closer to nature.[85] The shifting polarities that created analogues among race, class, and gender appear in employers' rationales for the racial division of labor on British ships. In the all-male workplace, gendered differences and the gendered division of labor were projected onto

Black men, thus invoking mutually reinforcing gendered as well as racial stereotypes. Gendered notions were reinforced by images of colonized men as bestial, exotic, infantilized, and dehumanized.

Categories of shipboard work were not, however, simply degraded because Black men did them and because Black men were considered less than men. Rather, shipboard tasks that were already defined as unmanly—deskilled or feminized—were assigned to Black men. Catering, for example, was gendered as feminine even when white men did it, for on ships as ashore, the work of reproduction, food preparation, cleaning, and personal service, was considered "women's work." Men who did it were stigmatized as unmanly: Joseph Cotter, militant General President of the National Union of Ships' Stewards, Cooks, Butchers and Bakers in the early 1920s, had a reputation among trade unionists for emotional outbursts that earned him the affectionate moniker, "Crazy Joe."[86] Consistent with the feminized stereotype, catering and housekeeping crews of certain lines were alleged havens for homosexuals and transvestites.[87] The connection between feminization and racialization was reinforced by the colonial legacy in which Black men performed personal service for white men as houseboys, house servants, and, in the Americas, house slaves.[88] As late as the mid-twentieth century, Black seamen could be insulted by white officers' expectations that they launder scivvies and carry luggage.[89]

Gendered differentiation reinforced the other ways in which employers justified divisions among their diverse workforce. Black men's relegation to the stokehold was accompanied by a redefinition of the job as unskilled, for which they were paid less than white men. Natural "racial" attributes superseded skill as the qualification for the job: "tropical races" were said to withstand the heat of the furnaces better, making extra pay unnecessary. Indeed, imputed tolerance for heat in itself signified inferiority. Employing Black men was represented as a racially rational "solution to the shortage and unsuitability of Europeans for work in the fiery heat of a steamer's stokehold in tropical waters.... It would be strange indeed if a man born and bred in the Tropics were not better able to stand heat than a Nordic specimen."[90]

When Black men did it, the work was also bestialized, described as "a job ... which requires ... the brute force of a gorilla."[91] If, as feminist scholars argue, male workers have salvaged a sense of masculinity from deskilled labor by measuring their work against "women's work," white sailors were perhaps consoled for the deskilling of deck sailoring by Black men's relegation to stoking and catering. At a meeting of the Newport

Trades Council, a Mr. G. Williams, speaking for the majority, declared, "They had to recognise the fact that the Asiatic was not as good a man as the Britisher, and so not worth the same money."[92]

The racialization of shipboard work resembled the process whereby certain types of labor were defined as women's work—"gendered feminine"—while other work has been gendered masculine. The gendering of skill has involved several simultaneous processes: historically, male workers have monopolized skilled work and relegated women to unskilled jobs and to the home. When specific tasks have been deskilled, women have been recruited to perform them. In addition, women's skills have not been recognized as skills, because they have been seen as "natural" attributes.[93] Much of women's work outside the home has been defined and devalued as mere extensions of their "natural" maternal and domestic function: childcare, food processing, and clothing production.[94] Finally, there is something of a dialectic or a feedback effect: when women do a job, it is frequently defined as unskilled, or as less skilled than when men do it.[95] The racialization of certain shipboard tasks and the workers who did them was not only similar to but arguably part of the same process of naturalizing and devaluing—a process that deprecated Black men's work along with their masculinity.

Understanding this reveals the agenda behind shipowner R. H. Thornton's seemingly innocuous praise for "the genuine seafaring peasantry of the Indian, African or Chinese coasts, who," he argued, possessed "an hereditary aptitude for the sea"—a natural aptitude, not a skill for which employers might expect to pay well.[96] Colonized men's suitability for heat and heavy work were only prominent examples of a complex series of imputedly inborn racial characteristics. A mid-twentieth-century description of "Types of Indian Seamen" reads like a seed catalogue, with Islamic Malabaris described as "superb seamen and amenable to discipline," Islamic Sylhetis able to "stand up well to hard work and cold weather," and Ratnagiris with "fine constitutions."[97] Since some definitions of working-class masculinity were linked to skill, while femininity was characterized by lack of skill or natural attributes, there appear to be not just similarities but mutual reinforcement among the feminization, "racialization," and deskilling of shipboard jobs.

Turn-of-the-century definitions of masculinity, indeed, involved contradictory demands for independence and self-discipline, initiative, and emotional and sexual control. Class distinctions were also infused with racial and gendered connotations. Thus, it was not difficult for British maritime employers to measure their employees, Black and white, against an internally contradictory as well as race- and class-specific ideal of British manhood and find them all wanting, particularly when power and profit were at stake. Working-class men's imputed "rowdiness," "loafing," "irregular habits," and "hooliganism," for example, were portrayed as evidence of insufficient manhood, even of effeminacy.[98]

Employers' dichotomous view of Black seamen was echoed in an equally inconsistent view of white seamen—particularly British seamen. Shipowners not only promoted racial stereotypes about colonized people but also exploited a mythology of British race, "the Imperial Race, the Island Race, the Island Breed."[99] During and after World War I, they celebrated merchant seamen's wartime heroism, invoking the "reckless courage and daring" of Drake, Frobisher, and Raleigh.[100] Romanticizing seafaring as essential to Britain's posterity, shipowners exaggerated their industry's importance beyond its waning economic significance, attempting to identify the national interest with their private agendas: "Our losses on the sea must be made up. . . . We are a maritime race. The sea is in our being."[101]

Praise for seamen's wartime sacrifices coexisted uncomfortably with fierce complaints about the wages the maritime hero could now command, constituting a threat to profits and to class distinctions: wage increases, employers complained, had enabled "the industrial classes . . . to compete for commodities, and thus artificially add to the cost of living."[102] Employers sought state assistance in their efforts to flood the labor market with underpayable apprentices in terms that identified British "racial" characteristics with maritime skills: "Thanks to the hereditary salt in the blood, we have an unlimited supply of embryo seamen."[103] Comparing maritime Britain to Athens and Carthage, they invoked turn-of-the-century fears of impending racial and imperial decline, calling for "a steady supply of respectable British lads to respond to the call which is in their blood."[104] "Our home-bred seamen have first call for employment on British ships. . . . It is their birthright."[105]

Shipowners justified hiring colonized seamen by arguing that they possessed virtues that white seamen lacked—docility, diligence, sobriety. Conversely, and contradictorily, employers argued that they must underpay and minutely control these docile, industrious workers because they were deficient in masculinity: the very traits that made them tractable, thus superior to white seamen, also made them inferior—"in an emergency they are practically useless"—for it was in this hour of crisis that the

Englishman excelled:[106] "Not a winter passes but brings evidence of their ability to meet with an every-day, undramatic heroism the cold-blooded perils of the sea. Meanwhile, from the standpoint of domesticity, they are a somewhat casual and shiftless community."[107] By splitting white seamen from Black and defining each as deficient in some essential characteristics of manhood, employers justified replacing white sailors with colonized contract workers and paying both categories less.[108]

Employers correctly stressed the intimate connections between British merchant seafaring and British imperialism. The gendered racial division of labor that took shape aboard British ships was a response to Britain's faltering imperial power in the face of foreign challengers. The growing presence of Black seamen in British ships was the result of employers' efforts to maintain their declining profits by splitting the labor force along racial lines and threatening each group with replacement by the other should their demands escalate. Shipboard labor relations also reflected imperial race relations and domestic class and gender relations. Employers found a ready source of cheaper labor in colonized seafarers, and an easily adaptable rationale in the colonial mythology of racial and cultural difference, itself infused with gendered and class-specific assumptions. In addition to defaming Black seamen as less than men—as effeminate, childlike, bestial—employers justified these inequalities with reference to the "lower standard of living" in the colonies. The attendant implication that Black men were physically and culturally inferior justified withholding the prerogatives of manhood: autonomy, authority, civic rights, and a wage sufficient to support a wife and home.

Arguments about racial proclivities were used not to drive Black sailors out of the industry—far from it—but to enforce the division of shipboard labor along racial lines. Gendered stereotypes legitimated a division of labor and racial wage hierarchy that not only saved employers money, prolonging the life of the deteriorating industry, but enabled them to better control and more flexibly deploy their workforce, white as well as Black. Contrasting images of British sailors as a "maritime race" with "salt in the blood" and stereotypes of feminized and childlike "tropical races," shipowners refashioned racial images borrowed from the colonial setting in pursuit of their immediate purposes of power and profit. Manipulating images derived from domestic and colonial race, class, and gender relations, they strove to extend the vulnerability of colonized labor to workers in Britain.

This process was apparent in Black men's assignment to women's work and to unskilled work, and in the defamation of white seamen. While the racial and gender inferiority of women and the colonized were emphasized to justify male ruling-class dominance, the class-specific "drunkenness" and "indiscipline" of working-class white men were stressed to justify hiring Black crews. Like the feminization of colonized men, splitting Black from white sailors was part of the process of dichotomizing, naturalizing, and hierarchizing that accompanied political and economic domination, or, as Black activist J. W. Ford of the *Negro Worker* put it, "a system of racial oppression, slander and lies."[109]

At sea as on land, manmade divisions of race and gender masqueraded as natural ones, undermining working people's potential solidarity and sustaining employers' power and imperial domination. White seafarers' fears of emasculation, of deskilling and loss of control in the process of industrial and technological change, were assuaged through the racialization of shipboard "women's work." The relations of race, class, gender, and skill that structured British society in the metropole and in the colonies also shaped the shipboard experience of the "maritime race."

LILLIAN NAYDER

9

Sailing Ships and Steamers, Angels and Whores
History and Gender in Conrad's Maritime Fiction

While Laura Tabili uses historical records to analyze race, gender, and class relations in the British merchant marine, Lillian Nayder examines how such relations are represented by Joseph Conrad, one of the most widely read authors of maritime literature. In particular, she explores the way that Conrad uses gendered schemes to rewrite social history, displacing the threat of class conflict with that of subordination to the feminine. Nayder contends that Conrad, responding to the industrialization of British shipping at the end of the nineteenth century, depicts the shift from sail to steam as an "emasculating" development, as the subservient sailing ship gives way to the unruly and self-propelled steamer. Although Conrad's maritime world is traditionally viewed as an exclusively male arena, Nayder invites us to read his stories of adventure and conquest as domestic narratives as well.

IN WHAT IS PERHAPS Joseph Conrad's best-known novel, *Lord Jim* (1900), the steamer *Patna* is badly disabled during a collision in the eastern seas, and the officers and crew disgracefully abandon their ship, leaving eight hundred Muslim passengers to fend for themselves. When Jim, the first mate, is tried for his actions, the assessor at his trial speculates that the ship hit "something floating awash, say a water-logged wreck."[1] But the sunken object with which the steamship collides is never properly identified. As Conrad's narrator explains, it proves impossible for the court to determine "how the *Patna* came by her hurt" (56). Yet while the specific object that damages the *Patna* is not identified, the general social conditions that place the ship in peril are clear enough. Immediately before the collision occurs, the disgruntled engineer surfaces from below with "the tale of his complaints" (22) and confronts the sailors, whom he perceives as members of a useless and predatory leisure class.[2] When the ship is struck, the engineer is himself attacked, falling to the deck "as though he had been clubbed from behind" (26). By using class conflict and social violence to frame the collision scene, Conrad subtly suggests that the antagonism between engineers and sailors on board the steamer is what threatens to wreck the ship of state.

A Victorian sailor as well as a novelist,[3] Conrad participated in the industrial revolution that transformed the British merchant marine in the second half of the nineteenth century—the gradual replacement of sailing ships with the more reliable and profitable steamers.[4] For Conrad, as for many of his contemporaries, the industrialization of the merchant marine appeared to have dire social consequences. On the one hand, the transformation from sail to steam was held responsible for the declining caliber of the men, who no longer seemed willing or able to respond to emergencies at sea—who had, in effect, lost the skills, endurance, and courage possessed by those "trained before the mast."[5] "A few months in steam rusts a sailor," Frank T. Bullen explained in 1900, for "what is wanted in a steamer is only a burly labourer who is able to steer."[6] On the other hand, problems of class conflict and social unrest in the merchant marine were attributed to the introduction of the "black gangs" hired to work the new steam engines.

Although life on sailing ships was by no means as harmonious as Conrad and other sea writers would have us believe, and although the widely celebrated solidarity among sailors has been effectively called into question in recent years, there is little doubt that class tensions were exacerbated by the advent of steam and the new division of labor it necessitated. While the engineers and firemen were "usually drawn from a still lower class in the social scale than the deck hands,"[7] they were better fed and more highly paid than both the deck hands *and* the officers, and had eight hours off between watches rather than four.[8] Thus, it is not surprising that the steamship divided workers against themselves. And because the proper operation of steamships largely depended on the efforts of the specialized workers who ran the engines, dissatisfied engineers proved more willing to challenge the authority of the captain and officers than disgruntled sailors had been. Unlike the deck hands, furthermore, the engineers were trained on shore and, in consequence, remained "in close touch with powerful trade unions" back home.[9] For Conrad, the new social relations established on steamships embodied the pitfalls of an industrialized economy in which traditional forms of authority are undermined and the self-interest of a decadent working class prevails. As he explains in his *Notes on Life and Letters* (1921), the firemen and trimmers who maintain marine boilers are an "unthrifty" and "unruly" mob, "a crowd of men *in* the ship but not *of* her."[10]

Conrad responded to this revolution at sea by idealizing life on the sailing ship.[11] Rewriting history in such a way that the harsh realities of life under sail are obscured, Conrad promotes an ideal that both maritime historians and literary critics have set out to demythologize. Complaining of the "nostalgic sentimentality" with which Conrad treats his sailing ships, on which the men are consistently unified, content, and obedient, they have undertaken to reconstruct the social history that underlies Conrad's glorified "distortions," pointing to the dangers, degradation, and isolation to which Victorian sailors were exposed, as well as to the growing problems of incompetence and undermanning.[12] They describe Conrad's idealized vision of social obedience and solidarity at sea as a wish fulfillment of sorts, "a plea for order and community . . . in the face of the 'modernizing habits' of individualism and class antagonism."[13] As Fredric Jameson notes, the sea in Conrad's fiction is "the privileged place of the strategy of containment," a place where threatening social realities are repressed. The dreary life of the capitalist workplace and its antagonistic class relations are left behind by Conrad's mariners, among whom "human relations [are] presented in all their ideal formal purity."[14]

What these critics and historians fail to note, however, is that Conrad retells and recasts maritime social history by sexualizing his social anxieties as well as by idealizing and repressing class relations. In response to what he perceives as the socially destructive transition from sail to steam, Conrad not only mythologizes the solidarity and obedience of sailors; he also transforms class conflicts at sea into problems of gender relations. Adhering to an ideological pattern well established in English fiction by the late nineteenth century, Conrad assuages his primary, social anxieties by feminizing the working class. In Conrad's maritime fiction, as in the domestic fiction of Dickens and the Brontës, "class conflict comes to be represented as a matter of sexual misconduct," a problem more easily solved than that of social unrest, by means of the discipline and surveillance of women.[15]

Throughout his sea narratives, Conrad draws on the polarized stereotypes of Victorian womanhood in order to provide a reassuring explanation of the shift from sail to steam. Although he conceives of this shift in socioeconomic terms, as the inevitable change from traditional, precapitalist social relations to the antagonistic class relations of an industrialized economy, he represents this shift in sexual terms. In effect, the difference between sail and steam becomes the difference between two types of feminine behavior, that of the angel and the whore.[16] Confronted with the specter of social unrest and the rise of a resentful proletariat at sea, Conrad resolves his fears by imagining class relations as marital relations. He turns from the political conflicts between a captain and his men to the romantic conflicts between a captain and his ship, displacing the dangers of working-class resentment with the threat of female insubordination. Although Conrad's maritime world is generally understood to be an "exclusively masculine community" where "women have no entry,"[17] Conrad invites us to read his adventure stories as domestic narratives that explore the tensions between captains and their troublesome "wives."[18]

I

This is not a marriage story. It wasn't so bad as that with me. My action, rash as it was, had more the character of divorce — almost of desertion. For no reason on which a sensible person could put a finger I threw up my job — chucked my berth — left the ship of which the worst that could be said was that she was a steamship and therefore, perhaps, not entitled to that blind loyalty which.... However, it's no use trying to put a gloss on what even at the time I myself half suspected to be a caprice.

—Joseph Conrad, *The Shadow-Line* (1916–17)

Conrad critics have long noted his antipathy to steamers, attributing it to the industrial nature of these ships. Observing that Conrad's maritime fiction consistently disparages steamships, they point out that he watched as steam power replaced sailors with engineers, and thus brought to sea the conflicts characteristic of factory life on shore.[19] "There is not much difference now between a deck and a factory hand," Conrad complained to his friend Captain A. W. Phillips in 1924.[20] In particular, the sounds of the steamer's engine room in Conrad's stories are menacing; they remind us that the ship has been industrialized, and that a party of disgruntled workers is present below deck. In *Lord Jim*, for example, "short metallic clangs burst ... out suddenly in the depths of the ship, the harsh scrape of a shovel, the violent slam of a furnace-door, exploded brutally, as if the men handling the mysterious things below had their breasts full of fierce anger" (19).

But if the "short metallic clangs" from below serve to acknowledge unpleasant social realities, the sexualized throbbing of the engine room serves to obscure them—to divert our attention from social to sexual dangers. Operated by an engineer who is "flushed" and "feminine" in appearance, the machinery—with its "slow," "gentle," yet "powerful movements"—recalls "the functions of a living organism."[21] Characterized by her "big body," the steamer "pulsates" and "throbs" as she "shoulders [her] arrogant way against the great rollers."[22] Thus, if the engine room in Conrad's steamer is the site of class unrest, it is also the locus of a threatening female sexuality.

As both literary critics and historians have shown, female sexuality was perceived as a subversive source of power in the Victorian period. Figures of sexually powerful yet demonic women abound in Victorian writing, where they challenge and resist patriarchal authority. The ideal Victorian woman was a de-eroticized being, her sexual activity limited to a purely reproductive function within the bounds of marriage. The so-called angel in the house, a Victorian icon, is meek and self-sacrificing, an asexual woman who serves rather than threatens the patriarchal status quo. Although her husband's sexual drive is active and spontaneous, her own is dormant. Only women considered pathological or deviant exhibit the sexual aggression allotted to men. This point is emphasized by the Victorian physician William Acton, an international expert on venereal disease and prostitution, in whose view "the majority of women (happily for them) are not very much troubled with sexual feeling of any kind": "What men are habitually, women are exceptionally. It is too true, I admit, as the divorce courts show, that there are some few women who have sexual desires so strong that they surpass those of men. . . . I admit, of course, the existence of sexual excitement terminating even in nymphomania, a form of insanity which those accustomed to visit lunatic asylums must be fully conversant with."[23]

In light of such beliefs, it seems only appropriate that the narrator of *The Shadow-Line* chooses to "divorce" a sexualized steamer at the outset of his story. Despite the seemingly irrational nature of his decision, he has good reason to "chuck his berth": "she was a steamship and therefore, perhaps, not entitled to . . . [his] loyalty." In particular, the narrator explains, it is the steamer's "internal propulsion" that has driven him away: "if it had not been for her internal propulsion," he observes, she would have been "worthy of any man's love."[24]

An emblem of female sexuality—powerful, autonomous, and devouring—the steamer's "internal propulsion" renders her "unworthy" of love in Conrad's eyes; what Conrad dislikes about the steamer, he explains in

The Mirror of the Sea (1905), is "the power she carries within herself."[25] Adapting for his own ends the stereotype of the powerful, sexualized female, Conrad engenders his social concerns in *The Shadow-Line*. At the outset of the narrative, Conrad refers to the "rebellious discontent" of those on board the steamer (8) and dramatizes a hostile encounter between the first mate and the second engineer (6). When his protagonist leaves the steamer and assumes command of a sailing ship, he meets a more experienced captain, who warns him of the deskilling caused by the advent of steam and fumes about mariners who are "afraid of the sails" (31). But these issues of incompetence and insubordination in the merchant marine are no sooner raised than they are obscured. Although the new captain "can't muster more than three hands to do anything" on board his sailing ship (102), Conrad attributes the noncompliant state of the men to disease rather than inability or insurrection. Rather than pursuing the class implications initially raised by his narrative—the captain's fear that his men want to tear him "limb from limb" (96)—Conrad recasts it as a cautionary tale about female empowerment and rebellion.

In *The Shadow-Line*, Conrad's fear of female sexuality and the threat it poses to male authority is suggested by his depiction of the steamer, with her "internal propulsion." But informing his treatment of the steamer is a powerful, sexualized woman on shore. This woman has seduced the captain of a sailing ship—the man whom the narrator is hired to replace. Recounting the story of his predecessor's seduction, as it was told to him by the first mate, Mr. Burns, the narrator simultaneously acknowledges and displaces the class anxieties that inform Conrad's fiction:

> In Haiphong . . . [the captain] got himself, in Mr. Burns' own words, "mixed up" with some woman. Mr. Burns had had no personal knowledge of that affair, but positive evidence of it existed in the shape of a photograph taken in Haiphong. Mr. Burns found it in one of the drawers in the captain's room.
>
> In due course I, too, saw that amazing human document (I even threw it overboard later). There he sat with his hands reposing on his knees . . . and by his side towered an awful, mature, white female with rapacious nostrils and a cheaply ill-omened stare in her enormous eyes. She was disguised in some semi-oriental, vulgar, fancy costume. She resembled a low-class medium or one of those women who tell fortunes by cards for half-a-crown. And yet she was striking. A professional sorceress from the slums. (58–59)

Although this passage articulates Conrad's fears of the urban working class and the power its members have assumed over traditional figures of authority, his anxieties are expressed in a pointedly sexual way. "Towering" over the captain, the "low-class.... sorceress" has established her dominion over the man who, in Conrad's view, should be her master. In comparing her to a "low-class medium.... from the slums," Conrad draws upon a figure familiar to his original readers, one in whom the dangers of working-class revolt are linked with those of feminist rebellion. In the spiritualist movement of the late nineteenth century, the seance served a subversive political function: it enabled women to appropriate the power and autonomy generally reserved for men. By assuming a masculine or an upper-class persona, the female medium could circumvent the rigid Victorian norms of social class and gender and could speak with the voice of authority. Furthermore, the medium's trance—her possession by various spirits—helped to redefine conceptions of female sexuality, extending the limits of women's sexual life in a socially acceptable way.[26]

Unlike the captain who has preceded him, and who is seduced and emasculated by a sexualized woman, the narrator of *The Shadow-Line* maintains his authority by associating with an asexual and angelic female figure. Having divorced an internally powered steamer, he wisely "remarries" a sailing ship the second time around. Whereas Conrad represents the steamer as a demonic and rebellious female body, he imagines the sailing ship as an angelic and subservient female soul. Sailing ships "lead ... a sort of unearthly existence," Conrad tells his readers. Made of "gossamer," they are angelic beings "held to obedience"—wholly dependent on the masculine winds and on the seamen for their movements. They thus provide a marked contrast to the steamer, which is largely independent of "man power"[27] and is both autonomous and promiscuous in Conrad's eyes. Like a "loose" woman, the steamer can be "loaded" by anyone, and in virtually any way: "Her cargo is not stowed in any sense; it is simply dumped into her through six hatchways, more or less ... with clatter and hurry and racket and heat, in a cloud of steam and a mess of coal-dust." But the sailing ship resembles a "modest bride," "diffident, lying very quiet, with her side nestling shyly against the wharf," and must be "loaded" with care.[28]

In Conrad's fiction, this female ideal serves an important, though largely unspoken, function—it enables the captain to bolster his patriarchal authority in the face of diminishing social control. Thus, in *The Shadow-Line,* Conrad's idealized conception of the "modest" sailing ship allows him to "solve" the problem of unrest and disaffection among the men. Although the captain "can't muster more than three hands to do anything," the ship is ready to serve her master. When the narrator gains his appointment as captain and is introduced to his "lover" (46), he is immediately empowered by her, since her will is utterly subordinate to his own: "A ship! My ship! She was mine, more absolutely mine for possession and care than anything in the world; an object of responsibility and devotion. She was there waiting for me, spellbound, unable to move, to live, to get out into the world (till I came), like an enchanted princess" (40).

Like his predecessor's relationship to the human seductress, the narrator's relationship to his ship is described in sexual terms. Nonetheless, their physical intimacy is rendered nonthreatening: while the narrator receives physical satisfaction from his ship, the ship herself—like the de-eroticised and subservient Victorian wife—merely suffers through her "loading":

> That illusion of life and character which charms one in men's finest handiwork radiated from her. An enormous baulk of teak-wood timber swung over her hatchway; lifeless matter, looking heavier and bigger than anything aboard of her. When they started lowering it the surge of the tackle sent a quiver through her from water-line to the tucks up the fine nerves of her rigging, as though she had shuddered at the weight. It seemed cruel to load her so....
>
> Putting my foot on her deck for the first time, I received the feeling of deep physical satisfaction. Nothing could equal the fullness of that moment, the ideal completeness of that emotional experience.... My rapid glance ran over her, enveloped, appropriated the form concreting the abstract sentiment of my command.... In all the parts of the world washed by navigable waters our relation to each other would be the same—and more intimate than there are words to express in the language. (49–50)

Utterly passive and dependent on her male lover, the sailing ship waits for him, "unable to move, to live" until he arrives. An object that can be "enveloped," "appropriated," and "possessed," she provides only the "illusion" of life, and thus the captain can safely enjoy her charms; she gives concrete form to his "abstract sentiment of... command."[29]

She is, furthermore, not simply an object, but a "man made" one at that, an example of "men's finest handiwork." As such, she defuses the dangers posed to social order by the growth of industrialism and by what Conrad perceives to be the uncontrollable force of female nature. As fine handiwork, Conrad's sailing ship is distinguished from the manufactured steamers, whose parts came from iron foundries and whose construction required highly specialized manufacturing facilities that gradually destroyed the local shipbuilding communities that Conrad valued.[30] At the same time, the ship's "man-made" status safely mediates her femininity; she is the product of male culture rather than a threatening manifestation of female nature. Subscribing to the patriarchal ideology that associates women with nature and men with culture, Conrad speaks of woman as "a force of nature, blind in its strength and capricious in its power." Like electricity, she can be "captured" by a man and used to "light . . . him on his way," to "warm . . . his home," and to "cook his dinner for him"; yet "the greater demand he makes on [her] . . . the more likely [she] is to turn on him and burn him to a cinder."[31] But ships, unlike women, are born of men, and hence dissociated from the destructive force of Mother Nature; Conrad describes them as a "perfect brood" to which "the thundering peal of hammers beating upon iron . . . gives birth."[32] Indebted to their fathers rather than their mothers for life, they bear witness to the strength of patriarchy instead of undermining it.

Despite her preindustrial and patriarchal origins, however, the sailing ship in *The Shadow-Line* temporarily behaves like the rapacious woman on shore; once under way, she too resists the captain's control. He feels "bewitched" (84) because he has difficulty sailing her beyond the Island of Koh-ring, and because once he succeeds in getting her out to sea, so many of his men have been laid low by fever that she threatens to "take the wheel out of [the helmsman's] hands" (112). "We won't be able to do anything with her," the captain warns his men: "She's running away with us now. All we can do is to steer her" (123). Yet if *The Shadow-Line* registers the threat posed to the captain's authority, it ultimately affirms his ability to put down insubordination. Despite the captain's anxieties about "handling" the "wildly rushing ship full of dying men" (124–25), her struggle for autonomy is foiled by her very design. Unlike a steamer operating upon her own power, by means of "internal propulsion," the sailing ship depends upon men for her movement. Thus, the captain can control his ship by manipulating her sails. "Haul[ing] the mainsail close up," "squar[ing] the mainyard," fastening the leech-line, and "letting go all the sheets and halliards by the run," he safely brings the ship into port (109, 126).

In *The Shadow-Line*, the physical anatomy of the sailing ship ensures her subordination; so, too, does her economic purpose. Unlike the engineers and firemen on Conrad's steamers, who persistently complain of their wages, and who jealously compare their earnings to those of sailors and officers, his idealized ship is a female worker who selflessly labors for the good of her master.[33] "Backed by the fidelity of ships"—"willing" and "untiring servants"—men "wrest from [the ocean] the fortune of their house, the dominion of their world."³⁴ Though, in "The Nigger of the *Narcissus*" (1897), Mr. Baker tells his men that they must "take care of the ship," the ship ultimately serves the men, and Conrad compares her labor to "the unselfish toil of a delicate woman."³⁵ As we will see, such "unselfish toil" is rare among Conrad's women, who serve to displace not only the threat of class unrest in the merchant marine but also the problem of economic exploitation as well.

II

Many years ago . . . strong men with childlike hearts were faithful to [the sea], were content to live by its grace—to die by its will. That was the sea before the time when the French mind set the Egyptian muscle in motion and produced a dismal but profitable ditch. Then a great pall of smoke sent out by countless steamboats was spread over the restless mirror of the Infinite. . . . The hearts changed; the men changed. The once loving and devoted servants went out armed with fire and iron, and conquering the fear of their own hearts became a calculating crowd of cold and exacting masters.

—Conrad, *An Outcast of the Islands* (1896)

Representing the transition from sail to steam as if it reenacts the Fall of mankind, Conrad attributes the loss of maritime "innocence" in the nineteenth century to the construction of the Suez Canal—"the time when the French mind set the Egyptian muscle in motion and produced a dismal but profitable ditch." As Conrad suggests, the opening of the canal in 1869 did, indeed, revolutionize the merchant marine by enlarging the steamer's sphere. Shortening the sea distance from Britain to Bombay by nearly six thousand miles, and between Britain and Shanghai by three thousand, the canal gave steam the economic advantage over sail on the longer trade routes to the East as well as the shorter routes to the Continent.³⁶ Yet insofar as Conrad idealizes the economic "innocence" of life under sail, he misrepresents this transition. Although the merchant marine always operated for profit and made possible the lucrative expansion of the empire, Conrad suggests that before the advent of steam, those who "followed the sea" had higher motives: childlike, faithful, and content with their hard lot, they were above financial calculations. For the sailors in his sea fiction, work is an end in itself, an "artistic" activity undertaken for pleasure rather than profit.³⁷ Obscuring the economic and power relations among masters, officers, deck hands, and shipowners, and eliding the turbulent labor history of the merchant marine, Conrad promotes a spiritual ideal of sail in which mariners and shipowners follow a "calling" or "vocation" and are alike "untainted by the pride of possession":³⁸

No seaman ever cherished a ship, even if she belonged to him, merely because of the profit she put in his pocket. No one, I think, ever did; for a ship-owner, even of the best, has always been outside the pale of that sentiment embracing in a feeling of intimate, equal fellowship the ship and the man, backing each other against the implacable, if sometimes dissembled, hostility of their world of waters.[39]

Into this "intimate, equal fellowship" between man and sailing ship at sea, the captain's wife intrudes, bringing with her the divisions and antagonisms that Conrad associates with the advent of steam, the profit motive, and claims to private property. While the men on Conrad's sailing ships are financial innocents, their wives certainly are not, and to them Conrad attributes the exploitation of maritime labor. Insofar as Conrad acknowledges the existence of exploited workers under sail, they are men victimized by greedy female "masters." Thus, while Conrad displaces class conflict with feminist rebellion, he also depicts women as members of a powerful leisure class, the unproductive "passengers" on board his ship of state.[40] The wives in Conrad's maritime fiction are often characterized as heartless managers, and their husbands as the laborers whom they oppress and exploit.

Not surprisingly, the labor problems that Conrad associates with industrialism are most obvious on his steamers. Yet even here the wife is held responsible for the exploitation of the men. In "Typhoon" (1900–1901), the sufferings of the working class on board the steamer *Nan-Shan* are suggested in two ways—by the condition of the men in the engine room, who are choked with ashes and who "toil . . . mutely, as if [their] tongue[s] had been cut out" (346), and by the injuries sustained during a violent storm by the two hundred coolies whom Captain MacWhirr is transporting to their homes in Fo-Kien "after a few years of work in various tropical colonies" (297). But instead of criticizing the merchant marine as an agent of industry and empire—for treating those in the engine room as mute beasts of burden, and the coolies as human "cargo" (362)—Conrad discredits these figures by feminizing them and recasts the problem of exploitation as a marital one. Conrad portrays the languid coolies on the deck of the *Nan-Shan* as they pose in "girlish" attitudes, plaiting their hair (307), and he notes that the third engineer below, with coal dust settled on his eyelids, has "something of a feminine, exotic and fascinating aspect" (340). He then collapses the economic and social distinctions among those characters who retain their masculinity by shifting our attention to the exploitation of men by women—in particular, that of the working-class captain by his socially superior wife. While her husband risks his life at sea in order to finance her pleasures, Mrs. MacWhirr spends her days shopping and luxuriates in her suburban home at his expense:

> He paid five-and-forty pounds a year for [her house], and did not think the rent too high, because Mrs. MacWhirr . . . was admittedly ladylike, and in the neighborhood considered as "quite superior." . . . She reclined in a plush-bottomed and gilt hammock-chair near a tiled fireplace, with Japanese fans on the mantel and a glow of coals in the grate. . . . Lifting her hands, she glanced wearily here and there into the many pages [of her husband's letter]. . . . She had a movement of impatience. He was always thinking of coming home. He had never had such a good salary before. What was the matter now? (303, 358)

The exploitation of male workers by the members of this female leisure class is even more apparent in those stories in which Conrad's captains bring their wives to sea. In *Chance* (1913), for example, the male community on the sailing ship *Ferndale* is "brotherly," a spiritual order in which social oppression and the claims of private property are unknown—but only until the arrival of Captain Anthony's wife. Flora's presence on her husband's ship divides the men against their captain and establishes a class system among them. The class divisions that result from her presence are suggested by the structural alterations that are made to the ship's cabin in order to accommodate her:

> Renovated certainly the saloon of the *Ferndale* was to receive the "strange woman." . . . The workmen had gone only last night; and the last piece of work they did was the hanging of the heavy curtains which looped midway the length of the saloon—divided it in two if released, cutting off the after end with its companionway leading direct on the poop, from the forepart with its outlet on the deck; making a privacy within a privacy, as though Captain Anthony could not place obstacles enough between his new happiness and the men who shared his life at sea. (251)

In his history of domestic relations, Friedrich Engels attributes the origins of the class system to the invention of monogamy, which in his view created the first form of private property: the wife.[41] Like Engels, Conrad associates monogamous marital relations with the origins of a class system—but men rather than women constitute the underclass. With Flora on board, the officers are "kept out of the cabin against the custom of the service" (200–201), "chucked out of the saloon as if [they] weren't good enough to sit down to meat with that woman" (207), and the men are slighted and ignored. The captain himself is relegated to this masculine lower class, failing to give his usual commands from the moment his wife comes on board (192). The captain's happiness proves elusive, as he, like his men, is excluded from his rightful place in the cabin. Economically exploited by his wife and unable to sexually possess her, "the poor captain hangs out to port on a couch," although "the starboard cabin is the bedroom one" (214). Parodying the notion that women, by virtue of their sex, are "the predestined victim[s] of conditions created by men's selfish passions . . . and abominable tyranny" (43), Conrad instead dramatizes "subjugated masculinity" (68). Flora is described as a "not very congenial passenger" aboard the *Ferndale* (212), as yet another member of the feminine leisure class; appropriately, her cabin is "fitted up afresh like a blessed palace . . . as if the Queen were coming with us" (214).

But while Conrad represents the wives on his ships as queens who dominate and divide the male community, he represents the ships themselves as female workers who serve their masters rather than exploiting them. Although Conrad characterizes the ship in *The Shadow-Line* as "a high-class vessel," she is "high-class" in a very restricted sense—as "a creature of high-breed." What the narrator perceives as her superiority over the "low-class" woman from the slums is, in reality, the mark of her subservience to him: "Amongst her companions," "all bigger than herself, she looked like an Arab steed in a string of cart-horses" (49).[42] And while, in "Typhoon," Mrs. MacWhirr reclines in luxury, the *Nan-Shan* "labor[s] heavily in . . . mountainous black waters" (351), "paying with [her] hard tumbling the price of her life" (355). Like Mrs. MacWhirr, she is described in the act of "spending," yet her expenditure is the mark of her self-sacrifice.

Furthermore, the ship—unlike the wife—is shared by all the men on board her and is passed on from one captain to the next. Unlike the exclusive relation between a captain and his wife, which "taints" the male community with conceptions of private property, the relation between the ship and men is polyandrous. As common property, she enables the male community to remain stable and brotherly. A ship "bonds" men together, Conrad explains in *The Mirror of the Sea*: "and therein a ship, though she has female attributes and is loved very unreasonably, is different from a woman."[43] Unlike a wife, a ship provides a home to all the men aboard her, and as a result they feel a common pride in their beloved rather than fighting among themselves for possession of her. "We all watched [the ship]," the narrator in "The Nigger of the *Narcissus*" notes. "We loved her. . . . We admired her qualities aloud, we boasted of them to one another, as though they had been our own."⁴⁴ As anthropologists and social historians point out, such polyandrous societies are generally matriarchal in structure, with the power of women based on "mother-right" (matrilineality), the right of the mother rather than the father to lay claim to the children. But in Conrad's stories, the polyandrous community is patriarchal rather than matriarchal. This is the case because the ship produces rather than reproduces; although she has a multitude of husbands, she can lay no claim to mother-right.⁴⁵

In Conrad's fiction, the idealized conception of life under sail seems imperiled not by class unrest and exploitation but by a woman's presence; by replacing ungovernable women with subservient ships in his sailors' affections, Conrad maintains his maritime ideal. In "Youth" (1898), the captain's wife is deposited on shore, and her feminine functions are assumed by the *Judea,* a ship that mothers all the men on board her; "it seemed as though we had been born in her, reared in her," the narrator remarks.⁴⁶ And though, in *Chance,* the captain's wife remains on board, she gradually assumes the economic and sexual role performed by the *Ferndale.* Originally a passenger, Flora becomes a worker (229) and, ultimately, a public resource. Admired by the chief mate, she is handed down to him upon the death of Captain Anthony. A childless woman remade in the image of the idealized ship, Flora can safely remain on board. Using Flora to resolve as well as displace class conflict and economic inequity in the merchant marine, Conrad represents her as a "treasure" shared by men, rich and poor alike (321).

Such representations lend force to the revisionist arguments of feminist literary critics, who call attention to the "ideological work" performed by gender in nineteenth-century fiction. According to these critics, English novelists responded to the alienation of labor caused by industrial capitalism by using gender relations to "solve" economic and social problems. On the one hand, they idealized the domestic labor performed by sisters, wives, and daughters, which they represented as "nonalienated" work "performed as selflessly and effortlessly as love is given."⁴⁷ On the other hand, they freed their novels from troubling political realities by sexualizing them, focusing their plots on the "misconduct" and "illicit desires" of fallen female characters rather than on the violence and discontent of male workers.⁴⁸ Understood as a response to the problems of industrialization and the transition from sail to steam, Conrad's maritime fiction shows that these strategies operate in a literary realm too often defined as purely masculine. Read as domestic narratives of a sort, his seafaring

Sailing Ships and Steamers, Angels and Whores

tales reveal the ideological uses to which sexual stereotypes are put in nineteenth-century literature; in so doing, they collapse the polarity critics have traditionally established between masculine adventure stories and domestic fiction, with its presumably "feminine" concerns.[49] It may appear that Conrad's heroes are "free from the complexities of relations with . . . women."[50] Yet their relations with their ships, under both sail and steam, demonstrate that tales of maritime adventure and stories of courtship and marriage can be one and the same.

MELODY GRAULICH

10

Opening Windows toward the Sea

Harmony and Reconciliation in American Women's Sea Literature

Like Lillian Nayder, Melody Graulich argues that sea literature has for too long been defined as both a male and a masculine genre. Even those recent critics, she claims, who bring a sensitivity to gender to their analysis of sea fiction still envision it as a body of literature centered exclusively on men. Graulich, in contrast, recovers a women-authored tradition of maritime fiction. In her examination of American literary texts produced from the mid– to late nineteenth century, Graulich identifies a distinctly female vision of the sea, which she terms a "synthesizing image of harmony." This vision, she suggests, focuses on the reconciling of opposites and on the balancing of alternatives. The form of this literature is appropriately tidal, and its setting is often the shore, the locus for male/female interconnection. Hers is a fitting work to conclude a volume that stresses the integration of land-based and maritime history and culture, and that argues for the transcendence of the symbolic, oppositional figures of "iron men" and "wooden women."

> the sea is another story
> the sea is not a question of power
> —Adrienne Rich, "Diving into the Wreck"

> The waves are full of whispers wild and sweet;
> They call to me
> —Celia Thaxter, "Off Shore"

Opening the Window

IN 1877 IN *The Story of Avis*, Elizabeth Stuart Phelps opened her heroine's window toward the sea: "The window toward the sea was open and the rhythm of the tide beat a strange duet with [Avis's friend's] gentle, happy breathing on the pillow at her side. It seemed to her a great song without words, full of uncaptured meanings, deep with unuttered impulse. She would have liked to fit expression to it."[1]

Throughout the late nineteenth century, many women writers captured the meanings of the great song without words, the sea's duet with the breathing of their loved ones. Like Kate Chopin's famous heroine, Edna Pontellier, the literary daughter of Phelps's Avis, these writers found that "the voice of the sea is seductive; never ceasing, whispering, clamoring, murmuring, inviting the soul."[2] Like Harriet Beecher Stowe's Mara Lincoln of *The Pearl of Orr's Island* (1862), the book which Jewett said most influenced her own work, these writers "looked pensively into the water" to discover that "every incident of life came up out of its depths to meet" them.[3]

Stowe calls the sea a "great, reflecting mirror" (319), and Mara is forced to look to the sea—to nature rather than to culture—to find herself. Reading Plutarch's *Lives* with the minister who is educating her, she asks, "[are] there . . . any lives of women?" The good man replies, "No, my dear, . . . in the old times, women did not get their lives written, though I don't doubt many of them were much better worth writing than the men's" (152). Reading today literary criticism on the tradition of American sea literature, one could still ask Mara's question.

W. H. Auden, for instance, tells us that at sea, "I precedes we," that fictional seamen seek to be "free from both the evils and responsibilities of communal life," to escape "necessity" in the "search for possibility," to test themselves by striving against the "primitive potential power" of nature.[4] Seeking absolute freedom, the seaman may end up alienated, feeling like a "stranger, . . . alone, above, apart."[5] Another critic says the sea represents "the restless, aggressive, ambitious, enterprising impulse—the impulse to know, to own, to domineer," adding that "Americans believed that the sea was too harsh and anti-social an environment for women."[6] This historical commonplace bespeaks literary historical assumptions, assumptions also evident in the critical insistence that sea literature focuses on metaphysical questions with "universal significance," questions about the meaning of human existence, the nature of good and evil, the moral and psychological freedom life allows, the possibility for heroism in the world, and what is Truth.[7] There are critics whose emphasis on community in the sea novel questions the male gender stereotypes implicit in the previous quotes, but even they present the sea as male territory.[8]

Just as Plutarch's assumptions about history and heroism led him to overlook women's lives, so have assumptions about what defines sea literature led us to overlook the fact that American women have repeatedly used the sea's mirroring image to reflect upon women's lives, that their voices echo each other. Echoing a writer from across the sea, Virginia Woolf, I see this essay as a voyage out, in which I begin defining a tradition of women's sea literature by exploring the sea as a significant recurring symbol in nineteenth-century women's writing. I look at the work of Stowe, Louisa May Alcott, Sarah Orne Jewett, Emily Dickinson, Celia Thaxter, Rebecca Harding Davis, Phelps, and Chopin.

Predestination and Free Will

In many ways, women's sea literature does contrast with the male tradition. Focusing on the seashore, on islands, on reefs, women writers also ponder questions about identity when gazing seaward, but their vision is qualified, framed by an awareness of their ties to others. To Avis, as to Whitman, the "sea whispered me," but it did so in harmony with the breathing of her friend. Their "universal" questions are social, not metaphysical; they do not challenge the universe but explore the construction and meaning of human relationships. They question binary oppositions and try to break down boundaries. Acknowledging necessity but seeking to harmonize it with vision and possibility, they offer a transformative interpretation of the sea, as did the anonymous nineteenth-century quiltmaker who designed the "Storm at Sea" quilt. A brief look at her design can make the women's view of the sea's synthesizing force a "heap plainer," as Eliza Calvert Hall would say. Hall, an Appalachian mountain writer, does not use sea imagery, but her narrator from *Aunt Jane of Kentucky* (1907) offers insights into quilt patterns, which in turn help us see the patterns in women's sea literature.

> How much piecin' a quilt's like livin' a life! And as for sermons, why, they ain't no better sermon to me than a patchwork quilt. . . . Many a time I've set and listened to Parson Page preachin' about predestination and free will, and I've said to myself, ". . . if I could jest git up there in the pulpit with one of my quilts, I could make it a heap plainer than parson's makin' it with all his big words."
>
> You see, you start out with jest so much caliker; you don't go to the store and pick it out and buy it, but the neighbors will give you a piece here and a piece there, and you'll have a piece left over every time you cut out a dress, and you jest take whatever happens to come. And that's like predestination. But when it comes to the cuttin' out, why you're free to choose your own pattern. You can give the same kind of pieces to two persons and one'll make a "nine-patch" and the other one'll make a "wild-goose-chase," and there'll

be two quilts made out o' the same kind of pieces and jest as different as they can be. And that is jest the way with livin'. The Lord sends us the pieces but we can cut 'em out and put 'em together pretty much to suit ourselves, and there's a heap more in the cuttin' out and the sewin' than there is in the caliker.[9]

Like Aunt Jane, the women sea watchers recognize the interrelationship of freedom and predestination. Self-expression takes place within a network of human ties: others give you the pieces. Free will and autonomy are created by piecing together, by discovering one's own pattern within givens or restrictions, a pattern that may well have been handed down from a mother or an aunt. With that reconciling view comes a definition of individuality *and* an acknowledgment of alternative patterns and points of view, a balance between self and other.[10]

While Parson Page, like dozens of ministers in nineteenth-century women's texts, uses his "big words" to impose his distanced abstractions on his audience, Aunt Jane provides a concrete example to ground her conceptualizing. Following her example, I turn to the "Storm at Sea" quilt design. Before reading on, discover your own patterns in the design.

Some people see waves; others see squares. Some see four-pointed stars; others, eight-pointed stars. Some tilt at windmills; some eyes run in circles. If you look long enough, you perhaps feel dizzy. Although you are probably taken in by the quilt's optical illusions, each side of every piece is perfectly straight. Look again and see if you can find the repeating geometric block, made up of squares and triangles, forty-five and ninety-degree angles. How does the quilt designer transcend, transform, predictable geometry and straight lines to create the quilt's dynamic energy?

Aunt Jane suggests that quilts speak more directly than sermons, that they can be "read." This storm at sea speaks of harmony and turbulence, reconciling opposites, accepting the mysterious and sometimes contradictory patterns of nature and human existence. We experience the calm and order of the tides in its straight lines, its regular pattern, and its repetitive geometry, while the illusive waves imply the energy and passion of storm. The quilt designer expresses both thematically, through the merger of the two faces of the sea, and formally, through the use of illusion, the idea of synthesis. A larger picture grows fantastically out of the ordinary bits of fabric; we see something more than the sum of the parts. The world of facts, of necessity, of geometry, is merged with the world of intuition, of possibility, of vision. Through its transformations, the design calls our attention to perception, to the inevitability of alternative visions.

"Storm at Sea" quilt, made by Melody Graulich (1992) from a traditional nineteenth-century design. Composed entirely of straight-edged pieces, the quilt in its overlapping design suggests the reconciling, harmonizing vision of women sea writers.

Sharing the desire of Aunt Jane and the anonymous quilt designer to reconcile vision and necessity, women sea writers use sea imagery—often stormy—to explore conflicting needs and desires, emotions, loyalties, and commitments.[11] Their works contain patterns of free will and predestination, self and other, which often overlap, as the waves overlap the shore.

Women's seashore literature explores the tidal boundaries of female identity and of the female body. The frequent oceanic mergers with the sea—with *la mère*—in *both* men's and women's literature recall infants' fusion with their mothers, with no recognition of boundaries between self and other. While men develop gender identity by separating from their primary caregivers, their mothers, women come to understand themselves as women by identifying with and against their mothers. For men like Ishmael on his masthead, the sea raises threats to the attainment of an individuated self. Women also must develop an ego that recognizes its own needs and desires, but boundaries are blurred.¹² Women perpetually negotiate what I will call a "self," recognizing the need to be differentiated but also seeking connection. And so a woman's evolving sense of self—and of her sexuality, a repeated theme in seashore literature—is tidal. The "continual crossing of self and other" is mirrored in the seashore and tides, a landscape of crossings.¹³

In this essay I focus on women characters who struggle to achieve a "reconciled self," a self that recognizes the tidal flow of identity, acknowledges both freedom and predestination, and achieves transformation. Like female identity, the form of women's seashore literature is tidal; apparently conflicting themes and alternate ways of seeing ebb and flow—and eventually cross. The sea washes into women's texts at moments when the heroine, author, or text is poised between alternatives, at moments of decision. Women's sea literature commonly reflects the most complex question for nineteenth-century women writers: how to reconcile autonomy with responsibility to others.¹⁴ Seen from the room with a sea view, freedom is qualified by an awareness of bonds to others and their rewards and costs. Although they may, like Dickinson, imagine that they "dwell in possibility," women dwell on the shore, unable to leave behind the communal, everyday world or its responsibilities.¹⁵ The seashore, where the land and the sea are brought into relationship, becomes an apt symbolic landscape for tales of emotional conflict and reconciliation, for scenes of synthesis or transformation, for authors and characters—and even literary historians—seeking to harmonize apparent opposites.

The seashore reminds women of the need—the necessity—of reconciling forces that seem to be in opposition, of finding compromises. Of course, tidal identities and broken-down binary boundaries are more complex than my summary has made them sound. But we can only make such discoveries by walking along the seashore with Stowe and the others.¹⁶

Stowe's Maternal Lessons

Stowe's *The Pearl of Orr's Island* initially seems to accept the conventional, even stereotypical, gender differences in sea literature by contrasting the "natures" of two children whose lives are intimately connected to the sea. Mara speculates on what causes the differences between her life and Moses': "He was handsome, clever, and had a thousand other things to do and to think of—he was a boy, in short, and going to be a glorious man and sail all over the world, while she could only hem handkerchiefs and knit stockings, and sit at home and wait for him to come back" (149). While this passage suggests differences in the social construction of gender, in nurture, Stowe more commonly insists that Moses and Mara have different natures.[17] Self-absorbed Moses goes off adventuring, challenging all limits; willful and domineering, he does not question putting *I* before *we*. Mara rambles along the seashore or "sit[s] at the open window that looked forth toward the ocean" and devotes herself to others (360). Both children are born of the sea, orphaned by shipwrecks, and sea imagery defines selfhood for both: Mara is "a pearl washed ashore by a mighty, uprooting tempest" "whose poor little roots first struck deep in the salt, bitter waters" (25, 8), while stormy metaphors describe Moses' "solitary freedom in his lonely seafaring life," his reluctance to be "anchored in society" (188). With his "love of contradiction and opposition," Moses tries to grow through separation, while Mara, like her creator, defines self and freedom in relation to their opposites (189). Self and other are interdependent; freedom and fate must somehow be harmonized.

Even as it supports easy gender dichotomies, Stowe's text brings polarities into question. Facing Mara's death, Moses guiltily realizes, "You always lived for me and I lived for myself" (389). Mara's reply absolves him of responsibility by appealing simultaneously to nature and nurture:

> Moses, I always knew I loved most. It was my nature; God gave it to me, and it was a gift for which I give him thanks—not a merit. I knew you had a larger, wider nature than mine,—a wider sphere to live in, and that you could not live in your heart as I did. Mine was all thought and feeling, and the narrow little duties of this little home. Yours went all round the world. (390)

Yet Mara manages to change Moses' nature, to "soothe" the "storm" in his breast (392). By the book's end he becomes "tired of wandering," "want[s] a home of [his] own," questions the value of "go[ing] on alone" (400–401). Stowe has transformed man's "nature" by uniting it with woman's.

Stowe further explores transformation in the story's ending. Moses marries another seashore woman, Sally Kittridge, Mara's closest friend, with whom she had shared many nighttime talks as they listen to the "weird murmur of the sea" (333). Impulsive and willful like Moses, Sally manages to "do as she pleased," yet she too will be transformed by Mara's death (330). The changes in both characters are revealed as they sit in a seaside grotto, an image of maternity where many crucial moments, many rebirths, take place: as the "tide rose up and shut them in," the two "sat and talked, leaning on each other" (401). The novel closes, not with the common apocalypse of male texts, but with this seashore image of mutual interdependence, with reconciliation.

Unlike later sea writers like Dickinson and Chopin, Stowe's sexual sea imagery focuses on the maternal, and she presents reconciliation as the sea's maternal lesson. Like other women's sea novels, *The Pearl of Orr's Island* conflates the sea, the mother, and the self. Both children lose their mothers in sea tragedies: after witnessing her husband's shipwreck, Mara's mother dies birthing her daughter, while Moses is discovered clutched in the arms of his drowned mother, who had been lashed to a spar during a storm. While initially the "call which [Moses] most passionately and often repeated was for his mother," soon she vanishes from her son's heart as her ship vanished beneath the sea (54). Stowe initiates his growth into manhood with his separation from his mother.

Mara's story is quite different. Everyone wishes she would "grow up into her mother's place" (22), and several passages suggest her longing to reunite with her mother: she was "always homesick to go back where [she came] from" (26–27). Mara does not find the sea's voice "lonesome," but "like[s] to hear it" (288). The following passage explains why:

> There are souls sent into this world who seem to have always mysterious affinities for the invisible and the unknown. . . . The Germans call this yearning of spirit home-sickness. . . . As Mara looked pensively into the water, it seemed to her that every incident of life came up out of its depths to meet her. Her own face reflected in a wavering image, something shaped itself to her gaze in the likeness of the pale lady of her childhood, who seemed to look up at her from the waters with dark, mysterious eyes of tender longing. (296)

Nature here is a reflection of the presence of the "invisible and unknown," of God. Reflected simultaneously in the sea and in her mother, Mara realizes her true self and goes "home" when she dies, merging her spirit with that of God, who "has always been to [her] not so much like a father as like a deep and tender mother" (322).[18]

Moses too must accept transformation through maternal imagery. He must take into himself female values, and he cannot grow into a man until he spiritually reunites with his mother. Moses reads the letter that reveals his mother's story in the tidal vaginal grotto, the scene of rebirth. Initially he misinterprets the significance of his mother's past, seeing himself as the "heir of wealth and power," which leads to a definition of self Stowe clearly resists: "If I could have my own way now, —if I could have just what I wanted, and do just as I pleased exactly, I might make a pretty good thing of it" (268). Through Mara's intervention, in her role as feminized Christ, he realizes his need for the love and forgiveness associated with mothers, with Stowe's feminized God.

Moses also receives this lesson from a man, the nurturing Captain Kittridge, who calls gender dichotomies into question. In yet another scene in the grotto, where Moses feels himself separate, "alone," the good captain comforts him about Mara's death by describing how she sang hymns for him, "her voice . . . jest as sweet as the sea of a warm evening" (381, 385).

> I tell ye what 't is, Moses, fellers think it a might pretty thing to be a-steppin' high, and a sayin' they don't believe the Bible, and all that ar, so long as the world goes well. This 'ere old Bible—why it's jest like yer mother,—ye rove and ramble, and cut up through the world without her a spell, and mebbe think the old woman ain't so fashionable as some; but when sickness and sorrow comes, why there ain't nothin' else to go back to. Is there, now? (386)

Stowe expects both Mara and Moses to go back to their mothers, both women and men to grow into adulthood through acknowledging their interdependence with and faith in others. Her "Pearl," her novel born of the sea, simultaneously acknowledges gender differences and seeks to transform them.

The Reconciled Self

Like Stowe, Alcott and Jewett use the sea in stories about growth and development, suggesting that as girls cross into womanhood, they recognize needs and desires as overlapping rather than simply conflicting. Both authors allow their heroines glimpses of the sea at major turning points in their lives. Alcott sets only one scene in *Little Women* (1867) at the seashore, but it is a crucial one: in it Beth tells Jo about her upcoming death. Imagining bird metaphors for each of her sisters, Beth suggests that she and Jo are sea birds. Jo is "the gull, . . . strong and wild, fond of the storm and the wind, flying far out to sea, and happy all alone," while the sandpipers remind Beth of herself: "quite at home . . . not so wild and handsome [as the gulls] . . . but happy, confiding little things . . . busy, quaker-colored creatures, always near the shore and always chirping that contented little song of theirs."[19] These images will comfortably fit most readers' memories of the novel. We remember Jo for her "wildness," for her nonconformity, her independence, her rebellion, Beth for being "at home," domestic, dependent, submissive. Jo soars; Beth walks along the sand. They are opposites.

And yet Alcott's scene on the seashore asks us to reject easy oppositions, to see how Jo and Beth overlap, to recognize that each young woman has complex needs and desires. Independent Jo is far from happy all alone: "I can't let you go," she cries, holding her sister more tightly; "I'll keep you in spite of everything" (412). "Piously submissive" Beth has envied her sister's freedom and wanted more from her own life: "I couldn't seem to imagine myself anything but stupid little Beth, trotting about at home, of no use anywhere but there," she says (412, 413). In this passage Alcott suggests that separation and connection, self and other, freedom and restriction, are tidal themes. The scene stresses reconciliation.

Although Jo is not reconciled to Beth's death, Beth does convince her that they can never truly be separated. Through incorporating Beth into herself, Jo expands her understanding of what she wants from her own life. Many contemporary feminists have bemoaned that after Beth's death Jo seems to change from gull to sandpiper, that she learns too well her mother's lessons about the "sweetness of self-denial and self-control" (98).[20] I share those feelings, but I believe that the novel also demands that I recognize an alternative pattern, as Aunt Jane does. Indeed, Jane might be Alcott's model reader, for while Alcott certainly acknowledges the predestinations that limit our lives, she suggests that Jo gains a fuller understanding of the limits and consequences of the kind of freedom she has sometimes sought. "I'd rather do everything for myself," she initially says, "and be perfectly independent" (332). Later she realizes that "the life I wanted then seems selfish, lonely and cold to me now" (540). Perhaps *Little Women*'s popularity stems from its balanced articulation of women's psychological dilemmas: the themes of free will and predestination, self and other, ebb and flow throughout the text. The novel should be read not as a sermon but as a quilt, with swirling, overlapping patterns.

Sarah Orne Jewett's "A White Heron" (1886) also presents readers with overlapping, rather than alternative, ways of seeing a crucial choice. Sylvie must decide whether to give away the secret, and the life, of the white heron to earn the ornithologist's love; the bird, of course, is the symbol of her very selfhood. Jewett gives Sylvie, who has never seen the sea, a glimpse of it, a transcendent, epiphanic moment, to help her make her choice. She has just climbed the giant pine, described as a mast:

> Sylvia's face was like a pale star, if one had seen it from the ground, when the last thorny bough was past, and she stood trembling and tired, but wholly triumphant, high in the tree-top. Yes, there was the sea with the dawning sun making a golden dazzle over it, and toward the glorious east flew two hawks with slow-moving pinions . . . and Sylvia felt as if she too could go flying away among the clouds. . . . truly it was a vast and awesome world.[21]

Until this transformative moment, Sylvie has been embedded in the woodland shadows; here she envisions a future where boundaries between earth, sky, and sea can be crossed.[22] Sharing a sight of the sea with the hawks, and in the next few paragraphs with the heron itself, Sylvie recognizes possibility and freedom, and her vision elliptically suggests a blurred boundary between her own dreams and her grandmother's desire to have lived her son's wandering life: "I'd ha' seen the world myself if it had been so I could" (231). Worlds open to her. Although the rewards and costs of Sylvie's decision not to tell initially seem binary and quite clearcut—she recognizes her first loyalty is to bird, to life, to self, and loses the young man as a consequence—Jewett's technique is in fact tidal: the reader experiences a surge of pleasure as Sylvie stands her ground and refuses to tell, but Jewett immediately backs away and forces us to question her loss in the story's last paragraph by asking, "Were the birds better friends than their hunter might have been,—who can tell?" (239). And in suggesting, however subtly, that Sylvie might live a life that merges her uncle's and her grandmother's, Jewett presents her own vision of reconciliation.

Jewett's *The Country of the Pointed Firs* (1896), with its repeated imagery of land and sea, of crossings and circles, is about vision, about recognizing connections and synthesizing alternatives, about mothering, about how selfhood is achieved through ties to others. A memorable passage occurs when the narrator sits down in Mrs. Blackett's rocker to look out her window at her sea view. The narrator has earlier linked the elder woman's vision to the sea: she sees in her eyes "a look of anticipation and joy, a far-off look that sought the horizon; one often sees it in seafaring families" (48). Looking out the window gives the narrator a kind of double vision: when she sees the "quiet outlook upon field and sea and sky" she also gets a glimpse into the other woman's heart and life, a moment that allows the two women "to under[stand] each other without speaking" (54). Always seeking images of centering, the narrator realizes, "Here was . . . the heart of the old house on Green Island" (54).

Despite living on "so apparently neighborless and remote an island," Mrs. Blackett "was one of those who do not live to themselves"; she is indeed one center of Jewett's work (41). Later the narrator visits another island, Shell-Heap Island, the former home of the hermit Mrs. Todd always calls "Poor Joanna," who only "wanted . . . to get away from folks; . . . to be free" (65). While Mrs. Blackett's eyes reveal her "pleasant hopefulness," Joanna's reveal her illness: " 'Tis like bad eyesight, the mind of such a person: if your eyes don't see right there may be a remedy, but there's no kind of glasses to remedy the mind," says Mrs. Todd, the healer who regrets her failure with her friend (77–78). Yet the narrator visits Shell-Heap Island because she also wants to share Joanna's viewpoint, looking out over the sea "as Joanna must have watched it many a day" and thinking, "In the life of each of us . . . there is a place remote and islanded, and given to endless regret or secret happiness; we are each the uncompanioned hermit and recluse of an hour or a day" (82). The pastoral Green Island and the lonely Shell-Heap Island, Mrs. Blackett and Joanna, present opposing views, yet the narrator manages to see—and take in—both views, to imagine both viewpoints. Jewett's interest in seeing through others' eyes is not surprising, given her description of Stowe's influence on her work in her 1893 introduction to *Deephaven:*

> It was, happily, in the writer's childhood that Mrs. Stowe had written of those who dwelt along the wooded seacoast and by the decaying, shipless harbors of Maine. The first chapters of *The Pearl of Orr's Island* gave the younger author of *Deephaven* to see with new eyes, and to follow eagerly the old shore paths from one gray, weather-beaten house to another where Genius pointed her the way.[23]

This image of influence implies Jewett's understanding of female identity, for she suggests that as the two women crossed paths the older author helped the younger to find her own vision; Mrs. Todd and the narrator walk the same paths and share a similar relationship in *The Country of the Pointed Firs*. Influence and independence are not opposed. In fact, the richest vision comes when the two are synthesized, as Jewett shows in her collection's opening chapters, where the narrator realizes that by reconciling her needs for community and solitude she can see herself and those around her with new eyes.

"Mrs. Todd" is as much about the narrator and her needs as about the landlady. Like many another sea-gazing woman, the narrator encounters the sea through her window, one of those "small-paned high windows . . . like knowing eyes that watched the harbor and the far sea-line beyond" (1). But the narrator does not see the sea or even feel the "sea-breezes [that] blew into the low end-window"; instead, she smells "strange and pungent odors" in those sea breezes, odors that reveal the presence of her landlady walking among the herbs in her garden (3). This synthesizing image, originating in the sea, evokes Mrs. Todd's power to bring together, to unite, disparate forces and people, to "remedy . . . the common ails of humanity," lessons she appears to have learned from her mother (4). Like the "Storm at Sea" quilt, *The Country of the Pointed Firs* has overlapping centers, and the second chapter's final image of Mrs. Todd standing in the center of her braided rug emphasizes simultaneously her role in her community and her independent—and sometimes lonely—sense of self.

In her relationship with Mrs. Todd, the narrator comes to recognize the tidal nature of human needs. Serving as her landlady's clerk, she can find no time for her writing. She knows that her decision to write at the empty schoolhouse will have consequences for everyone, but her interior voice wins: it was "not until the voice of conscience sounded louder in my ears than the sea on the nearest pebble beach that I said unkind words of withdrawal to Mrs. Todd" (7). Yet "Mrs. Todd and I were not separated or estranged by the change in our business relations" (7). By voicing a need for a relationship with Mrs. Todd based on an acknowledgment of their mutual individual needs and of their affection for each other, the narrator earns a "deeper intimacy," leading to the wonderful moment when "the cool air came up from the sea . . . and [Mrs. Todd] stood outside the window . . . and told . . . all that lay deepest in her heart" (7). The balance and mutuality that the narrator and Mrs. Todd achieve is beautifully conveyed by the collection's last line: "We went home together up the hill, and . . . we held each other's hands all the way" (226). As Mrs. Blackett's and Joanna's lives and viewpoints are balanced and ultimately joined, so too are the narrator's and Mrs. Todd's. Indeed, I will press my metaphor a bit further and call the structure of *Firs* tidal; our attention flows back and forth between the two main characters, the narrator and Mrs. Todd, and finally focuses on the space where they meet, on the crossing between them, on their evolving relationship.

Yet most of the sea crossings in the collection have to do with a third important character, Mrs. Blackett, whose life is defined by a simultaneous need for affiliation *and* for her own island apart. Through her portrayal of Mrs. Blackett and the mothering relationship, Jewett makes clearest her understanding that female personality ebbs and flows between needs for connection and for independence and solitude. While crossing the sea to Green Island, Mrs. Todd glimpses her mother on shore and affectionately suggests how her identity relates to her mother's: "There, you never get over bein' a child long's you have a mother to go to" (35). But later in the same chapter, Mrs. Blackett recognizes her daughter's need to have her own life: "You wanted more scope, didn't you Almiry?" (52). Mrs. Todd and Mrs. Blackett have separate selves and needs, but their hearts reach out to each other across the water.

"The Foreigner" culminates Jewett's exploration of the fluid boundaries between mothers and daughters. Near the end of the narrator's stay in Dunnet Landing, a northeaster blows in, and, like the sea "stirred to its dark depths," Mrs. Todd frets; she begins to worry about the "danger offshore among the outer islands." Her fears for Mrs. Blackett lead her to tell the narrator a story about Mrs. Tolland, a "stranger" in Dunnet Landing, circling around and around, like the cat in her lap, until she reaches her story's center.

The heart of her story she has told few others. "'Twas such a gale as this the night Mis' Tolland died," she says, and yet Mrs. Todd's memory is stirred less by the storm than by her thoughts of her mother (183). As Mrs. Todd sat up with the dying woman, "the window open toward the sea," the two of them saw a ghostly face in the room, "a woman's dark face lookin' right at us" (184). It was Mrs. Tolland's mother come in from the storm to welcome her daughter to the world beyond, to assure her, as Mrs. Todd interprets, that she "ain't never goin' to feel strange an' lonesome no more" (186). Of course, these words echo Mrs. Blackett's. Mrs. Tolland and her mother go "away together," and Mrs. Todd concludes with a characteristic image of synthesis: "There's somethin' of us that must still live on; we've got to join both worlds together an' live in one but for the other" (186). Having shared her mysterious experience with the narrator, her story elliptically expressing her feelings of love for and acceptance by her mother, Mrs. Todd finds that the "storm's all over" (187). Like the "Storm at Sea" quilt, "The Foreigner" explores how storm and calm overlap, as do sea and land, mothers and daughters, and even narrative techniques. In this wonderful story, we can certainly see Jewett's debt to Stowe, for Mrs. Tolland's mother, with her accepting arms, recalls Mara's definition of God as a mother and the image of her mother looking up out of the sea.

Like Mrs. Todd's story, Dickinson's "Wild Nights! Wild Nights!" (about 1861) originates in a stormy night and explores a speaker's ability to reconcile storm and calm, predestination and free will.

> Wild Nights—Wild Nights!
> Were I with thee
> Wild Nights should be
> Our luxury!
>
> Futile—the Winds—
> To a Heart in port—
> Done with the Compass—
> Done with the Chart!
>
> Rowing in Eden—
> Ah, the Sea!
> Might I but moor—Tonight—
> In Thee![24]

The passion of the first stanza, with its nights so wild they must be repeated, with its excited "i's" and "e's" and eager, repeated rhyme, is balanced by the peaceful second stanza, with the heart sheltered in port, its navigations accomplished, and its calm low "o's" and "ar's" and relaxed off-rhyme. The third stanza, with both "o's" and "ah's" *and* "I's" and "e's" as well as its lovely final image of merger, brings storm and calm, passion and peace, self and other, into harmony. Even innocence and sensuality can be harmonized, as the speaker can row in Eden but dissolve in a satisfying, orgasmic "Ah" in the sea. Like the "Storm at Sea" quilt, "Wild Nights" reveals coexisting patterns. It hints at predestination with its conditional verbs: instead of being with the lover with whom she would like to share the "luxury" of "wild nights," the speaker is alone. Yet the poem focuses on imaginative free will, on transcendence: the seashore is a poetic landscape where Dickinson, like many of her seaside sisters, can indeed "dwell in possibility."

The Unreconciled Self

Try as they might to dwell in possibility, many shore dwellers find themselves stuck in the predestined pattern of self *or* other. In "Land-locked" (1874), for instance, Celia Thaxter's speaker yearns for the seashore denied to her, for the voice of the sea, for Dickinson's imaginative empowerment. Raised on the Isles of Shoals off New Hampshire's coast and nicknamed The Sandpiper by her friend Jewett, Thaxter was devoted to her mother, an island dweller like Mrs. Blackett. Jewett's treatment of the relationship between Mrs. Todd and her mother may echo Thaxter's life, and "The Foreigner" may have been inspired by Thaxter's story about encountering her mother's ghost.[25] But Thaxter married a man who insisted upon living on the mainland. Crossings defined her life, but she presents herself as torn between rather than reconciling dichotomous loyalties and needs. The title "Land-locked" conveys her feelings of imprisonment when she is separated from the sea—and perhaps her feelings about her marriage. "Longing for level line of solemn sea," she addresses herself to the river.[26] Bounded by land but able to "run . . . softly to the sea," it personifies her "yearning heart, that never can be still." Unable to follow the river, she dreams of the light and scent and voice of the sea, but it is human "voices on the gale / afar off calling low" that define her: "my name they speak!" Separated from the sea, from her mother, Thaxter yearns to be addressed, to be named as herself. "Land-locked," she is lost in the grid of predestination. The poem's final lines acknowledge her need for a reconciling vision as she reaches not for the sea but for the landscape of crossings: "I but crave / The sad, caressing murmur of the wave / That breaks in tender music on the shore."[27]

Thaxter's poem never explicitly mentions marriage, but the speaker's presentation of an unreconciled self—her sense of imprisonment, her uncertainty about identity, her frustration, and her thematic focus on dichotomies—links her poem to a number of sea texts that suggest that marriage and childbearing created a sense of division in nineteenth-century women. Indeed, Dickinson's speaker may have been able to hold onto her reconciled self only because her expression of sexuality is imaginary, Stowe because hers is maternal, and Jewett because hers focuses on bonds between women. Rebecca Harding Davis's *Earthen Pitchers* (1873–74), Elizabeth Stuart Phelps's *The Story of Avis* (1877), Jewett's *The Country Doctor* (1884), and Kate Chopin's *The Awakening* (1899) carry on a conversation about the balancing acts that nineteenth-century women faced: how to marry—and have children—without giving up self; how to develop voice, vocation, and sexuality when social constructions of gender denied them to most women; how simultaneously to validate and to escape the roles of their mothers, how to connect and to separate. In each work the sea has a strong voice and speaks to these questions, but while the authors articulate the tidal nature of their character's conflicts, the seashore's synthesizing landscape provides no answer. Their heroines cannot reconcile their opposing needs and emotions; they ebb *or* flow. As Aunt Jane might say, given the same pieces, the authors found different patterns in them, but no one could claim for her heroine an overlapping resolution or Jane's synthesizing vision. Having already devoted so much attention to Jewett, I will focus on the other three novels.

Earthen Pitchers is a classic nineteenth-century woman's story: Audrey, a singer, discovers she must give up art for marriage. Davis sets two critical scenes at the seashore which reveal but fail to harmonize Audrey's needs for self-expression and for love. "Wander[ing alone] down the beach . . . over-looking the sea," Audrey experiences an epiphanic realization of self, vocation, and voice.[28] The sea speaks to her in a "voice she could almost hear," then chooses her to express its message, singing "a lofty hymn, in which there was one word lacking left for her to supply. . . . The longing, the hope . . . for which no man has ever found words, oppressed and choked her. . . . *She* would find words for this unknown hope" (494).

Davis's sea imagery recalls the synthesizing vision of other writers: *self-expression* grows from an understanding of the fluid harmony between self and other, requiring a balance of listening and speaking, being responsive and then responding. Perhaps the "unknown hope" is for a reconciled self, one that acts upon individual needs yet remains responsive to those of others. In a passage that conflates her voice with the sea's, Audrey does find words: "Strains of simple, powerful harmony were heard, unknown before her; whether she sang them or not she did not know" (494). The passage's final image evokes the sea's maternal embrace and suggests that Audrey's art is born from her merger with the sea: "She went down and threw herself into the sea, floated out to deep water; the waves light and buoyant caressing her with fine supporting touches. To Audrey it had the solemnity of a baptism" (494). Most readers will recognize how this scene of rebirth foreshadows Edna Pontillier's sea swims, but they may not know Phelps's Corona, of *An Old Maid's Paradise* (1879), whose swims lead her to exclaim, " 'I am alive! alive!' "[29]

Like Dickinson, Phelps, and Chopin, Davis uses sea imagery to convey her heroine's passionate nature; in Audrey's relationship to the sea, she expresses both her art and her sexuality. Sea imagery conveys desire, for self-expression *and* for other. Having just experienced buoyant support and merger in nature, Audrey comes up out of the water imagining a similar relationship in her social life: in her "work," Audrey imagines that "the man she loved . . . would surely bid her God speed" (494). But her fantasy that she could harmonize work and love does not come to pass; her husband "cares little for music" (721). Davis explores her conflicts and her loss in a climactic seashore scene. Having accepted that her "birthright is to love," Audrey also accepts that "the sea [is only] water" (720, 721). But "when evening begins to gather, and the sunset colors the sky and the pools in the marshes behind them, blood-red, and the sea washes into their feet, dark and heavy, with subdued cries and moans, as though all the love and unappeased longing of the world had gone down into it, and sought to find speech in it, Audrey takes up her child" and sings to it. "For one brief moment the tossing waves, the sand dunes, the marshes put on their dear old familiar faces. Old meanings, old voices came close to her," and she felt she must answer (721). For one brief moment, Davis allows Audrey to harmonize her love for her child and her need for self-expression. "But . . . the voice was cracked. . . . whatever power she might have had was quite wasted and gone. She would never hear again the voice that had called to her" (721). Audrey experiences a doubled silence—she can neither speak nor hear—which ironically mocks her earlier vision of harmony. Unable to hold onto the vision of the reconciled self, she can see only one pattern in her life—predestination. She accepts what her society defines as her "birthright" and turns to her child to justify her existence.[30]

Davis wrote "with an ardor that was human, and a passion that was art," said Phelps, in a tribute that identified the themes they shared.[31] Like Audrey, Phelps's Avis would like to "fit expression" to the sea's "great song" (19); like Audrey, she comes to her realization of her vocation as an artist wandering by the sea; like *Earthen Pitchers, The Story of Avis* is filled with imagery of self-division, of "Civil Wars." Throughout her novel Phelps uses sea imagery to explore Avis's conflicts, her growth as an artist, her relationship to her mother, and her passion and sexuality. I will focus on only one key passage, which takes place during a winter storm and chronicles a moment of conflict and rebirth like others I have discussed. In it Avis shifts her loyalties from her mother, symbolized by a "gorge within the cliff, . . . a vein of deep purple lava," to her lover, symbolically connected to the phallic lighthouse, which may preserve ships but attracts birds to their deaths (42).³²

Avis's mother was the victim of a civil war. She wanted to be an actress but, she explains to Avis, "I married your papa: that is why I never acted" (24). Having had a "glimpse into her mother's heart," Avis grows up realizing that she must not marry, must not cultivate "self-oblivion"; one way of denying her mother's death-in-life and their separation is to complete her mother's life.³³ Phelps's description of the gorge, which "told the story of a terrible organic divorce," explains the self-division she sees as inevitable when women marry (42). "The two sides of that gorge are thrust apart by flood or fire. They were originally of one flesh. It was a perfect primeval marriage. The heart of the rock was simply broken" (46). In it Avis sees "an awful organic tragedy, differing from human tragedy only in being symbolic of it"; it reminds her of "the motherhood of earth" (46). This final phrase, linked to the "organic tragedy," implies Avis's guilty recognition that while marriage might be a social construction, maternity is not, that her birth exacerbated the conflict that led to her mother's self-denial.

Despite her resolve, Avis too becomes the victim of a civil war. Phelps explores overlapping patterns between mother and daughter imagistically through Avis's stormy experience in the gorge. She has walked out along a reef to the lighthouse, where her suitor, Ostrander, sees her "against the ice-covered rock like a creature sprung from it, sculptured, primeval, born of the storm" (43). Passages like this one serve two functions: they emphasize Avis's ties to her mother, who experienced her own storms, and they suggest Avis's passionate nature, her sexuality. The imagery expresses conflicting desires for connection: Avis is torn between her desire to express what her mother could not and her physical desires for a man.

These desires will continue to ebb and flow throughout the novel, but this scene, like others I have examined, does mark a turning point. Avis slips off the reef and hangs in a cleft between the purple rocks and the reef. She and Ostrander link hands and he pulls her up out of the sea in a remarkable scene of rebirth. Although Avis will resist marrying him for some time, he has, in effect, separated her from her mother and from her dedication to self. For the moment, the storm ends: "The surf upon the beach had died; only a slight sob came from the Harbor, like that of a creature in whom a great struggle had worn to a peaceful close" (61).

Yet Avis's great struggle, her civil war, is not over. Like Audrey, she will turn to her child, to her role as a mother, to justify her life; the two authors' stormy seas reflect their struggles to find a transcending pattern in the predestined pieces. Like Stowe, Phelps vacillates between nature and nurture explanations, between attacking marriage as it is socially constructed, as a "profession to a woman" (71), and questioning whether women themselves cannot synthesize opposing desires: "Success—for a woman—means absolute surrender, in whatever direction. Whether she paints a picture or loves a man, there is no division of labor possible in her economy" (69). Through sea imagery, Phelps explores tensions she cannot resolve.[34]

Many critics have seen Kate Chopin as "daring and reckless" in her portrayal of marriage and sexuality, like her heroine Edna, who "wanted to swim far out, where no woman had swum before" (28). Yet Chopin swims familiar seas, in company with others, and she suggests that the divisions Edna sets up between herself and other women reflect her self-divisions. *The Awakening* begins with an image of motherless Edna's isolation and of her divided self: "Even as a child [Edna] had lived her own small life all within herself. At a very early period she had apprehended instinctively the dual life—that outward existence which conforms, the inward life which questions" (15). Chopin constructs her text around a series of dichotomies Edna cannot reconcile: the two ineffective models, Mme. Ratignolle, the "mother-woman" who "esteemed it a holy privilege to efface [herself] as [an] individual," and Mlle. Reisz, the "defiant" and "disagreeable" artist with her "disposition to trample on the rights of others" (10, 26); the dreaming and waking lives; "blind contentment" and "life's delirium" (56); "days when she was very happy . . . [and] days when she was unhappy" (58); and a host of others, all related to the book's largest tension, between duties to self and to others.

As in earlier texts, "the voice of the sea" speaks of the woman's conflicts:

> The voice of the sea is seductive; never ceasing, whispering, clamoring, murmuring, inviting the soul to wander for a spell in abysses of solitude; to lose itself in mazes of inward contemplation.
>   The voice of the sea speaks to the soul. The touch of the sea is sensuous, enfolding the body in its soft close embrace. (15)

This passage, which begins Edna's "awakening," blurs together several of her conflicting desires: her sexual desire, connected to learning to swim, "the very passions themselves . . . aroused within her soul, swaying it, lashing it, as the waves daily beat upon her splendid body" (27); her paradoxical desire to find herself by seeking the "unlimited in which to lose herself" (29); her desire for communication; her desire to be alone, to define herself apart from society and from personal relationships; and her desire to achieve a tender, emotional connection, an embrace, buoyed up and supported as Audrey was.

The repetition of this passage in the book's closing, as Edna swims out to her death, suggests that these conflicts are never resolved. Unlike Audrey and Avis, Edna has earlier refused the idea that a mother must give up self for her children, but the ending clearly does not resolve her dilemmas. Contained in the ending are, in fact, conflicting messages. Perhaps "naked" Edna, "a new-born creature opening its eyes," experiences rebirth, a kind of liberation from cultural clothing that restricts her (113). Or perhaps her death echoes messages from Stowe or Alcott, suggesting that particularly for a woman total dedication to self ultimately leads to loss of self. Chopin does not offer synthesis but paradox—rebirth in death. Like *Little Women*, *The Awakening* should be read as a quilt, but here the patterns do not overlap but compete.

The paradox is further played out in maternal sea imagery. Another early passage is echoed in the novel's final scene, where Edna thinks "of the blue-grass meadow that she had traversed when a little child" (114), a meadow that "seemed as big as the ocean" (17). The motherless little girl had walked through it as "if swimming," "unguided" (17, 18). In Chopin's sexual imagery, in the sea's "close embrace," Edna is reunited with her mother, ironically with the mother who abandoned her by dying, and thus she recapitulates her mother's life. Leaving behind the landscape of crossings, leaving "the shore . . . far behind her," Edna dissolves all boundaries; rather than escaping her ties to others to achieve a separate self, she returns to an egoless union. The ending of *The Awakening* can be read as an ironic retelling of *The Pearl of Orr's Island* or "The Foreigner," for Chopin offers no Christian vision to transform Edna's death.

By 1899, when Chopin published *The Awakening*, American women writers had for many years considered what the seashore had to tell them about their lives. They listened to the sea, and they listened to each other. They created an enduring tradition. Although our seaside tour closes with the nineteenth century, the women's seashore tradition continues into our century. In 1900, when Mary Ellen Chase, aged 13, went to visit her favorite writer, Sarah Orne Jewett, she knew that she, too, would write books about the coast.[35] And so she did, along with Edith Wharton, Edna St. Vincent Millay, Sara Teasdale, Virginia Woolf, Rachel Carson, May Sarton, Paule Marshall, Adrienne Rich, Gloria Anzaldua, Gloria Naylor, and Ursula Le Guin, to name only a few of the writers whose works can be read through the woman's window on the sea.

Harmony

In 1949 in *The Second Sex,* Simone de Beauvoir borrowed assumptions from male writers that find women lacking. She explained that no woman wrote *Moby Dick* or *Ulysses*—both sea works—because "women do not contest the human situation, because they have hardly begun to assume it. This explains why their works for the most part lack metaphysical resonances and also anger; . . . they do not ask [the world] questions, they do not expose its contradictions."[36] In 1972, with a different set of assumptions and hopes, Adrienne Rich's speaker went "Diving into the Wreck" to find a mirroring mermaid; she carried "a book of myths / in which / our names do not appear."[37] With the benefit of years of opened windows, of feminist recovery, I have a wider seaview. I have tried to reveal the questions, to explore the contradictions and the reconciliations, to put together a shelf of books in which our names do appear.

When I began work on this essay some years ago, I focused on differences in female and male culture and literary traditions. Yet as I have thought more fully on those apparent differences, I have realized that female and male writers use sea settings and symbolism to reflect upon and struggle with many of the same concerns: free will and fate, self and other, alienation and connection, isolation and community, freedom and responsibility. Looking at similar themes from different vantage points—sisterhood and brotherhood—female and male sea writers highlight and emphasize different pieces of a shared puzzle.

In writing this essay, I have learned from the women seashore wanderers to call dichotomies into question, to question the use of binary oppositions as paradigms for understanding, to look for intersections. Binary thinking is the tool of the critic, who often who exaggerates and polarizes gender differences. As the writers I have discussed tell us, crossings are necessary and lead to richer and fuller understanding. For years we have borrowed de Beauvoir's model: we have explored women's literature in relation to the "established" or "dominant" tradition. Now that so many of us have rediscovered Rich's book of myths, it is time to reverse the pattern and wonder what we will discover in male writers when we look at them through the woman's window on the sea.[38] As Stowe suggests, Moses "changes" in relation to Mara. Focusing on stories of conflict and conquest, critics have generally overlooked Whitman as a sea writer, for instance. Poems like "Out of the Cradle Endlessly Rocking"—with its seashore setting, its singing bird, its maternal imagery, and its exploration of the loss of others—or "Song of Myself"—with its unthreatened imagery of self-discovery through merger and multiple unions—resonate within the women's tradition. I hope that someone will carry my seaside speculations along on a new voyage of crossings.

Jewett provides us with a synthesizing image of harmony to help me envision a more balanced and overlapping sea tradition. At the end of her visit to Green Island, the narrator has what she calls a "great pleasure." She listens to Mrs. Todd's brother William sing "Home, Sweet Home" with his mother: "they sang together, she missing only the higher notes, where he seemed to lend his voice to hers for the moment and carry on her very note and air" (53).

Notes

Introduction

1. Frederick William Wallace, *Wooden Ships and Iron Men: The Story of the Square-Rigged Merchant Marine of British North America* (London: Hodder & Stoughton, 1924).
2. Peter Linebaugh and Marcus Rediker, " 'The Many-Headed Hydra': Sailors, Slaves, and the Atlantic Working Class in the Eighteenth Century," in Colin Howell and Richard J. Twomey, eds., *Jack Tar in History: Essays in the History of Maritime Life and Labour* (Fredericton, N.B.: Acadiensis Press, 1991), 15-19; Julius S. Scott, "Afro-American Sailors and the International Communication Network: The Case of Newport Bowers," in ibid., 37-52. See also Mary Beth Norton, "The Evolution of White Women's Experience in Early America," *American Historical Review* 89 (June 1984): 595-601, on the transplanting of English gender ideology to North America.
3. Ralph Davis, *The Rise of the English Shipping Industry in the Seventeenth and Eighteenth Centuries* (London: Macmillan, 1962); Davis, *The Rise of the Atlantic Economies* (Ithaca: Cornell University Press, 1973); Immanuel Wallerstein, *The Modern World System II: Mercantilism and the Consolidation of the European World-Economy, 1600-1750* (New York: Academic Press, 1980); esp. chap. 6. For recent surveys of American and British maritime history, see K. Jack Bauer, *A Maritime History of the United States* (Columbia: University of South Carolina Press, 1988); and Ronald Hope, *A New History of British Shipping* (London: John Murray, 1990).
4. Thorsten Rinman and Rigmor Brodefors, *The Commercial History of Shipping* (Gothenburg: Rinman & Linden, 1983), 32.
5. The numbers of seafaring men have also been difficult to establish, given the highly mobile and casual character of so much maritime work during the period considered in this collection. For a start, see Ira Dye, "Early American Merchant Seafarers," *Proceedings of the American Philosophical Society* 120 (1976): 331-60; and V. C. Burton, "Counting Seafarers: The Published Records of the Registrar of Merchant Seamen, 1849-1913," *Mariner's Mirror* 71 (3): 305-20.
6. Among the more useful discussions of this shift are Thomas Laqueur, *Making Sex: Body and Gender from the Greeks to Freud* (Cambridge, Mass.: Harvard University Press, 1990) esp. chaps. 5 and 6; and Mary Poovey, *The Proper Lady and the Woman Writer* (Chicago: University of Chicago Press, 1984), chap. 1. Joan W. Scott provides a most helpful perspective in "Gender: A Useful Category of Historical Analysis," *American Historical Review* 91 (1986): 1053-75. See also Dianne Dugaw's essay in this volume.
7. Linda Kerber has provided a concise review of the relevant American historiography in "Separate Spheres, Female Worlds, Woman's Place: The Rhetoric of Women's History," *Journal of American History* 75 (June 1988): 9-39. For the British developments, see, among others, Catherine Hall, "The Early Formation of Victorian Domestic Ideology," in S. Burman, ed., *Fit Work for Women* (New York: St. Martin's Press, 1979), 15-32; Mary Poovey, *Uneven Developments: The Ideological Work of Gender in*

Mid-Victorian England (Chicago: University of Chicago Press, 1988); and Leonore Davidoff and Catherine Hall, *Family Fortunes: Men and Women of the English Middle Class, 1780–1850* (Chicago: University of Chicago Press, 1987).

8. For the male half of this imagery, Marcus Rediker has pointed out that the romanticized sailors populating the works of Samuel Eliot Morison and Herman Melville "belong (if anywhere) to the nineteenth century." Marcus Rediker, *Between the Devil and the Deep Blue Sea: Merchant Seamen, Pirates, and the Anglo-American Maritime World, 1700–1750* (Cambridge: Cambridge University Press, 1987), 5.

9. For men as for women, we still know much more about the middle class than about other groups in society. But for the beginnings of a history of working-class formulations of masculinity, see Steven Maynard, "Rough Work and Rugged Men: The Social Construction of Masculinity in Working-Class History," *Labour/Le Travail* 23 (spring 1989): 159–69; Sean Wilentz, *Chants Democratic: New York City and the Rise of the American Working Class, 1788–1850* (New York: Oxford University Press, 1984); Bruce Laurie, *Working People of Philadelphia, 1800–1850* (Philadelphia: Temple University Press, 1980); David Reynolds, *Beneath the American Renaissance: The Subversive Imagination in the Age of Emerson and Melville* (New York: Knopf, 1988), chap. 6; Elliot Gorn, *The Manly Art: Bare-Knuckle Prize Fighting in America* (Ithaca: Cornell University Press, 1986); and several of the essays in Ava Baron, ed., *Work Engendered: Toward a New History of American Labor* (Ithaca: Cornell University Press, 1991).

10. See, among others, Clyde Griffen, "Reconstructing Masculinity from the Evangelical Revival to the Waning of Progressivism: A Speculative Synthesis," in Mark C. Carnes and Clyde Griffen, eds., *Meanings for Manhood: Constructions of Masculinity in Victorian America* (Chicago: University of Chicago Press, 1990), 183–204; E. Anthony Rotundo, "Body and Soul: Changing Ideas of American Middle-Class Manhood, 1770–1920," *Journal of Social History* 16 (summer 1983): 23–38; Gorn, *The Manly Art*, esp. 252; John Higham, "The Reorientation of American Culture in the 1890s," in John Weiss, ed., *The Origins of Modern Consciousness* (Detroit: Wayne State University Press, 1965), 25–48; and several of the essays in J. A. Mangan and James Walvin, eds., *Manliness and Morality: Middle-Class Masculinity in Britain and America, 1800–1940* (New York: St. Martin's Press, 1987), and in Michael Roper and John Tosh, eds., *Manful Assertions: Masculinities in Britain since 1800* (London: Routledge, 1991).

11. Examples of such studies include Thomas Philbrick, *James Fenimore Cooper and the Development of American Sea Fiction* (Cambridge: Harvard University Press, 1961); Martin Green, *Deeds of Adventure: Dreams of Empire* (New York: Basic Books, 1979); and Patrick Brantlinger, *Rule of Darkness: British Literature and Imperialism, 1830–1914* (Ithaca: Cornell University Press, 1988).

12. For American seagoing women, see Linda Grant De Pauw, *Seafaring Women* (Boston: Houghton Mifflin, 1982); Edward R. Snow, *Women of the Sea* (New York: Dodd, Mead, 1962); Emma Whiting and Henry Beetle Hough, *Whaling Wives* (Boston: Houghton Mifflin, 1952); Julia C. Bonham, "Feminist and Victorian: The Paradox of the American Seafaring Woman of the Nineteenth Century," *American Neptune* 37 (July 1977): 203–18; Joan Druett, "Those Female Journals," *Log of Mystic Seaport* 40 (winter 1989): 115–25; Joan Druett, *"She Was a Sister Sailor": Mary Brewster's Whaling Journals* (Mystic, Conn.: Mystic Seaport Museum, 1992); John Battick, "The Searsport 36," *American Neptune* 44 (1984): 149–54; and Linda Maloney, "Doxies at Dockside: Prostitution and American Maritime Society, 1800–1900," in Timothy J. Runyan, ed.,

Ships, Seafaring, and Society: Essays in Maritime History (Detroit: Wayne State University Press, 1987), 217–25. On British women, see Basil Greenhill and Ann Giffard, *Women Under Sail* (Newton Abbot: David & Charles, n.d.). Perhaps the most widely read examples of published seagoing women's accounts include Dorothea Balano, *The Log of the Skipper's Wife*, ed. James W. Balano (Camden, Maine: Down East Books, 1979); Mary C. Lawrence, *The Captain's Best Mate*, ed. Stanton Garner (Providence: Brown University Press, 1966); and Eliza Azelia Williams, "Journal," in *One Whaling Family*, ed. Harold Williams (Boston: Houghton Mifflin, 1964).

13. Vilhelm Aubert, *The Hidden Society* (New Brunswick, N.J.: Transaction Books, 1982), chap. 8, "A Total Institution: The Ship," and chap. 9, "On the Social Structure of the Ship."

14. For example, see three works by Daniel J. Boorstin, *The Americans: The Colonial Experience* (New York: Random House, 1958), *The Americans: The National Experience* (New York: Random House, 1965), and *The Americans: The Democratic Experience* (New York: Random House, 1973); Louis Hartz, *The Liberal Tradition in America* (New York: Harcourt Brace, 1955); and David M. Potter, *People of Plenty: Economic Abundance and the American Character* (Chicago: University of Chicago Press, 1954).

15. For an important beginning of a gendered analysis of the British merchant marine, see the pioneering work of Valerie C. Burton, especially "The Work and Home Life of Seafarers, 1871–1921" (Ph.D. diss., University of London, 1988), and "The Myth of Bachelor Jack: Masculinity, Patriarchy, and Seafaring Labour," in Howell and Twomey, *Jack Tar in History*, 179–98.

The British scholarship attentive to the sea and shore connections, though lacking a sensitivity to gender, includes Kenneth R. Andrews, *Elizabethan Privateering* (Cambridge: Cambridge University Press, 1964); David Beers Quinn and A. N. Ryan, *England's Sea Empire, 1550–1640* (London: Allen & Unwin, 1983); Davis, *Rise of the English Shipping Industry*; J. H. Parry, *Trade and Dominion: The European Overseas Empires in the Eighteenth Century* (London: Weidenfeld and Nicolson, 1971); Christopher Lloyd, *The British Seaman, 1200–1860: A Social Survey* (London: Collins, 1968); and Peter Kemp, *The British Sailor: A Social History of the Lower Deck* (London: Dent, 1970).

16. Jesse Lemisch, "Jack Tar in the Streets: Merchant Seamen in the Politics of Revolutionary America," *William and Mary Quarterly*, 3d ser., 25 (July 1968): 371–407.

17. Prominent in what might be termed a "new social (and cultural) history of seafaring" in the United States are such works as Rediker, *Between the Devil and the Deep Blue Sea*; Peter Linebaugh, "All the Atlantic Mountains Shook," *Labour/Le Travail* 10 (1982): 87–121; Robert C. Ritchie, *Captain Kidd and the War against the Pirates* (Cambridge: Harvard University Press, 1986); Daniel Vickers, "The First Whalemen of Nantucket," *William and Mary Quarterly*, 3d ser., 40 (1983): 560–83; Vickers, "Nantucket Whalemen in the Deep-Sea Fishery: The Changing Anatomy of an Early American Labor Force," *Journal of American History* 72 (Sept. 1985): 277–98; and Runyan, *Ships, Seafaring, and Society*. Canadian maritime historians have been particularly active: for example, Rosemary Ommer and Gerald Panting, eds., *Working Men Who Got Wet* (St. John's: Memorial University, 1980); Judith Fingard, *Jack in Port* (Toronto: University of Toronto Press, 1982); Eric W. Sager, *Seafaring Labour: The Merchant Marine of Atlantic Canada, 1820–1914* (Kingston: McGill-Queen's University Press, 1989); and Howell and Twomey, *Jack Tar in History*.

Studies of sea literature which are particularly and usefully attentive to the historical context of maritime subcultures include Haskell Springer, ed., *America and the Sea: A Literary History* (Athens: University of Georgia Press, 1995); Philbrick, *James Fenimore Cooper and the Development of American Sea Fiction;* C. F. Burgess, *The Fellowship of the Craft: Conrad on Ships and Seamen and the Sea* (Port Washington, N.Y.: Kennikat Press, 1976); Bert Bender, *Sea Brothers: The Tradition of American Sea Fiction from "Moby-Dick" to the Present* (Philadelphia: University of Pennsylvania Press, 1988); and Patricia Carlson, ed., *Literature and Lore of the Sea* (Amsterdam: Rodopi, 1986).

18. Lewis R. Fischer and Helge W. Nordvik, "The Context of Maritime History," *International Journal of Maritime History* 1 (June 1989): vi–ix. Quotation from ix.

19. On pioneering work on sailors' homosexual behavior, see especially Arthur Gilbert, "Buggery and the British Navy, 1700–1861," *Journal of Social History* 10 (1976): 72–98; Gilbert, "Sexual Deviance and Disaster during the Napoleonic Wars," *Albion* 9 (1977): 98–113; George Chauncey Jr., "Christian Brotherhood or Sexual Perversion? Homosexual Identities and the Construction of Sexual Boundaries in the World War I Era," *Journal of Social History* 19 (1985): 189–212; Chauncey, *Gay New York: Gender, Urban Culture, and the Making of the Gay Male World, 1890–1940* (New York: Basic Books, 1994), esp. chap. 3; B. R. Burg, *Sodomy and the Perception of Evil: English Sea Rovers in the Seventeenth-Century Caribbean* (New York: New York University Press, 1983); and Burg, *An American Sailor in the Age of Sail: The Erotic Diaries of Philip Van Buskirk* (New Haven: Yale University Press, 1994).

1. Marcus Rediker, Liberty beneath the Jolly Roger

Earlier versions of this chapter were presented at the Center for Cultural Studies at the University of California at Santa Cruz, before an informal meeting of graduate students at Georgetown University, and in a public lecture at Mary Washington College. Thanks to the many who attended and made useful comments; special thanks to James Clifford, Joanna Hamilton, and Richard Warner for making the meetings possible. I would also like to thank Margaret Creighton, Wendy Goldman, Nancy Hewitt, Bridget Hill, Donna Hunter, John Markoff, Lisa Norling, Steve Sapolsky, and Joseph White for their thoughtful assistance.

1. *Boston News-Letter,* 19–26 Dec. 1720. On the trial, see *The Tryals of Captain John Rackam and Other Pirates* (Jamaica, 1721). I have analyzed Rackam's generation of pirates in *Between the Devil and the Deep Blue Sea: Merchant Seamen, Pirates, and the Anglo-American Maritime World, 1700–1750* (Cambridge: Cambridge University Press, 1987), chap. 6.

2. *Tryals of Captain John Rackam,* 15.

3. Captain Charles Johnson, *A General History of the Pyrates,* ed. Manuel Schonhorn (London, 1724, 1728; reprint, London: Dent; Columbia: University of South Carolina Press, 1972), 152.

4. Literary critic John Robert Moore argued in *Defoe in the Pillory and Other Studies* (Bloomington: Indiana University Press, 1939), 129–88, that Captain Johnson was in truth none other than Daniel Defoe. His claim soon gained wide acceptance, as reflected in the republication of *A General History of the Pyrates* in 1972 with Defoe as author. Recently, however, scholars have begun to doubt the attribution. Moore has been challenged by P. N. Furbank and W. R. Owens, *The Canonisation of Daniel Defoe*

Notes to Pages 3–8

(New Haven: Yale University Press, 1988), 100–121. Having worked on *A General History of the Pyrates* for more than fifteen years, I have come to the conclusion that its author had a deeper and more detailed knowledge of things maritime than Defoe could possibly have had.

5. The publishing history of *A General History of the Pyrates* can be followed in Philip Gosse, *A Bibliography of the Works of Captain Charles Johnson* (London: Dulau, 1927).

6. See "By his Excellency Woodes Rogers, Esq; Governour of New-Providence, &c. A Proclamation," *Boston Gazette*, 10–17 Oct. 1720; *Tryals of Captain John Rackam*, 16–19; Governor Nicholas Lawes to Council of Trade and Plantations, 12 June 1721, in Cecil Headlam, ed., *Calendar of State Papers, Colonial Series, America and the West Indies* (London: HMSO, 1933), 32:335 (italics in original); *American Weekly Mercury*, 31 Jan.–7 Feb. 1721; *Boston Gazette*, 6–13 Feb. 1721; and *Boston News-Letter*, 13–20 Feb. 1721.

7. It is possible that the author of *A General History of the Pyrates* used this pamphlet, as he did others, in preparing his text. See Schonhorn's commentary in *A General History of the Pyrates*, 670.

8. *Tryals of Captain John Rackam*, 16.

9. Linda Grant De Pauw notes that women frequently worked in artillery units during the American Revolution. See "Women in Combat: The Revolutionary War Experience," *Armed Forces and Society* 7 (1981): 214–17.

10. *Tryals of Captain John Rackam*, 18.

11. The narratives are in almost all respects plausible. Literary convention of the day played a part in constructing the narratives, to be sure, as in the invocation of the conflict between Mars and Venus in the life of Mary Read. But it has been established by scholars that, apart from one fictional chapter (on Captain Misson), the author of *A General History of the Pyrates* was indeed a "faithful Historian," remarkably reliable in presenting historical facts. For assessments, see Philip Gosse, *The History of Piracy* (New York: Tudor, 1932), 182; Hugh F. Rankin, *The Golden Age of Piracy* (New York: Holt, Rinehart & Winston, 1969), 161; Rediker, *Between the Devil and the Deep Blue Sea*, 258; and B. R. Burg, *Sodomy and the Perception of Evil: English Sea Rovers in the Seventeenth-Century Caribbean* (New York: New York University Press, 1983), 196. See also Schonhorn's introduction to *A General History of the Pyrates*, xxvii–xl.

12. Linda Grant De Pauw, *Seafaring Women* (Boston: Houghton Mifflin, 1982), 18, 71. Seafaring was only one of many lines of work formally to exclude women, for the sexual division of labor was clearly established and indeed growing in the eighteenth century, even if not yet as severe in some respects as it would become. Medieval guilds and the apprenticeship system had long ago segregated the majority of crafts by sex. See the excellent work by Bridget Hill, *Women, Work, and Sexual Politics in Eighteenth-Century England* (Oxford: Basil Blackwell, 1989), especially her comments at 49, 260.

13. Dianne Dugaw, ed., *The Female Soldier: Or, the Surprising Life and Adventures of Hannah Snell* (London, 1750; reprint, Los Angeles: Augustan Reprint Society, 1989), v. Linda Grant De Pauw has pointed out that during the American Revolution, "tens of thousands of women were involved in active combat," a "few hundred" of these—like Deborah Sampson, Sally St. Clair, Margaret Corbin, and a woman known only as "Samuel Gay"—fighting in uniform with the Continental line. See "Women in Combat," 209.

14. "Female Warriors," originally published in the *British Magazine*, was repub-

lished as an "unacknowledged essay" in Peter Cunningham, ed., *The Works of Oliver Goldsmith* (New York: Harper & Bros., 1881), 3:316–19.

15. Historians have only recently begun to study the process by which seafaring became a masculine activity; indeed, this collection was conceived to address this very issue. Given the limitations of current scholarship, the speculations that follow should be regarded as tentative.

16. Rudolf M. Dekker and Lotte C. van de Pol, *The Tradition of Female Transvestism in Early Modern Europe* (London: Macmillan, 1989), 80, 81; Julia Wheelwright, *Amazons and Military Maids: Women Who Dressed as Men in the Pursuit of Life, Liberty, and Happiness* (London: Pandora Press, 1989), 51, 53, 78. Maritime employers probably felt about women sailors the way employers of indentured labor felt about the ten thousand or so women who were transported as felons to Britain's American colonies between 1718 and 1775: they considered these women to be less skilled, less capable of heavy physical labor, and more likely to lose labor time to pregnancy. See A. Roger Ekirch, *Bound for America: The Transportation of British Convicts to the Colonies, 1718–1775* (Oxford: Clarendon Press, 1987), 48–50, 89.

17. Arthur N. Gilbert, "Buggery and the British Navy, 1700–1861," *Journal of Social History* 10 (1976): 87–88.

18. John Flavel, *A Pathetic and Serious Disswassive* . . . (Boston, 1725), 134; De Pauw, *Seafaring Women*, 162, 184–85. The women who regularly came aboard were passengers and increasingly the wives of officers, the great majority of whom were separated from the crew by chasms of gender and class. The trend of captains' wives accompanying them to sea reached a peak in the nineteenth century and declined in the twentieth.

19. The fear of female sexuality probably drew upon an older superstition about the magical, spiritual, and supernatural powers of women that arose during the terrifying early days of seafaring. Linda Grant De Pauw maintains that it is a "myth" and a shoreside invention that women were regarded as bad luck at sea, having little or nothing to do with the actual beliefs of seamen. But her argument is contradicted by too much evidence (some of which is her own) to be persuasive. See her *Seafaring Women*, 15–18.

20. Clive Senior, *A Nation of Pirates: English Piracy in Its Heyday* (London: David & Charles Abbott, 1976), 39.

21. *A General History of the Pyrates*, 212, 343; William Snelgrave, *A New Account of Some Parts of Guinea and the Slave Trade* (London, 1734; reprint, London: Frank Cass, 1971), 256–57.

22. Roberts and his crew may have known—and disapproved—of Bonny and Read. Another of their articles of agreement stated: "If any Man were found seducing any of the [female] Sex, and carry'd her to Sea, disguised, he was to suffer Death." See *A General History of the Pyrates*, 212.

23. *Tryals of Captain John Rackam*, 18.

24. "At a Court held at Williamsburg" (1727), HCA 1/99, fols. 2–8. Mary's husband, Thomas, was also involved in the piracy but somehow eluded arrest. For information on Thomas and Mary Harvey, identified as husband and wife, see Peter Wilson Coldham, *English Convicts in America*, vol. 1, *Middlesex, 1617–1775* (New Orleans: Polyanthos, 1974), 123. Mary was transported to the colonies in April 1725. Thomas was

sentenced in October and transported in November of the same year. The leader of the gang, John Vidal, requested and was granted the king's mercy, receiving pardon for his capital crime in September 1727. See H. R. McIlwaine, *Executive Journals of the Council of Colonial Virginia* (Richmond: Virginia State Library, 1930), 4:149, 150.

25. "Proceedings of the Court of Admiralty [in Virginia]" (1729), HCA 1/99. See also Coldham, *English Convicts in America*, 67 (Crichett) and 290 (Williams). No record exists to show whether the hangings actually took place.

26. By limiting the role of women aboard their ships, pirates may have made it more difficult to reproduce themselves as a community and hence easier for the state to wage its deadly assault upon them.

27. Julia Wheelwright has written: "Women who enlisted as soldiers and sailors were most often from the labouring classes where they were used to hard, physical work. They came from communities where the women were confident of their strength as they worked side by side with men in the fields" or other areas. See *Amazons and Military Maids*, 42; and Dekker and van de Pol, *Tradition of Female Transvestism*, 2.

28. Based on a study of 119 instances of cross-dressing found in the archives of the Dutch East India Company, Rudolf M. Dekker and Lotte C. van de Pol have concluded, "Throughout the early modern era passing oneself off as a man was a real and viable option for women who had fallen into bad times and were struggling to overcome their difficult circumstances." See *Tradition of Female Transvestism*, 1–2 (quotation), 11, 13, 42.

29. See Anne Chambers, *Granuaile: The Life and Times of Grace O'Malley, c. 1530–1603* (Dublin: Wolfhound Press, 1983), Sydney quoted at 85. See also De Pauw, *Seafaring Women*, 24–25. Mary Read, in turn, who kept an inn at Breda, may have influenced the Netherlands' most famous female cross-dresser, Maria van Antwerpen. See Dekker and van de Pol, *Tradition of Female Transvestism*, 40.

30. James Caulfield, *Portraits, Memoirs, and Characters of Remarkable Persons from the Revolution in 1688 to the End of the Reign of George II* (London: T. H. Whitely, 1820), 2:43–51.

31. Ibid., 4:111, 112.

32. Dugaw, *The Female Soldier*, vi, 1, 5, 6, 17, 19, 22–23, 39, 41. Hannah Snell's story was often told in celebration of the British nation, emphasizing the patriotism of her military service. The stories of Bonny and Read admitted no such emphasis, for the inescapable fact remained that they attacked *British* ships and *British* commerce, refusing the logic of nationalism in their depredations.

33. Dianne Dugaw, *Warrior Women and Popular Balladry, 1650–1850* (Cambridge: Cambridge University Press, 1989), 20.

34. Ibid., 1, 48.

35. See ibid., 124, 131, 122 (quotation). Dugaw's conclusion about the positive popular reaction to women warriors would appear to be at odds with that of Rudolf Dekker and Lotte C. van de Pol, but this may be a matter of different responses in England and the Netherlands. See Dekker and van de Pol, *Tradition of Female Transvestism*, 97–98.

36. Bonny and Read's cross-dressing and going to sea should be seen in the broader context suggested by Peter Linebaugh: "I think that to the many acts of survival and

getting by, we should add the power of seeming to be what you are not as among the characteristics of the thick, scarred, and calloused hide of the English proletariat." See "All the Atlantic Mountains Shook," *Labour / Le Travail* 10 (1982): 99.

37. De Pauw argues in "Women in Combat" (223) that in the eighteenth century, "engaging in hand-to-hand combat was not considered unfeminine behavior."

38. *Tryals of Captain John Rackam*, 16, 18.

39. *A General History of the Pyrates*, 151; *Tryals of Captain John Rackam*, 11; Douglas Hay, Peter Linebaugh, and E. P. Thompson, *Albion's Fatal Tree: Crime and Society in Eighteenth-Century England* (New York: Pantheon Books, 1975); E. P. Thompson, *Whigs and Hunters: The Origin of the Black Act* (New York: Pantheon Books, 1975); Peter Linebaugh, *The London Hanged: Crime and Civil Society in the Eighteenth Century* (Cambridge: Cambridge University Press, 1991).

40. *A General History of the Pyrates*, 597.

41. John Gillis, *For Better, for Worse: British Marriages, 1600 to the Present* (New York: Oxford University Press, 1985), 13, 14, 18, 37, 84, 85, 99 (quotation); Anonymous letter from South Carolina, Aug. 1716, Colonial Office Papers 5/382, fol. 47 (quotation), PRO, London. Richard Turnley, who not only refused to witness the wife sale but informed Governor Rogers, became an immediate object of revenge. With "many bitter Oaths and Imprecations," Bonny and Rackam swore that if they had been able to find him (and they went in search of him), they would "have whipp'd him to Death." See *A General History of the Pyrates*, 623, 626. The narrative also suggests that this particular wife sale was initiated not by the husband, as was customary, but rather by Anne Bonny herself. On wife sale, see E. P. Thompson, *Customs in Common* (London: Merlin Press, 1991), chap. 7; Samuel Pyeatt Menafee, *Wives for Sale* (Oxford: Oxford University Press, 1981); and Hill, *Women, Work, and Sexual Politics*, 216.

42. *A General History of the Pyrates*, 391. On the class dimensions of piracy, see Rediker, *Between the Devil and the Deep Blue Sea*, chap. 6; and "Hydrarchy and Libertalia: The Utopian Dimensions of Atlantic Piracy in the Eighteenth Century," paper presented to the conference on "Privateering and Piracy in International Perspective, 1750–1850," Institute for the History of European Expansion / Department of Dutch and Maritime History, Leiden University, and the Dutch Society for Maritime History, Middelburg, The Netherlands (1991).

43. See also Dugaw, *Warrior Women*, 73, 75, 155. The warrior woman ballad declined in England just as cross-dressing declined in the Netherlands. See Dekker and van de Pol, *Tradition of Female Transvestism*, 102–3.

44. Wheelwright, *Amazons and Military Maids*, 11, 78, 159; Dugaw, *Warrior Women*, 1, 3–4. On the subsequent editions of *A General History of the Pirates*, see Gosse, *Bibliography of the Works of Captain Charles Johnson*.

45. Natalie Zemon Davis, "Women on Top," in her *Society and Culture in Early Modern France* (Stanford: Stanford University Press, 1975), 131, 144; Wheelwright, *Amazons and Military Maids*, 15, 119 (quotation).

46. Daniel Defoe, *The Fortunes and Misfortunes of the Famous Moll Flanders* (London, 1722; reprint, New York: Penguin Books, 1978), 28, 33, 228, 208–9.

47. Christopher Hill, *A Tinker and a Poor Man: John Bunyan and His Church, 1628–1688* (New York: Knopf, 1989), 362; Linebaugh, *London Hanged*, 119–20; Dugaw, *The Female Soldier*, 40–41.

Notes to Pages 17–19

48. James R. Sutherland, " 'Polly' among the Pirates," *Modern Language Review* 37 (1942): 291–92; Joan Hildreth Owen, "*Polly* and the Choice of Virtue," *Bulletin of the New York Public Library* 77 (1974): 393. Gay's play helps to prove that warrior women were a major "imaginative preoccupation of the early modern era," as suggested by Dugaw, *Warrior Women*, 1; see also her interesting interpretation of *Polly*, 191–211.

49. John Gay, *Polly: An Opera, being the Second Part of the Beggar's Opera*, in John Fuller, ed., *John Gay: Dramatic Works* (Oxford: Clarendon Press, 1983), 2:95. The name Morano may refer to the Spanish word *moreno*, meaning brown, or it may refer to *marrano*, the term used to describe Jews who converted to Catholicism rather than leave Spain in 1492. This latter meaning would further play upon the theme of disguise.

50. Gay, *Polly*, 99, 140.

51. Ibid., 129.

52. On Aeolus, see Rudolf Wittkower, *Allegory and the Migration of Symbols* (New York: Thames & Hudson, 1977), 94; and Michael Grant and John Hazel, *Gods and Mortals in Classical Mythology* (Springfield, Mass.: G. & C. Merriam, 1973), 27–28. It is also possible that the malevolent god Typhon is the source of the winds, which would have made them "the allies of disorder, the powers of chaos." See Yves Bonnefoy, comp., *Mythologies* (Chicago: University of Chicago Press, 1991), 1:510.

53. Maurice Agulhon has noted how allegorical depictions of anarchy included a dagger and a torch, which signified crimes of destruction. See *Marianne into Battle: Republican Imagery and Symbolism in France, 1789–1880* (Cambridge: Cambridge University Press, 1981), 13. In fashioning this particular image, the unknown artist may have drawn upon Pieter Bruegel's eerily powerful painting *Dulle Griet*, which features the wild, disorderly, sword-toting virago named "Mad Margot" striding fearlessly across the mouth of the gates of hell, impervious to the devils, demons, and creatures all around her. See Leo van Puyvelde, *Pieter Bruegel's "Dulle Griet"* (London: Percy Lund Humphries, n.d.).

54. The art-historical literature on Delacroix's *Liberty* is enormous. Some of the most important works include Lee Johnson, ed., *The Paintings of Eugène Delacroix: A Critical Catalogue* (Oxford: Clarendon Press, 1981), vol. 1 (1816–31), 144–51; George Heard Hamilton, "The Iconographical Origins of Delacroix's 'Liberty Leading the People,' " in Dorothy Miner, ed., *Studies in Art and Literature for Belle Da Costa Greene* (Princeton: Princeton University Press, 1954), 55–66; Hélène Adhémar, "La Liberté sur les Barricades de Delacroix: Étudiée d'après des documents inédits," *Gazette des Beaux-Arts* 43 (1954): 83–92; N. Hadjinicolaou, " 'La Liberté guidant le peuple' de Delacroix devant son premier plan," *Actes de la Recherche en Social Sciences* (June 1979): 3–26; Hélène Toussaint, *La Liberté guidant le peuple de Delacroix* (Paris: Éditions de la Réunion des musées nationaux, 1982); T. J. Clark, *The Absolute Bourgeois: Artists and Politics in France, 1848–1851* (Princeton: Princeton University Press, 1973), 17–20, 22, 25–26, 29; and Marcia Pointon, "*Liberty on the Barricades:* Women, Politics, and Sexuality in Delacroix," in her *Naked Authority: The Body in Western Painting, 1830–1908* (Cambridge: Cambridge University Press, 1990), 59–82.

55. Marina Warner, *Maidens and Monuments: The Allegory of the Female Form* (London: Weidenfeld & Nicolson, 1985), 272.

56. The four winds under the charge of Aeolus were usually depicted as children or

beardless men, which might help to explain Delacroix's choice of the youth. See J. S. Cooper, *An Illustrated Encyclopaedia of Traditional Symbols* (New York: Thames & Hudson, 1978), 192.

57. It is curious that art historians have not explored the possible maritime meanings of the symbolism in the painting, especially in light of Delacroix's proximity to the sea in his youth, where he would have seen bare-breasted women as figureheads on a variety of ships. The artist would likely have known that many sailors considered these figures to have protective supernatural powers, in particular the capacity to silence the tempests they faced at sea. See Margaret Baker, *The Folklore of the Sea* (London: David & Charles, 1979), chap. 1; and Horace Beck, *Folklore and the Sea* (Middletown, Conn.: Wesleyan University Press, 1973), 15–16.

58. Lynda Nead, *The Female Nude: Art, Obscenity, and Sexuality* (London: Routledge, 1992), 2 (quotation), 9, 47. The distinction between the naked and the nude was pressed by Kenneth Clark, *The Nude: A Study in Ideal Form* (Princeton: Princeton University Press, 1953), 3–29. When, a generation later, the new definition of femininity had taken hold, Eduard Manet would scandalize the art establishment afresh by painting women who were naked rather than nude. See T. J. Clark, "Preliminaries to a Possible Treatment of 'Olympia' in 1865," *Screen* 21 (1980): 18–41.

59. See Warner, *Maidens and Monuments*, chaps. 6, 8, 12.

60. There is also the story of the "Maid of Saragossa," well known for her courage during the defense of her Spanish home against the French in 1808. For discussion of these sources, see Pointon, "Liberty on the Barricades," 64; Hamilton, "Iconographical Origins," 63–64; and Johnson, *Paintings of Delacroix*, 147. The influences discussed here do not displace or diminish the widely acknowledged importance of artists such as Gericault, Gros, and Guerin to Delacroix's painting.

61. The female image of piracy may be seen as a forerunner of a specifically radical image of liberty that emerged during the French Revolution. Lynn Hunt has pointed out that this image—armed, "bare-breasted and fierce of visage," woman as an active agent of change—existed in tension with a conservative image of a woman "seated, stolid, tranquil, and often without lance or liberty cap," woman as a passive reflection of stability. See Lynn Hunt, *Politics, Culture, and Class in the French Revolution* (Berkeley: University of California Press, 1984), 93. On the genesis of liberty as a symbol in France, see Agulhon, *Marianne into Battle*, chap. 1. The radical image would in turn make its way into the socialist tradition. Eric Hobsbawm, "Man and Woman in Socialist Iconography," *History Workshop Journal* 6 (1978): 121–38. See also Maurice Agulhon, "On Political Allegory: A Reply to Eric Hobsbawm," *History Workshop Journal* 8 (1979): 167-73.

62. Gosse, *Bibliography of the Works of Capt. Charles Johnson*.

63. See three articles by George Heard Hamilton: "Eugène Delacroix and Lord Byron," *Gazette des Beaux-Arts* 23 (1943): 99–110; "Hamlet or Childe Harold? Delacroix and Byron," *Gazette des Beaux-Arts* 26 (1944): 365–86; and "Iconographical Origins," 63, where Hamilton notes that Byron was much on Delacroix's mind during the winter of 1830-31. *The Corsair* can be found in Ernest Hartley Coleridge, ed., *The Works of Lord Byron* (New York: Octagon Books, 1966), 3:227–96.

64. Bartholomew Roberts and his crew, active between 1719 and 1722, were probably the most successful—and widely feared—band of pirates to roam the seas in the

early eighteenth century. Roberts was killed in an engagement with HMS *Swallow* off the coast of West Africa in 1722. His crew was captured, and many hanged at Cape Coast Castle. Edward Teach, better known as Blackbeard, was a pirate captain active in the Caribbean and western Atlantic between roughly 1715 and 1719, when he, too, was killed in an engagement with the Royal Navy. For additional information on each, see Philip Gosse, *The Pirates' Who's Who, Giving Particulars of the Lives & Deaths of the Pirates & Buccaneers* (London, 1924; reprint, New York: Burt Franklin, 1968).

65. The suggestion that Mary Read fought in the War of the League of Augsburg, which began in 1689 and was concluded by the Peace of Ryswick in 1697, would seem to be an error. It is more likely that she fought in the War of Spanish Succession (1702–13), which means that she was probably born between 1690 and 1695, and therefore in her late twenties during the period of her piracy.

66. The King's Proclamation was issued on 5 Sept. 1717. News of it began to circulate in New World ports late in the year.

67. Woodes Rogers was a gentleman mariner who was commissioned by the Crown to bring the Bahama Islands, a pirate haunt, under royal authority in 1717. He arrived in the islands in July 1718. See "Woodes Rogers," in Sir Leslie Stephen and Sir Sidney Lee, eds., *Dictionary of National Biography* (Oxford: Oxford University Press, 1964), 17:147–48.

68. What appears to be the same mutiny is described briefly in "The Memoriall of the Merchants of London Trading to Africa," Admiralty Papers 1/3810, PRO, London.

69. Most pirates did not keep people against their will. See Rediker, *Between the Devil and the Deep Blue Sea*, 266.

70. Dueling at "sword and pistol" was a ritual among pirates. See ibid., 265.

71. Several historians have claimed that Anne Bonny's father was named William Cormac and her mother named Peg Brennan, though I have not been able to locate the original sources upon which these identifications have been made. It is also claimed that Anne Bonny's father went to Charleston rather than other parts of the Carolinas, which seems likely. According to historian Thomas Truxes, South Carolina was in the early eighteenth century becoming the most important American destination for Irish passengers and servants. See his *Irish-American Trade, 1660–1783* (Cambridge: Cambridge University Press, 1988), 143. More specifically, Charleston would have been the easiest place for an attorney to find work and eventually to make his way into mercantile pursuits and the ownership of a plantation. It was also the likeliest place from which to develop ties to planters in Jamaica, mentioned below.

72. Providence was the pirates' main settlement in the Bahama Islands.

2. Dianne Dugaw, Female Sailors Bold

The ballad excerpt in the epigraph comes from Helen Creighton, *Songs and Ballads from Nova Scotia* (Toronto: J. M. Dent, 1932), 68–70. This ballad celebrates a disguising woman sailor, Anne Jane Thornton, who made herself known in London in 1835. See "Extraordinary Circumstance," *London Times*, 9 Feb. 1835, p. 1, col. 5; "Ship News," 10 Feb. 1835, p. 4, col. 2; and "Police," 11 Feb. 1835, p. 6, col. 5. An account quickly appeared, *The Interesting Life and Wonderful Adventures of that Extraordinary Woman Anne Jane Thornton, the Female Sailor . . . Written by herself* (London: n.p., 1835). Several ballads about her were also printed on both sides of the Atlantic, this one still being sung in our own day.

1. I have called this transposing pattern—which also includes women soldiers along with women sailors—the Female Warrior Motif. The imaginative pattern and its ideology derive from the epic and its conventions for heroic (masculine) behavior at war and at sea. For my extended study of this heroine in ballads and other literature, see Dianne Dugaw, *Warrior Women and Popular Balladry, 1650–1850* (Cambridge: Cambridge University Press, 1989; reprint, Chicago: University of Chicago Press, 1996). For other recent studies of disguising women, see Julie Wheelwright, *Amazons and Military Maids: Women Who Dressed as Men in the Pursuit of Life, Liberty, and Happiness* (London: Pandora Press, 1989); and Rudolf Dekker and Lotte van de Pol, *The Tradition of Female Transvestism in Early Modern Europe* (London: Macmillan, 1989).

2. The idea of transvestism has received considerable scholarly attention in the past few years. In addition to those studies of women sailors and soldiers already cited, see Marjorie Garber's *Vested Interests: Cross-Dressing and Cultural Anxiety* (New York: Routledge, 1992). In response to Garber's psychology-based diagnosis of "cultural anxiety," I would urge a longer view that contextualizes the meaning of transvestism in the culture of the twentieth century by putting it in a larger historical context.

3. Michel Foucault and his followers discuss the emergence of the modern ideology of sexuality and its social and institutional contexts. His discussion of the "persecution of peripheral sexualities" by means of "a new specification of individuals," that is, by an understanding of behavior as arising from one's personal "sensibility," is pertinent. See *The History of Sexuality*, vol. 1, *An Introduction*, translated by Robert Hurley (New York: Vintage Books, 1980), 42–44.

4. Judith Butler observes that "it becomes impossible to separate out 'gender' from the political and cultural intersections in which it is invariably produced and maintained." *Gender Trouble: Feminism and the Subversion of Identity* (New York: Routledge, 1990), 3. Butler's questioning of "stable signifiers" and "a universal basis" for gender categories can be linked to Foucault's historicizing of concepts of "sexual identity."

5. See Dugaw, *Warrior Women*, 121–42, on these differences—in particular, the experience and sensibility of lower-class people in the early modern era, the trope of masquerading both as a pastime and as a way of conceptualizing identity, and the decentralized character of military institutions and seafaring.

6. On this waning, see ibid., 65–90. See also Dianne Dugaw, "'Rambling Female Sailors'": The Rise and Fall of the Seafaring Heroine," a version of this chapter published in the *International Journal of Maritime History* 4 (June 1992): 179–94.

7. The development of this idea in the eighteenth century and its widespread percolation to all levels in the nineteenth is a subject too complex to cover here. On the eighteenth century as a period important in the construction of modern subjectivity (with particular attention to gender), see Felicity A. Nussbaum, *The Autobiographical Subject: Gender and Ideology in Eighteenth-Century England* (Baltimore: Johns Hopkins University Press, 1989). On delicacy and the eighteenth-century sensibility, see Jean Hagstrum, *Sex and Sensibility: Ideal and Erotic Love from Milton to Mozart* (Chicago: University of Chicago Press, 1980), 5–23, 195–99. On passivity as a feminine ideal, see Ellen Pollak, *The Poetics of Sexual Myth: Gender and Ideology in the Verse of Swift and Pope* (Chicago: University of Chicago Press, 1985), 42ff. On the corset and the

nineteenth-century physiology and ideology of female frailty that accompanied it, see Mel Davies, "Corsets and Conception: Fashion and Demographic Trends in the Nineteenth Century," *Comparative Studies in Society and History* 24 (1982): 611–41. For discussion of the education of women to conform to these values, see Nancy Armstrong, *Desire and Domestic Fiction: A Political History of the Novel* (Oxford: Oxford University Press, 1987). See also Mary Poovey, *The Proper Lady and the Woman Writer: Ideology as Style in the Works of Mary Wollstonecraft, Mary Shelley, and Jane Austen* (Chicago: University of Chicago Press, 1984). For discussion of the politics of female delicacy in England against the backdrop of the French Revolution, with specific application to women aboard ships, see Claudia L. Johnson, *Jane Austen: Women, Politics, and the Novel* (Chicago: University of Chicago Press, 1988), 149–54. Johnson discusses the seafaring "Mrs. Crofts" of Jane Austen's *Persuasion*.

8. For general discussion of female delicacy with regard to this heroine and ballad tradition, see Dugaw, *Warrior Women*, 65–90, 124–31, 140-42.

9. For a collection and catalogue of these ballads, see Dianne Dugaw, "The Female Warrior Heroine in Anglo-American Popular Balladry" (Ph.D. diss., University of California, Los Angeles, 1982), 340–886.

10. On this context for ballads, see Dugaw, *Warrior Women*, 15–31.

11. See ibid., 31–90, for extended discussion of this ballad tradition and its transformation over time.

12. Walker actually published short and long versions of a single text under the same imprint, both versions claiming to be firsthand accounts from the "Female Soldier" herself. For discussion of these, see Dianne Dugaw, introduction to *The Female Soldier (1750)* (Augustan Reprint Society, no. 257, Los Angeles: William Andrews Clark Memorial Library, 1989), v.

13. Apart from Walker's account, little is known about Snell. Her name appears in pension records of her time. She moved for some years in public notice, appearing on stage at Sadler's Wells and operating an inn at Wapping. She wed a carpenter named Eyles in Berkshire. Eventually, she declined in health and at the age of 69 died in Bedlam Hospital in 1792. See *The Female Soldier* (1989), v–vi. See also *Dictionary of National Biography*, 18:613–14; and Rev. Daniel Lysons, *The Environs of London: Being an Historical Account of the Towns, Villages and Hamlets within 12 Miles of That Capital*, 4 vols. (London: T. Cadell, Jun. and W. Davies, 1792–96), 2:164.

14. See my discussion in *The Female Soldier* (1989), vi–x.

15. Ibid., 15.

16. Ibid., 2.

17. Ibid., 1.

18. For a discussion of Richardson's work and importance, see Margaret A. Doody, *A Natural Passion: A Study of the Novels of Samuel Richardson* (Oxford: Oxford University Press, 1974).

19. *The Female Soldier*, 40–41.

20. James Woodforde, *The Diary of a Country Parson*, ed. John Beresford, 5 vols. (London: Humphrey Milford, Oxford University Press, 1924-31), 1:224–25. The entry is for 21 May 1778. Woodforde's parsonage was in Weston Longeville, Norfolk. He has some misinformation about Snell's life.

21. Mary Anne Talbot, "The Intrepid Female: Or, surprising life and adventures of

Mary-Anne Talbot, otherwise John Taylor," published by R. S. Kirby in 1804 and circulated both as a single piece and as part of a variously titled miscellany published between 1803 and 1820. All page numbers cited in the text are taken from *Kirby's Wonderful and Eccentric Museum, &c.*, 6 vols. (London: R. S. Kirby, 1820), 2:160–225.

22. An introduction to "The Intrepid Female" describes the account as "Narrated by herself to the Editor of the Scientific Museum, and now first made public" (160).

23. Talbot's boarding-school education undoubtedly introduced her to that ethos of female behavior represented in novels and conduct books, an ethos quite apart from the lower-class world of seafaring. Moreover, appealing for help from bourgeois book-buyers and aristocratic patrons required not only that Talbot present herself as suffering and in need of succor but also that she do so in terms matching the expectations of her readers.

24. Talbot's story may actually stand behind a late-eighteenth-century ballad called "The Female Drummer." For versions, see Dugaw, "Female Warrior Heroine," 846–53.

25. Dogged by further misfortunes, Talbot lived from 1804, until she died in 1808, "in the capacity of a domestic" in the house of Kirby, her publisher. See Menie Muriel Dowie, ed., *Women Adventurers: The Adventure Series*, vol. 15 (London: Unwin Bros., 1893), 194–95.

26. Julie Wheelwright sketches aspects of this tension in Snell's story in *Amazons and Military Maids*, 141–43.

27. Richardson's *Clarissa, or the History of a Young Lady* tells, as a novelistic tragedy, the story of the kidnapping and rape of a young bourgeois woman by a rakish upper-class man, and her subsequent languishing death. Published in 1747–48, *Clarissa* constructs an image of female heroism in the context of male brutishness and sexual predation.

28. We do well to remember the material conditions of Talbot's world when we ask why she remained disguised rather than disclose herself. She may have considered it more dangerous to disclose herself on a foreign battlefield or on board a schooner than to remain in disguise. Or perhaps she recognized that late-eighteenth-century Europe had no social or economic place for a woman in her situation. Today a woman can survive autonomously—albeit marginally—*as a woman*. Talbot had almost no such opportunity of being a beautician, secretary, or waitress. She had little incentive to reveal herself as long as her disguise worked.

29. This implies the constructed nature of gender identity and power in any world.

30. Talbot's "manliness" extended to relationships with women. Like many ballads and other stories of transvestite heroines, "The Intrepid Female" includes a courtship episode that sets into a wonderful confusion the "naturalness" of heterosexual attraction. (On this trope in the conventional female warrior story, see Dugaw, *Warrior Women*, 143–62. See also Dianne Dugaw, "Mary Lacy's Ladies: being a Consideration of the Divers Adventures with the fair Sex of this Woman Sailor and others like Her, who disguised as Men to Fight, Work, and Romance in Days Gone By; with Discussion of these Heroines in the further Light of Concerns of Lesbian Women of our own Time," *CSWS Review* [Eugene, Oreg.: Center for the Study of Women in Society, University of Oregon, 1993]: 8–12). Talbot also refers matter-of-factly to a householding arrangement with a woman (217). Though we can only surmise a sexual side to

this seemingly marital relationship, it could be what our era would call a lesbian relationship. I am reluctant to label Talbot a lesbian because this concept depends upon a post-Victorian view of sexuality and identity to which Talbot and her world did not subscribe. It is as anachronistic to imagine her possessing our "psychology" of "sexual orientation" as it is to see her dogged by thoughts of her physical limitations as a woman. These ideas arise when identity is defined by such allegedly natural traits of the body as race, sexual behavior, and gender.

31. Talbot's masking of her gender made this traversing of the economy as a marketable male individual possible. She thereby bypassed the externally imposed restrictions placed upon women. Known as a woman—which she was by Bowen, and in her life on shore after disclosing her "adventures"—Talbot was prevented from using those attributes that made possible her advancement as a man. Had she lived later or been educated more fully in "womanly" ideals, she would have displayed and experienced, one suspects, characteristics of emotional delicacy, physical and psychological frailty, and intellectual doubt. As a woman, she would remain at the margins of the social and material economy.

32. On servants and the controversy about recognizing social rank in the eighteenth century, see Janet Todd, "Pamela: or, the Bliss of Servitude," *British Journal for Eighteenth-Century Studies* 6 (1983): 135–48. The classic studies of modern British class structure are background for my discussion, especially E. P. Thompson, *The Making of the English Working Class* (London: Victor Gollancz, 1963); and Harold Perkin, *The Origins of Modern English Society, 1780–1880* (London: Routledge & Kegan Paul; Toronto: University of Toronto Press, 1969).

33. On the shift in the construction of sexuality and gender from an external and social system of codes to an internal and individual system, see John D'Emilio and Estelle B. Freedman, *Intimate Matters: A History of Sexuality in America* (New York: Harper & Row, 1988), 41ff. D'Emilio and Freedman locate this shift in attitude in the early nineteenth century.

34. Dowie, *Women Adventurers*.

35. Ibid., xxi–xxii.

36. Ibid., x–xi.

37. Ibid., xviii. *A General History of the Pyrates*, by "Captain Charles Johnson," has been (questionably) attributed to Defoe. See Captain Charles Johnson, *A General History of the Pyrates*, ed. Manuel Schonhorn (London, 1724, 1728; reprint, London: Dent; Columbia: University of South Carolina Press, 1972).

38. Ibid., xx.

39. Ibid., xviii.

40. Cecilia Lucy Brightwell, *Memorials of the Life of Amelia Opie* (Norwich: Fletcher & Alexander; London: Longman, Brown, 1854), 18. The entire episode is found on pages 17–21. All excerpts cited in the text are from this source. To appreciate the complexity of Opie's view, it is useful to realize that in her own politics she was a reformer, not a reactionary. See Janet Todd, ed., *A Dictionary of British and American Women Writers, 1660–1800* (Totowa, N.J.: Rowman & Allanheld, 1985), 236–37.

41. This intriguing invocation of foodways to mark "otherness" calls to mind Claude Lévi-Strauss's *Le Cru et le cuit* (Paris: Plon, 1964), translated by John and Doreen Weightman as *The Raw and the Cooked* (New York: Harper & Row, 1969).

42. The woman's name suggests that she is Hispanic or perhaps Portuguese. However, Opie supplies nothing further on this aspect of her identity.

43. See Dugaw, *Warrior Women*, 140–42, for discussion of this reform movement. On representations of lower-class people in eighteenth- and early-nineteenth-century art and literature, see John Barrell, *The Dark Side of the Landscape: The Rural Poor in English Painting, 1730–1840* (Cambridge: Cambridge University Press, 1980); Ann Bermingham, *Landscape and Ideology: The English Rustic Tradition, 1740–1860* (Berkeley: University of California Press, 1986). On reforming the lower classes, see Barrell, 65–85, 118, 137; Bermingham, 70–77.

44. Bermingham discusses the ownership of property as a requirement for humanity on 71–72. For links to nature, see 14–25.

45. The best-known interrogation of this subject-object construction is the work of Michel Foucault. On this aspect of his thought, see Jerrold Seigel, "Avoiding the Subject: A Foucaultian Itinerary," *Journal of the History of Ideas* 51 (1990): 273–99. See also Michel Foucault, "The Subject and Power," afterword to Hubert L. Dreyfus and Paul Rabinow, *Michel Foucault: Beyond Structuralism and Hermeneutics*, 2d ed., with an interview with Michel Foucault (Chicago: University of Chicago Press, 1983 [1982]), 211–12.

46. On a new eighteenth-century conception of society and nature, Bermingham remarks, "To be mistaken for what one is not represented an alarming breakdown in the sign system—a breakdown more easily avoided than repaired." *Landscape and Ideology*, 23.

47. Carrie Grover was raised in rural Nova Scotia and Maine. Toward the end of her life, she became interested in the songs traditional in her family, contacting Alan Lomax at the Library of Congress. These remarks, together with several songs, are on Tape 4463 in the Library of Congress Archive of Folksong.

3. Ruth Herndon, The Domestic Cost of Seafaring

1. "Serving time" was a common phrase used to refer to indentured servitude.

2. Town council meeting of 20 Jan. 1775, Jamestown Town Council Records, 2:117–18.

3. Town council meeting of 30 Jan. 1775, Westerly Town Council and Probate Records, 4:250.

4. On the eighteenth-century masculine ideal (for New Englanders, at least) of heading a household, see E. Anthony Rotundo, *American Manhood: Transformations in Masculinity from the Revolution to the Modern Era* (New York: Basic Books, 1993), 2–3, 10–18. Rotundo does not elaborate on the racial bias of this concept, but it was clearly a prescription made by and for white men. See below, section 2.

5. Linda K. Kerber, "The Revolutionary Generation: Ideology, Politics, and Culture in the Early Republic," *The New American History*, ed. Eric Foner (Philadelphia: Temple University Press, 1990), 31.

6. Stephanie Coontz, *The Social Origins of Private Life: A History of American Families, 1600–1900* (London: Verso, 1988), 79.

7. Town council meetings of 5 Sept. 1796 and 3 Oct. 1796, Hopkinton Town Council Records, 3:86–87.

Notes to Pages 58–60

8. Anthony Rotundo sums up this cultural construction of male responsibility thus: "The shortcomings of a youth were charged directly to the father who brought him forth into the community." *American Manhood*, 3.

9. For a discussion of the responsibilities of town councilmen and of the institutions of social control that they used, see Ruth Wallis Herndon, "Governing the Affairs of the Town: Continuity and Change in Rhode Island, 1750–1800" (Ph.D. diss., American University, 1992), chaps. 8, 9.

10. Town council meeting of 21 Apr. 1752, Jamestown Town Council Records, 1:53.

11. Lisa Norling, "Ahab's Wife: Women and the American Whaling Industry, 1820–1870," this volume.

12. Town council meeting of 31 Dec. 1757, Providence Town Council Records, 4:167.

13. Lisa Norling, "Contrary Dependencies: Whaling Agents and Whalemen's Families, 1830–1870," *Log of Mystic Seaport* 42 (spring 1990): 7.

14. The Jamestown town clerk identified Primus Thompson as "Indian"; but the Westerly town clerk identified him as "Mustee or Molatto." This lack of precision about Primus's racial heritage was commonplace. Eighteenth-century Rhode Island town clerks routinely blurred racial distinctions. Many clerks referred to the same person as "mulatto" in one place and "Indian" in another, or used the terms "Indian" and "Negro" to describe the same person within one document.

15. Daniel Vickers, "The First Whalemen of Nantucket," *William and Mary Quarterly* 40 (Oct. 1983): 560–83; Daniel Vickers, "Nantucket Whalemen in the Deep-Sea Fishery: The Changing Anatomy of an Early American Labor Force," *Journal of American History* 72 (Sept. 1985): 277–96, esp. 286–87.

16. W. Jeffrey Bolster, "'To Feel Like a Man': Black Seamen in the Northern States, 1800–1860," *Journal of American History* 76 (Mar. 1990): 1173–99. For Rhode Island blacks turning especially to seafaring, see 1182. For a substantially revised version, see "'Every Inch a Man': Gender in the Lives of African American Seamen, 1800–1860," this volume.

17. In Rhode Island, at least 25 percent of the public indentures recorded in the town records between 1750 and 1800 were for Native American and African American children and adults. This figure is far out of proportion to the population for these two racial groups, which together never exceeded 10 percent. See Herndon, "Governing the Affairs of the Town," 245 and note.

18. Vickers, "Nantucket Whalemen in the Deep-Sea Fishery," 295–96.

19. Marcus Rediker, "The Anglo-American Seaman as Collective Worker, 1700–1750," in Stephen Innes, ed., *Work and Labor in Early America* (Chapel Hill: University of North Carolina Press, 1988), 257–58; and Marcus Rediker, *Between the Devil and the Deep Blue Sea: Merchant Seamen, Pirates, and the Anglo-American Maritime World, 1700–1750* (Cambridge: Cambridge University Press, 1987), 82–83, 124, 146–49, 155–56, 304–5.

Rediker notes that "seafaring jobs were most easily found in late spring, summer, and fall." "The Anglo-American Seaman as Collective Worker," 257; and *Between the Devil and the Deep Blue Sea*, 82. This fits with the transiency records in Rhode Island, which show that warnouts of vagrants peaked in the winter and again in the spring. When maritime work dried up in the winter, ex-seamen became transients on land; when such work appeared again in the spring, the stream of transients began again as men headed for the ports. Jamestown, which suffered a yearly influx of transients as seamen passed through town on the way to neighboring Newport, warned out more people in May than in all the other months combined between 1750 and 1800. Herndon, "Governing the Affairs of the Town," 224.

20. Peter J. Coleman, "The Insolvent Debtor in Rhode Island, 1745-1828," *William and Mary Quarterly* 22 (July 1965): 422n. Cited in Jesse Lemisch, "Jack Tar in the Streets: Merchant Seamen in the Politics of Revolutionary America," *William and Mary Quarterly* 25 (July 1968): 376 and note.

21. The language of the Rhode Island town records makes it clear that white leaders did not expect blacks and Indians to adhere to white standards of household structure, nor did they acknowledge as legally binding household arrangements that people of color made among themselves. Clerks rarely used the term *bastard* to refer to a child born to an unmarried black or Indian woman; the term is used primarily to identify children of white women who were (apparently) expected to adhere to (white) marital conventions. Clerks most often used the term *alias* to preface the married names of Indian and black women and to indicate that no recognized legal marriage had been conducted. In 1796, for example, the South Kingstown Town Council interrogated two impoverished Indian women, mother and daughter. The mother's name is recorded as "Mary Fowler alias Mary Cummock" to identify Mary's mother (Sarah Cummock) and Mary's mate (James Fowler). Mary's daughter's name is rendered "Mary Fowler, Jr. alias Champlin alias Mary Cummock" to identify her mother (Mary Fowler) and her grandmother (Sarah Cummock) as well as her own mate (John Champlin). The clerk described the daughter's household thus: "She hath lived with a person of the name of John Champlin, a mustee man, as his wife eleven years . . . and has had six children by him, but never was married to him according to the form used by the white people in these parts." Town council meeting of 14 May 1796, South Kingstown Town Council Records, 6:229-30.

22. Vickers, "Nantucket Whalemen in the Deep-Sea Fishery," 283; Vickers, "The First Whalemen of Nantucket," 579.

23. Rediker, *Between the Devil and the Deep Blue Sea*, 159, 207-22, 241-42; and "The Anglo-American Seaman as Collective Worker," 259, 267.

24. *Acts and Laws of the English Colony of Rhode Island and Providence Plantations in New England, in America* (Newport: Samuel Hall, 1767), 197.

25. Town council meeting of 29 Sept. 1781, Providence Town Council Records, 5:193.

26. Town council meeting of 9 Jan. 1775, South Kingstown Town Council Records, 6:32-33.

27. Town council meeting of 27 Nov. 1784, East Greenwich Town Council Records, 4:9.

28. Marcus Rediker found that between 1700 and 1750, the average age of the common seaman was 27. *Between the Devil and the Deep Blue Sea*, 12, 156, 299-300; Vickers, "Nantucket Whalemen in the Deep Sea Fishery," 294. Bolster argues that in the early nineteenth century, black seamen were an exception and tended to be older than their white counterparts. "'To Feel Like a Man,'" 1190.

29. John Eldred will and inventory, 17 Jan. 1785, Jamestown Town Council Records, 2:176-80. At his death, Eldred left three slaves and several pounds of silver plate in his personal estate to testify to his wealth. His election to public office is recorded in the annual spring town election meetings in Jamestown Town Meeting Records, vol. 1.

30. Town meeting of 25 Aug. 1761, Jamestown Town Meeting Records, 1:96.

Notes to Pages 62–66

31. Town meetings of 21 Jan. 1765 and 28 Nov. 1785, Warwick Town Meeting Records, 2:302, 3:226.

32. Town meeting of 16 Apr. 1794, Glocester Town Meeting Records, 2:40.

33. Town meeting of 29 Aug. 1758, East Greenwich Town Meeting Records, 2:n.p.

34. Recorded with Robert Scott's will, 1785, Providence *Wills*, 6:504-5. The careful, detailed wording of the document and its inclusion in the town clerk's records testify to the unusual case of a single woman taking over responsibility for a man's estate.

35. Town council meeting of 23 May 1791, Glocester Town Council Records, 2:56.

36. *Acts and Laws of Rhode Island* (1767), 217.

37. Town council meeting of 6 Aug. 1750, Tiverton Town Council Records, 2:32.

38. Town council meeting of 4 Feb. 1760, Warren Town Council Records, 1:190.

39. The Providence Town Council bound out Robert Leonard Jr. on 1 Apr. 1782 during his father's absence and released him from indenture, at his father's request, on 11 Oct. 1783. Town council meetings of 1 Apr. and 2 Apr. 1782 and 11 Oct. 1783, Providence Town Council Records, 5:206-7, 5:247-48.

40. In 1798, the state legislature codified town responsibility for the poor in "An Act providing for the Relief, Support, Employment and Removal of the Poor." This act opened with the stipulation "That every town in this State shall be holden to relieve and support all poor and indigent persons, lawfully settled therein, whenever they shall stand in need thereof." *The Public Laws of the State of Rhode Island and Providence Plantations* (Providence: Carter & Wilkinson, 1798), 348.

41. For the concept of mutual responsibilities and privileges in New England towns, see Josiah Henry Benton, *Warning Out in New England, 1656-1817* (Boston, 1911; reprint, Freeport, N.Y.: Books for Libraries Press, 1970), esp. 4–5. For a full discussion of poor support in Rhode Island towns, see Herndon, "Governing the Affairs of the Town," chap. 7.

42. *Acts and Laws of Rhode Island* (1767), 228–29. Women also took on the legal settlements of their husbands and lost their settlement of birth or servitude when they married.

43. Ibid., 229.

44. "Transient" conveyed different meanings in the eighteenth century than it does today. Then, the word referred neither to travelers nor (usually) to homeless vagrants, although a small fraction of footloose people counted in the transient population. Instead, "transient" usually described a person who had been dwelling in a town for some time but who had not qualified as a legal inhabitant. Inhabitants had rights and privileges, but transients remained in residence only by the permission of town leaders. Councilmen typically warned out (removed) transients only when other inhabitants complained about the transients' poverty, illness, or misbehavior. Most transients lived in a town long enough to put down roots before they were warned out: the average residence for transients questioned by the Rhode Island councils in the eighteenth century was a little less than five years. See Ruth Wallis Herndon, "Women of 'No Particular Home': Town Leaders and Female Transients in Southeastern New England, 1750–1800," in Larry Eldridge, ed., *Women and Freedom in Early America* (New York: New York University Press, forthcoming 1996).

45. Throughout New England, towns required poor newcomers to appear before the town council and produce certificates from their hometowns. This document, which the town clerk filed with official papers, was issued by the hometown council

and promised that the hometown would take back the bearer and family if the need arose. The certificate also made council examinations unnecessary. But many transients were either ignorant of this requirement or deliberately ignored it and spent their time trying to avoid the authorities in one town or another. Without proof of legal residence, needy transients found no welcome anywhere and were usually warned out once a town council had spotted them. Prosperous newcomers who purchased freehold estates and qualified as voters were not required to bring a certificate, which was demanded only of poor, landless people. For a discussion of warning out and departure certificates in Rhode Island, see Herndon, "Governing the Affairs of the Town," chap. 9.

46. Town council meeting of 21 Dec. 1772, South Kingstown Town Council Records, 6:9.

47. Town council meeting of 11 Oct. 1783, Providence Town Council Records, 5:248–49.

48. In Providence, for example, town clerks indicated a seafaring history for 15 percent of transient people interrogated by the town council between 1750 and 1790. The actual percentage is probably higher, because clerks did not always note the complete details of a transient's past.

49. Town council meeting of 10 Dec. 1764, South Kingstown Town Council Records, 5:157.

50. Town council meeting of 8 Oct. 1785, Providence Town Council Records, 5:340.

51. Town council meeting of 18 Apr. 1787, Cumberland Town Council Records, 3:151–52.

52. Town council meeting of 30 Jan. 1775, Westerly Town Council and Probate Records, 4:250.

53. Town council meeting of 19 June 1757, Exeter Town Council Records, 2:15.

54. Town council meeting of 11 June 1764, Warwick Town Council Records, 2:248. Stuckley's profession as a mariner is noted in town council meeting of 14 Oct. 1765, Warwick Town Council Records, 2:265.

55. Town council meeting of 27 Mar. 1762, Jamestown Town Council Records, 1:143.

56. Rhode Island law authorized town councils to bind out poor children in public indentures, as if the councilmen were themselves parents of the children. *Acts and Laws of Rhode Island* (1767), 232; *Public Laws of Rhode Island* (1798), 319–22.

57. Town council meeting of 21 May 1765, Jamestown Town Council Records, 1:202. £4 Rhode Island Old Tenor translated to $.50 silver in 1765, or the equivalent of one day's wages for a common laborer.

58. See n. 45.

59. Town council meetings of 18 July and 23 July 1768, Middletown Town Council Records, 2:35.

60. See Bolster, "'To Feel Like a Man,'" 1183, and Rediker, "The Anglo-American Seaman as Collective Worker," esp. 281–82.

4. Lisa Norling, Ahab's Wife

Abbreviations:

AAS American Antiquarian Society, Worcester, Massachusetts
KWM Kendall Whaling Museum, Library, Sharon, Massachusetts

Notes to Pages 70–72

MattHS	Mattapoisett Historical Society, Mattapoisett, Massachusetts
MSM	G. W. Blunt White Library, Mystic Seaport Museum, Mystic, Connecticut
NBFPL	New Bedford Free Public Library, Special Collections, New Bedford, Massachusetts
NHA	Nantucket Historical Association, Peter Foulger Research Center, Nantucket, Massachusetts
ODHS	Old Dartmouth Historical Society Whaling Museum, Library, New Bedford, Massachusetts
PPL	Providence Public Library, Nicholson Whaling Collection, Providence, Rhode Island

I am indebted to Marcus Rediker, the commentator, and Margaret Creighton and W. Jeffrey Bolster, the other panelists, for their helpful comments on the version of this chapter presented at the Organization of American Historians conference, 23 Mar. 1990. Some of the ideas discussed here also appear, in somewhat different form, in my article "Contrary Dependencies: Whaling Agents and Whalemen's Families, 1830–1870," *Log of Mystic Seaport* 42 (spring 1990): 3–12.

1. Eric W. Sager, *Seafaring Labour: The Merchant Marine of Atlantic Canada, 1820–1914* (Kingston: McGill-Queen's University Press, 1989), 238.

2. See especially the discussion of gender in nineteenth-century seafaring culture in Margaret Creighton, "Davy Jones's Locker Room: Gender and the Sailors' Sphere, 1830–1870," this volume; also Caroline Moseley, "Images of Young Women in Nineteenth-Century Songs of the Sea," *Log of Mystic Seaport* 35 (1984): 132–39; E. Norman Flayderman, *Scrimshaw and Scrimshanders / Whales and Whalemen* (New Milford, Conn.: N. Flayderman, 1972), 36–61; and Margaret Baker, *Folklore of the Sea* (North Pomfret, Vt.: David & Charles, 1979), esp. 19–20.

3. Virtually every study of a range of maritime industries confirms this, although no scholar (to my knowledge) has directly addressed the unusually strict sexual division of labor without falling back on the very stereotypes and conventions that this anthology begins to challenge. See Daphne Spain, *Gendered Spaces* (Chapel Hill: University of North Carolina Press, 1992), for both a survey of anthropological and sociological studies of the gendered segregation of space and her own analysis of this in nineteenth- and twentieth-century America. In chap. 4, "The Spatial Division of Labor," Spain identifies "hunting large aquatic fauna" and "smelting of ores" as the only two 100-percent male occupations out of the fifty lines of work she examines (184–85).

4. Joseph McDevitt provides a classic example of the importance of marital alliances when he describes the double linking in the late eighteenth century of the Rotches and the Rodmans of Nantucket and New Bedford, two of the most prominent families in the upper reaches of the whaling industry, through the marriages of a Rotch daughter to a Rodman son and a Rotch son to a Rodman daughter. Joseph Lawrence McDevitt Jr., "The House of Rotch: Whaling Merchants of Massachusetts, 1734–1828" (Ph.D. diss., American University, 1978), app. 1, B, p. 551. On the phenomenon more generally, see Peter Dobkin Hall, "Marital Selection and Business in Massachusetts Merchant Families, 1700–1900," in Rose Laub Coser, ed., *The Family: Its Structures and Functions*, 2d ed. (New York: St. Martin's Press, 1974), 226–40.

5. The secondary sources on whalemen in the South Pacific, including their inter-

actions with native women, are multitudinous. See Briton Cooper Busch, *Whaling Will Never Do for Me: The American Whaleman in the Nineteenth Century* (Lexington: University Press of Kentucky, 1994), 135–57; Joan Druett, "More Decency and Order: Women and Whalemen in the Pacific," *Log of Mystic Seaport* 39 (summer 1987): 65–74; Robert W. Kenny, "Yankee Whalers at the Bay of Islands," *American Neptune* 12 (1952): 22–44; and Alan Moorehead, *The Fatal Impact: The Invasion of the South Pacific, 1767–1840* (New York: Harper & Row, 1987). See also the especially frank contemporary account of David Porter, *Journal of a Cruise made to the Pacific Ocean . . . in the United States Frigate Essex, in the Years 1812, 1813, and 1814*, vols. 1–2 (Philadelphia: Bradford & Inskeep, 1815). See the first edition only: the later editions were censored.

6. Robert G. Albion, William A. Baker, and Benjamin W. Labaree, *New England and the Sea* (Middletown, Conn.: Wesleyan University Press, for the Marine Historical Assoc., Mystic Seaport, 1972), 114–18; Elmo Hohman, *The American Whaleman* (New York: Longmans, Green, 1928); Alexander Starbuck, *History of the American Whalefishery . . . to the Year 1876* (Boston, 1876); and Leonard Bolles Ellis, *History of New Bedford and Its Vicinity, 1602–1892* (Syracuse, 1892).

7. Daniel Vickers, "Maritime Labor in Colonial Massachusetts: A Case Study of the Essex County Cod Fishery and the Whaling Industry of Nantucket, 1630–1775" (Ph.D. diss., Princeton University, 1981), 284–93.

8. See in particular Hohman, *The American Whaleman*, on the details of the proletarianization of the forecastle.

9. My understanding of this is based primarily on Jeanne Boydston, *Home and Work: Housework, Wages, and the Ideology of Labor in the Early Republic* (New York; Oxford University Press, 1990); Mary Ryan, *Cradle of the Middle Class: The Family in Oneida County, New York, 1790–1865* (Cambridge: Cambridge University Press, 1981), esp. chaps. 1, 4, 5; E. Anthony Rotundo, *American Manhood: Transformations in Masculinity from the Revolution to the Modern Era* (New York: Basic Books, 1993), chaps. 1, 8; Mary Blewett, *Men, Women, and Work: Class, Gender, and Protest in the New England Shoe Industry, 1780–1910* (Urbana: University of Illinois Press, 1988); Alice Kessler-Harris, *Out to Work: A History of Wage-earning Women in the United States* (New York: Oxford University Press, 1982), chaps. 2, 3; Leonore Davidoff and Catherine Hall, *Family Fortunes: Men and Women of the English Middle Class, 1780–1850* (Chicago: University of Chicago Press, 1987), esp. chaps. 4, 5; and Wally Seccombe, "Patriarchy Stabilized: The Construction of the Male Breadwinner Wage Norm in Nineteenth-Century Britain," *Social History* 11 (Jan. 1986): 53–76.

10. Ira Dye, "Early American Merchant Seafarers," *Proceedings of the American Philosophical Society* 120 (Oct. 1976): 331–60; John F. Battick, "A Study of the Demographic History of the Seafaring Population of Belfast and Searsport, Maine, 1850–1900," in Rosemary Ommer and Gerald Panting, eds., *Working Men Who Got Wet* (St. John's: Memorial University, 1980), 231–61; Marcus Rediker, *Between the Devil and the Deep Blue Sea: Merchant Seamen, Pirates, and the Anglo-American Maritime World, 1700–1750* (Cambridge: Cambridge University Press, 1987), 156–58, 299–300.

11. Alonzo M. Taber to William Loring Taber, 13 Jan. 1852, William Loring Taber Papers, MattHS.

12. Ezra Goodnough quoted in Margaret S. Creighton, *Rites and Passages: The Experience of American Whaling, 1830–1870* (Cambridge: Cambridge University Press, 1995), 48.

13. Leonard S. Gifford to Lucy Roberts, 30 Nov. 1851, Leonard S. and Lucy Gifford Papers, MSS 98, subgrp. 1, ser. A, folder 1, ODHS.

14. Ellen K. Rothman, *Hands and Hearts: A History of Courtship in America* (New York: Basic Books, 1984), chap. 2; Karen Lystra, *Searching the Heart: Women, Men, and Romantic Love in Nineteenth-Century America* (New York: Oxford University Press, 1989), chap. 7.

15. Rotundo, *American Manhood*, chap. 1; Ryan, *Cradle of the Middle Class*, chap. 4.

16. Samuel Braley, journal entries 29. Nov. 1851, 25 May 1850, 27 Oct. 1850, "Journal kept on Board ship *Arab* of Fairhaven, 1849–1853," KWM.

17. Charles Peirce to Eliza T. Peirce, 27 June 1870, [?] Dec. 1871, 29 Mar. 1874, Charles Peirce Papers, MSS B85-41.1, ODHS.

18. George Richmond to Leonard Gifford, 19 June 1854, Leonard S. and Lucy Gifford Papers, MSS 98, subgrp. 1, ser. A, folder 2, ODHS.

19. Matthew Howland to Philip Howland, 18 Mar. 1856, Philip Howland Papers, KWM.

20. Orrick Smalley to Thomas Knowles, 18 June 1861, 30 Apr. 1862, MSS 55, subgrp. 2, ser. C, subser. 5, folder 1, ODHS.

21. Henry Swain to Thomas Knowles, 2 Aug. 1862, MSS 55, subgrp. 2, ser. L, subser. 5, folder 1, ODHS.

22. Philip Howland to Thomas Knowles, 29 Sept. 1866, MSS 55, ODHS.

23. Eliza Ann Codd to Charles G. & Henry Coffin, [?] Oct. 1846, [?] Nov. 1847, Charles G. & Henry Coffin Papers, MSS 152, NHA. Information on birth of child from *Vital Records of Nantucket, Massachusetts, to the Year 1850* (Boston: New England Historic Genealogical Society, 1925–28), vol. 1: Mary Eliza Codd born to Eliza Ann and John 10 Mar. 1847.

24. Christopher McKee, "Fantasies of Mutiny and Murder: A Suggested Psycho-History of the Seaman in the United States Navy, 1798–1815," *Armed Forces and Society* 4 (Feb. 1978): 297.

25. The fourteen voyages used in the computations, by agent and date, are: George Howland & Sons, New Bedford: bark *Golconda*, Capt. G. A. Baylies, 1827–29; *Golconda*, Capt. John D. Samson, 1829–32; *Golconda*, Capt. Hezekiah Adams, 1836–39 (MSS 7, subgrp. 1, ser. B, subser. 8, vol. 2, ODHS); Swift & Allen, New Bedford: ship *Tacitus*, Capt. S. S. Hathaway, 1844–lost 1845; ship *Gratitude*, Capt. Preserved Wilcox, 1845–48; bark *Harvest*, Capt. Thomas Bailey, 1847–50; ship *Jireh Swift*, Capt. William Earl, 1853–57 (MSS 5, ser. C, subser. 1, vols. 1–2, ODHS); William Tallman Russell, New Bedford: ship *Braganza*, Capt. Michael Baker, 1834–37 (MSS 6, ser. C, vol. 3, ODHS); C. R. Tucker, Dartmouth: ship *Benjamin Tucker*, Capt. Shubael Worth, 1839–43 (NBFPL); Davis & Cory, Westport: ship *Harbinger*, Capt. Ephraim Gifford 2d, 1842–44 (MSS 80, subgrp. 3, ser. F, subser. 1, vol. 1, ODHS); Tucker & Cummings, Dartmouth: bark *A. R. Tucker*, Capt. Oren Higgins, 1857–61 (NBFPL); Thomas Knowles & Co., New Bedford: bark *Edward*, Capt. Orrick Smalley, 1860-64 (MSS 55, subgrp. 2, ser. C, subser. 5, folder 2, ODHS); C. A. Church, Westport: brig *Leonidas*, Capt. James L. Skiff, 1860–63 (NBFPL); Benjamin B. Howard, New Bedford: ship *John Coggeshall*, Capt. Aaron Dean, 1860–64 (misc. vol. 118, MSM).

26. Hannah Ashley diary, 3 Feb., 2 June, 3 Aug., 5 Oct. 1864, and list of payments in back of volume, privately owned collection, Acushnet, Mass.

27. William Troy account with the bark *Harvest*, 1847–50, MSS 5, subgrp. 3, ser. C, subser. 1, vol. 1, ODHS.

Notes to Pages 77–80

28. "Your affectionate wife" to Orlando H. Houston, 21 Oct. 1855, MSS 80, subgrp. 3, ser. K, subser. 4, ODHS.

29. Orrick Smalley to Thomas Knowles, 30 Apr. 1862, MSS 55, subgrp. 2, ser. C, subser. 5, folder 1, ODHS.

30. Phebe B. Cottle to Charles G. & Henry Coffin, 9 Apr. 1844, MSS 152, folder 15, NHA.

31. Emeline Parsons to William C. Parsons, 8 May 1848, MSS 80, subgrp. 3, ser. K, subser. 4, ODHS; Sylvia Leonard to John Leonard, undated ca. 1857, privately owned collection, New Bedford, Mass.

32. Anthropologist Gayle Rubin argues that "as long as the relations specify that men exchange women, it is men who are the beneficiaries of the product of such exchanges—social organization." Rubin, "The Traffic in Women: Notes on the 'Political Economy' of Sex," in Rayna F. Reiter, ed., *Toward an Anthropology of Women* (New York: Monthly Review Press, 1975), 174.

33. Harriet Allen diary, 11 Mar. 1863, Log 401-A, KWM.

34. See, for examples of women's businesses, advertisements in the local newspapers; also the records of R. G. Dun & Co. reporting on the creditworthiness of New Bedford and Nantucket proprietors and business people, both male and female. Baker Library, Harvard University, Boston. See also Linda M. Maloney, "Women in Maritime America: The Nineteenth Century," in Paul Adam, ed., *Seamen in Society* (Bucharest: International Commission of Maritime History, 1980), pt. 3, 113–21.

35. Elisabeth Anthony Dexter, *Career Women of America, 1776–1840* (Francestown, N.H.: Marshall Jones Co., 1950); Emily Weeks, "Women of Nantucket," *Nantucket Historical Proceedings* (1912): 31–47.

36. For specific examples of women being charged with prostitution, theft, and illegally purveying liquor, see the New Bedford City Watch, Daily Record Book, 1 June 1848–24 Mar. 1850, NBFPL; see also the reference to the cases reported in William W. Sanger, *The History of Prostitution* (1858), cited in Maloney, "Women in Maritime America," 119.

37. "Sister Sally" to Horatio Wood, 9 Apr. ca. 1861; Perry Lawton to George J. A. Allen, 30 July 1844; both in MSS 80, subgrp. 3, ser. K, subser. 4, ODHS.

38. Cook & Snow Ledger Book, 1855–70, NBFPL; New Bedford Port Society annual reports for years 1837 and 1838, on deposit at ODHS; Sarah A. Cory to George G. Cory, 14 Aug. 1853, MSS 80, subgrp. 3, ser. K, subser. 4, ODHS.

39. Eliza Stanton account in Cook & Snow Ledger Book, 1855–70, NBFPL; Sarah A. Cory to George G. Cory, 14 Aug. 1853, MSS 80, subgrp. 3, ser. K, subser. 4, ODHS; Hannah Ashley diary, privately owned collection, Acushnet, Mass.; Sylvia Sowle to Robert P. Sowle, 8 Nov. 1854, MSS 80, subgrp. 3, ser. K, subser. 4, ODHS.

40. Julia Fisk diary, 1859, and Silas W. Fisk correspondence, VFM 1007, MSM.

41. For references to women running or working on family farms, see the account of Hannah Blackmer in Genevieve M. Darden, comp. and ed., *My Dear Husband: Being a Collection of Heretofore Unpublished Letters of the Whaling Era* (New Bedford: Descendants of Whaling Masters, 1980), 13–20; information on Mary Ann Braley in Pamela Miller, untitled TS ca. 1982, esp. chap. 3, KWM; Caroline Gifford to her husband Charles, 1865–70, MSS 56, ser. G, subser. 7, folders 1–3, ODHS; Caroline Omey to Philip H. Omey, 5 Apr. 1861, MSS 80, subgrp. 3, ser. K, subser. 4, ODHS; and Hannah Ashley diary, 1863, privately owned collection, Acushnet, Mass.

Notes to Pages 81–84

42. Abby Grinnell to Stephen Grinnell, 6 Sept. 1845, MSS 80, subgrp. 3, ser. K, subser. 4, ODHS.

43. Henry Beetle to Eliza Beetle, 2 Oct. 1851; 10 Sept. 1854, Beetle Family Papers, PPL.

44. For an example of tax payment, see Harriet Allen diary, 15 May 1865; for the purchase of insurance for David's share of the oil, see 28 Sept., 2 May, 13 May 1863; for examples of borrowing and loaning cash, see 5 Aug., 11 Aug., 11 Sept. 1863, Log 401-A, KWM.

45. Caroline Gifford to Charles Gifford, 19 Jan. 1870, 21 Aug. 1867, MSS 56, ser. G, subser. 7, ODHS.

46. Selina J. Coffin to George Coffin, 2 Nov. 1858, MSS 80, subgrp. 3, ser. K, subser. 4, ODHS; Caroline Gifford to Charles Gifford, 30 Sept. 1866, MSS 56, ser. G, subser. 7, ODHS.

47. On "imperial motherhood," see Mary Ryan, *Empire of the Mother: American Writing about Domesticity, 1830–1860* (New York: Harrington Park Press, 1985), 97–114.

48. Betsey King to James King Jr., 10 Feb. 1850, MSS 80, subgrp. 3, ser. K, subser. 4, ODHS.

49. Myra Weeks to William Weeks, 10 July 1842, MSS 80, subgrp. 3, ser. K, subser. 4, ODHS.

50. For examples of each activity, see Susan Gifford diary, 4 Dec. 1859, 15 Apr., 26 Jan., 28 May 1860, 19 Dec. 1859, 7 Aug., 9 Apr., 20 Jan., 25 July 1860, 24 Nov. 1859, 13 Oct., 22 Feb., 16 June, 19 Oct. 1860, privately owned, on deposit ODHS.

51. Susan's year-long diary begins on the day John left, 15 Nov. 1859. During the first month, 15 Nov.–15 Dec., Susan recorded entries for all but four days. According to her record of her activities (she may, of course, have omitted some), she went out at least once on twenty-three days. She remained at home for an entire day five times, though on two of those days visitors came in, so that Susan interacted just with other members of her household only three days of the entire month. Most of the individuals in her diary are listed by first name only, so it is very difficult to assess how many were related to Susan by blood or marriage. While I was able to identify six of the women and five of the men as kin, many others were probably related also, given the nature of kinship in the small village of Mattapoisett (including what seems to have been a typically high rate of endogamous marriage). Quotation from diary entries: 15 May 1860 and, addressed directly to John, 15 Nov. 1859.

52. Hannah Ashley diary, 1864, privately owned collection, Acushnet, Mass. Social interaction patterns analyzed for the months of January, March, and June.

53. Hannah bore her first and only child, Williams Crapo Ashley, on 8 Mar. 1864. She remained at her in-laws before, during, and after the birth.

54. Harriet Allen diary, 2 Jan., 17 Apr.–1 May 1863, Log 401-A, KWM.

55. On female "gadding," see Laurel Thatcher Ulrich, "Housewife and Gadder: Themes of Self-Sufficiency and Community in Eighteenth-Century New England," in Carol Groneman and Mary Beth Norton, eds., *"To Toil the Livelong Day": America's Women at Work, 1780–1980* (Ithaca: Cornell University Press, 1987), 21–34.

56. Nancy A. Childs to John D. Childs, 8 Jan. 1847, MSS 80, subgrp. 3, ser. K, subser. 4, ODHS.

57. Information compiled from New Bedford vital records, probate records, and city directories; New Bedford Free Public Library index to crew lists; 1850 federal

Notes to Pages 84–88

census, household enumeration for New Bedford; and the letters from Libby Spooner to Caleb Spooner (3 Dec. 1858) and from Gideon Spooner to Shubael and Caleb Spooner (7 Dec. 1858), both in MSS 80, subgrp. 3, ser. K, subser. 4, ODHS.

58. As elegantly put by Laurel Thatcher Ulrich: "the fragile threads of ordinary need that bound families together." Ulrich, *A Midwife's Tale: The Life of Martha Ballard Based on Her Diary, 1785–1812* (New York: Knopf, 1990), 100; see also Nancy Grey Osterud, *Bonds of Community: The Lives of Farm Women in Nineteenth-Century New York* (Ithaca: Cornell University Press, 1991), 85.

59. Information compiled from O. S. Cleveland to Wilcox & Richmond, 6 Sept. 1856, Papers of the New Bedford Ship *Hope*, 1851–57, VFM 1066, MSM; Starbuck, *History of the American Whalefishery*, 494–95; Nantucket vital records and census material.

60. William Loring Taber to Susan Taber, 7 Jan., 6 Feb. 1853, William Loring Taber Correspondence, MattHS.

61. William Loring Taber to Susan Taber, 6 Feb., 15 July, 13 July 1853, MattHS.

62. For the best description of the administrative and managerial activities in the industry, see David Moment, "The Business of Whaling in America in the 1850s," *Business History Review* 31 (autumn 1957): 261–91.

63. Mrs. Eliza Lewis to Wilcox & Richmond, n.d. ca. 1854, VFM 1066, MSM.

64. William Loring Taber to Susan Taber, 9 Dec. 1852, MattHS.

65. Mrs. J. E. Chase to Swift & Allen, 12 June 1862, MSS 5, subgrp. 3, ser. F, subser. 1, folder 65, ODHS.

66. Robert Greaves to Mrs. Cornelius Marchant, 2 May 1857, MV F. no. 225, DCHS.

67. Ruth Barker Post to Captain Francis Post, 26 Jan. 1851, quoted in Darden, *My Dear Husband*, 49; Samuel Braley, journal entries 21 Dec. 1850, 12 Aug. 1851, 8 Nov. 1850, "Journal Kept on Board ship *Arab* of Fairhaven, 1849-1853," KWM.

68. Charles Peirce to Eliza Peirce, 16 Mar. 1863, 17 Feb. 1862, Charles Peirce Papers, MSS B85-41.1, ODHS.

69. Samuel Braley, journal entries 21 Dec., 11 Oct. 1850, "Journal Kept on Board ship *Arab*," KWM; Jared Gardner to Harriet Gardner, 3 June 1840, Gardner Family Papers, AAS.

70. Again, these trends have been glimpsed in a preliminary survey of fourteen voyages and must be considered suggestive rather than conclusive. Further analysis of a larger sample, with more complete identification of third-party creditors, has yet to be done.

71. Boydston, *Home and Work*; Nancy Folbre and Marjorie Abel, "Women's Work and Women's Households: Gender Bias in the U.S. Census," *Social Research* 56 (autumn 1989): 545–69; Veronika Bennholdt-Thomsen, "Towards a Theory of the Sexual Division of Labor," in Joan Smith, Immanuel Wallerstein, and Hans-Dieter Evers, eds., *Households and the World Economy* (Beverly Hills: Sage, 1984), 252–71.

72. Charles Peirce to Eliza Peirce, 16 Mar. 1863, Charles Peirce Papers, MSS B85-41.1, ODHS.

73. In October: "I want you to be carefull of your health and dont cut any more wood"; and in March 1847: "when I begin to write, my mind is far, far away where I wish to be to cut some wood." Henry Beetle to Eliza Beetle, 25 Apr., 29 Apr., 18 Sept., 1 Oct. 1846, 5 Mar. 1847, Beetle Family Papers, PPL.

Notes to Pages 88–93

74. Sarah Pierce to Captain Elijah Chisole, 24 Dec. 1852, MSS 80, subgrp. 3, ser. K, subser. 4, ODHS.

75. Libby Spooner to Caleb Spooner, 3 Dec. 1858, MSS 80, subgrp. 3, ser. K, subser. 4, ODHS.

76. Caroline Gifford to Charles Gifford, 7 June 1866; Eleanor Gifford postscript on letter Caroline Gifford to Charles Gifford, 1 Sept. 1867, MSS 56, ser. G, subser. 7, ODHS; information on David Lewis Gifford drawn from David Lewis Gifford Papers, MSS 56, ser. G, subser. 8, ODHS.

77. Myra Weeks to William Weeks, 10 July 1842, MSS 80, subgrp. 3, ser. K, subser. 4, ODHS; Edward R. Ashley to parents, 1 Dec. 1855, privately owned collection, Acushnet, Mass.

78. William A. Ashley to Hannah Ashley, 15 June, 2 Sept. 1864, 23 Sept. [1864?], privately owned collection, Acushnet, Mass.

79. See Julia C. Bonham, "Feminist and Victorian: The Paradox of the American Seafaring Woman of the Nineteenth Century," *American Neptune* 37 (July 1977): 203–18; Druett, "More Decency and Order"; Druett, "Those Female Journals," *Log of Mystic Seaport* 40 (winter 1989): 115–25.

80. Charles Weeks to his (unnamed) wife, 24 Nov. 1829, MSS [unnumbered], KWM.

81. William Loring Taber to Susan Taber, 15 July 1853, 20 Nov. 1856, MattHS.

82. Anthropologist Rayna Rapp has argued that "it is through their concept of family that people are recruited to the material relations of households. Because people accept the meaningfulness of family, they enter into relations of production, reproduction, and consumption with one another. . . . In all of these activities, the concept of family both reflects and masks the realities of household formation and sustenance." Rayna Rapp, Ellen Ross, and Renate Bridenthal, "Examining Family History," in Judith L. Newton, Mary P. Ryan, and Judith R. Walkowitz, eds., *Sex and Class in Women's History* (London: Routledge, 1983), 234.

5. Haskell Springer, The Captain's Wife at Sea

1. I use the word *journal* for these documents, not just as a reflection of the dominant terminology among the writers themselves, by which they meant a variety of personal and not-so-personal records, but also to designate a personal account that is not written under the assumption or hope of privacy. A few of my sources seem to be addressed only to the writer or insist on calling themselves diaries; for those I use *diary*. Seven of the thirty-six have been published in whole or in part. The rest are in manuscript, typed transcript, or microfilm form at various museums and libraries, except for one in private hands. For the fullest list of whaling logs and journals kept by women, see Joan Druett, *Petticoat Whalers: Whaling Wives at Sea, 1820–1920* (Aukland: Collins, 1991); see also Stuart C. Sherman, *Whaling Logbooks and Journals, 1613–1917: An Inventory of Manuscript Records in Public Collections* (New York: Garland, 1986).

The published journals are: Dorothea Balano, *The Log of the Skipper's Wife*, ed. James W. Balano (Camden, Maine: Down East Books, 1979); Mary Brewster, *"She Was a Sister Sailor": The Whaling Journals of Mary Brewster, 1845–1851*, ed. Joan Druett (Mystic, Conn.: Mystic Seaport Museum, 1992); Sarah Congdon Hazard, "Around the Horn: Journal of the Captain's Wife," *Newport History* 38 (1965): 131–49; Mary C.

Lawrence, *The Captain's Best Mate*, ed. Stanton Garner (Providence: Brown University Press, 1966); Henrietta De Blois, "Off to the Pacific" (Newport, R.I. *Mercury,* 21 Feb.–15 Aug. 1885); Philip F. Purrington, ed., *Mrs. Ricketson's Whaling Journal* (New Bedford: Old Dartmouth Historical Society, 1958); Eliza Azelia Williams, "Journal of a Whaling Voyage to the Indian and Pacific Oceans . . . ," in Harold Williams, ed., *One Whaling Family* (Boston: Houghton Mifflin, 1964). In addition, selections from the journal of Alice Drinkwater appear in Julianna FreeHand, *A Seafaring Legacy* (New York: Random House, 1981).

2. The phrase "itch to record" is found, quoted, in Arthur Ponsonby, *English Diaries* (Freeport, N.Y.: Books for Libraries Press, 1971), 7 (first published 1923). Ponsonby's introduction comments on motives, including most of those I have listed, behind diaries and other personal records.

3. Mary Jane Moffat, foreword to *Revelations: Diaries of Women,* ed. Mary Jane Moffat and Charlotte Painter (New York: Random House, 1974), 5.

4. Elizabeth Hampsten, *Read This Only to Yourself: The Private Writings of Midwestern Women, 1880–1910* (Bloomington: Indiana University Press, 1982), 2. Hampsten's introduction is an excellent essay on women's personal writings, though the texts she uses are so different from those included here that a number of her observations do not apply.

5. For such activities, and historical background, see Margaret S. Creighton, *Rites and Passages: The Experience of American Whaling, 1830–1870* (Cambridge: Cambridge University Press, 1995); Linda Grant De Pauw, *Seafaring Women* (Boston: Houghton Mifflin, 1982); Joan Druett, cited above (n. 1); Fred B. Duncan, *Deepwater Family* (New York: Pantheon Books, 1969); William H. Rowe, *The Maritime History of Maine* (New York: Norton, 1948); Edward R. Snow, *Women of the Sea* (New York: Dodd, Mead, 1962); A. B. C. Whipple, *The Whalers* (Alexandria, Va.: Time-Life Books, 1979); and Emma Whiting and Henry Beetle Hough, *Whaling Wives* (Boston: Houghton Mifflin, 1952). Scholarly articles using women's writings at sea as evidence are: Julia C. Bonham, "Feminist and Victorian: The Paradox of the American Seafaring Woman of the Nineteenth Century," *American Neptune* 37 (July 1977): 203–18; Margaret S. Creighton, "The Captain's Children: Life in the Adult World of Whaling, 1852–1907," *American Neptune* 38 (July 1978): 203–16.

6. [Abram G. Briggs], "A Private Log of the Ship Eliza Adams," 1872-75, 29 Nov. 1872, MS, New Bedford Whaling Museum.

7. Lucy P. Smith, 7 June 1870, MS, Nicholson Whaling Collection, Providence Public Library (hereafter PPL).

8. [Abram G. Briggs], 15 Apr. 1873. This was one of his milder comments. He could also be vicious: "We came here for the express purpose to land the Capt's Cow, so she could calf again" (25 Nov. 1874). From the private journal of the fourth mate on the whaler *Gazelle,* by contrast, comes evidence of a rare successful interaction. Usually full of disparaging comments about the undoubtedly neurotic Mrs. Worth, on one occasion the man could not disguise his enjoyment at being with her—though he tried: "Had a very long gam with the old woman this afternoon. Very edifying, so much so that most of my watch below went away before I was aware of it. Conversed about love and murder, society, churches, men, and about the price of nutmegs." (Quoted and discussed in Whiting and Hough, *Whaling Wives,* 106-7.)

9. Sallie Smith, "Sallie G. Smith's Diary kept on board of the Barque Ohio of New Bedford[.] Sailed July 6th 1875 for a whale voyage in the Atlantic Ocean," 26 Aug. 1875, MS, G. W. Blunt White Library, Mystic Seaport Museum, Mystic, Conn. (hereafter MSM).

10. Elizabeth M. Morey, journal on whaling ship *Phoenix*, 1853–55, 4 June 1854, MS, Peter Foulger Museum, Nantucket Historical Association (hereafter NHA).

11. Margaret Youle Fraser, "Journal on Board of Ship *Sea Witch*," 1852-53, 12 Nov. 1852, MS, Peabody Essex Museum, Salem, Mass. (hereafter PEM).

12. Williams, *One Whaling Family*, 19.

13. Emma McInnes, "Log kept on board bark Josephine," 1891–92, 1 June [miswritten 4 June] 1892, MS, Kendall Whaling Museum, Sharon, Mass. (hereafter KWM).

14. Anon. journal, bark *Clement*, 1838, MS, PEM.

15. Bethia K. Sears, "A Journal kept by B. K. Sears, on board Ship 'Wild Ranger' on her passage from Boston to San Francisco, commencing October, 4, 1855," 25 Oct. 1855, MS, PEM.

16. Morey journal, 10 Sept. 1853. She was alluding to the old sailor custom of initiating first-time crossers of the equator with ceremonies (often sadistic or vulgar) in which "King Neptune" came aboard.

17. Mrs. Alonzo Follansbee journal, 1837–39, TS, PEM.

18. Harriet Allen diary, 26 Sept. 1869, MS, KWM.

19. Anne Augusta Fitch Brown on board the merchant bark *Agate*, 1870, microfilm, MSM.

20. Hannah Rebecca Crowell Burgess journals, 1852–56, MS, Sandwich Historical Society, Sandwich, Mass.

21. Mrs. William Brewster, "Journal, of a voyage to sea[.] Sailed from Stonington November 4th, 1845 Ship *Tiger*"; MS, MSM.

22. MS, MSM.

23. MS, PPL.

24. MS, NHA.

25. The New Bedford *Whaleman's Shipping List and Merchant's Transcript* (27 Mar. 1855), for example, reprinted from the *Observer*, Dover, Maine, excerpts of a letter from Susan Fisher on the *Cowper* in the North Pacific, saying the remarks "will afford a novel interest to our readers." Under the heading "Interesting Journal of a Whaling Voyage from New Bedford kept by a Newport Lady," the Newport *Mercury* (21 Feb.–15 Aug. 1885) printed Henrietta De Blois's account of her life on the *Merlin* from 1856 to 1859. Susan Fisher's story is most accessible in Whiting and Hough, *Whaling Wives*, 25–32.

26. A brief attempt to deal with Eliza Brock's journal as literature is Sherri Federbush, "The Journal of Eliza Brock at Sea on the Lexington," *Historic Nantucket* 30 (July 1982): 13–17.

27. See the frontispiece in Garner, *The Captain's Best Mate*.

28. Mrs. Wanton H. Sherman, journal on whaleship *Nimrod*, 1848–49, MS, PPL. For Balano, see n. 1, above.

29. Sarah Taber journals, 1848–51, 1851–55, MSS, Mariner's Museum, Newport News, Va.

30. As did Mrs. Follansbee in her journal, 1: 51–52.

Notes to Pages 101–119

31. This point is missed by Sherri Federbush, who calls the locution Mrs. Brock's "favorite phrase." So, too, an unawareness of other conditioning factors leads her to misunderstand the journal's genre. See Federbush, "Journal of Eliza Brock," 14, 16.

32. None I have read, however, is written exclusively or even predominantly to a divine audience (a so-called journal of conscience) or is openly confessional, as such a document would more likely be.

33. Williams, *One Whaling Family*, 41.

34. Mary Hayden Russell, "Sea Letter," [?] Jan. 1823, TS, NHA.

35. Lucy P. Smith, 1 Oct. 1870.

36. Pamela Miller, *And the Whale Is Ours: Creative Writing of American Whalemen* (Boston & Sharon: David R. Godine and Kendall Whaling Museum, 1979), 16.

37. Lydia Abby Beebe, "Diary on board Bark Brewster," 1863–65, 30 Dec. 1863, MS, NHA.

38. Hannah Rebecca Crowell Burgess, 25 Feb. 1854.

39. Mrs. Obed Swain, "Journal on Ship Catawba of Nantucket," 1852–55, 19 May 1854, MS, NHA.

40. Lucy P. Smith, 20 Apr., 12 Oct. 1871.

41. Williams, *One Whaling Family*, 366.

42. Sarah Cole, "A Journal of a Whaling Voyage to the Pacific Ocean On Board Bark Vigilant," 1860–62, 14 Sept. 1860, MS, PEM.

43. The opening page of Mrs. Brewster's journal records her foster mother's threat to bar her from her door forever should she go to sea.

44. Sand quoted in Moffat and Painter, *Revelations*, 16.

6. Margaret S. Creighton, Davy Jones' Locker Room

This essay is reprinted, with some modifications, from the *International Journal of Maritime History* 4 (June 1992): 195–218.

1. On the West, see Susan Armitage and Elizabeth Jameson, *The Women's West* (Norman: University of Oklahoma Press, 1987); and Glenda Riley, *A Place to Grow: Women in the American West* (Arlington Heights, Ill.: Harlan Davidson, 1992). On the Civil War, see Catherine Clinton and Nina Silber, eds., *Divided Houses: Gender and the Civil War* (New York: Oxford University Press, 1992).

2. Discussions of gender and nineteenth-century history abound. Especially lucid discussions of American masculinity in the 1800s can be found in Mark C. Carnes and Clyde Griffen, eds., *Meanings for Manhood: Constructions of Masculinity in Victorian America* (Chicago: University of Chicago Press, 1990); and E. Anthony Rotundo, *American Manhood: Transformations in Masculinity from the Revolution to the Modern Era* (New York: Basic Books, 1993).

3. On the meaning of home and domesticity to middle-class white Americans in the nineteenth century, see Nancy F. Cott, *The Bonds of Womanhood: "Woman's Sphere" in New England, 1780–1835* (New Haven: Yale University Press, 1977).

4. See Alan Villiers, *The War with Cape Horn* (New York: Scribner, 1971). The quotations are drawn from Villiers, *The Way of a Ship* (New York: Scribner, 1953), 188. Other maritime histories that portray the opposition of sea and shore include Captain S. Samuels, *From the Forecastle to the Cabin* (New York: Harper & Bros., 1887), 1; John D.

Whidden, *Ocean Life in the Old Sailing Ship Days* (Boston: Little, Brown, 1909), 3; and Carl C. Cutler, *Greyhounds of the Sea: The Story of the American Clipper Ship* (New York: Halcyon House, 1930), 376.

5. Alexander Starbuck, *History of the American Whale Fishery* (1877; reprint, Secaucus, N.J.: Castle Books, 1982), 2; Robert Carse, *The Moonrakers: The Story of the Clipper Ship Men* (New York: Harper & Bros., 1961), xiii; Villiers, *War with Cape Horn*, xxiv.

6. Anthony Rotundo, who has identified this gender ideal as the "masculine primitive," claims that it was taken up by many middle-class whites in the mid- to late 1800s. See E. Anthony Rotundo, "Learning about Manhood: Gender Ideals and the Middle-Class Family in Nineteenth-Century America," in J. A. Mangan and James Walvin, eds., *Manliness and Morality: Middle-Class Masculinity in Britain and America, 1800–1940* (New York: St. Martin's Press, 1987), 35–51.

7. See David Leverenz, *Manhood and the American Renaissance* (Ithaca: Cornell University Press, 1989), 279–306; Robert Martin, *Hero, Captain, and Stranger: Male Friendship, Social Critique, and Literary Form in the Sea Novels of Herman Melville* (Chapel Hill: University of North Carolina Press, 1986); and Bert Bender, *Sea-Brothers: The Tradition of American Sea Fiction from Moby-Dick to the Present* (Philadelphia: University of Pennsylvania Press, 1988).

8. These conclusions concur with recent studies of men ashore. Mainland men and women were deemed by "scientific" literature, medical studies, and reform tracts in the mid-1800s to be naturally unalike and constitutionally oppositional. But real men endorsed various ideals of manhood and exhibited diverse masculine behaviors, some of which could be considered "feminine." See Rotundo, *American Manhood*.

9. The slant of this essay owes a great deal to scholarship that identifies shared as well as polarized aspects of male and female values and behaviors. See Linda K. Kerber, "Separate Spheres, Female Worlds, Woman's Place: The Rhetoric of Women's History," *Journal of American History* 75 (June 1988): 9–39; Elizabeth Jameson, "Women as Workers, Women as Civilizers: True Womanhood in the American West," in Armitage and Jameson, *The Women's West*, 160; and Nancy F. Cott, "On Men's History and Women's History," in Carnes and Griffen, *Meanings for Manhood*, 205–11.

10. George Blanchard diary, *Solomon Saltus*, 16 Aug. 1847, Whaling Museum Library, Old Dartmouth Historical Society, New Bedford, Mass. (hereafter NBWM). The poem can be found in Blanchard diary, *Pantheon*, 4 Feb. 1843, NBWM. Other descriptions of the challenges of sea life include Alexander Hoxie, *Maria*, 2 Mar. 1833, quoted in Edouard Stackpole, *The Sea Hunters: The New England Whalemen during Two Centuries, 1635–1835* (Philadelphia: J. B. Lippincott, 1953), 407; James Allen diary, *Alfred Gibbs*, 20 Nov. 1870, Nicholson Whaling Collection, Providence Public Library, Providence, R.I. (hereafter PPL); and Benjamin Boodry diary, *Arnolda*, 10–11 Jan. 1853, NBWM. (Diarists' ships are cited with their entries.)

11. John F. Sears, *Sacred Places: American Tourist Attractions in the Nineteenth Century* (New York: Oxford University Press, 1989), 4–10; Elizabeth McKinsey, *Niagara Falls: Icon of the American Sublime* (Cambridge: Cambridge University Press, 1985).

12. Robert Weir diary, *Clara Bell*, 23 Nov. 1855, 24 Apr. 1856, Manuscript Collection, G. W. Blunt White Library, Mystic Seaport Museum, Mystic, Conn. (hereafter MSM).

13. Orson Shattuck diary, *Frances*, 16 Jan. 1851, NBWM; Blanchard diary, *Solomon Saltus*, 18 Nov. 1845.

14. See, for example, the diaries of Abram Briggs, *Eliza Adams*, 4 Oct. 1872, NBWM; J. T. Langdon, *St. Peter*, 25 Feb. 1850, PPL; and William Allen, *Samuel Robertson*, c. 1844, NBWM.

15. Blanchard diary, *Solomon Saltus*, 28 Dec. 1845.

16. Samuel Chase diary, *Arab*, 19 Dec. 1842, Collection of the Maine Historical Society, Portland, Maine (hereafter MeHS).

17. Edwin Pulver diary, *Columbus*, 30 June 1852, PPL.

18. Margaret S. Creighton, "Fraternity in the American Forecastle, 1830–1870," *New England Quarterly* 63 (Dec. 1990): 531–57.

19. William Abbe diary, *Atkins Adams*, 17 June 1859, NBWM.

20. Silliman Ives diary, *Sunbeam*, 28 Jan. 1870, NBWM.

21. William Allen diary, *Samuel Robertson*, c. 1845, NBWM. For details of whaling recruitment, see Margaret S. Creighton, *Rites and Passages: The Experience of American Whaling, 1830–1870* (New York: Cambridge University Press, 1995), chap. 1.

22. Pulver diary, 31 Jan. 1856; Lewis Williams diary, *Northern Light*, 12 Dec. 1859, Peabody Essex Museum, Salem, Mass. (hereafter PEM); Charles Nordhoff, *Whaling and Fishing* (New York: Dodd, Mead, 1895), 14–29.

23. See Rotundo, *American Manhood*; and Margaret Marsh, "Suburban Men and Masculine Domesticity, 1870–1915," in Carnes and Griffen, *Meanings for Manhood*, 111–27.

24. Rotundo, *American Manhood*, 250–51.

25. Elmo Paul Hohman, *The American Whaleman: A Study of Life and Labor in the Whaling Industry* (New York: Longmans, Green, 1928), 57–58; Creighton, *Rites and Passages*, chap. 2. As voyages progressed around the globe, and as desertions and discharges (and sometimes deaths) took their toll on the forecastle population, this group became more racially and ethnically diverse.

26. Albert N. Buel diary, *Java*, 22 Oct. 1857, PPL.

27. Marshall Keith diary, *Brewster*, n.d., PPL; Orson F. Shattuck diary, *Frances*, 19 Oct. 1850, NBWM.

28. Ives diary, *Sunbeam*, 10 July 1868.

29. For a more thorough discussion of the Neptune ritual, see Creighton, "Fraternity in the American Forecastle," 533–40.

30. Stephen Curtis journal, *Mercury*, c. Feb. 1842, New Bedford Free Public Library (hereafter NBFPL).

31. Mary Ann Clawson, *Constructing Brotherhood: Class, Gender, and Fraternalism* (Princeton: Princeton University Press, 1989), 185–86, 243–44, describes how anti-Masonic sentiment, which rose in the 1820s to 1840s, was fueled in part by women concerned that Masons appropriated some of the roles of the family. It is not unlikely that some of the women in seamen's reform societies were similarly concerned.

32. See Margaret S. Creighton, "American Mariners and the Rites of Manhood," in Colin Howell and Richard Twomey, eds., *Jack Tar in History: Essays in the History of Maritime Life and Labour* (Fredericton, N.B.: Acadiensis Press, 1991), 143–63.

33. For discussions of female types in sailors' songs, see Caroline Mosely, "Images of Young Women in Nineteenth-Century Songs of the Sea," *Log of Mystic Seaport* 35 (1984): 132–39. Analyses of female types in male shoreside cultures can be found in Elliott Gorn, *The Manly Art: Bare-Knuckle Prize Fighting in America* (Ithaca: Cornell

University Press, 1986), 142; and in Carroll Smith-Rosenberg, "Sex as Symbol in Victorian Purity: An Ethnohistorical Analysis of Jacksonian America," *American Journal of Sociology* 34 (1978): 242. Further discussion of the sailor's "whore" was presented by Valerie Burton in "The Whore-piping Sailor: Deconstructing a Myth of Male Sexuality," paper delivered at the Gender and Seafaring Forum, Memorial University, St. John's, Newfoundland, 17 Oct. 1991.

34. Isaac Baker diary, *Taskar*, 29 May 1842, PEM.

35. Creighton, "American Mariners."

36. See, e.g., Walter Brooks diary, *Gladiator*, 26 Feb. 1854, MSM; and Ezra Goodnough diary, *Ann Parry*, 23 Mar. 1847, PEM.

37. George Brown Goode, *The Fisheries and Fishery Industries of the United States* (Washington, D.C.: Government Printing Office, 1887), sec. 5, vol. 2, 231.

38. On the sailor's "pleasure," see ibid.

39. B. R. Burg's recent discussion of the homoerotic records of a Navy sailor in this period may push more scholars into exploring this important subject. See B. R. Burg, *An American Seafarer in the Age of Sail: The Erotic Diaries of Philip C. Van Buskirk* (New Haven: Yale University Press, 1994).

40. Records that refer to sexual activity on shipboard include the Logbook of master, *Joseph Starbuck*, 7 Sept., 15 Sept. 1838, Peter Foulger Museum, Nantucket Historical Association (hereafter NHA); Silas Fitch diary, *Charles Phelps*, 29–31 Jan. 1843, MSM; George Ray to Paita Consul, 21 May 1835, in Crew List of *Emily Morgan*, NBFPL; and Hiram Bailey to Charles G. Coffin and Henry Coffin, 15 Sept. 1844, NHA, coll. 152.

41. On romantic friendship ashore, see E. Anthony Rotundo, "Romantic Friendship: Male Intimacy and Middle Class Youth in the Northern States, 1800–1900," *Journal of Social History* 23 (1989–90): 1–25.

42. Elias Trotter diary, *Illinois*, 26 Aug., 29 Nov., 14 Dec. 1845, NBWM.

43. Karen Lystra maintains that romantic lovers built unique bonds that "emphasized their individuality, their distinctiveness, their separateness." This sort of romantic love would have been contrary to forecastle norms. See *Searching the Heart: Women, Men, and Romantic Love in Nineteenth-Century America* (New York: Oxford University Press, 1989), 9.

44. On the increased rewards of whaling masters in the eighteenth century, see Daniel Vickers, "Maritime Labor in Colonial Massachusetts: A Case Study of the Essex County Cod Fishery and the Whaling Industry of Nantucket, 1630–1775" (Ph.D. diss., Princeton University, 1981), 277.

45. Gorn, *The Manly Art*, 142, considers the ways that working-class men rejected middle-class domesticity.

46. E. Anthony Rotundo, "Boy Culture: Middle-Class Boyhood in Nineteenth-Century America," in Carnes and Griffen, *Meanings for Manhood*, 15–36.

47. Mark C. Carnes, *Secret Rituals and Manhood in Victorian America* (New Haven: Yale University Press, 1989), 119.

48. William Hutchinson Rowe, *The Maritime History of Maine: Three Centuries of Shipbuilding and Seafaring* (New York: Norton, 1948), 228.

49. Benjamin Boodry diary, *Arnolda*, 1 May 1853, NBWM.

50. Edmund E. Jennings diary, *Mary & Susan*, 29 Nov. 1877, PPL; Marshall Keith diary, *Cape Horn Pigeon*, 18 Oct. 1866, NBWM.

51. Jennings diary, 29 Nov. 1877; Samuel N. Braley diary, *Arab*, 8 Dec. 1849, Kendall Whaling Museum, Sharon, Mass. (hereafter KWM); George Bowman diary, *Albion*, 1 July 1869, PPL.

52. John Alden diary, *Albatross*, 5 June 1847, PEM; John Jones diary, *Eliza Adams*, 3 Jan. 1852, KWM.

53. See Richard Hixson diary, *Maria*, 21 Oct. 1834, Houghton Library, Harvard University; J. Hersey diary, *Esquimaux*, 18 Mar. 1843, KWM; F. Cady diary, *Julian*, 27 June 1847, KWM; and anon. diary, *Brunette*, 24 July 1842, PPL.

54. "Lady Whalers," *Whalemen's Shipping and Merchant's Transcript*, 1 Feb. 1853; for information on the rising number of women on merchant vessels, see Julia C. Bonham, "Feminist and Victorian: The Paradox of the American Seafaring Woman of the Nineteenth Century," *American Neptune* 37 (1977): 203–18.

55. Julie S. Matthaei, *An Economic History of Women in America: Women's Work, the Sexual Division of Labor, and the Development of Capitalism* (New York: Schocken Books, 1982), 101–19.

56. Cott, *Bonds of Womanhood*, 63–100; Jackson Lears, *No Place of Grace: Antimodernism and the Transformation of American Culture, 1880–1920* (New York: Pantheon Books, 1981), 15.

57. These diaries and letters support the argument that men and women were emotionally intimate, despite the distance between them. On the closeness of nineteenth-century middle-class whites, see Karen Lystra, *Searching the Heart*, 9–11. On the debates surrounding male-female companionship, see the classic essay by Carroll Smith-Rosenberg, "The Female World of Love and Ritual," *Signs* 1 (1975): 1–29; see also Carnes, *Secret Rituals*, 206, and Marsh, "Suburban Men."

58. Braley diary, 27 Jan. 1850; Keith diary, 1 Oct., 15 Aug. 1866.

59. Braley diary, 22 Nov. 1849; Edward N. Jenney diary, *Alfred Gibbs*, 12–14 Nov. 1859, NBWM; Henry Beetle to Eliza Beetle, 18 July 1845, PPL.

60. Jonathan Bourne Jr. to Mrs. John D. Willard, 6 Mar. 1858, Bourne Letterbook, NBWM.

61. Swift and Allen to Capt. Josiah Chase, 30 Sept. 1861, NBWM.

62. Lisa Norling, "Contrary Dependencies: Whaling Agents and Whalemen's Families, 1830–1870," *Log of Mystic Seaport* 42 (spring 1990): 10. One owner who expressed especially strong feelings about gamming was George Howland. See George Howland Sr. to Capt. Hezekiah Adams, May 1836, Howland Family Collection, NBWM.

63. Swift and Allen to Capt. James E. Stanton, 16 Dec. 1859, NBWM.

64. Hugh H. Davis, "The American Seaman's Friend Society and the American Sailor, 1828–1838," *American Neptune* 39 (1979): 45–57; Wheelock Craig, "An Address on the Occasion of the Twenty-seventh Anniversary of the New Bedford Port Society" (New Bedford: n.p., 1857), 1; anon., *Sixth Annual Report of the American Seaman's Friend Society* (New York: George P. Scott, 1834), 26.

65. On the diversity of young men who used and abused women in the early American city, see Patricia Cline Cohen, "Unregulated Youth: Masculinity and Murder in the 1830s City," *Radical History Review* 52 (winter 1992): 33–54.

66. See Laura Tabili, "'A Maritime Race,'" and Lillian Nayder, "Sailing Ships and Steamers, Angels and Whores," both in this volume.

67. Joseph P. Goldberg, *The Maritime Story: A Study in Labor-Management Relations*

Notes to Pages 138–140

(Cambridge, Mass.: Harvard University Press, 1958); Bruce Nelson, *Workers on the Waterfront: Seamen, Longshoremen, and Unionism in the 1930s* (Urbana: University of Illinois Press, 1988).

7. W. Jeffrey Bolster, "Every Inch a Man"

An earlier and substantially different version of this chapter appeared in the *Journal of American History* 76 (Mar. 1990): 1173–99. I would like to thank David Thelen, Susan Armeny, and the *JAH* readers for launching it; Lisa Norling, Bob Brugger, and Margaret Creighton for careful readings that helped put new wine in old bottles; Ron Walters and Molly Bolster for keeping the faith the first time around; and the National Endowment for the Humanities for supporting a larger project of which this is a part.

1. Frederick Douglass, *Life and Times of Frederick Douglass, Written By Himself: His Early Life As A Slave, His Escape From Bondage, And His Complete History* (1892; reprint, New York: Collier Books, 1962), 125.

2. Ibid., 199. Beginning in 1796 the federal government issued certificates to American sailors, black and white, as protection against impressment.

3. Ibid., 199, 125.

4. "Protest Against Kidnapping and the Slave Trade," in Herbert Aptheker, ed., *A Documentary History of the Negro People in the United States*, 2 vols. (New York: Citadel Press, 1951), 1:21. The numbers of black (including mulatto) mariners were derived from crew lists and from abstracts of applications for seamen's protection certificates. New York and Philadelphia crew lists, Records of the U.S. Customs Service (hereafter USCS), RG 36, National Archives (hereafter NA); Providence crew lists, RG 28, U.S. Customs House Papers, Manuscript Collection, Rhode Island HIstorical Society (hereafter CHP, RIHS), Providence, R.I.; Salem, Massachusetts, crew lists and abstracts of applications for seamen's protection certificates for New London, Connecticut, both in Records of the U.S. Customs Service, RG 36, NA, Boston Branch, Waltham, Mass. For pioneering work using such records, see Ira Dye, "Seafarers of 1812—A Profile," *Prologue: The Journal of the National Archives* 5 (spring 1973): 3-13; Ira Dye, "Early American Merchant Seafarers," *Proceedings of the American Philosophical Society* 120 (Oct. 1976): 331–60; U.S. Department of Commerce, Bureau of the Census, *Historical Statistics of the United States: Colonial Times to 1970*, 2 vols. (Washington, D.C., 1975), 1:24–37; and Edwin M. Snow, *Census of the City of Providence, Taken in July, 1855; With a Brief Account of the Manufacturers, Trade, Commerce, and Other Statistics of the City; and an Appendix, Giving an Account of Previous Enumerations of the Population of Providence* (Providence, 1856), 73.

5. For the gendered identity of blacks in the nineteenth century, a virtually unexplored topic, see James Oliver Horton, "Freedom's Yoke: Gender Conventions among Antebellum Free Blacks," *Feminist Studies* 12 (spring 1986): 51–76. This pathbreaking article compares the masculine and feminine ideals of northern free black society with those of antebellum white American society. The data from that article, however, were drawn primarily from black newspapers, and the resulting bias is naturally toward a respectable, "middle-class" version of black masculinity. See also Jim Cullen, "'I's a Man Now': Gender and African American Men," in Catherine Clinton and Nina Silber, eds., *Divided Houses: Gender and the Civil War* (New York: Oxford University

Notes to Pages 140–141

Press, 1992), 76–91; and Steven Maynard, "Rough Work and Rugged Men: The Social Construction of Masculinity in Working-Class History," *Labour / Le Travail* 23 (spring 1989): 159–69.

6. "Respectability" and "reputation" were first presented as ways of conceptualizing gendered identity among African Americans by Peter J. Wilson, "Reputation and Respectability: A Suggestion for Caribbean Ethnography," *Man* 4 (1969): 70–84; and Peter J. Wilson, *Crab Antics: The Social Anthropology of English-Speaking Negro Societies of the Caribbean* (New Haven: Yale University Press, 1973). See also Roger D. Abrahams, *The Man-of-Words in the West Indies: Performance and the Emergence of Creole Culture* (Baltimore: Johns Hopkins University Press, 1983); and Roger D. Abrahams, "Reputation vs. Respectability: A Review of Peter J. Wilson's Concept," *Revista / Review Interamericana* 9 (1979): 448–53. James Kelly, *Voyage to Jamaica, and Seventeen Years' Residence in That Island: Chiefly Written With a View to Exhibit Negro Life and Habits* (Belfast, 1838), 29–30, quoted in Edward Brathwaite, *The Development of Creole Society in Jamaica 1770–1820* (Oxford: Clarendon Press, 1971), 301.

7. For notable exceptions, see Dye, "Seafarers of 1812"; Dye, "Early American Merchant Seafarers"; Harold D. Langley, "The Negro in the Navy and the Merchant Service, 1798–1860," *Journal of Negro History* 52 (Oct. 1967): 273–86; and Martha S. Putney, *Black Sailors: Afro-American Merchant Seamen and Whalemen prior to the Civil War* (Westport, Conn.: Greenwood Press, 1987). For omission of black sailors, see Samuel Eliot Morison, *The Maritime History of Massachusetts, 1783–1860* (Boston: Houghton Mifflin, 1921); Robert G. Albion, *The Rise of New York Port, 1815–1860* (New York: Scribner, 1939); Margaret Creighton, *Dog Watch and Liberty Days: Seafaring Life in the Nineteenth Century* (Salem, Mass.: Peabody Museum, 1982); Robert G. Albion, William A. Baker, and Benjamin W. Labaree, *New England and the Sea* (Middletown, Conn.: Wesleyan University Press, 1972); and Marcus Rediker, *Between the Devil and the Deep Blue Sea: Merchant Seamen, Pirates, and the Anglo-American Maritime World, 1700–1750* (Cambridge: Cambridge University Press, 1987).

8. One notable exception is Gerald W. Mullin, *Flight and Rebellion: Slave Resistance in Eighteenth-Century Virginia* (New York: Oxford University Press, 1972), esp. 98–103.

9. For the (exceptional) recognition of black sailors as part of the African American community, see Gary B. Nash, *Forging Freedom: The Formation of Philadelphia's Black Community, 1720–1840* (Cambridge: Harvard University Press, 1988); and Shane White, "'We Dwell in Safety and Pursue Our Honest Callings': Free Blacks in New York City, 1783–1810," *Journal of American History* 75 (Sept. 1988): 445–70. One author specifically excluded mariners from his study "because they were an unstable floating element in the city's population." See Robert Ernst, "The Economic Status of New York City Negroes, 1850–1863," in August Meier and Elliott Rudwick, eds., *The Making of Black America: Essays in Negro Life and History* (New York: Atheneum, 1969), 250–61, esp. 254. Black sailors' lives receive little more than mention in Leon F. Litwak, *North of Slavery: The Negro in the Free States, 1790–1860* (Chicago: University of Chicago Press, 1961); Leonard P. Curry, *The Free Black in Urban America, 1800–1850: The Shadow of the Dream* (Chicago: University of Chicago Press, 1981); Robert J. Cottrol, *The Afro-Yankees: Providence's Black Community in the Antebellum Era* (Westport, Conn.: Greenwood Press, 1982); William D. Pierson, *Black Yankees: The Development of an Afro-American Subculture in Eighteenth-Century New England* (Amherst: University of Massachusetts Press, 1988);

and Theodore Hershberg, "Free Blacks in Antebellum Philadelphia: A Study of Ex-Slaves, Freeborn, and Socioeconomic Decline," *Journal of Social History* 5 (winter 1971–72): 183-209.

10. William S. Swift, *The Negro in the Offshore Maritime Industry*, pt. 3 in Lester Rubin, William S. Swift, and Herbert R. Northrup, eds., *Negro Employment in the Maritime Industries; A Study of Racial Policies in the Shipbuilding, Longshore, and Offshore Maritime Industries* ([Philadelphia], 1974); James Barker Farr, "Black Odyssey: The Seafaring Traditions of Afro-Americans" (Ph.D. diss., University of California, Santa Barbara, 1982), 229.

11. For an important article calling for the integration of race and gender in working-class history, see David Roediger, "Race and the Working-Class Past in the United States: Multiple Identities and the Future of Labor History," *International Review of Social History* 38, suppl. (1993): 127–43, esp. 138.

12. Samuel Taylor Coleridge, *The Piccolomini; or, the First Part of Wallenstein*, act 1, scene 6, epigraph in Richard Henry Dana, *Two Years before the Mast: A Personal Narrative of Life at Sea* (1840; reprint, New York: Penguin Books, 1981), 35.

13. Charles A. Valentine, "Deficit, Difference, and Bicultural Models of Afro-American Behavior," *Harvard Educational Review* 41 (May 1971): 135-57; Eric R. Wolf, "Specific Aspects of Plantation Systems in the New World: Community Sub-Cultures and Social Classes," in *Plantation Systems of the New World: Papers and Discussion Summaries of the Seminar Held in San Juan, Puerto Rico* (Washington, D.C., 1959), 141–42. My analysis of culture and society also draws on Peter H. Fricke, "The Socialization of Crews Aboard British Dry Cargo Merchant Ships" (Ph.D. diss., University of Wales, Cardiff, 1974), 87–95; William Roseberry, "Balinese Cockfights and the Seduction of Anthropology," *Social Research* 49 (winter 1982): 1013–29; and Gerald M. Sider, *Culture and Class in Anthropology and History: A Newfoundland Illustration* (Cambridge: Cambridge University Press, 1986).

14. Rediker, *Between the Devil and the Deep Blue Sea*, 286; William Butterworth, *Three Years Adventure of a Minor in England, Africa, the West Indies, South Carolina and Georgia* (Leeds, [1831]), 205–11, esp. 211; William C. Nell, *The Colored Patriots of the American Revolution, With Sketches of Several Distinguished Colored Persons: To Which Is Added a Brief Survey of the Conditions and Prospects of Colored Americans* (Boston, 1855), 314, emphasis mine; S. G. Howe, *Report of the Freedmen's Inquiry Commission, 1864: The Refugees from Slavery in Canada West* (1864; reprint, New York, 1969), 75.

15. Elmo Paul Hohman, *History of American Merchant Seamen* (Hamden, Conn.: Shoe String Press, 1956), 4; Frederic R. Sanborn, *Origins of the Early English Maritime and Commercial Law* (New York: Century, 1930), 63, 64, 96.

16. Greg Dening, *Islands and Beaches: Discourse on a Silent Land, Marquesas 1774–1880* (Honolulu: University Press of Hawaii, 1980), 158–59.

17. Ira Berlin, *Slaves without Masters: The Free Negro in the Antebellum South* (New York: Pantheon Books, 1974), 111; Cottrol, *Afro-Yankees*, 153–54, 161; Frank T. Bullen, *The Cruise of the Cachelot* (1898; reprint, New Haven: Leete's Island Books, 1980), 4.

18. Providence crew lists, 1819–21, 1831–35, RG 28, CHP, RIHS; Edward Carrington & Co., "Seamen's Ledgers," 1819–21, 1831–35, Carrington Papers, ibid.; Herman Melville, *Billy Budd, Sailor (An Inside Narrative)* (Chicago: University of Chicago Press, 1962), 43–44.

19. "Joseph M. Smith vs. Barque *Triton*," Aug. 1840, Final Record Book 8, U.S. District Court at Providence, Records of the U.S. District Court, RG 21, NA, Boston Branch; Paul C. Nicholson, comp., *Abstracts from a Journal Kept aboard the Ship Sharon of Fairhaven on a Whaling Voyage in the South Pacific, 1841–1845* (Providence, 1953), 9–10.

20. Jay Coughtry found that the embargo had a similar impact on black seamen in Newport. See Jay Coughtry, *The Notorious Triangle: Rhode Island and the African Slave Trade, 1700–1807* (Philadelphia: Temple University Press, 1981), 60.

21. Lamont D. Thomas, *Paul Cuffe: Black Entrepreneur and Pan-Africanist* (Urbana: University of Illinois Press, 1986); Henry S. Sherwood, "Paul Cuffe," *Journal of Negro History* 8 (Apr. 1923): 153–229. For the lack of intergenerational success among seamen of color, see Cuffe's son's autobiography, *Narrative of the Life and Adventures of Paul Cuffe, A Pequot Indian* (Vernon, Conn., 1839). George Henry, *Life of George Henry. Together With a Brief History of the Colored People in America* (1894; reprint, Freeport, N.Y.: Books for Libraries Press, 1971), 62.

22. William J. Brown, *The Life of William J. Brown of Providence, R.I., with Personal Recollections of Incidents in Rhode Island* (Providence, 1883), 49; Noah H. Landau, "The Negro Seaman," *Negro Quarterly* 1 (winter/spring 1943): 334; Charles C. Andrews, *The History of the New York African Free-Schools, From Their Establishment in 1787, to the Present Time; Embracing A Period of More than Forty Years; Also A Brief Account of the Successful Labors of the New-York Manumission Society: With An Appendix* (1830; reprint, New York, 1969), 85–96; Thomas Hamilton, *Men and Manners in America* (1833; reprint, New York, 1968), 55–58.

23. Brown, *Life of Brown*, 126.

24. Seebert J. Goldowsky, *Yankee Surgeon: The Life and Times of Usher Parsons, 1788–1868* (Boston: Francis A. Countway Library of Medicine, 1988), 410; J. Ross Browne, *Etchings of a Whaling Cruise: With Notes of a Sojourn on the Island of Zanzibar* (New York, 1846), 108; James Kelly, *Voyage to Jamaica and Seventeen Years' Residence in That Island: Chiefly Written with a View to Exhibit Negro Life and Habits* (Belfast, 1838), 29–30.

25. Providence crew lists, 1803–56, CHP, RIHS; cf. New York and Philadelphia crew lists, USCS, RG 36, NA.

26. Brig *John Josiah Arnold* crew list, outbound, 1803, Providence crew lists, CHP, RIHS; Elbridge S. Brooks, *The Story of the American Sailor* (Boston, 1888), 189.

27. James M. Rose and Barbara W. Brown, *Tapestry: A Living History of the Black Family in Southeastern Connecticut* (New London, Conn.: New London County Historical Society, 1979), 124.

28. *Proceedings of the Black State Conventions, 1840–1865*, ed. Philip S. Foner and George E. Walker (Philadelphia: Temple University Press, 1980), 2:207–8; William P. Powell, "Coloured Seamen—Their Character and Condition, No. 1," *National Anti-Slavery Standard*, 14 Sept. 1846, reprinted in *The Black Worker to 1869*, vol. 1 of Philip S. Foner and Ronald L. Lewis, eds., *The Black Worker: A Documentary History from Colonial Times to the Present* (Philadelphia: Temple University Press, 1978), 198; William P. Powell to William Lloyd Garrison, 10 Nov. 1853, Garrison Papers, Rare Book Room, Boston Public Library. See also William P. Powell to Sydney Howard Gay, 12 Dec. 1850, in C. Peter Ripley, ed., *The Black Abolitionist Papers* (Chapel Hill: University of North Carolina Press, 1985), 1:234.

29. David Montgomery, *Workers' Control in America: Studies in the History of Work,*

Technology, and Labor Struggles (Cambridge: Cambridge University Press, 1979), 13; E. Anthony Rotundo, "Body and Soul: Changing Ideals of American Middle-Class Manhood, 1770–1920," *Journal of Social History* 16 (summer 1983): 23.

30. Owen Chase, *Narrative of the Most Extraordinary and Distressing Shipwreck of the Whaleship Essex* (New York, 1821), reprinted in Thomas Farel Heffernan, ed., *Stove by a Whale* (Middletown, Conn.: Wesleyan University Press, 1981), 18–19; John Malvin, *North into Freedom: The Autobiography of John Malvin, Free Negro, 1795–1880*, ed. Allan Peskin (Kent, Ohio: Kent State University Press, 1988), 37.

31. Dorothea M. Balano, *The Log of the Skippers Wife* (Camden, Maine: International Marine Press, 1979), 69.

32. All of these traits, representative of Atlantic maritime culture, can be found in the journals, logs, and published memoirs of seamen. For the best accounts, see Dana, *Two Years before the Mast*, 72–73, 78–79, 120-22, 250, 431; Rediker, *Between the Devil and the Deep Blue Sea*, 153–253; and Creighton, *Dog Watch and Liberty Days*, 40–41, 48–50, 60–68.

33. Dana, *Two Years before the Mast*, 330; Franklin cited in William MacLeish, *The Gulf Stream: Encounters with the Blue God* (Boston: Houghton Mifflin, 1989), 87; *Clayton et al. v. The "Harmony,"* 5 Federal Cases 994 (1807).

34. *Judicial Cases Concerning American Slavery and The Negro*, ed. Helen Tunicliff Catterall, 5 vols. (Washington, D.C.: Carnegie Institute, 1926–37), 2:376.

35. Elliot J. Gorn, *The Manly Art: Bare-Knuckle Prize-Fighting in America* (Ithaca: Cornell University Press, 1986), 34–35; Peter Fryer, *Staying Power: Black People in Britain since 1504* (Atlantic Highlands, N.J.: Humanities Press, 1984), 443–57.

36. Gorn, *Manly Art*, 19–20, 34–35; Reginald Horsman, "The Paradox of Dartmoor Prison," *American Heritage* 26 (Feb. 1975): 13–17, 85; Ira Dye, "American Maritime Prisoners of War, 1812–1815," in Timothy J. Runyan, ed., *Ships, Seafaring, and Society: Essays in Maritime History* (Detroit: Wayne State University Press, 1987), 293–320; Ira Dye, "The American Prisoners of War at Dartmoor" (paper); William Jeffrey Bolster, "African-American Seamen: Race, Seafaring Work, and Atlantic Maritime Culture, 1750–1860" (Ph.D. diss., Johns Hopkins University, 1991), 184–257.

37. Gorn, *Manly Art*, 26–29.

38. Elliot J. Gorn, "'Gouge and Bite, Pull Hair and Scratch': The Social Significance of Fighting in the Southern Backcountry," *American Historical Review* 90 (Feb. 1985): 20. Gorn's otherwise marvelous analysis of violence and honor within the male culture of the backcountry is strangely silent on race, making no mention of black fighters or interracial fights, and no analysis of racially specific forms of combat.

39. William Grimes, *Life of William Grimes*, in *Five Black Lives*, ed. Arna Bontemps (Middletown, Conn.: Wesleyan University Press, 1971), 92; Dana, *Two Years before the Mast*, 429–30.

40. Butterworth, *Three Years Adventure of a Minor*, 301–7; Robert Farris Thompson, foreword to J. Lowell Lewis, *Ring of Liberation: Deceptive Discourse in Brazilian Capoeira* (Chicago: University of Chicago Press, 1992), xii–xiv. See also Sidney Kaplan and Emma Nogrady Kaplan, *The Black Presence in the Era of the American Revolution* (Amherst: University of Massachusetts Press, 1989), 50–51; and Austin Steward, *Twenty-two Years a Slave & Forty Years a Freeman* (1856; reprint, New York, 1968), 274–77.

41. *Sailor's Magazine* 18 (Aug. 1846): 382. On the Five Points district, see "Midnight

Notes to Pages 157–160

Domicilary Visits," *New York Times*, 21 Jan. 1866, p. 6, col. 3; and "Boarding Houses for Colored Seamen in New York," *Sailor's Magazine* 41 (1869): 250.

42. For the concept of "bourgeois interior," see Norman Clark, *Deliver Us from Evil* (New York: Norton, 1976), 12–13. Brown, *Life of Brown*, 90, 35.

43. Stanley Lebergott, *Manpower in Economic Growth: The American Record since 1800* (New York: McGraw-Hill, 1964), 74, 149–50, 241–47; Donald R. Adams Jr., "Wage Rates in the Early National Period: Philadelphia, 1785-1830," *Journal of Economic History* 28 (Sept. 1968): 409–22; Morison, *Maritime History of Massachusetts*, 110.

44. Relative pay for black and white sailors on many ships can be determined by comparing Providence crew lists, CHP, RIHS, with Edward Carrington & Co., "Seamen's Ledgers," 1819–1835, Carrington Papers, RIHS. For ship's articles with wage data, see Ships' Articles, 1840s, 1850s, CHP, RIHS; and New York crew lists, 1856, USCS, RG 36, NA. *The John, Abner Mosher, Master, (An Appeal from New Providence)*. Appendix, 1809, Pamphlet, Manuscript Collection, RIHS. Moses Grandy, *Narrative of the Life of Moses Grandy, Late a Slave in the United States of America* (Boston, 1844), reprinted in William Loren Katz, ed., *Five Slave Narratives: A Compendium* (New York: Arno Press, 1968), 26.

45. "A Narrative of the Life and Adventures of Venture, a Native of Africa" (New London, Conn., 1798), in Bontemps, *Five Black Lives*, 1–34.

46. Brown, *Life of Brown*, 6–29; Providence crew lists, 1803–7, CHP, RIHS; Herman Melville, *Moby Dick: Or, The White Whale* (1851; reprint, New York: Penguin Books, 1961), 115.

47. Brown, *Life of Brown*, 103; Jay Coughtry, *Creative Survival: The Providence Black Community in the Nineteenth Century* (Providence, [1981]), 40–42; Gary Nash, "Forging Freedom: The Emancipation Experience in the Northern Seaports, 1775–1820," in Gary Nash, ed., *Race, Class, and Politics: Essays on American Colonial and Revolutionary Society* (Urbana: University of Illinois Press, 1986), 284–87. Delaware, Maryland, and Virginia provided at least one-third of Philadelphia's black seamen in the first half of the nineteenth century. Philadelphia crew lists, 1803, 1820, 1830, 1850, USCS, RG 36, NA.

48. Coughtry, *Creative Survival*, 52; *Early Negro Writing*, ed. Dorothy Porter (Boston, 1971), 42–44, 51–61.

49. Lamont D. Thomas, *Paul Cuffe: Black Entrepreneur and Pan-Africanist* (Urbana: University of Illinois Press, 1988); Philip S. Foner, *History of Black Americans from Africa to the Emergence of the Cotton Kingdom* (Westport, Conn.: Greenwood Press, 1975), 339–40; Eleanor McDougall, ed., *Memoirs of Elleanor Eldridge* (Providence, 1838), 33–41; Henry Highland Garnet to Louis Alexis Chamerovzow, 2 Oct. 1854, in Ripley, *Black Abolitionist Papers*, 2:410; Sterling Stuckey, "A Last Stern Struggle: Henry Highland Garnet and Liberation Theory," in Leon F. Litwak and August Meier, eds., *Black Leaders of the Nineteenth Century* (Urbana: University of Illinois Press, 1988), 129–49, esp. 130.

50. Register of Seamen's Protections, Library, RIHS; Register of Members, First Baptist Church, Providence, Manuscript Collection, ibid.

51. Brown, *Life of Brown*, 6; "Return of Coloured Persons Being Housekeepers," 24 June 1822, fol. 118, vol. 112, Providence Town Papers, Manuscript Collection, RIHS; *The Providence Directory, Containing the Names of the Inhabitants, Their Occupations, Places of*

Business, and Dwelling-Houses; With Lists of the Streets, Lanes, Wharves, &c. (Providence, 1832); Charles Ball, *Fifty Years in Chains; or, The Life of an American Slave* (New York, 1858), 418; Deposition of Charles Williams, *Thomas Saunders v. John Carmen and Bartholomew Bukup*, Oct. term 1830, roll 30, frame 583, Admiralty Case Files of the U.S. District Court for the Southern District of New York, 1790–1842, RG 21, NA.

52. On seamen's ages, see table 7.3. On Prince Brown, see Providence crew lists, 1803–10, CHP, RIHS.

53. *The John*, Abner Mosher, Master; Ronald G. Walters, ed., *A Black Woman's Odyssey through Russia and Jamaica: The Narrative of Nancy Prince* (1850; reprint, New York: Markus Wiener, 1990), 3.

54. Deposition of John Gardner, 30 Sept. 1831, Richard Ward Greene Papers, Manuscript Collection, RIHS; Depositions of John Gardner and Mary Gardner, *State v. Fuller and Nobles*, 1835, ibid.

55. Nathaniel Ames, *Nautical Reminiscences* (Providence, 1832), 38; Coughtry, *Creative Survival*, 39. My discussion of black seafarers' families has profited greatly from a magisterial work: Herbert G. Gutman, *The Black Family in Slavery and Freedom, 1750–1925* (New York: Random House, 1976). Providence crew lists, 1803–56, CHP, RIHS; Philadelphia crew lists, USCS, RG 36, NA.

56. George Edward Clark, *Seven Years of a Sailor's Life* (Boston, 1867), 12; Jesse Lemisch, "Jack Tar in the Streets: Merchant Seamen in the Politics of Revolutionary America," *William and Mary Quarterly* 25 (July 1968): 377. On black seamen's ages and relation to home ports, see Providence crew lists, 1803–56, CHP, RIHS; Philadelphia crew lists, USCS, NA.

57. Log of the ship *Resource*, 29 Dec. 1803, Manuscript Collection, RIHS.

58. Thomas Larkin Turner diary, 16 Feb. 1832, Manuscript Collection 95, vol. 14, Mystic Seaport Museum; John Hope Franklin, *The Free Negro in North Carolina, 1790–1860* (Chapel Hill: University of North Carolina Press, 1943), 141.

59. Roediger, "Race and the Working-Class Past in the United States," 141.

60. Charles Benson Papers, vol. 1, 13 May 1862; vol. 3, 2 July 1878, Peabody Essex Museum, Salem, Mass.

61. Benson Papers, vol. 4, 11 Aug. 1880.

62. Registers of Signatures of Depositors in Branches of the Freedman's Savings and Trust Company, 1865–74, microfilm 816, roll 13, frame 158, Records of the Office of the Comptroller of the Currency, RG 101, NA; "Report of the Colored Sailors' Home," *Sailors' Magazine* 37 (Feb. 1865): 169-70.

63. David Roediger, *The Wages of Whiteness: Race and the Making of the American Working Class* (London: Verso Books, 1991); Roediger, "Race and the Working-Class Past in the United States," 127–43.

64. Richard J. Cleveland, *Voyages and Commercial Enterprises of the Sons of New England* (New York, 1855), 26; Elmo P. Hohman, *Seamen Ashore: A Study of the United States' Seamen's Service and of Merchant Seamen in Port* (New Haven: Yale University Press, 1952), 3.

65. My work on occupational mobility among Providence's white seamen, 1803–56, indicates that virtually any white man making multiple voyages between 1803 and 1840 would be promoted. See also David Montgomery, "The Working Classes of the Pre-Industrial American City, 1780–1830," *Labor History* 9 (1968): 3–22, esp. 16.

Notes to Pages 166–172

66. Hohman, *History of American Merchant Seamen*, 7, 21–22; Elmo P. Hohman, *The American Whaleman: A Study of Life and Labor in the Whaling Industry* (New York: Longmans, Green, 1928), 48–49.

67. Jacob A. Hazen, *Five Years before the Mast; or, Life in the Forecastle, Aboard of a Whaler and Man-of-War* (Philadelphia, 1854), 184; Browne, *Etchings of a Whaling Cruise*, 23; Gaddis Smith, "Black Seamen and the Federal Courts, 1789–1860," in Runyan, *Ships, Seafaring, and Society*, 321; Richard Henry Dana, *Two Years before the Mast* (1840; reprint, Boston, 1869), 116–17.

68. Browne, *Etchings of a Whaling Cruise*, 495; Cottrol, *Afro-Yankees*, 120–21, 151–52.

69. Bolster, "African-American Seamen," 597–621.

8. Laura Tabili, "A Maritime Race"

Permission to cite and quote materials from the papers of the National Union of Seamen (NUS) and from its journal, *The Seaman*, has been granted by the copyright holder, the National Union of Rail, Maritime and Transport Workers (RMT).

1. *Negro Worker* 1 (Oct.–Nov. 1928): 2; J. W. Ford, "Lessons of the Vestris Disaster and a Programme of Organisation and Action," *Negro Worker* 1 (Dec. 1928): 3–7; "In the matter of the Merchant Shipping Act 1894 and in the matter of the British Steamship '*Vestris*' of the Port of Liverpool, official no. 1331451, Minutes of Proceedings, 1st day, 22 April 1929," University of Warwick, Modern Records Center, National Union of Seamen MSS 175/7/LE/41; "Rescued Passengers Declare the Ship Was Unseaworthy," *New York Times*, 15 Nov. 1928, 1, 3. More than twenty children were lost, and only five women were among those rescued, including a "plucky" stewardess, Mrs. Clara Ball.

2. Ford, "Lessons of the Vestris Disaster."

3. *New York Times*, 14 Nov. 1928, 1; 15 Nov. 1928, 1–2.

4. "In the matter of the Merchant Shipping Act."

5. *New York Times*, 15 Nov. 1928, 3.

6. *New York Times*, 15 Nov. 1928, 1.

7. Ford, "Lessons of the Vestris Disaster."

8. Shipowners continued to wield disproportionate political power both within government and as a pressure group outside it. Labour Research Department, *Shipping*, Studies in Labour and Capital, no. 4 (London: Labour Publishing Department, 1923), 31.

9. *The Syren and Shipping*, 1 May 1918, 264.

10. Eric Sager, *Seafaring Labour: The Merchant Marine of Atlantic Canada, 1820–1914* (Kingston: McGill–Queen's University Press, 1989), 1, 6. For a similar argument with reference to shipboard relations in World War II, see Tony Lane, *The Merchant Seamen's War* (Manchester: Manchester University Press, 1989), 8.

11. Jeffrey Bolster, writing of the antebellum U.S. industry, accepts this notion of "rough-hewn . . . equality" but argues that extrinsic economic and social factors account for its demise by the late nineteenth century, when black seamen were excluded from U.S. ships, except, significantly, for caterers and stewards. "'Every Inch a Man': Gender in the Lives of African American Seamen, 1800–1860," this volume.

12. Literary critic Abdul JanMohamed writes that the "native" becomes the "recip-

ient of the negative elements of the self that the European projects onto him," the "mirror that reflects the colonialist's self-image." "The Economy of Manichean Allegory: The Function of Racial Difference in Colonialist Literature," in Henry Louis Gates Jr., ed., *Race, Writing, and Difference* (Chicago: University of Chicago Press, 1985), 83, 85–86, 84, 99. Robert Berkhofer called this "the paradigm of polarity": "As fundamental white ways of looking at themselves changed, so too did their ways of conceiving of Indians." Robert F. Berkhofer Jr., *The White Man's Indian: Images of the American Indian from Columbus to the Present* (New York: Random House, Vintage Books, 1978), xv–xvi. Also see Edward Said, *Orientalism* (New York: Random House, Vintage Books, 1979), 7. The content of masculinity and femininity varied between the working class and the middle class: proper "feminine" conduct for middle-class Victorian ladies was unfeasible for their working-class counterparts. See Leonore Davidoff, "Class and Gender in Victorian England: The Diaries of Arthur J. Munby and Hannah Cullwick," *Feminist Studies* 5 (spring 1979): 87–141, esp. 88, 91, 130. On the view of colonized people as part of the natural world, see Mary Louise Pratt, "Scratches on the Face of the Country; or, What Mr. Barrow Saw in the Land of the Bushmen," in Gates, *Race, Writing, and Difference*, 138–62. Cultural critics use the term *naturalize* to denote the appeal to "essential differences" in justifying social relations: "*Natural* in this context has two related meanings: the relationship was taken for granted; it was a given. It was also part of nature as opposed to the civilized, the man-made, which was unnatural." Davidoff, "Class and Gender in Victorian England," 99; also see Joanna DeGroot, "'Sex' and 'Race:' The Construction of Language and Image in the Nineteenth Century," in Susan Mendus and Jane Rendall, eds., *Sexuality and Subordination: Interdisciplinary Studies of Gender in the Nineteenth Century* (London: Routledge & Kegan Paul, 1989), 95. Also see V. Spike Peterson, "Transgressing Boundaries: Theories of Knowledge, Gender, and International Relations," in *Millennium: Journal of International Studies* 21, 2 (1992): 183–206, esp. 185–86, 193, 203, 206.

13. Catherine Hall, "The Economy of Intellectual Prestige: Thomas Carlyle, John Stuart Mill, and the Case of Governor Eyre," *Cultural Critique* 12 (spring 1989): 192–95; John Mackenzie, "The Imperial Pioneer and Hunter and the British Masculine Stereotype in Late Victorian and Edwardian Times," in J. A. Mangan and James Walvin, eds., *Manliness and Morality: Middle-Class Masculinity in Britain and America, 1800–1940* (Manchester: Manchester University Press, 1986), 177, 180–82, 186; J. A. Mangan, "The Grit of Our Forefathers: Invented Traditions, Propaganda, and Imperialism," in John Mackenzie, ed., *Imperialism and Popular Culture* (Manchester: Manchester University Press, 1986), esp. 115, 120, 122; Ann Laura Stoler, "Carnal Knowledge and Imperial Power: Gender, Race, and Morality in Colonial Asia," in Micaela di Leonardo, ed., *Gender at the Crossroads of Knowledge: Feminist Anthropology in the Postmodern Era* (Berkeley: University of California Press, 1991), 52, 56, 75; Satya P. Mohanty, "Drawing the Color Line: Kipling and the Culture of Colonial Rule," in Dominick LaCapra, ed., *The Bounds of Race: Perspectives on Hegemony and Resistance* (Ithaca: Cornell University Press, 1991), esp. 314, 329, 332, 334–36; C. I. Hamilton, "Naval Hagiography and the Victorian Hero," *Historical Journal* 23, 2 (1980): 397 and passim; and see introduction to Michael Roper and John Tosh, *Manful Assertions: New Masculinities in Britain* (London: Routledge, 1991), 1–24.

14. Cynthia Cockburn, *Machinery of Dominance: Women, Men, and Technical Know-*

How (Boston: Northeastern University Press, 1988); Sonya Rose, *Limited Livelihoods: Gender and Class in Nineteenth-Century England* (London: Routledge, 1992), esp. chap. 6; Rosemary Pringle and Ann Game, *Gender at Work* (Boston: Allen & Unwin, 1983), 7–8, 16, 18, 34–35, 39, 119–42 (quotation about political definition of skill on 34); Ellen Ross, "Fierce Questions and Taunts: Married Life in Working-Class London, 1870–1914," *Feminist Studies* 8 (fall 1982): 575–602. On deskilling, see Harry Braverman, *Labor and Monopoly Capital: The Degradation of Work in the Twentieth Century* (New York: Monthly Review Press, 1974); and Sager, *Seafaring Labour*, 8, 246, 261, 264–65.

15. Lisa Norling, "Ahab's Wife," this volume. Jeffrey Bolster points out that seafaring wages facilitated African American family and community formation in " 'Every Inch a Man,' " this volume. See also Mrs. Mary Fazel to India Office, Sept. 1925, Great Britain, India Office Records, Economic and Overseas Department, L/E/9/953. On the absence of women from Anglo-American seafaring, see Sager, *Seafaring Labour*, 250–51; and Rediker, *Between the Devil and the Deep Blue Sea: Merchant Seamen, Pirates, and the Anglo-American Maritime World, 1700–1750* (Cambridge: Cambridge University Press, 1987), 255–56, n. 3. In my research on the period 1900–1950 I have found no evidence that women served aboard British merchant ships in any significant numbers.

16. Rediker, among others, characterizes the merchant ship as, in Erving Goffman's phrase, a "total institution," a self-sustaining social system, in *Between the Devil and the Deep Blue Sea*, 211–12; Sager writes that the steward's job in a sailing ship "combined the role of waiter, domestic servant and assistant cook," while cooks themselves were often "teenagers" "substituting for apprenticeships" and "easily terrorized" by adult crew members, in *Seafaring Labour*, 112. On women's labor as reproductive labor, see, among many, Heidi Hartmann, "The Unhappy Marriage of Marxism and Feminism," in Lydia Sargent, ed., *Women and Revolution: A Discussion of the Unhappy Marriage of Marxism and Feminism* (Boston: South End Press, 1981), 1–41; and Roisin McDonough and Rachel Harrison, "Patriarchy and Relations of Production," in Annette Kuhn and Annemarie Wolpe, eds., *Feminism and Materialism* (London: Routledge & Kegan Paul, 1978), 1–41.

17. In sailing ships, which seldom carried more than two dozen men, including officers, the role of cook was low in status and defined as unskilled—not least in cookery itself. Sager, *Seafaring Labour*, 106–7; Rediker, *Between the Devil and the Deep Blue Sea*, 83, 85, 123. Bolster also found that by the late nineteenth century, these so-called feminine tasks were performed by African American seafarers in the American industry. " 'Every Inch a Man,' " this volume.

18. Andrew Porter, *Victorian Shipping, Business, and Imperial Policy: Donald Currie, the Castle Line, and South Africa* (New York: St. Martin's Press, 1986), 246. Although stokehold and deck crews' relative wages varied in the course of the interwar period, so that at times firemen's wages were somewhat higher than those of regular seamen, black seamen were often paid "customary" lower wages. Eric Taplin, *Liverpool Seamen and Dockers, 1870–1890* (Hull: University of Hull Press, 1974), 14; R. H. Thornton, *British Shipping* (Cambridge: Cambridge University Press, 1939), 82–83, 86, 250.

19. There is a growing literature on the feminization of colonized people, especially of colonized men. See Uma Chakravarti, "Whatever Happened to the Vedic Dasi? Orientalism, Nationalism, and a Script for the Past," in Kumkum Sangari and Sudesh

Notes to Pages 174–175

Vaid, eds., *Recasting Women: Essays in Indian Colonial History* (New Brunswick, N.J.: Rutgers University Press, 1990), 47, 49; Mrinalini Sinha, "Gender and Imperialism: Colonial Policy and the Ideology of Moral Imperialism in Late Nineteenth-Century Bengal," in Michael S. Kimmel, ed., *Changing Men: New Directions in Research on Men and Masculinity* (Beverly Hills: Sage, 1987), 217–31; John Roselli, "The Self-Image of Effeteness: Physical Education and Nationalism in Nineteenth-Century Bengal," *Past and Present* 86 (Feb. 1980): 121–48; Patrick Brantlinger, *Rule of Darkness: British Literature and Imperialism, 1830–1914* (Ithaca: Cornell University Press, 1988); Hall, "Economy of Intellectual Prestige," 179–80, 188–89.

20. The British fleet had historically been "far in excess of our capacity to man with our own seafaring peasantry," necessitating a large proportion (80,000 of 280,000 in 1910) of "foreigners, between whom and their employers few mutual obligations . . . exist." Thornton, *British Shipping*, 82.

21. British merchant tonnage quintupled between 1860 and 1914, comprising one-third of world tonnage by 1914. After 1900, only monopolistic conference arrangements with the German, Dutch, Belgian, and U.S. industries enabled the overcapitalized industry to limp toward 1914. Labour Research Department, *Shipping*, 14–16; Adam Willis Kirkaldy, *British Shipping: Its History, Organization, and Importance* (New York: Augustus M. Kelly, 1970 [1914]), 168, 207. Thornton reported that "by 1910 Great Britain owned about 40 per cent of the tonnage of the whole world." *British Shipping*, 82, 87. Also see Derek Aldcroft, *The British Economy*, vol. 1, *Years of Turmoil, 1920–1951* (Atlantic Highlands, N.J.: Humanities Press, 1986), 34–35; Sidney Pollard, *The Development of the British Economy, 1914–1967* (New York: St. Martin's Press, 1969), 75–76; Peter Linebaugh, "Labour History without Labour Process," *Social History* 7 (Oct. 1982): 327; and John Mackenzie, *Propaganda and Empire: The Manipulation of British Public Opinion, 1880–1960* (Manchester: Manchester University Press, 1984), 187.

22. Hardly an impartial observer, Thomas Brassey was a Liberal M.P. concerned with imperial defense, and a lobbyist for the shipping industry and government subsidies in the mid–nineteenth century. He wrote approvingly in 1877, "The scale of wages is probably less than it would have been if foreigners had been prohibited from sailing under the British flag." Brassey estimated that "foreigners" accounted for 13 percent of all seamen, or 20 percent of able seamen, in the 1870s. *British Seamen* (Longmans, Green, 1877), 35–37, also 373, 378. Shipowner R. H. Thornton, too, admitted that widespread employment of "Eastern" crews was a cost-cutting measure. *British Shipping*, 221–22. Until the repeal of the Navigation Acts in 1849, three-quarters of crew members of ships sailing into British ports were required to be British sailors. Bob Hepple, *Race, Jobs, and the Law* (Harmondsworth: Penguin Books, 1968), 63.

23. Brassey, *British Seamen*, 6, 10, 16, 164–65; Thornton, *British Shipping*, 213–27; National Union of Seamen (NUS) Correspondence, MSS 175 / 3 / 14 / 1&2, University of Warwick, Modern Records Centre (MRC); Porter, *Victorian Shipping*, 90, 246; Taplin, *Liverpool Seamen and Dockers*, 70; Harris Joshua and Tina Wallace, with the assistance of Heather Booth, *To Ride the Storm: The 1980 Bristol "Riot" and the State* (London: Heinemann, 1983), 14–15.

24. J. Grignon, consul at Riga, 1872, and A. De Capel Crowe, consul at Copenhagen, 1872, both quoted in Brassey, *British Seamen*, 6–7, also 315.

25. Trade union delegation to the Board of Trade, Mar. 1914, Great Britain. Records

of the Board of Trade Mercantile Marine Department, MT9/1087.M835119, Public Record Office (PRO).

26. In the early twentieth century the union provided German, Danish, and Scandinavian translators at some meetings. Papers of the International Transportworkers' Federation (ITF), MSS 159/B/63/, MRC. The union opened branches in New York, Antwerp, Bremerhaven, Hamburg, and other foreign ports. General Secretary Edmund Cathery, 339 East India Dock Road, Poplar, to the Registry of Friendly Societies, FS 12/189 (NUS 1493T), PRO.

27. *Seaman*, Apr. 1911, 47–48, ITF Papers, MSS 159/5/3/497. Although Wilson was speaking specifically about Chinese seamen in this instance, the principle held. Because the Chinese were not formally colonized by Britain, their experience in some ways resembled that of colonized people, but there were also significant differences that scholars have yet to explore adequately. See Ng Kwee Choo, *The Chinese in London* (London: Oxford University Press, for the Institute of Race Relations, 1968); J. P. May, "The Chinese in Britain, 1860–1914," in Colin Holmes, ed., *Immigrants and Minorities in British Society* (London: Allen & Unwin, 1978), 111–24; and Colin Holmes, *John Bull's Island: Immigration and British Society, 1871–1971* (London: Macmillan Educational, 1988).

28. For the derivation of the term *lascar*, see Hugh Tinker, *A New System of Slavery: The Export of Indian Labour Overseas, 1830–1920* (London: Oxford University Press, for the Institute of Race Relations, 1974), 41.

29. For a fascinating and poignant study of Bengali seafarers, see Caroline Adams, *Across Seven Seas and Thirteen Rivers: Life Stories of Pioneer Sylheti Settlers in Britain* (London: Tower Hamlets Arts Project, 1987), esp. 1, 15–30.

30. Hepple, *Race, Jobs, and the Law*, 63; Tony Lane, *Grey Dawn Breaking: British Merchant Seafarers in the Late Twentieth Century* (Manchester: Manchester University Press, 1986), 17; Brassey, *British Seamen*, 36.

31. Adams reports, for example, that the corruptible *ghat serang* system was codified into law during the British occupation. *Across Seven Seas*, 20–21.

32. India Office Records (IOR), L/E/7/936; and see Board of Trade Papers, MT9/2735; Catherine Betty Abigail Behrens, *Merchant Shipping and the Demands of War* (London: HMSO, 1955), 157; India Office Revenue no. 171, 20 Nov. 1903, R&S 819/1903, L/E/7/481; and A. Colaco, ed., *A History of the Seamen's Union, Bombay* (Bombay: Pascoal Vaz, 1955), 58, ITF Papers, MSS 159/5/3/588.

33. In the same years, while the proportion of "British" seamen remained fairly stable, the proportion of "foreign seamen" on standard articles—among whom many black seamen, British and otherwise, were classed—fell steadily. Since approximately a third of men listed as "British" were officers, and these were usually white, lascars, who were of course confined to the lower ranks, constituted more like a third of the rank and file. See table 8.1. For detailed definitions of categories, see Great Britain, Board of Trade, *Census of Seamen* (London: HMSO, 1937, 1938, 1939), esp. 1937, 4, 6, 7.

34. On comparative wages, see Great Britain, *Parl. Deb.*, Commons, 5th ser., 218 (1928): 1331–32; also *Monthly Labor Review* 9 (Oct. 1919): 157. White seamen's monthly wages fluctuated between £11 in 1917 and £8 2s in 1932. Hours were gradually reduced from 84 to 64 per week, and 45 in port. See Leslie Hughes Powell, *The Shipping Federation: A History of the First Sixty Years, 1890–1950* (London: Shipping Federation, 1950), 46–

Notes to Pages 176–178

47. In the interwar years, wages for men on Asiatic articles averaged 35 shillings per month, or £1 15s. Memorandum from the All-India Seamen's Federation, "Indian Seamen in the Merchant Navy," per S. Alley, Board of Trade Papers, MT9 / 3657 M.14184.

35. Minutes by Hoskin, 5 Aug. 1929, and Board of Trade minutes, 3 Oct. 1927, MT9 / 2735 M.4184.

36. W. E. Home, *Merchant Seamen: Their Diseases and Their Welfare Needs* (New York: Dutton, 1922), 87.

37. Federation of Nigeria, *Report of the Board of Enquiry into the Trade Dispute between the Elder Dempster Lines, Ltd., and the Nigerian Union of Seamen* (Lagos: Federal Government Printer, 1959), esp. 31–34, 79–81, 118–24.

38. Charles Ainsworth to the *Telegraph*, reprinted in the *Seaman*, 29 Nov. 1933, 2. See also an advertisement for a Chinese crew placed by a Mr. A. H. Sam of Cardiff in March of 1908 urging, "You only require about two more [Chinese] hands than Europeans, but the difference in costs, not only in wages, is balanced by the cheaper scale of provisions the crew demands." NUS Correspondence, MSS 175 / 3 / 14 / 1&2.

39. P. G. Kanekar, *Seamen in Bombay: Report of an Enquiry into the Conditions of Their Life and Work* (Bombay: Servants of India Society, 1925), ITF Papers, MSS 159 / 5 / 3 / 587, 17; Colaco, *History of the Seamen's Union, Bombay*, 87–88.

40. Goan stewards, subjects of Portugal, were exempt on grounds of "race" and "custom" from full wages payable to aliens in British ships. The British merchant marine employed more Chinese seamen than any other national industry and paid them half of a white man's wage. Board of Trade Papers, MT9 / 2737 M.4541. In 1909 Chinese seamen were paid £3 10s per month, as opposed to £5 10s for Europeans. NUS Correspondence, MSS 175 / 3 / 14 / 1&2.

41. D. C. Jones, *The Social Survey of Merseyside* (Liverpool: Liverpool University Press, 1932), 2:102, 98; J. G. Dendy, chief superintendent for the Port of London, to Hoskin at the Board of Trade, 7 Aug. 1923, IOR L / E / 7 / 1152. Tramps employed the bulk of black seamen sailing on standard National Maritime Board articles. See Taplin, *Liverpool Seamen and Dockers*, 14; R. Bean, "Employers' Associations in the Port of Liverpool, 1890–1914," *International Review of Social History* 21 (1976): 366–67; and Board of Trade, *Census of Seamen* (London: HMSO, 1937, 1938, 1939).

42. The phrase "dirty little tramps" is from Behrens, *Merchant Shipping*, 163. The Board of Trade claimed in 1935 that tramp shipping "employs few, if any Lascars." Board of Trade Memorandum, Weston to Turner, 6 Aug. 1935, enclosure app. 4, National Maritime Board to Tramp Shipping Subsidy Committee, July 1935, IOR, L / E / 9 / 955; also see Board of Trade, *Census of Seamen* (1937), 4; Thornton, *British Shipping*, 223; Bean, "Employers' Associations in the Port of Liverpool," 366–67; and Lane, *Grey Dawn Breaking*, 9–10.

43. See Tony Lane, "Neither Officers nor Gentlemen," *History Workshop Journal* 19 (spring 1985): 131; Taplin, *Liverpool Seamen and Dockers*, 14; and Thornton, *British Shipping*, 82–83, 86, 250.

44. Thornton, *British Shipping*, 250.

45. Lane, *Grey Dawn Breaking*, 32–33.

46. Sager, *Seafaring Labour*, 10–11.

47. Lillian Nayder suggests that Conrad and others perceived the deskilling associated with steamships as emasculating, in "Sailing Ships and Steamers, Angels and

Whores," this volume. Also see Robert Foulke, "Life in the Dying World of Sail, 1870–1910," in Patricia Ann Carlson, ed., *Literature and Lore of the Sea* (Amsterdam: Rodolpi, 1986), 72–115, esp. 84–85. These processes were features of the Second Industrial Revolution on the Continent, which coincided with the phase of "mature industrialization" in Britain itself. See Eric Hobsbawm, *Industry and Empire* (Harmondsworth: Penguin Books, 1968), 172–94.

48. Brassey's figures suggest that the proportion of "non-seafaring" jobs—stoking, catering, and engineering—went from 10 percent on sailing ships to 50 percent on steamships. In 1873 there were 130,877 "Crews in Sail," from which Brassey deducted 10 percent, or 13,087, for "Stewards&c.," in order to arrive at the number of "real" sailors. Of "Crews in Steam," who constituted only 71,362, or barely one-third of total crews, he deducted 50 percent, or 35,681, for "Engineers, Stokers, Stewards, &c." Of the total 153,471 "real" sailors, Brassey estimated that 19,840, or 20 percent, were "foreigners." *British Seamen*, 35–36. Sager reported that in many steamships there were "more waiters than deckhands," and that deck sailors were frequently "outnumbered by engine room and service workers." *Seafaring Labour*, 248–49, 262–63; also James C. Healey, *Foc'sle and Glory Hole: A Study of the Merchant Seaman and His Occupation* (New York: Greenwood Press, 1969), 29–34.

49. Captain Kent, "Sailors: Past and Present," *Syren and Shipping*, 27 June 1917, 805.

50. Brassey reported contradictory testimony in *British Seamen*, 11, 17.

51. Thornton, *British Shipping*, 83, 213, 223. Somewhat contradictorily, Thornton defended the twentieth-century workforce, "each of whom knows his job and does it with unflurried precision," 214.

52. Ibid., 83, 87; Joshua, Wallace, and Booth, *To Ride the Storm*, 14–15; Porter, *Victorian Shipping*, 246; Taplin, *Liverpool Seamen and Dockers*, 14; India Office Records, L/E/9/935, app. 4, July 1935, National Maritime Board to Tramp Shipping Subsidy Committee, enclosed in Board of Trade memorandum, Weston to Turner, 6 Aug. 1935; Kirkaldy, *British Shipping*, 205. Sager confirms that between 1863 and 1914, firemen earned more than certificated or licensed "able seamen" (ABs) and much more than unlicensed "ordinary" seamen, both because of the skill involved and the unpleasantness of the work. *Seafaring Labour*, 247–48.

53. Joe Stack, "Shooting Ashes on the Old George Washington," *The Hawsepipe*, newsletter of the Marine Workers' Historical Association 8 (Feb.–Mar. 1989): 12. Although this is a description of an American ship, the work process was much the same, as was the racial division of labor.

54. Both quotations from Thornton, *British Shipping*, 250.

55. Stack, "Shooting Ashes on the Old George Washington," 12. "The stokehold watch will be composed of about three-fifths firemen and two-fifths trimmers." Thornton, *British Shipping*, 250.

56. For an example of how food and other supplies could be used to manipulate and to signify status, see Federation of Nigeria, *Report of the Board of Enquiry*, 16–20, 28, and passim; for women's status and power in relation to food distribution, see Judith K. Brown, "Iroquois Women: An Ethnohistorical Note," in Rayna Reiter, ed., *Toward an Anthropology of Women* (Monthly Review Press, 1975), 235–51; and, in very different circumstances, Ross, "Fierce Questions and Taunts."

57. Sager, *Seafaring Labour*, 248–49, 262–63; Healey, *Foc'sle and Glory Hole*, 29–34.

Notes to Pages 180–182

58. On large liners, the varied responsibilities of the chief steward were comparable to those of a hotel manager. In some liners, catering crews were supervised separately by the chef or chief cook. A pecking order prevailed among stewards and caterers, shaped by minute distinctions among tasks and among the classes of passengers served. Peeling vegetables, for example, carried less prestige than cooking but more than scrubbing pots. See Sager, *Seafaring Men*, 248–49, 262–63; and Healey, *Foc'sle and Glory Hole*, 29–34.

59. Thornton, *British Shipping*, 82.

60. Joshua, Wallace, and Booth, *To Ride the Storm*, 14–15; Taplin, *Liverpool Seamen and Dockers*, 14.

61. Lane reports that many of the men called "Somalis" were actually from the Sudan, Aden, the Yemen, or Zanzibar. *Grey Dawn Breaking*, 18, 21, 167–69, 174. Also see David Byrne, "The 1930 'Arab riot' in South Shields: A Race Riot That Never Was," *Race and Class* 18, 3 (1977): 263.

62. Kanekar, *Seamen in Bombay*, 11; "Types of Indian Seamen," *Syren and Shipping*, 3 Jan. 1945, 117.

63. Lane, *Grey Dawn Breaking*, 32–33, 153–55, 175. A similar division of labor was found on American ships. See *Hawsepipe* 11 (Jan.–Feb. 1992): 11, 19.

64. Thornton, *British Shipping*, 82–83, 85–86, 119, 213–15, 225–27, 250; Brassey, *British Seamen*, 6, 10, 60, 164–65, 315, 373, 378; NUS Correspondence, MSS 175 / 3 / 14 / 1&2.

65. Peter N. Davies, *The Trade Makers: Elder Dempster in West Africa, 1852–1972* (London: Allen & Unwin, 1973), 154.

66. Lane, *Grey Dawn Breaking*, 19, 32–33, 153–55, 162–63, 167–75; *Maritime Board Year Book*, 1923, 7; and see 1935, 1936, 1937, 1938, 1939, 1940, 1949; Francis E. Hyde, *Shipping Enterprise and Management, 1830–1939: Harrisons of Liverpool* (Liverpool: Liverpool University Press, 1967), 153; "Inspection of Lascars' Food," R&S 54 / 1908, IOR L / E / 7 / 604; Home, *Merchant Seamen: Their Diseases*, 87; Federation of Nigeria, *Report of the Board of Enquiry*, 16–20, 28, 31–34, 79–81, 118–24, and passim; compare this process to the gendering of work discussed by Sallie Westwood in *All Day, Every Day: Family and Factory in the Making of Women's Lives* (Urbana: University of Illinois Press, 1985), esp. chap. 2, "The Domestication of Labour."

67. John Gillis, *Youth and History: Tradition and Change in European Age Relations, 1770–Present* (New York: Academic Press, 1974), esp. 102–15, 133–42, 171–73; John Mackenzie, "Imperial Pioneer," esp. 177, 179.

68. Hermon McKay to Tony Lane, *Grey Dawn Breaking*, 162–63.

69. Officers internalized these distinctions. Lane, *Grey Dawn Breaking*, 19, 152, 167–71; Lane, "Neither Officers nor Gentlemen," 137.

70. In the mid-1970s, one ship still featured four separate messes for a crew of twenty-eight, one each for able seamen, stewards, engine-room crews, and officers. Commented seaman Tony Santamara, "They wanted to divide us up," and the result was indeed ill-feeling among different messes. Tramps might mix their deck crews, but stokehold crews were usually ethnically homogeneous. Lane, *Grey Dawn Breaking*, 18, 21, 167–74; Byrne, "1930 'Arab riot,'" 263. Segregated quarters for different crews were new with steam. Sager, *Seafaring Labour*, 249.

71. Kanekar, *Seamen in Bombay*, 22; "Types of Indian Seamen," *Syren and Shipping*, 3 Jan. 1945, 117.

72. Home Office Aliens Department file on the 1919 riots, HO45 / 11017 / 377969.

73. See *Maritime Board Year Book*, 1923–49. The National Maritime Board was a wartime organization that brought shipowners to the bargaining table with the seamen's unions under government sponsorship. After the Armistice, the body became voluntary. See Powell, *Shipping Federation*, 38–39.

74. Kirkaldy, *British Shipping*, 269–70; and see J. O'Connor Kessack, quoted in the *Seaman*, 17 Apr. 1914.

75. *Seaman*, 29 Nov. 1933, 2, quoting a letter from G. C. Howe, master mariner, published by the *Telegraph*, 24 Nov. 1933; see also *Hawsepipe* 6 (Mar. 1987): 1; and M. J. Daunton, "Jack Ashore: Seamen in Cardiff before 1914," *Welsh History Review* 9, 2 (1975): 190–91.

76. Pay differentials by no means matched these manning differentials, for the real motive was of course to get more labor power at bargain prices. *Maritime Board Year Book*, 1923, 7; and see 1935, 1936, 1937, 1938, 1939, 1940, 1949; Hyde, *Shipping Enterprise and Management*, 153. Tony Lane's informants suggested that a 2:1 ratio of lascars to white seamen was customary. *Grey Dawn Breaking*, 19.

77. Federation of Nigeria, *Report of the Board of Enquiry*, 16–20, 28, and passim.

78. Lane, *Grey Dawn Breaking* 162; Hepple, *Race, Jobs, and the Law*, 64; "we have all heard of fatalistic Indians," quoted in Behrens, *Merchant Shipping and the Demands of War*, 156.

79. *Seaman*, Apr. 1911, 47–48; Thornton, *British Shipping*, 213–23; Brassey, *British Seamen*, 6, 10, 16, 164–65, 315, 373, 378.

80. Thornton, *British Shipping*, 221. While Thornton asserted that these crews were paid NBM rates, all-black crews were exempt by statute from NMB rates. See *National Maritime Board Year Book* for any year from 1923 through 1949.

81. John Springhall argues that these behaviors constituted an "alternative" culture of working-class masculinity, in "Building Character in the British Boy: The Attempt to Extend Christian Manliness to Working-Class Adolescents, 1880–1914," in Mangan and Walvin, *Manliness and Morality*, 69–70.

82. Thornton, *British Shipping*, 225–26.

83. *Syren and Shipping*, 30 July 1919, 424.

84. Joanna DeGroot, "'Sex' and 'Race,'" 91–92, 95, 97, 100. Noting the similarities in culturally dominant portrayals of colonized people and of women, DeGroot argues that "nineteenth century representations and discourses of sexual identity and difference drew upon and contributed to comparable discourses and representations of ethnic, 'racial,' and cultural identity and difference," 89, 100.

85. Davidoff, "Class and Gender in Victorian England," 130 and passim.

86. All workers in service and catering were treated as social inferiors by officers and engineers. Sager, *Seafaring Labour*, 262–63. On Cotter, see NSFU, "Minutes of Proceedings of a Conference with Representative Cooks and Stewards," at St. George Hall, Westminster, 19 Oct. 1921, remarks by J. Havelock Wilson, NUS MSS 175 / 4 / 17. See also *Syren and Shipping*'s criticism of Cotter's opposition to conscription and to the union boycott of the Stockholm Peace Conference, in *Syren and Shipping*, 20 Mar. 1918, 803.

87. Lane, *Grey Dawn Breaking*, 153–55, 175.

88. Joanna DeGroot makes this point in "'Sex' and 'Race,'" 94.

Notes to Pages 184–186

89. Federation of Nigeria, *Report of the Board of Enquiry*, 17–18; Lane, *Grey Dawn Breaking*, 163.

90. Thornton, *British Shipping*, 221.

91. *Irish Times* of 19 Nov., quoted in *Negro Worker* 1 (Dec. 1928): 4.

92. *Seaman*, 9 Jan. 1914, 6.

93. Barbara Taylor, "'The Men Are as Bad as Their Masters'. . . Working Women and the Owenite Economic Offensive, 1828–1834," in *Eve and the New Jerusalem: Socialism and Feminism in the Nineteenth Century* (New York: Pantheon Books, 1983), 83–117; Rose, *Limited Livelihoods;* Pringle and Game, *Gender at Work*, esp. 16, 23, 120; Westwood, *All Day, Every Day*. A well-known example from British history were the "dilution" workers who replaced skilled workmen conscripted into the military in World War I. See, for example, Gail Braybon, *Women Workers in the First World War: The British Experience* (London: Croom Helm, 1981).

94. Jane Lewis argued that women's work both inside and outside the home was so similar that it was naturally devalued, in "Sexual Divisions: Women's Work in Late Nineteenth Century England," in S. Jay Kleinberg, ed., *Retrieving Women's History: Changing Perceptions of the Role of Women in Politics and Society* (Oxford: Berg/UNESCO, 1988). Yet Rose, Westwood, and Pringle and Game have documented the ways in which male workers and employers have systematically and deliberately pushed women out of skilled work, identified masculinity with certain types of skills, and redefined certain types of work as "women's work" while defining women's skills as nonskills. They argue that in itself "the definition of skill is gender-biased. . . . by and large women's 'skills' are not recognized as such." See Westwood, *All Day, Every Day*, 13–38; Pringle and Game, *Gender at Work*, esp. 7–40; and Rose, *Limited Livelihoods*.

95. Cockburn, *Machinery of Dominance;* Pringle and Game, *Gender at Work*, 16.

96. Thornton, *British Shipping*, 221–22.

97. "Types of Indian Seamen," *Syren and Shipping*, 3 Jan. 1945, 117–23.

98. Social Darwinists justified Victorian economic disparities by arguing that working-class people were an inferior breed. See, among others, Anna Davin, "Imperialism and Motherhood," *History Workshop Journal* 5 (spring 1978): 9–66; Springhall, "Building Character in the British Boy," 54–55, 58.

99. The industry carried emotional, historical, and nationalistic resonances for many Britons. See Michael Howard, "Empire, Race, and War in pre-1914 Britain," in Hugh Lloyd-Jones, Valerie Pearl, and Blair Warden, eds., *History and Imagination: Essays in Honour of H. R. Trevor-Roper* (London: Duckworth, 1981), 342–45; Hamilton, "Naval Hagiography," 397; and Frederick Cooper and Ann Stoler, "Tensions of Empire: Colonial Control and Visions of Rule," *American Ethnologist* 16 (Nov. 1989): 615.

100. *Syren and Shipping*, 9 July 1919, 115; 6 Aug. l9l9, 509–10.

101. Ibid., 3 Apr. 1918, 15.

102. Ibid., 20 June 1917, 735; 10 Apr. 1918, 83; 17 Apr. 1918, 138; 26 June 1918, 712; 16 Apr. 1919, 174; and see Hugh Clegg, *A History of British Trade Unions since 1889*, vol. 2, 1911–1933 (Oxford: Clarendon Press, 1985), 141, 164. *Syren and Shipping* denounced government "readiness . . . to truckle to labour tyranny," 18 June 1919, 1055. Also see 13 Aug. 1919, 646; 20 Aug. 1919, 691; 9 Apr. 1919, 114; 24 Apr. 1919, 199.

103. *Syren and Shipping*, 27 Mar. 1918, 851; 24 Apr. 1919, 199.

104. They warned sternly of "the decline of Athens" and of Carthage, due to "the

decline of the training of the rank and file of the seafaring population," ibid., 17 Apr. 1918. On prewar fears, see Michael Howard, "Empire, Race, and War"; and Anna Davin, "Imperialism and Motherhood." This was a "business proposition," an investment in Britain's global position. *Syren and Shipping*, 10 Apr. 1918, 83.

105. *Syren and Shipping*, 18 June 1919, 1056.

106. The quote is from Ainsworth, *Seaman*, 29 Nov. 1933, 2.

107. Thornton, *British Shipping*, 221–22, 225–26; and see Davidoff, who argues that working-class men represented "'true' masculinity" to their effete middle-class counterparts. "Class and Gender in Victorian England," 131.

108. On splitting, see Davidoff, "Class and Gender in Victorian England," 92, 95.

109. Ford, "Lessons of the Vestris Disaster."

9. Lillian Nayder, Sailing Ships and Steamers, Angels and Whores

1. Joseph Conrad, *Lord Jim* (New York: Modern Library, 1921), 29. Page numbers follow subsequent quotations in the text.

2. "The sailors had a good time of it up here," the second engineer tells them, "and what was the use of them in the world he would be blowed if he could see. The poor devils of engineers had to get the ship along anyhow, and they could very well do the rest too.... It's all very fine for you—you get a power of pieces out of her one way and another; but what about me—what do I get?" (22, 25).

3. In his *Last Essays*, Conrad describes himself as "a seaman trained to his duties under the British flag and, in regard to the performance of such duties, having a good record for more than sixteen years of sea life, both in sail and steam." See "Memorandum: On the Scheme for Fitting Out a Sailing Ship for the Purpose of Perfecting the Training of Merchant Service Officers Belonging to the Port of Liverpool," in *Last Essays* (Garden City, N.Y.: Doubleday, Page, 1926), 67.

4. For discussions of the transition from sail to steam and the technological developments that made this transition possible, see Robert Foulke, "Life in the Dying World of Sail, 1870–1910," *Journal of British Studies* 3 (1963): 105–36; and Charles K. Harley, "The Shift from Sailing Ships to Steamships, 1850–1890: A Study in Technological Change and Its Diffusion," in Donald N. McCloskey, ed., *Essays on a Mature Economy: Britain after 1840* (Princeton: Princeton University Press, 1971), 215–31.

5. Frank T. Bullen, *The Men of the Merchant Service: Being the Polity of the Mercantile Marine for 'Longshore Readers* (New York: Frederick A. Stokes, 1900), 257–59. In order to remedy the problem of deskilling, Conrad advocated training officers for the merchant marine on sailing ships rather than steamers, although he acknowledged that his proposal, written in 1919, would be perceived as "hopelessly out of date." In his view, the ship on which merchant officers are trained should have "no labour-saving appliances" and "no auxiliary propulsion of any kind." See "Memorandum: On the Scheme for Fitting Out a Sailing Ship," 69, 70, 79.

6. Bullen, *Men of the Merchant Service*, 259, 274.

7. R. J. Cornewall-Jones, *The British Merchant Service: Being a History of the British Mercantile Marine from the Earliest Times to the Present Day* (London: Sampson Low, Marston, 1898), 275.

8. Bullen, *Men of the Merchant Service*, 309, 318; Eric Sager, *Seafaring Labour: The*

Merchant Marine of Atlantic Canada, 1820–1914 (Montreal: McGill-Queen's University Press, 1989), 247–48. Laura Tabili discusses the varying rates of wages paid on steamers, and the relation of wages to the division of labor, in "'A Maritime Race,'" this volume.

9. Bullen, *Men of the Merchant Service*, 309.

10. Conrad, "Certain Aspects of the Admirable Inquiry into the Loss of the *Titanic*," in *Notes on Life and Letters* (Garden City, N.Y.: Doubleday, Page, 1925), 238.

11. Edward W. Sloan provides numerous examples of this response among Victorians in "Men of Sail in the Age of Steam: Responses to a Maritime Revolution," MS, G. W. Blunt White Library, Mystic Seaport Museum, Mystic, Conn.

12. Foulke, "Life in the Dying World of Sail," 105, 109, 133.

13. Michael Levenson, "The Modernist Narrator on the Victorian Sailing Ship," *Browning Institute Studies* 11 (1983): 101–2.

14. Fredric Jameson, *The Political Unconscious: Narrative as a Socially Symbolic Act* (Ithaca: Cornell University Press, 1981), 210–13.

15. Nancy Armstrong, *Desire and Domestic Fiction: A Political History of the Novel* (Oxford: Oxford University Press, 1987), 178. Tabili discusses a related strategy—the feminization of the racial "other"—in "'A Maritime Race,'" this volume.

16. For discussions of these dichotomous female stereotypes, see Lynda Nead, *Myths of Sexuality: Representations of Women in Victorian Britain* (Oxford: Basil Blackwell, 1988); and Kate Millett, "The Debate over Women: Ruskin vs. Mill," in *Suffer and Be Still: Women in the Victorian Age*, ed. Martha Vicinus (Bloomington: Indiana University Press, 1972), 121–39.

17. Bernard C. Meyer, *Joseph Conrad: A Psychoanalytic Biography* (Princeton: Princeton University Press, 1967), 307.

18. Conrad's misogynistic representations have been noted by a host of critics and biographers who have discussed his views of women from psychoanalytic, economic, and political angles, and who have observed his tendency to scapegoat the female sex. In his psychoanalytic biography, for example, Meyer associates Conrad's early loss of his mother with his "reiterated insistence upon the destructive and devouring nature of a woman's love" (117). Claire Kahane, a feminist critic, argues that Conrad projects male aggression onto the domineering African woman in *Heart of Darkness*. Rather than blaming Kurtz for his "voraciousness," Conrad blames the object of Kurtz's desire. See "Seduction and the Voice of the Text: *Heart of Darkness* and *The Good Soldier*," in Dianne Hunter, ed., *Seduction and Theory: Readings of Gender, Representation, and Rhetoric* (Urbana: University of Illinois Press, 1989). For an economic critique of Conrad's treatment of women, based on the work of Engels, see Karen Klein, "The Feminine Predicament in Conrad's *Nostromo*," in John Hazel Smith, ed., *Brandeis Essays in Literature* (Waltham, Mass.: Brandeis University, Dept. of English and American Literature, 1983), 101–16. Eileen Sypher approaches the subject on neo-Marxist grounds in "Anarchism and Gender: James's *The Princess Casamassima* and Conrad's *The Secret Agent*," *Henry James Review* 9 (1988): 1–15. Heliena Krenn examines Conrad's portraits of women in the context of imperialism in *Conrad's Lingard Trilogy: Empire, Race, and Women in the Malay Novels* (New York: Garland, 1990).

19. See, for example, Robert Foulke, "Life in the Dying World of Sail, 1870–1910," in Patricia Ann Carlson, ed., *Literature and Lore of the Sea* (Amsterdam: Rodopi, 1986), 84–

87. This essay differs substantially from the article published under the same title in *Journal of British Studies*, cited above.

20. Letter to Captain A. W. Phillips, 12 Jan. 1924, in G. Jean-Aubry, *Joseph Conrad: Life and Letters* (Garden City, N.Y.: Doubleday, Page, 1927), 2:334.

21. Joseph Conrad, "Typhoon," in *Great Short Works of Joseph Conrad* (New York: Harper & Row, 1967), 340–41. Page numbers follow subsequent quotations in the text.

22. Conrad, *The Mirror of the Sea* (Garden City, N.Y.: Doubleday, Page, 1925), 37, 64–65.

23. William Acton, *The Functions and Disorders of the Reproductive Organs in Youth, in Adult Age, and in Advanced Life Considered in Their Physiological, Social, and Psychological Relations*, 4th ed. (1865), 112; quoted by Lynda Nead, *Myths of Sexuality*, 50. For discussions of female sexuality as it was conceptualized in the Victorian period, see, in addition to Nead, Nina Auerbach, *Woman and the Demon: The Life of a Victorian Myth* (Cambridge: Harvard University Press, 1982); Sander L. Gilman, *Difference and Pathology: Stereotypes of Sexuality, Race, and Madness* (Ithaca: Cornell University Press, 1985); and Helena Michie, *The Flesh Made Word: Female Figures and Women's Bodies* (New York: Oxford University Press, 1987).

24. Joseph Conrad, *The Shadow-Line*, ed. Jeremy Hawthorn (Oxford: Oxford University Press, 1985), 5. Page numbers follow subsequent quotations in the text. Although *The Shadow-Line* was not published until 1916–17, Conrad began formulating his ideas for the work in 1899; it was originally entitled *First Command*.

25. Conrad, *Mirror of the Sea*, 63.

26. Alex Owen, *The Darkened Room: Women, Power, and Spiritualism in Late Victorian England* (Philadelphia: University of Pennsylvania Press, 1990), 4, 11, 218.

27. Conrad, *Mirror of the Sea*, 37, 64.

28. Ibid., 47, 132. The sexual implications of boarding and loading ships were widely recognized by Victorians and employed in the popular maritime ballads of the day. The following poem, found by Joan Tyler Mead in a journal kept on the American ship *Peruvian* and dating from 1865, is one example; as Mead notes, the poem uses "a *double entendre* of shipboard terminology" to describe "a sailor's unfortunate encounter with a diseased prostitute":

> As I went a cruising St Frances Street
> a Lofty Frigate I chanced to meet
> She was well riged and fit for sea
> and all she wanted was her company
> I asked her if I could go to sea on board
> That verry same day she sent me word
> that I was welcom that night on board
> I boarded her the truth I tell
> I found her bosen had riged her well
> and when I entered her cabin fine
> I found her lined with good Venus wine . . .
> it was my misfortune as I am told
> our ship took fire down in the hold
> come all you sailors that cruise that street
> beware of this frigate you may oft times meet
> for she is but a fire ship in disguise
> and if she dont burn you then dam my eyes.

Notes to Pages 196–201

See Mead's "'Spare me a few minutes i have Something to Say': Poetry in Manuscripts of Sailing Ships," in Carlson, *Literature and Lore of the Sea*, 28–29.

29. Similarly, in *The Rescue* (1920), a novel that Conrad began writing in 1896, the love that Captain Lingard bears for his ship is predicated upon her unconditional obedience to his will and her dependence upon him for her very life:

> To him she was always precious—like old love; always desirable—like a strange woman; always tender—like a mother; always faithful—like the favourite daughter of a man's heart. . . . She—the craft—had all the qualities of a living thing: speed, obedience, trustworthiness, endurance, beauty, capacity to do and to suffer—all but life. He—the man—was the inspirer of that thing that to him seemed the most perfect of its kind. His will was its will, his thought was its impulse, his breath was the breath of its existence.

See *The Rescue: A Romance of the Shallows* (Garden City, N.Y.: Doubleday, Page, 1925), 10–11.

30. In *The Mirror of the Sea*, Conrad expresses his esteem for "the devoted generations of ship-builders" who have created noble and graceful vessels "from some pure nooks of their simple souls" (117). As Sloan notes in "Men of Sail in the Age of Steam," "In the days of sail . . . local men with experience in ships, skill in carpentry, [and] a modest amount of capital . . . could build a sailing ship in their own seafaring community." But these local industries were gradually put out of business by steamers, which required "centralization of the industrial process and a substantial amassing of funds" for their manufacture (2–3).

31. Joseph Conrad, *Chance* (New York: Bantam Books, 1985), 235–36. Page numbers follow subsequent quotations in the text. For a discussion of women's tie to nature in patriarchal systems of belief, see Sherry B. Ortner, "Is Female to Male as Nature Is to Culture?" in Michelle Zimbalist Rosaldo and Louise Lamphere, eds., *Woman, Culture, and Society* (Stanford: Stanford University Press, 1974), 67–87.

32. Joseph Conrad, "The Nigger of the *Narcissus*," in *Great Short Works of Joseph Conrad* (New York: Harper & Row, 1966), 93.

33. She thus resembles the middle-class wives and mothers described by Mary Poovey in her discussion of Victorian gender ideologies, women whose domestic labor was idealized as "immune to . . . alienation," "a nonalienated expression of a selfless self." See *Uneven Developments: The Ideological Work of Gender in Mid-Victorian England* (Chicago: University of Chicago Press, 1988), 14, 101.

34. Conrad, *Mirror of the Sea*, 120, 136–37.

35. Conrad, "Nigger of the *Narcissus*," 93.

36. Harley, "Sailing Ships to Steam Ships," 223–25.

37. "Like all true art," Conrad writes in *The Mirror of the Sea*, "the general conduct of a ship and her handling . . . had a technique which could be discussed with delight and pleasure by men who found in their work, not bread alone, but an outlet for the peculiarities of their temperament" (31).

38. Conrad, *Mirror of the Sea*, 31, 136.

39. Ibid., 137.

40. Conrad, "Nigger of the *Narcissus*," 113.

41. Friedrich Engels, *The Origin of the Family, Private Property, and the State* (New York: International Publishers, 1972 [1884]), 124–29.

42. As Jeremy Hawthorn notes in his introduction to *The Shadow-Line*, Conrad's

novel suggests that "the world would be better if women were like well-made ships: beautiful to look at and under the control of an appreciative captain" (xxii).

43. Conrad, *Mirror of the Sea*, 19.

44. Conrad, "Nigger of the *Narcissus*," 93.

45. The classic discussion of polyandry and the power it grants to women is found in Engels, *Origin of the Family, Private Property, and the State*. That polyandry can, indeed, function to maintain the patriarchal order is demonstrated by Sidney Ruth Schuler in her study of marriage customs in Nepal. Schuler points out that polyandry, like preferential primogeniture, is a "traditional means by which families avoid division of land and limit legitimate reproduction, in order to produce a single set of male heirs" (6). Although Western travelers often associated polyandry with the "freedom" of women in their societies, it does not necessarily improve their status within a patriarchal community (3–4). See *The Other Side of Polyandry: Property, Stratification, and Nonmarriage in the Nepal Himalayas* (Boulder: Westview Press, 1987). For other discussions of polyandry, see Laura L. Betzig, *Despotism and Differential Reproduction: A Darwinian View of History* (New York: Aldine, 1986); and Nancy E. Levine, *The Dynamics of Polyandry: Kinship, Domesticity, and Population on the Tibetan Border* (Chicago: University of Chicago Press, 1988).

46. Conrad, "Youth," in *Great Short Works of Joseph Conrad*, 189.

47. Poovey, *Uneven Developments*, 101.

48. Armstrong, *Desire and Domestic Fiction*, 178.

49. According to Martin Green, for example, the adventure tales of Defoe, Kipling, and Conrad focus on "the colonial enterprise," while the domestic narratives of Austen and Eliot concern themselves with "home life, marriage, and sex." See *Dreams of Adventure, Deeds of Empire* (New York: Basic Books, 1979), 63.

50. Patrick Brantlinger, *Rule of Darkness: British Literature and Imperialism, 1830–1914* (Ithaca: Cornell University Press, 1988), 11.

10. Melody Graulich, Opening Windows toward the Sea

1. Elizabeth Stuart Phelps, *The Story of Avis*, ed. Carol Farley Kessler (New Brunswick, N.J.: Rutgers University Press, 1985), 19. Page numbers follow subsequent quotations in the text.

2. Kate Chopin, *The Awakening*, ed. Margaret Culley (New York: Norton, 1976), 15. Page numbers follow subsequent quotations in the text.

3. Harriet Beecher Stowe, *The Pearl of Orr's Island* (Boston: Houghton Mifflin, 1896), 296. Page numbers follow subsequent quotations in the text.

4. W. H. Auden, *The Enchàfed Flood: The Romantic Iconography of the Sea* (New York: Random House, 1950), 16, 14, 20.

5. The phrase comes from Edmund Tyrone's long soliloquy about his life at sea in Eugene O'Neill, *Long Day's Journey Into Night* (New Haven: Yale University Press, 1956), 153.

6. Richard C. Vitzthum, *Land and Sea: The Lyric Poetry of Philip Freneau* (Minneapolis: University of Minnesota Press, 1978), 5, 15.

7. "Universal significance" is Thomas Philbrick's phrase from *James Fenimore Cooper and the Development of American Sea Fiction* (Cambridge, Mass.: Harvard University

Press, 1961), 264, but many others share Philbrick's view. Auden, for instance, says, "The sea is where the decisive events, the moments of eternal choice, of temptation, fall, and redemption occur. The shore life," he adds, "is always trivial" (14).

8. In *Literary Democracy* (New York: Viking Press, 1981), Larzar Ziff argues that "Melville's sailors go to sea principally to find the community denied them on land" (264). In *Sea-Brothers: The Tradition of American Sea Fiction from Moby-Dick to the Present* (Philadelphia: University of Pennsylvania Press, 1988), Bert Bender suggests sea fiction is largely about the development of bonds between men, a theme D. H. Lawrence had emphasized much earlier in *Studies in Classic American Literature*.

9. Eliza Calvert Hall, *Aunt Jane of Kentucky*, ed. Melody Graulich (Albany, N.Y.: New College and University Press, 1992), 34.

10. The quilt design is a useful way of conceptualizing women's lyric style. As many critics have suggested, women writers tend to minimize plot and explore what Jewett called "recognitions," small moments of illumination that the reader must piece together to discover a larger meaning, to create epiphanies or suggestions rather than superimposing abstract meanings on experience. Moments of isolation and separation can be transcended by piecing together the small, everyday meanings of life. See, for instance, Joanna Russ, "What Can a Heroine Do? or, Why Women Can't Write," in Susan K. Cornillon, ed., *Images of Women in Fiction: Feminist Perspectives* (Bowling Green, Ohio: Bowling Green University Press, 1972), 3–20.

11. Although I don't have the space to devote here, I hope in future pieces to develop further the parallels between nineteenth-century material culture, women's art, and literature. The seashore inspired many quilt designs, often capturing the movement of waves; the best known is probably the "Mariner's Compass." For a visual overview of sea quilts and their relationship to women's lives, see the film *Hearts and Hands*, by Pat Ferraro, Elaine Hedges, and Julie Silber. Other women's arts used materials gathered by the sea; Mrs. Martin from Jewett's *The Country of the Pointed Firs*, for instance, has a frame made from seashells. Like Hawthorne's Pearl, Stowe's Mara Lincoln gathers shells and seaweed to make jewelry.

Further studies might also look at women painters like Anna Mary Richards Brewster, who at age 14 sold her painting of the waves, *The Wild Horses of the Sea* (c. 1884), and painted seascapes throughout her life. Her work provides interesting contrasts and parallels to Winslow Homer's. See Charlotte Rubenstein, *American Women Artists* (New York: Avon Books, 1982).

12. In "On Female Identity and Writing by Women," *Critical Inquiry* 8 (winter 1982): 347–61, Judith Kegan Gardiner argues that female personality is "fluidly defined," "cyclical as well as progressive." "The self is defined through social relationships; issues of fusion and merger of the self with others are significant, and ego and body boundaries remain flexible" (352). Gardiner is adapting the work of sociologist Nancy Chodorow to literary study; see *The Reproduction of Mothering: Psychoanalysis and the Sociology of Gender* (Berkeley: University of California Press, 1978). These theories of identity formation are based on middle-class, post-industrial white women's lives. While I believe that much of what I say about sea imagery in women's literature crosses racial and class boundaries in the twentieth century, my focus in this study is on nineteenth-century white women.

Diane Freedman's *An Alchemy of Genres: Cross-Genre Writing by American Women*

Notes to Pages 209–214

Poets (Charlottesville: University of Virginia Press, 1992) has influenced my thinking about boundaries in women's literature.

13. Gardiner, "Female Identity," 355.

14. To cite one example, Louisa May Alcott succinctly reveals this conflict when, in an early novel, *Moods*, she claims, "The duty we owe to self is greater than the duty we owe to others," an assertion she promptly undercuts in *Little Women*.

15. Emily Dickinson, "I dwell in Possibility," in *The Complete Poems of Emily Dickinson*, ed. Thomas H. Johnson (Boston: Little, Brown, 1952), 327. The opening stanza reads:

> I dwell in Possibility
> A fairer House than Prose—
> More numerous of Windows—
> Superior—for Doors—

16. Before I move into discussions of specific texts, I would like to point out that critics before me have discussed in individual works on writers like Stowe or Jewett some of the themes I encounter, but so far as I know, no one has yet explored a tradition of sea literature among these writers or connected their themes in a systematic fashion to sea imagery. I acknowledge my debts to earlier critics of nineteenth-century women's literature, notably Elizabeth Ammons, Josephine Donovan, Lisa MacFarlane, Marjorie Pryse, Sarah Sherman, Jane Tompkins, and Barbara White.

17. Here is a representative passage:

> All that there was developed of him, at present, was a fund of energy, self-esteem, hope, courage, and daring, the love of action, life and adventure; his life was in the outward and present, not in the inward and reflective; he was a true ten-year-old boy, in its healthiest and most animal perfection. What she was, the small pearl with the golden hair, with her frail and high-strung organization, her sensitive nerves, her half-spiritual fibres, her ponderings, and marvels, and dreams, her power of love, and yearning for self-devotion, our readers may, perhaps, have seen. (148)

18. Through Mara's death, Stowe once more breaks gender dichotomies and offers a transformative vision. In a dream, Mara's grandfather walks along the seashore to find his lost "pearl" and sees "*Him* a-coming—Jesus of Nazareth, jist as he walked by the sea of Galilee" (397). With his "long hair . . . hanging down on his shoulders," Christ takes up the pearl and puts it on his forehead, where "it shone out like a star, and shone into [the old man's] heart" (397). As Christ and Mara merged into one "melt" into the skies, so do they merge into the old man's heart, leaving him "so happy, and so calm!" (397).

19. Louisa May Alcott, *Little Women* (New York: Macmillan, 1962), 413. Page numbers follow subsequent quotations in the text.

20. See, for instance, Judith Fetterley, "*Little Women*: Alcott's Civil War," *Feminist Studies* 5 (1979): 369–83.

21. Sarah Orne Jewett, *The Country of the Pointed Firs and Other Stories*, ed. Mary Ellen Chase, intro. Marjorie Pryse (New York: Norton, 1981), 236. Page numbers follow subsequent quotations in the text.

22. For a contemporary treatment of this same theme, see Faith Ringgold's children's book, *Tar Beach*, where the adolescent heroine imagines herself flying over the

George Washington Bridge. Based on one of Ringgold's quilts and firmly placed in African American experience, *Tar Beach* suggests that some of the themes I've explored here cross racial boundaries, as do other twentieth-century seashore novels by black women, Paule Marshall's *Praisesong for the Widow* and *Daughters* and Gloria Naylor's *Mama Day*. For further evidence of such racial crossings, see the opening poem in Gloria Anzaldua's *Borderlands* and the discussion of it in Freedman, *Alchemy of Genres*.

23. Sarah Orne Jewett, *Deephaven and Other Stories*, ed. Richard Cary (New Haven: College & University Press, 1966), 32. As this passage implies, *Deephaven*, a novel about two young women's growth in a seaside town, can be read as yet another sea novel of transformation and synthesis.

24. Emily Dickinson, "Wild Nights! Wild Nights!" in *Complete Poems*, 114.

25. See Sarah Way Sherman, *Sarah Orne Jewett, an American Persephone* (Hanover, N.H.: University Press of New England, 1989), 58.

26. Thaxter, *Poems by Celia Thaxter* (Cambridge, Mass.: Riverside Press, 1874), 9-10.

27. Although I don't have the space to explore them here, Thaxter's prose works, *Among the Isles of Shoals* (1873) and *An Island Garden* (1894), can be read through my window on women's sea literature, suggesting further genre crossings.

28. Rebecca Harding Davis, *Earthen Pitchers, Scribners Monthly* (1873-74): 352. Page numbers follow subsequent quotations in the text.

29. Phelps quoted in Josephine Donovan, *New England Local Color Literature: A Women's Tradition* (New York: Frederick Ungar, 1983), 68.

30. For an insightful exploration of how this story reveals Davis's personal conflicts, see Tillie Olsen's "A Biographical Interpretation," in Davis, *Life in the Iron Mills and Other Stories*, ed. Tillie Olsen (Old Westbury, N.Y.: Feminist Press, 1985).

31. Phelps quoted in Olsen, "A Biographical Interpretation," 174. Olsen also suggests that Davis "inspired" *The Story of Avis*.

32. As we've already seen in Jo and Beth, Thaxter, and Sylvie, sea birds wing their way through women's sea texts, themselves images of transcendence and merger of earth / sea and sky; both *The Story of Avis* and *The Awakening* are filled with symbolic birds.

33. *The Story of Avis* is autobiographical in many ways; in it Phelps conflates her mother's life with her own, a merger not surprising given that the daughter took her mother's name upon her mother's death. The first Elizabeth Stuart Phelps was, of course, also a writer, and *Avis* can be read as a rewriting of her short story, "The Angel Over the Right Shoulder" (1852), which ends with the mother's hope that she can give her daughter a life "all mended by her own experience." Believing that she has lost her own artistic genius by the end of the novel, Avis, too, looks to her daughter to live the life she could not.

34. A few years later, Jewett would respond to *The Story of Avis* with *A Country Doctor*, whose heroine, Nan Prince, has her own mother problems and seaside experiences; when confronted with a choice between career and marriage, she chooses career, a choice Jewett makes easier by suggesting that Nan is genetically unstable and therefore should never bear children. Unlike her mother, Nan is a far less stormy—and less sexual—character than Avis, and her conflicts are minimized. Unlike Avis, Nan simply chooses not to struggle; she is a conscientious objector to the civil war. For

Jewett's criticisms of *The Story of Avis* and comments that suggest that she might have seen *A Country Doctor* as a response to Phelps's text, see Donovan, *New England Local Color Literature,* 47. For Phelps's imagistic critique of the lack of sexuality and passion in Jewett's work, see ibid., 48.

35. Mary Ellen Chase, introduction to *The Country of the Pointed Firs and Other Stories.*

36. Simone de Beauvoir, *The Second Sex* (New York: New English Library, 1969), 443.

37. Adrienne Rich, *Diving into the Wreck* (New York: Norton, 1973), 23.

38. Of course, feminist critics have done this in other contexts. Jane Tompkins's *Sensational Designs* is only one example.

Index

abolitionists, and African American manhood, 152, 159

African Americans (*see also* race; sailors, African American): in antebellum American cities, 139–40; and benevolent associations, 159; and economic mobility, 141, 148–49, 158–59; and manhood, 152–53; in maritime employment, 60–61, 67, 138–68; motivations to sail, 152, 158–59, 166; and racial equality, 152–53, 165; and schools, 149

African sailors. *See* merchant marine, British: contract labor in, racial divisions in, recruitment of colonial labor in

aftercabin (*see also* captains, merchant and whaling; officers, merchant and whaling; ships, sail and steam), 89, 200–201; compared to forecastle, 132, 135; description of, 130–31

age, of sailors, 73; in antebellum U.S. (table), 161; as component of maritime culture, 125–28; and Rhode Island laws of settlement, 65–66

Alcott, Louisa May, 206, 212, 214, 224

American Seamens' Friend Society, 134

Anzaldua, Gloria, 224

Aptheker, Herbert, 141

Arab sailors. *See* merchant marine, British: contract labor in, racial divisions in, recruitment of colonial labor in

Asian Articles. *See* merchant marine, British: contract labor in

Asian sailors. *See* merchant marine, British: contract labor in, racial divisions in, recruitment of colonial labor in

Awakening, The (Chopin), 219, 223–24

ballads of female warriors and sailors, 11, 15, 19, 34–40

Baltimore, and African American sailors, 139, 160, 164, 168

Beggar's Opera, The (Gay), 17

Bible, the, 95, 105, 128, 132

Billy Budd (Melville), 148

Bolster, W. Jeffrey, 60

Bonny, Anne, 1–21, 48, 237n. 71; narrative of, 28–33; portraits of, 2, 6

Boston, and African American sailors, 140, 164, 166, 168

British sailors. *See* sailors, Black, on British ships; sailors, white British

broadside, "The Female Sailor," 36

Bullen, Frank T., 147, 190

Byron, Lord George Gordon, 22

cabin boys, 95, 131, 147, 149, 173, 182

Cape Horn, 121

captains, merchant and whaling (*see also* discipline, shipboard; women at sea: as captains' wives): blacks as, 148–49, 153, 159; Conrad's depiction of, 194–96, 199–201; and crews, 61, 109, 113; and racial prejudice, 148; and shipowners, 75–78, 120, 132–34; shipboard accommodations of, 130–31; and shore community, 60, 62; Stowe's depiction of, 212; and wives at sea, 89, 93, 95, 109, 113–15, 132–34

captains, pirate, 9–10, 13, 14

Caribbean, as site of piracy, 5, 18, 22

Carnes, Mark, 130

Carse, Robert, 119

Carson, Rachel, 224

chanteys, sea, 135

Chase, Mary Ellen, 224

Chinese sailors. *See* merchant marine, British: contract labor in, racial divisions in, recruitment of colonial labor in

Chopin, Kate, 205, 206, 219, 221, 223–24

Civil War, U.S., 47, 119

class (*see also* femininity; labor, maritime; masculinity): Conrad's depiction of, 190–92, 194–95, 198, 200–202; and gender, x, 11–15, 35, 37–54, 57–59, 120–22, 125–26, 130, 135, 172–74, 180–88, 191; intersections with gender and race, 152–53, 165–68, 169, 172–74, 179–84; and race, 60–61, 144–53; racializing of, 169–88; relations within maritime industries, 72–78, 114, 129–30, 147, 169, 170–83, 190–91, 199–201; social construction of, vii, 11–15, 46, 147, 172

Index

Coleridge, Samuel Taylor, 146
Coloured Sailors' Boarding House (New York), 152, 156–57, 164
Conrad, Joseph, ix, 189–203
Consolato del mare (medieval shipping code), 146
contract labor. *See* merchant marine, British: contract labor in
cooks, sea, 131, 158, 270nn. 16, 17; and African American manhood, 144, 147–49, 151, 154, 158, 163–66
Coontz, Stephanie, 58
Country of the Pointed Firs, The (Jewett), 214–18, 219
crews. *See* merchant marine, British; merchant marine, U.S.; sailors
cross-dressing: by female pirates, 5–8, 10–13; by female sailors, 1, 34–54; tradition of, among working-class women, 10–11, 34, 35, 42, 48
Cruel War Is Raging, The (folksong), 37

Dana, Richard Henry, ix, 154
Davies, (Mrs.) Christian, 11, 47
Davis, Rebecca Harding, 206, 219–21
de Beauvoir, Simone, 225
Deephaven (Jewett), 215
Defoe, Daniel, 4, 16, 230n. 4
Dekker, Rudolf M., 10
Delacroix, Eugène, *Liberty Leading the People*, 18–22, 236n. 57
Dening, Greg, 147
De Pauw, Linda Grant, 8
desertion, 73, 78, 192
diaries. *See* journals
Dickens, Charles, 191
Dickinson, Emily, 100, 206, 209, 218, 221
discipline, shipboard: and captain's authority, 61, 109, 113–14, 130, 166, 200; compared to slavery, 166; on pirate ships, 9; race and class specificity of, 174–75, 181–83, 187; and rank, 190–91, 200
"Diving into the Wreck" (Rich), 204, 225
Douglass, Frederick, 139
Dowie, Menie Muriel, 47–48, 50
drama, eighteenth-century British, influence of female pirates on, 17–18
Dugaw, Dianne, 8, 11, 15

Earthen Pitchers (Davis), 219–21
Engels, Friedrich, 200

engineers (*see also* steam technology), 173, 178, 189–90, 192–93, 199
English sailors. *See* merchant marine, British: contract labor in, racial divisions in, recruitment of colonial labor in
families of sailors (*see also* femininity; masculinity; women; women at sea; women on shore): in combined households, 59–60, 83–84; dependence on advances of wages, 78; dependence on town support, 57–60, 63–64, 66–69; as motivation for seafaring, 74, 133, 157–63; relations with shipowners, 75–78, 85–86, 133–34; in shipboard culture, 86–88, 131–32; vulnerability of, 66–67, 78–79, 84, 160–62
Farr, James Barker, 141
Female Sailor Bold, The (folksong), 37
Female Soldier, The (Walker), 38, 42, 43, 49
femininity (*see also* gender; love, romantic; sexuality; subjectivity, female): chastity as element of, 40, 195; and class, 15–16, 37–54, 194–95; conceptions of, xii, 36–38, 44–45, 48, 70, 73–77, 90–92, 153, 183, 188, 193; delicacy as element of, 35–37, 48, 195; dependence as element of, 57–58, 63, 64, 68–69; and masculinity, 172; middle-class, 15–16, 35–37, 42–54; motherhood as element of, 82–83; "wooden" style of, vii; working-class, 11–12, 19, 37–38, 40–41, 47–53
fiction, maritime. *See* literature, sea
firemen. *See* stokers
forecastle (*see also* fraternity; sailors, male; ships, sail and steam), 72, 77, 87, 120, 126–27, 160; compared to aftercabin, 132, 135; description of, 128–30; egalitarianism in, 140, 146, 150; racial interactions in, 146, 150; as working-class space, 138
"Foreigner, The" (Jewett), 217, 224
fraternal societies, on shore, 130
fraternity, among sailors, 9, 69, 126–30, 140, 146–47, 149–50, 152, 171; Conrad's ideas of, 191, 199, 201–2

gamming, 124, 128, 133
Gay, John, 17
gender (*see also* femininity; masculinity; subjectivity, female): associated with land and sea, ix–x, xii, 70, 71, 118, 120–21, 136, 228n. 8; and class, x, 11–15, 35, 37–54, 57–59, 120–22, 125–26, 130, 135, 172–74, 180–88, 191; defined, ix, xi–xii, 45–46; intersections with

Index

race and class, 152–53, 165–68, 169, 172–74, 179–84; and race, 138, 140–41, 153–65, 199; Victorian ideology of, 70, 92, 104, 164, 183, 195–96
General History of the Pyrates, A, 3, 5, 7, 15, 21, 22–33, 48, 231n. 11; frontispiece of Dutch version, 18, 20
Gilbert, Arthur N., 9
Gillis, John, 14
Globe Hotel. *See* Coloured Sailors' Boarding House
Goldsmith, Oliver, 8
greenhand. *See* forecastle; labor, maritime; sailors, male
Grover, (Mrs.) Carrie, 54

Hamilton, George Heard, 22
Henneberry, Ben, 35
Hill, Christopher, 16
Hohman, Elmo P., 165
homosexuality. *See* sexuality
households. *See* families of sailors
Huckleberry Finn, 105

impressment: of African Americans, 158, 161; and class, 46; and cross-dressing females, 43, 44; protection against, 261n. 2
Indian (North American) sailors. *See* sailors, Indian (North American)
Indian sailors. *See* merchant marine, British: contract labor in, racial divisions in, recruitment of colonial labor in
"Intrepid Female, The," 42–43
"iron" men, stereotype of (*see also* masculinity), vii, x

Jack Monroe (folksong), 37
Jefferson, Thomas, and impact of embargo on African American sailors, 148
Jewett, Sarah Orne, 206, 212, 214–18, 219, 224, 226, 285–86n. 34
Johnson, Capt. Charles, 1, 3, 15, 18, 230–31n. 4
journal keepers, women: Allen, Harriet, 98, 111–12, 116; Balano, Dorothea, 101, 102, 104, 105, 112–15, 116–17; Brewster, Mrs. William, 99; Brock, Eliza, 100; Brown, Anne, 98, 104; Burgess, Hannah, 98, 116; Cole, Sarah, 116; Crapo, Lucy Ann, 104; Follansbee, Mrs. Alonzo, 98, 100, 114; Fraser, Margaret, 96, 107–9, 113–14; Lawrence, Mary, 99, 100, 116; Morey, Elizabeth, 96, 97, 105; Morrell, Abby Jane, 100; Russell, Mary Hayden, 103; Sears, Bethia, 96, 98, 106–7; Sherman, Mrs. Wanton, 101; Smith, Lucy, 95, 115; Smith, Sallie, 102; Swain, Harriet, 110; Taber, Sarah, 101; Williams, Eliza, 96, 104, 110, 115
journals (*see also* writing, by women at sea), 94, 122; African American sailors', 150, 163

Kerber, Linda, 57–58
Kirby, R. S., 42, 43, 50
Kirby's Wonderful and Eccentric Museum, 42

labor, maritime (*see also* age, of sailors; discipline, shipboard; fraternity; merchant marine, British; merchant marine, U.S.; pirates, female; pirates, male; sailors [all entries]; steam technology; whaling): and class conflict, 13–15, 46, 129–30, 174–75, 191–92, 199–202; degradation of, 165–68, 174–78, 190; distinctive subculture of, viii–ix, 13–15, 126–27, 130–31, 140, 144–47, 153–55; feminization of, 163–64, 173, 180, 183–85; gender division of, ix, 8–9, 71, 95–96, 125, 132, 163, 173, 184, 188, 247n. 3; hierarchy in, 61–62, 72–73, 77, 144, 147–51; persistence in, 73, 159, (table) 162; and race, 144, 147, 148–49, 154, 165–68, 169–88; racial division of, 181–82, 183–84, 185–88; and recruitment of foreign sailors, viii, 174–78; respectability of, 159, 165–66; skill in, 44, 153–54, 163, 173–74; transiency of, 16, 64–69, 79, 153, 243n. 19; uncertainty of, 60, 157; and unions, 137, 175; wage structure of, 76–77, 157–58, 166, 170, 173–77
"Land-locked" (Thaxter), 219
Lane, Tony, 178
lascar sailors. *See* merchant marine, British: contract labor in, racial divisions in, recruitment of colonial labor in
Le Guin, Ursula, 225
Lemisch, Jesse, xi
Liberty Leading the People (Delacroix painting): compared to frontispiece of *Historie der Engelsche Zee-Roovers*, 18–19; illustration, 21
Linebaugh, Peter, 16
literature, men's sea. *See* Conrad, Joseph; Melville, Herman
literature, sea (*see also* ballads; drama; literature, women's sea; poetry; writing, by women at sea): as masculine genre, 205

Index

literature, women's sea (*see also* Alcott, Louisa May; Chopin, Kate; Davis, Rebecca Harding; Dickinson, Emily; Jewett, Sarah Orne; Phelps, Elizabeth Stuart; Stowe, Harriet Beecher; Thaxter, Celia), 204–26; compared to men's, 206, 225; distinctive features of, 207–9, 225; Walt Whitman in tradition of, 226

Little Women (Alcott), 213, 224

logs (*see also* journals), 102, 118, 120; definition of, 100

Lomax, Alan, 54

Lord Jim (Conrad), 189, 192

love, romantic (*see also* sexuality; ships, sail and steam: as female): between officers and wives or sweethearts, 73–74, 88–90, 107–8, 110, 112–13, 131–33; between sailors and women, 128–29; between shipmates, 128–29; in Stowe's writing, 210–12

mariners. *See* captains; officers

Marshall, Paule, 224

masculinity (*see also* fraternity; gender; love, romantic; sexuality): anti-authoritarianism as element of, 14–15, 130, 183; and class, 46, 156–57, 181, 183, 186; combat as element of, 120, 155–56, 183; courage as element of, 13–14, 154, 187; and domestic ties, 131–35; independence as element of, 69, 73; "iron" style of, vii, x; middle-class, x, 34, 120, 121–22, 172, 183; and patriarchy, 57–59, 153; physical prowess as element of, x, 12–13, 125, 140–41, 154–56; providership as element of, 59–60, 64–69, 70, 73–76, 140–41, 157–63; and race, 138, 140–41, 152–53, 181, 186; reputation as element of, 140–41, 153–54; skill as element of, 172–73; social construction of, ix–x, 44–45, 55, 70, 119, 124–25, 138, 153, 172; stoicism as element of, 126, 154, 185, 186–87; in Stowe's writing, 210–12; working-class, x, 156–57, 183

masters. *See* captains, merchant and whaling

mates. *See* officers, merchant and whaling

McKee, Christopher, 76

Melville, Herman, ix, 70, 91, 120, 148, 158

merchant marine, British (*see also* discipline, shipboard; labor, maritime): and British imperial power, 169, 171–72; class conflict in, 175, 180–81, 190–92; conflation of class, gender, and race in, 169, 170, 173, 180–88; contract labor in, 175–78; history of, viii, 171, 174–75, 198, 271n. 21; racial divisions in, 180–88, 199; recruitment of colonial labor in, 174–78; and seamen employed in British ships (table), 177; tramp ships in, 177–78; and unions, 175, 182, 184; wage structure of, 170, 173–74

merchant marine, U.S. (*see also* discipline, shipboard; labor, maritime; whaling): allotment of berths by race (table), 142–43; history of, viii, 136, 165–88; race relations in, 141, 144–53; "whitening" of, 165–68

middle class. *See* African Americans; class: relations within maritime industries; femininity; gender: Victorian ideology of; masculinity

Millay, Edna St. Vincent, 224

Miller, Pamela, 105

Mills, Anne, 11; portrait of, 12

Mirror of the Sea, The (Conrad), 194, 201

Moby Dick, 70–71, 91, 103, 224

Moll Flanders (Defoe), 16

Montgomery, David, 153

motherhood: experience of, at sea, 104; and mother-daughter love, 217–18; Victorian conception of, 82

mulatto. *See* African Americans; sailors, African American

musicians, African American, on U.S. warships, 144

Nantucket, as whaling port, 59, 60, 72, 79

Narrative of a Voyage to the Ethiopic and South Atlantic Ocean, Indian Ocean, Chinese Sea, North and South Pacific Ocean, in the Years 1829, 1830, 1831, 100

navy, British, 1, 47; and homosexuality, 9

navy, U.S., 76; African American officers in, 147; African American sailors in, 149–50; and manning regulations, 149

Naylor, Gloria, 224

Neptune Ceremony, 123–24, 127

New Bedford: and African American sailors, 139; as whaling port, 72, 77

New Bedford Port Society, 80, 134

New England, decline of shipping in, 165

New Orleans, and African American sailors, 147

New York, and African American sailors, 139, 142–43, 146, 149, 150, 152, 156, 159, 160, 164, 168

"Nigger of the *Narcissus*, The" (Conrad), 198, 201

Index

Nordhoff, Charles, 124
Norling, Lisa, 59, 133

officers, merchant and whaling (*see also* after-cabin; captains, merchant and whaling; discipline, shipboard; families of sailors; women on shore): African American, and white sailors, 147, 149; demographics of, 72, 77; and gender and space on shipboard, 130–35; white, and African American crews, 150, 154, 156
"Off Shore" (Thaxter), 204
Old Maid's Paradise (Phelps), 220
One Whaling Family, 110
Opie, Amelia, 48–54
Outcast of the Islands, An (Conrad), 198
"Out of the Cradle Endlessly Rocking" (Whitman), 226
owners, ship (*see also* families of sailors; labor, maritime; women at sea): and American whaling, 73; and British labor relations, 174–88; and maritime law, 146–47; and relations with captains and officers, 75–76, 84, 132–33; and shipboard social relations, 129, 171

Pacific Ocean, as feminine, 122, 123
Pamela (Richardson), 17, 40
patriarchy: colonial definition of, 57–58; Conrad on, 193, 202; and dependence, 58; and masculinity, 57–59, 153
Pearl of Orr's Island, The (Stowe), 93, 205, 210–12, 215, 224
Phelps, Elizabeth Stuart, 204, 206, 219, 221–23, 285n. 33
Philadelphia, and African American sailors, 139, 143, 156, 159
piracy, allegorical image of, as source for image of liberty, 18–20, 22, 236n. 61; illustrations, 20, 21
pirates, female (*see also* Bonny, Anne; Read, Mary; sailors, female; cross-dressing): cultural influence of, 15–22; and discipline, 9–10; and gender, 10, 11–12, 15; Grace O'Malley as, 11; illustrations of, 2, 4, 6, 20; and liberty, 15; in masculine subculture, 3, 7–8, 10, 12–15; numbers of, 10; and pregnancy, 3, 7
pirates, male: and discipline, 9–10; and liberty, 1, 15; masculine subculture of, 13–15; views of women on ships, 9–10, 233n. 26
poetry of the sea, 218, 219, 226

Polly, an Opera, being the second part of the Beggar's Opera (Gay), 17
pregnancy: of captains' wives, 95–96, 104, 133; of female pirates, 3, 7; of female sailors, 11
Providence, R.I., and African American sailors, 139, 142, 158, 159, 160, 161–62, 167, 168

quadroon. *See* sailors, African American
quilt patterns, sea imagery in, 206–8

race (*see also* African Americans; labor, maritime; masculinity; merchant marine, British; merchant marine, U.S.): and class, 60–61, 144–46, 169–88; conception of, in early-twentieth-century British empire, 171; and gender, 138, 140–41, 153–65, 199; intersections with class and gender, 152–53, 165–68, 169, 172–74, 179–84, 199; maritime, British people as a, 186
Rackam, Calico Jack, 2, 5, 7, 13–14; in *A General History of the Pyrates*, 26, 32–33
Read, Mary, 2–22; narrative of, 23–28; portrait of, 2, 4
Real, Anna Maria, 48–53
Rediker, Marcus, 60, 61, 146
reformers, social: and American sailors, 127, 133–34, 156–57; and British working class, 50
religion: on shipboard, 95, 132, 133; in women's writing, 97–98, 102–3
Revolution, American: portrait of black sailor in, 145; and sailors, xi, 61; and service in Continental Army, 67, 145, 152
Revolution, French, and femininity, 37
Rhode Island: sailors, seamen's families, and town leaders in, 55–69
Rich, Adrienne, 204, 224, 225
Richardson, Samuel, 17, 40, 43
Roediger, David, 163, 165
Rolls of Oleron (medieval shipping code), 146
Rotundo, E. Anthony, 153

sailors, African American (*see also* discipline, shipboard; families of sailors; fraternity), 60, 67, 138; in all-black crews, 150–52, 166; and boxing, 155; contrasted with white sailors, 139–40, 150, 155, 162–63, 165; and families, 160–62, 164; and head butting, 155–56; in maritime employment, 60–61, 67, 138–68; and masculinity, 138–68; and middle-class status, 159–60, 168; motiva-

Index

sailors, African American (*continued*)
tions to sail, 152, 158–59, 166; numbers of, 139, 141, 160; and occupational mobility, 148–49, 154, 160, 163; portrait of, 146; as prisoners of war, 155; as providers, 140, 144, 157–66, 168; racial equality on shipboard, 140, 144, 146–50; and wages, 144, 148, 157–58

sailors, Black, on British ships (*see also* merchant marine, British), 170–71, 173–74, 175–78, 180–82, 183–85, 187–88

sailors, female (*see also* cross-dressing; pirates, female; warriors, female): in ballad and biography, 34–54; illustrations of, 12, 36, 39; in merchant or naval service, 38, 43; narratives of, 23–33; numbers of, 1, 8; as pirates, 1–22

sailors, Indian (North American), 55–56, 59, 60, 61, 64

Sailor's Magazine, 134, 156

sailors, male (*see also* discipline, shipboard; families of sailors; fraternity): administration of estates while at sea, 62–63; ages of (table), 161; allotment of berths by race of (table), 142–43; and masculinity, 57, 65, 69, 73; persistence at sea (table), 162; and public support, 57, 58, 68; and Rhode Island town leaders, 55, 59, 61, 66; views of women on ships, 9, 232n. 19

sailors, white American male (*see also* discipline, shipboard; families of sailors; fraternity): attitudes toward women on ships, 95–96, 121; images of women in shipboard material culture, 127; and masculinity, 118–21, 124, 126–27, 136; and race, 141, 147–48, 150–51, 156, 162–64; and shore communities, 73, 84–85; views on women, 125, 128, 136; and wages, 157–58; as working class, 130

sailors, white British (*see also* merchant marine, British), 175–76, 180–81, 183, 186

sea: connection between shore and, xi, xii, 34, 55, 70, 84–85, 90, 173, 204; depictions of, in women's writing, 115–17, 204–26; as male space, x, 70, 89, 96, 119, 205; seamen's perceptions of, 121–23

seafaring. *See* labor, maritime; merchant marine, British; merchant marine, U.S.; pirates, female; pirates, male; sailors (all entries); steam technology

seamen. *See* sailors

seashore, literary importance of, 204, 206, 208–9, 224

Second Sex, The (de Beauvoir), 225

separate spheres. *See* gender

servants, indentured, 61, 64, 65, 68

sexuality (*see also* love, romantic): conceptions of female, in Victorian era, 193; Conrad's depiction of female, 192–95, 201–2; Conrad's depiction of male, 196, 201–2; female, 40, 48, 52, 114–15, 218, 221–23, 280n. 28; homosexuality, xiii, 9, 128, 141, 184, 240n. 30; male, 9, 114–15, 127, 156

Shadow-Line, The (Conrad), 192, 193–97, 201

shipping. *See* merchant marine

ships, sail and steam (*see also* aftercabin; forecastle; labor, maritime; steam technology; women at sea): class distinctions on, 130–31, 170, 193; as female, 71, 127, 192–98, 201–3, 281n. 29; fictional representations of, 192–98, 201–2; as gendered space, 71, 92, 94, 95–96, 117–35; hierarchy on, 147; as racialized space, 151, 170; as "total institution," x, 61, 71, 147, 171

shore communities, connection to seafaring, xi, xii, 55–69, 70–91, 173, 204

slavery, 67, 139, 152

Snell, Hannah, 11, 16–17, 38–43, 47, 49–51, 53, 233n. 32, 239n. 13; portrait of, 39

sodomy, 128

soldiers, female. *See* warriors, female

"Song of Myself" (Whitman), 226

spiritualism, 195

Springer, Haskell, 135

Starbuck, Alexander, 119

steam technology, 178–80, 192–93; and class conflict, 190–92; Conrad on, 190–203; transition from sail to, 136, 173, 178–79, 190, 198, 202–3

stewards: African American, 144, 149, 158, 163–66; and gender identity, 164; and women's work, 113, 131, 163–64, 173, 180, 184–85

stokers, 170, 173, 174, 178–79, 182–84, 191

"Storm at Sea" (quilt pattern), 206–7, 216, 218; illustration of, 208

Story of Avis, The (Phelps), 204, 219, 221–23

Stowe, Harriet Beecher, 93, 95, 205, 206, 209, 210–12, 215, 218, 223, 224, 225

subjectivity, female (*see also* femininity): and class, 41–42, 44–47, 48–53; constructed in women's sea journals, 94, 98, 115; as di-

vided, 219–25; harmonizing, 206–7, 226; in reconciled female self, 212–18; as tidal ebb and flow, 209–18
Suez Canal, 198
Sydney, Sir Henry, 11

Talbot, Mary Ann, 42–47, 49, 50, 53, 239–41nn. 21, 23, 24, 25, 28, 30, 31
Teasdale, Sara, 224
Thaxter, Celia, 204, 206, 219
Transiency of sailors. *See* labor, maritime: transiency of
transvestism. *See* cross-dressing
Tryals of Captain John Rackam and Other Pirates, The, 7
Turner, Frederick Jackson, xi
"Typhoon" (Conrad), 199, 201

Valentine, Charles, 146
van de Pol, Lotte C., 10
Velasquez, Loreta Janeta, 47
Vestris, SS, wreck of (1928), 169–70, 171, 172, 173, 182
Vickers, Daniel, 60
Victorian gender ideology. *See* gender
Villiers, Alan, 119–20
Voyage to Jamaica (James Kelly), 150

Walker, Robert, 38, 40, 49
Wallace, Frederick William, vii
warriors, female (*see also* cross-dressing), 8, 43, 44, 238n. 1; in working-class ballads, 11, 15, 37, 50
War with Cape Horn, The (Villiers), 119
whales: described in shipboard accounts, 101–2, 105–6; as signifier of gender, 121–23
whalemen. *See* sailors
whaling, American: gendered nature of, 71, 90–91, 118–37; industry, history of, 72, 136; paternalism in, 75–78; role of women on shore in, 78–91; social relations of work in, 60, 72–73; 147; voyages, women on, 95–106, 110–12, 115–17; wage system of, 76–77
Wharton, Edith, 224
"White Heron, A" (Jewett), 214
Whitman, Walt, 206, 226
"Wild Nights! Wild Nights!" (Dickinson), 218
women (*see also* families of sailors; femininity; women at sea; women on land): Conrad's depiction of, 199–202; as viewed by sailors, 9, 126–28, 131–36; and work, 185, 277n. 94
Women Adventurers (Dowie), 47
women at sea (*see also* labor, maritime; writing, by women at sea): as captains' wives, 89, 92–117, 199–202; as pirates, 1–15; roles of, 94–96, 101, 110–11, 112; as sailors, 8, 34, 35, 37–38, 42–47, 49–50; superstitions about, 9, 96–97, 232n. 19; on whaleships, 95–106, 110–12, 115–17, 132–34
women on shore (*see also* families of sailors): communities of, 59–60, 82–85, 91, 209, 251n. 51; maritime industries' reliance on, 78–79, 81, 85–87, 90–91, 173; occupations of, 79–88, 159–62; public support of, 63, 66, 68; support of families by, 74, 79–81, 86–88, 91, 162, 253n. 82
"wooden" women, stereotype of (*see also* femininity), vii, 127
Woodforde, James, 41, 51
Woolf, Virginia, 95, 206, 224
working class. *See* class: relations within maritime industries; femininity; gender: and class; labor, maritime; masculinity
writing, by women at sea (*see also* femininity; journal keepers, women; subjectivity, female), 92–117, 253n. 1; audience of, 102–4, 106–8, 110, 115; gendered form of, 94, 98–101, 117; marital relations in, 106–9, 110–15; relations with sailors, 96; and self-image, 96, 101, 106, 112, 115, 117; subjects of, 97–98

"Youth" (Conrad), 202

Library of Congress Cataloging-in-Publication Data

Iron men, wooden women : gender and seafaring in the Atlantic World, 1700–1920 / edited by Margaret S. Creighton and Lisa Norling.
    p. cm.—(Gender relations in the American experience)
  Includes bibliographical references and index.
  ISBN 0-8018-5159-9 (hardcover : alk. paper).—
ISBN 0-8018-5160-2 (pbk. : alk. paper)
    1. Women and the sea. 2. Seafaring life. I. Creighton, Margaret S., 1949– .
II. Norling, Lisa. III. Series.
G540.I76 1996
910.4′5—dc20   95-30921
                                                                                   CIP